EASTERN BENGAL BALLADS

Eastern Bengal Ballads

(Ramtanu Lahiri Research Fellowship Lectures for 1924-26, inTwo Parts)

Vol. II : Part I

Compiled and Edited by

Dineshchandra Sen, Rai Bahadur, B.A. D.Litt. (Hons.)

GYAN PUBLISHING HOUSE

NEW DELHI-110002

Eastern Bengal Ballads

ISBN: 81-212-0906-4 (Set)
ISBN: 81-212-0908-0 (Vol. II)

Published in 2006 in India by
Gyan Publishing House,
5, Ansari Road, Daryaganj, New Delhi-110002
E-mail: books@gyanbooks.com

Laser Typesetting at: Vinayak Printers, Delhi
Printed at: Salasar Imaging System, Delhi

To

Those who love Bengal

CONTENTS

	PAGE
General Introduction	ix-xl
Preface to the ballad of the Washer-maiden ...	1-8
The ballad of the Washer-maiden ...	9-30
Preface to the ballad of the Young Herdsman ...	33-40
The ballad of the Young Herdsman ...	41-63
Ditto ditto (Second Version) ...	63-76
Preface to the ballad of Kanchanmala ...	76-84
The ballad of Kanchanmala or the Bride of a Blind Baby	85-114
The ballad of Kanchanmala—Another version ...	115-116
Preface to the ballad of Santi	119-122
The ballad of Santi	123-128
Preface to the ballad of Bhelua, the Beautiful One	130-137
The ballad of Bhelua, the Beautiful One ...	138-188
Preface to the ballad of Rani Kamala Devi by Adhar Chandra	191-196
The ballad of Rani Kamala Devi	197-211
Preface to the ballad of the Adventurous Career of a Young Dacoit	215-220
The ballad of the Adventurous Career of a Young Dacoit	221-256
Preface to the ballad of the Santal Insurrection	259-264
Ballad of the Santhal Insurrection ...	265-271
Preface to the ballad of Nizam Dacoit ...	275-281
The ballad of Nizam Dacoit	285-298
Preface to the ballad of Isha Khan Mashnadali of Jangalbari	301-335

	PAGE
The ballad of Isha Khan Mashnad Ali ...	337-375
Preface to the ballad of Surat Jamal and Adhua	379-390
The ballad of Surat Jamal and Adhua, a Love-tale and Tragedy	391-419
Preface to the ballad of Firoj Khan Dewan ...	423-426
The ballad of Firoj Khan Dewan	427-454

LIST OF ILLUSTRATIONS.

		PAGE
1.	The Washer-maiden	10
2.	Herdsman Lover	47
3.	Kanchanmala	93
4.	Santi	125
5.	Rani Kamala	199
6.	Inscription on Isha Khan's Cannon ...	314
7.	Laksman Hazra's Capital reduced to a swamp	315
8.	Isha Khan's Cannon	316
9.	Sher Shaha's Cannon	316
10.	Mosque and ruins of house of Isha Khan's immediate descendants	335
11.	Isha Khan observing the Hindu princess from his *Kosha*	351
12.	Kedar Roy and his two nephews ...	356
13.	The bereaved mother and Karimulla ...	356
14-21.	Eight figures of ships and boats ...	454

GENERAL INTRODUCTION.

1. *The Value of the Bengali Ballads.*

Since the publication of the first volume of Eastern Bengal Ballads, we have been able to secure many more of them, full of literary and historical interest. They are as plenty as are the field-flowers and lie strewn all over the country. The Eastern part of the district of Mymensingh, however, owing to its political isolation from the rest of Bengal during the centuries immediately preceding the Muhammadan conquest, and its cultural freedom, untrammelled by the canons of Brahminic renaissance, has preserved the best of these ballads,—a fact which will be evidenced by the love-episodes, contained in the two volumes of ballads, already published by the University. I have described the causes leading to the peculiar advantage of Mymensingh over other districts of Bengal in this respect in my Introduction to the first volume.

The first volume of the ballads was very well received by scholars and orientalists in Europe and India. Lord Ronaldshay, who is as great a scholar as he is an administrator, not only wrote a Foreword to the same but drew the attention of the literary public to these rural songs, by making extracts from them in a learned and interesting article, published in "the Nineteenth Century and After" and in his recent work, "The Heart of Aryyavarta." Scholars like Romain Roland, Sylvain Levi, Grierson and Pargiter have warmly applauded them and the long review published in the Times Literary Supplement has established the claims of Bengali ballads to a lasting and solid literary fame. Lord Lytton, the worthy scion of an illustrious family of worldwide renown in the domain of Art and Literature, has shown his appreciation of this literary treasure of the province that he has been called upon to rule, by granting a pecuniary aid towards its collection. Mr. E. F. Oaten, the Director of Public Instruction, Bengal, has, ever since the publication of the first volume of ballads, taken a keen interest in this popular literature of Bengal and publicly expressed his high estimate of its merits.

With the help granted by the Government and the University of Calcutta, we have been able to get on our staff four ballad-collectors, at the head of whom stands Babu Chandra Kumar De, whose love for the rural literature of his country is boundless and beyond all praise. His example has inspired the other three men, and a lively spirit has been roused in the countryside for the preservation of these gems of Bengali literature.

2. *Ballad of Manwoor Khan.*

We have now secured a good many historical ballads, only three or four of which could be published in the present volume. Owing to want of space and urgency for bringing out a second volume, we could not insert in it all of the numerous ballads we have got about Isha Khan, one of the most sturdy champions of liberty in this side of India in the 16th century. The ballad of Manwoor Khan, a great-grandson of Isha Khan that we have secured, is another valuable historical record, which throws much sidelight on the political condition of the country during the latter part of Shah Jehan's rule, unfolding many incidents in the life of Shah Shuja, the unfortunate son of that monarch. These facts are mostly unknown to historians and though the ballad often becomes legendary in character, mixed up with popular fancy, it must be regarded as actually true in its historical aspects, so far as the main points of its description are concerned. Eastern Bengal is still full of traditions about Shah Shuja. A mosque in Tipperah was built by Govinda Manikya, Raja of Tipperah, and a personal friend of the prince, the cost being borne by the sale of a valuable diamond-ring, which the latter had presented to the Tipperah-Raja. The cost of maintenance of this mosque is met from the endowment of a village, called 'Shuja-Nagar' in Tipperah, named after him,—a gift of Govinda Manikya for the purpose. Prince Shuja was one of the most conspicuous figures at Dacca towards the end of the seventeenth century, where his vicissitudes of fortune and incidents of life have left a lasting impression on the popular mind.

It appears that Shah Shuja, while staying at Dacca in the garden-house of Lall Bagh, was enamoured of a princess, named Sunai, a daughter of Nawab Amir Aly. He proposed to marry her, offering her a dowry of two lakhs of rupees with other presents. But as he was stout and of unwieldy features, his limbs lacking the nimble manly grace of a gallant—worthy of a fashionable lady's love, he could not win the heart of the handsome maiden of Dacca. Her mother, however, favoured the proposal owing to the high status, which such a connection would give her daughter, and marriage-negotiations had considerably advanced. But she absconded in the meantime with Manwoor Khan, who was accomplished and handsome, though his position as Dewan of Jangalbari was certainly far inferior to that of the prince.

Shah Shuja's dogged pursuit of Manwoor Khan, described in this ballad, bristles with interest. With his own army which was considerable, reinforced by recruits from Murshidabad, he pursued Manwoor Khan, who had been making a precipitous retreat, pursuing a tortuous river-course to avoid Shah Shuja. In a boat, rowed by thirty-two oarsmen, Manwoor Khan passed through the canal of Demra and reached the great expanse of Sitalakha. Having crossed the latter, he came to the Kyatara from where he sent princess Sunai to Jangal Bari, his capital. He next turned his course and arrived at Naraingunj. As soon as Shah Shuja got a report of this, he came with forty armed boats in pursuit of Manwoor Khan who now fled to Barisal. But before Shah Shuja could reach the latter place, Manwoor had fled to Jhalakathi. From Jhalakathi to Khulna and thence to Keshabpur, the pursuer chased the pursued and to very many other places till a full year rolled by. Shah Shuja was wearied of his adventurous pursuit, involving a heavy cost for the maintenance of the army. Food was not always available for them in the out-of-the-way places, visited during the fruitless search, and he was obliged to dismiss them, retaining only fifty picked warriors. But so great had been his rage at his disappointment in love that he did not give up his pursuit inspite of all hardships. Manwoor Khan, in the meantime, had reached the small island of Sandwip in the Bay of Bengal. Shah Shuja all unexpectedly arrived there so that his enemy was taken by absolute surprise. The latter entered a Musjid there, of which the sacred walls offered him shelter—where he could not be molested by his enemy. The prince did not violate the rules of the sanctuary but surrounded it with his fifty men, confident that Manwoor Khan would find no way of escape and would eventually be starved to death. Full twenty-one days passed and there was no sign of any living being in the mosque. Shah Shuja, at this stage, ordered its doors to be opened by force, being certain that Manwoor Khan, the young Dewan of Jangal Bari, had died.

But when the door was broken open, the commanding figure of the Dewan, though reduced by hunger, was observed at the gateway, wielding his sword with a dexterity which baffled the attempts of many of the prince's soldiers to get hold of his person. Wonder-struck at this valorous conduct of his famished foe, Shah Shuja gazed with surprise and admiration at the handsome and majestic appearance of the Dewan. He ordered his men to withdraw and graciously pardoned the Jangal Bari-chief. They now became fast friends and conceived the plan of jointly attacking the Burmese king of Chittagong, which was not very far from Sandwip.

Shah Shuja gained a victory here, mainly owing to a stratagem, by which Manwoor Khan had killed the Burmese king Rahangam and succeeded in spreading a consternation in his army.

The prince and Manwoor Khan looted the palace, which yielded valuable treasure, a part of which was given to the Dewan. Two boats, full of valuables, were sent to Jangalbari.

The Burmese citizens were mostly driven away from Chittagong by the heroes. Those amongst them, who embraced Islam, were allowed to live there. Many good Muhammadans were brought from the neighbouring countries and made to settle at Chittagong under Shah Shuja's orders. They obtained Lakhraj (rent-free) lands as gifts from the prince, "Even now," Says the ballad-maker, "these lands stand as lakhraj-properties of their owners,—at one time granted by

Shah Shuja." The town was given the name of Islamabad, after Islam had thus obtained a firm footing there. Many towns and markets were established in the district by the two glorious heroes, and these have since flourished.

After this adventure, the prince and the Dewan came back to Naraingunj where they parted—Manwoor going to his own town of Jangalbari and the prince to Rajmahal. "At this time," Says the ballad-maker in a sad tone, "Shah Shuja was destined to meet his tragic end, well known in the pages of history."

From a poem by Syed Alwal, we come to know of the developments that took place at Arakan, where prince Shaq Shuja had fled after his defeat at the hands of Aurangzeb. But this is no episode of our ballad-literature. So we refrain from noticing it here. We have, however, come across some lines of an old ballad, in which there is a humorous reference to a daughter of Shah Shuja falling in love with a Burmese Prince during his stay in that country.

We are sorry, for shortness of .space we could not insert the ballad of Manwoor Khan in this volume.

3. *Struggle of the Bhuian Rajas for Independence.*

A spirit of revolt against the Delhi-suzerain seems to have been rampant in Bengal in the 16th and 17th centuries. The Bāra Bhuians, or the twelve sub-lords of Bengal were practically independent and wielded a great power. Besides the Nawabs of Bengal themselves often tried to throw off the imperial yoke when an opportunity presented itself. Daud Khan and Katlu Khan had lost their lives in such attempts, but Sher Shah became successful.

Isha Khan, one of the Bhuian lords, had many a tough fight with the Imperial army, led by Shahbaz Khan and Man Sinha. The conciliatory spirit, that characterised the administration of Akbar, eventually subdued the chief of Jangalbari by an offer of friendship. His great-grandson, Manwoor Khan, as is proved by the accounts given above, conducted his hostilities against Shah Shuja with courage and tact, having even dared to carry off a princess, who was practically betrothed to the latter. The ballad of Feroz Khan proves in an undoubted manner how acutely the yoke of Delhi oppressed the souls of these Baiswara Rajput chiefs, converted to Islam. It is said that the young Dewan lost all taste for food and spent sleepless nights over the thought of his political thraldom, which obliged him to pay an annual revenue to the Delhi-Court. He decided to stop payment of the revenue and was on the eve of a revolt, convinced that such a course would, in all probability, involve his ruin. The story of Chand Rai and that of his brother Kedar Rai are a record of incessant struggle to assert independence, and at least one of them lost his life in an affray with the Imperial army under Man Siñha. But the figure of Pratap Aditya rises far above these glorious rebels in bravery and indomitable spirit of an unyielding patriotism. The words with which he answered the Delhi-ambassador when the latter handed him fetters and a sword as alternatives, wishing him to accept either at his choice—the one indicating his submission to the throne of Delhi and the other his wish to meet the Imperial army in battle—are characteristically significant. Pratap Aditya said, "I return the fetters. With these bind the feet of your own master at Delhi. I accept the sword; after my victory, I will wash off its blood-stain in the waters of the Jumna."

The sub-lords of Bengal were verily like wild leopards and in their struggle for independence, they hardly showed a spirit of compromise. Pratap Aditya, after winning many victories in the field, was at last killed by Man Sinha. The last of these champions of freedom was Raja Sitaram Rai, the relics of whose palace are still to be seen at Mahmudpur in the district of Jessore. But these are not all ; we learn from Vaishnaba history that Raja Vira Hambir of Vaishnupur had attempted to lead an expedition against the Nawab of Murshidabad, and Raja Chand Rai of Gaur Dwar (not the hero of Sripur) was so powerful that the Pathan king Katlu Khan did not venture to send his revenue-collectors to his city for recovering his arrear-dues. The Rajmala records the victories that some of the old monarchs of Tipperah won over the kings of Gaur, helped by the Imperial force.

During the 16th and 17th centuries Bengal was in a troubled state and the Hindu sub-lords had practically become independent, defying the powers of the Nawab of Gaur and sometimes aspiring to the still higher glory of throwing off the Delhi-yoke.

Bengali women have often shown heroic and romantic traits of character in these ballads, but the character of Sakhina attains a towering eminence not only by her devotion to husband, which was so great that she did not even shrink from fighting with her own father for its sake, but by the triumphant victory that she won over the Delhi army, disguised as a young soldier. All the while, however, the feminine grace of her character was in evidence, which reached its flowering point at her death, caused by a letter of divorce. The field of Kellatajpur in the sub-division of Kishoregunj (Mymensingh) still bears the spot, where the heroic woman fought like a lioness and died of a broken heart like a fragile woman that she was.

4. *Connection of the Ballads with old Bengali-Literature, especially with the Vaishnava Literature.*

These ballads have opened our eyes to an altogether new chapter in the history of Bengali literature. The rustic songs are permeated by deep poetry, presenting to us vividly the varying shades of popular mentality in Bengal. The poets of the Renaissance have written classical works, which are now recognised as land-marks in our literature. But however highly some of them might have been admired when their authors lived, the true test of their excellence and abiding interest lies in the relation which they bear to the ballads. However Sanskritised they may be in form, the more they approach the spirit and the language of the ballads, the greater is their appeal to the popular mind. Their gorgeous exterior dazzled the eyes of their contemporaries at one time, but their genuineness and claims to permanent poetic fame should be judged not by their rich loans from Sanskrit, but from the way in which they have been able to depict popular sentiments of which these ballads are the nurseries.

Take for instance the Vaishnava literature of Bengal. A student unfamiliar with the ballads will hardly be able to trace the history of Bengal Vaishnavism. The ballads show romantic love, kindred to that which the Sahajiyas have developed. Chandidas says, "Every one of our time aspires to be a Sahajiya. But how many of us know the true significance of that creed?" This statement of the great poet of the fourteenth century, proves that the Sahajiya creed was in a flourishing condition in Bengal during this period. For illustration of this fact one should read the ballads of the young Herdsman, the Washer-maiden, Kanchanmala and Lila, published in this volume. They show men and women, strikingly the latter, inspired by a spirit of romantic love. They are beautiful poems, having a natural flavour of their own, and belonging as they do to the secular plane, they do not seem to owe anything directly to the Sahajiya propaganda which bears the hall-mark of the spiritual. But all the same they evince a kindred spirit and prove beyond doubt that the atmosphere of Bengal of that age was permeated by a spirit of freedom in sexual relation, which though it reached the highest and the best conceivable perfection, was not yet reckoned as a spiritual force. The whole province of Bengal lay under the spell of this romantic love, showing a higher sacrifice for the beloved than is to be found even in mediæval knight-errantry. It gives rise to stormy emotions of the soul and is assuredly a result of *tapasyā* for which I do not find an adequate expression in English.

The ballads show that Bengal was slowly preparing itself for the message of Chaitanya Deva—the message of divine love. Great hardship and self-sacrifice, verging on martyrdom are in evidence everywhere, this being a dominant feature especially in the characters of the heroines. This form of secular but highly romantic love was idealised by Chandidas till Chaitanya came forward to give it a spiritual interpretation and elevate it to a superior plane. He said, "Yes, Radha loved Krishna and abandoned all for her beloved cowherd. But Radha is the human soul and Krishna is none other than the Great One, who wants all men to love Him with all their might." The ballads bear no trace of Vaishnava influence whatever. In their crude language and complete independence of all religious ideas and propagandism, they stand alone as theoffspring of a school a different from all others. Though romantic, they seldom rise above the earth, and one familiar with

Vaishnava poetry will find them in no sign of any connection with the ballads. Chronologically speaking, some of the ballads might be anterior to Chandidas, but most of them are of a later period. No wave of Vaishnava thought seems to have reached the rustic huts, where the ballads were sung. How are we then to account for the fact that occasionally we find the very lines of Chandidas and other Vaishnava poets occurring in them? The situation and environment of lovers described in these ballads occasionally show a striking similarity with the incidents of Radha-Krishna love. The ballads are evidently, as I have stated, a quite independent literature. How are we to account for the unmistakably striking agreement between the two in verbal forms?

Now we are going to illustrate our remark by some specific cases, which show this concurrence most prominently. It is well known that of all Vaishnava poets, Chandidas uses the archaic language of the country-folk with the most happy effect. Though a great Sanskrit scholar himself, his poems seldom indulge in classical display, but they throb with the life and sentiments of the people; and his finest lyrics are those wherein he depicts the joys, sorrows and felicitous emotions of his race and cares not for displaying a mastery over Sanskritic style or the canons of Sanskrit poetics, as he does in the first offspring of his poesy—the Krishna Kirtan. This rural element in his thought and language constitutes the strength and special feature of his poetry. Here in this literature of ballads, we find many sentences and phrases, which will at once recall the poetry of Chandidas. I will mention some striking cases of these. In the song of the Washer-maiden (12-30), we have the line "জিহ্বার সঙ্গে দাঁতের পীরিতি, আর ছলাতে কাটে" (It is like the friendship between the teeth and the tongue, the former do not fail to bite the latter on some pretext or other). We have a similar line in Chandidas almost in the very words of the ballad-maker, "জিহ্বার সঙ্গেতে দাঁতের পীরিতি, সময় পাইলে কাটে." In the same ballad, the line "তোমার চরণে আমার শতেক পরণাম" (Canto 24) will remind one of the famous song of Chandidas, "তোমার চরণে বঁধু শতেক পরণাম। তোমার চরণে বঁধু লিখ আমার নাম॥ লিখিতে দাসীর নাম লাগে যদি পায়। মাটিতে লিখিয়া নাম, চরণ দিও তায়." One of the most popular songs of Chandidas begins with the lines, "সুখের লাগিয়া এ ঘর বাঁধিনু অনলে পুড়িয়া গেল। অমিয়া-সাগরে সিনান করিতে সকলি গরল ভেল." The whole idea contained in the above is breathed in the following lines of the ballad of Bhelua;—the imagery is not the same, but the idea is strikingly similar, whereas the language of the ballads is simpler, more direct and homely, "গাছের তলায় আইলাম ছায়া পাইবার আশে। পত্র ছেইদ্যা রৌদ্র লাগে আপন কর্ম্মদোষে।" "ঘরেতে পাতিলাম শয্যা নিদ্রার কারণ। সেই ঘরে লাগিল আগুণ কপালে লিখন." The ballad of the Washer-maiden describes a situation where the princely youth, her lover, exposes himself to rain, and she, while feeling extreme pain at the suffering of her lover for her sake, cannot come out to meet him, as the elders of the house have not yet gone to sleep, and she deplores her lot in a soliloquy (2, 6-10). A situation like this gives the occasion for Chandidas's popular song, "এ ঘোর রজনী মেঘের ঘটা, কেমনে আইলা বাটে। আঙ্গিনার মাঝে, বঁধুয়া ভিজিছে, দেখে যে পরাণ ফাটে." The one seems evidently like the counter-part of the other. The lines "কাট্যা গেছে কাল মেঘ চাঁদের উদয়। এই পথে যেতে গেলে কুলমানের ভয়॥" (Washer-maiden, 2-18) will remind one of Chandidas's "কহিও বঁধুরে সই কহিও বঁধুরে। গমন বিরোধী হ'ল পাপ শশধরে॥" The many exquisite lines addressed to the flute and the effect of its sound, that we find in the Herdsman-lover (4, 47-62) are just like those which we so often meet with in Chandidas's lyrics,—the sweetest one being the song in the Krishna Kirtan, which begins with, "কে না বাঁশী বাএ, বড়ায়ি যমুনাণঙ্গ কূলে."

Not only Chandidas, but many other Vaishnava poets have written in a style in which the phraseology of our ballad-poetry occurs again and again. The unmatched beauty of Jnana Das's famous line, "ঢল ঢল কাঁচা অঙ্গের লাবণী অবনী বহিয়ে যায়" has many a parallel in the ballad-literature. For instance, "অঙ্গের লাবণী সোনাইর বাইয়া পড়ে ভূমে" (Dewan Bhabana, 2-12), "হাঁটিতে ভাঙ্গিয়া পড়ে অঙ্গের লাবণী" (Bhelua, 2, 23) and "হাটিতে মাটিতে ভাসে অঙ্গের লাবণী" (Isha Khan, 2, 17). The line "কাল দিন চল্যা গেল কাল হ'ল কাল" (Washer-maiden, 9-42), sounds like an echo of Vidyapati's "কাল অবধি বঁধু গেল। ..ভেল পরভাত পুছই সবহুঁ। কহ কহ রে সখি কালি কবহুঁ॥" Lochan Das's song "এস এস বঁধু এস," etc., popularised by Bankim Chandra in his "*Kamala Kanter Daptar*" has the line, "ফুল নহ যে কেশের করি বেশ." This idea we find again and again in the ballad-literature, for example, in "ফুল যদি হইতারে বঁধু ফুল হইতা তুমি। কেশেতে ছাপাইয়া রাখতাম, ঝার্যা বান্তাম বেণী॥" (Mahua 8-22), in "পুষ্প হ'লে প্রাণের বঁধু খোপায় রাখতাম তোরে।" (Dewan Bhabana, 4-26) and in "পুষ্প হ'লে বঁধুয়ারে গাথ্যা রাখতাম গলে" (Kamala p. 162). Gopal Uré, whose Yātrā-songs enjoyed a great popularity among the Bengalis in the early part of the nineteenth century, has some beautiful lines, the original of which comes to us as a surprise from the ballads. "ভোমরা আছিলা তুমি হৈলা গোবরিয়া" occurs in the Washer-maiden's song (S-19), composed about the 14th century, and the corresponding line in the very language of the ballad-poetry, we find in "গোবরা পোকা হইয়া বসিলি পদ্মে" of Gopal Uré.

We believe that the ballad-poetry did not supply the Vaishnava poets with these fine ideas. Nor did the ballad-makers copy from Vaishnava-poetry. Both got the ideas and the beautiful language in which we find them couched, from the rich phraseology of emotional poetry with which Bengal in those days abounded—a sequel to the romantic love with which the very atmosphere of this country was charged, due partly to the culture spread by the Sahajiyas. The ballad-makers and the Vaishnava-poets attacked a common source, the rural poetical phraseology current in the air of Bengal ; so that every poet who studied life, and not the Sanskrit classics alone, got the vivid images and this finished poetical language first-hand from his own hearth and home. The material was before the poets, if they only cared to utilise and not contemptuously reject it as a rustic thing beneath notice.

The ballad-literature shows us how deep-rooted in the soil is the Vaishnava-religion, founded by Chaitanya. It took centuries for the Bengali-people to fit them by emotional culture for receiving the love-messages of the apostle of Nadia. The higher emotion developed by the Bengali race, leading to noble sacrifices and martyrdoms, as we find in the ballads, was not "a rosy path of dalliance" with them. It was not a mere fashion of the age favoured by the dandies of society. It was a *tapasya*, a spiritual training under the garb of sexual romance, making the youth of both the sexes undergo all sacrifices and renunciations in the spirit of saints. Sexual love was thus gradually idealised, and when Chaitanya came forward to declare that it had no saving power except as an allegory of Divine Love, the people found no difficulty in receiving his interpretation, as the soil was already prepared for it.

Vaishnavism of Bengal, therefore, did not come from the south,—the home of Ramanuja ; neither did it come from Madhyacharya, *alias* Ananda tirtha, born in 1191 A.D., though it is popularly ascribed to him. It was a product of the soil, over which the very life-blood of men and women was shed for centuries and which was fertilised by tears—the offspring of self-less action. The ballad-literature of Bengal mirrors the *tapasya* of the people in the domain of emotion. And it was for this reason that Chaitanya's religion found a ready response in the country, and the lyrics of Vaishnava-masters had such a powerful appeal for the people. This Vaishnava-religion of Bengal arose out of the ashes of the martyrs of both sexes in the cause of love—Chaitanya turning the angle of vision from earth to a higher world.

But the connection of the ballads with our old literature does not cease here. If we scrutinise these popular songs, we will find in them the ground-work of the whole fabric of our past literature. We find lines and passages in them, which correspond to the texts of the aphorisms of Dāk and Khanā, the Maināmati songs, the Bengali Ramayanas, the Kabikankan Chandi, in fact, of all the best works of the old school. This establishes the indigenous character and homogeneity of our old literature. It seems that the common stock of the felicitous language of emotion, perfected in the countryside, did not supply the ballad-maker and the Vaishnava-poet alone with rich material, but also all other poets of the old school in every sphere of our literature. The ballads prove the existence of a common source, which offered to the old Bengali writers ideas and also the suitable language to convey them. We will illustrate our remark by references. In the Herdsman-lover (11-12), we find the lines, "ভরা কলসীর জল জমীনে ফেলিয়া। জলের ঘাটে যায় কন্যা কলসী লইয়া." The parallel will be found in the line of the aphorisms of Dāk "পানি ফেলি পানিকে যায়" (Typical Selections, Vol. I, p. 8). The lines, "তুমি হও তরুরে বঁধু আমি হই লতা। বেইড়া রাখব যুগল চরণ ছাইড়া যাবে কোথা ॥" (Kanka-o-Lila, p. 250) agrees almost *verbatim* with the appeal of Aduna to Gopichandra in the Mainamati-Songs:—"তুমি হবু বটবৃক্ষ আমি তোমার লতা। রাঙ্গা চরণ বেড়িয়া রমু ছাড়িয়া যাইবা কোথা." The lines "মুষ্টিতে আটয়ে লীলার চিকণ কাঁকালি" (Kanka-o-Lila, Canto V) and "মুষ্টিতে ধরিতে পারি কটিখানি সরু" (Kamala, 3-7) have their parallel in "মুষ্টিতে ধরিতে পারি সীতার কাঁকালি" (Kṛttivasa) and the lines "মনে বিষ মুখে মধু এতেক কহিয়া। ভেলুয়ার নিকটে গেল বিদায় মাগিয়া ॥" (Bhelua, p. 50) will remind one of "মনে বিষ মুখে মধু জিজ্ঞাসে ফুল্লরা। ক্ষুধা তৃষ্ণা দূরে গেল রন্ধনের ত্বরা ॥" of Kabikankan. We have quoted only stray passages to prove our point. Some of the finest passages of many a distinguished Bengali poet of the old school will be accounted for and traced in the current phraseology of popular literature, composed by illiterate rustics. The spring of poetry was in the heart of the masses—in the artless souls of the rural people. From this source flowed the current of Vaishnava-thought, purified by philosophy and science on the one hand, and some of the exquisite ideas of our Renaissance-literature enlivened by words of Sanskritic importation on the other. The ballads open the portals of the history of our cultural development in various spheres of literary activities and possess more than their poetic value, unfolding the latent forces that created and developed our literature.

The few historical ballads, given in this volume, may be found lacking in poetical interest. But they are valuable as illuminating some of the obscure corners of the history of Bengal. We have reserved a number of ballads of this kind for insertion in the third volume.

The song of the Washer-maiden, that of Kanchanmala, of Lila and the incomplete ballad of the Herdsman-lover are, however, the finest examples of lyrical poetry in the field of ballads, occasionally rising to a sublime epic-height by the grandeur of the character of the heroines.

An instance of glorious poetry occurs in the ballad of Rani Kamala, which we have found in an incomplete shape based on an historical incident, mixed up with a mystic legend-lore. The ovation it gives to the Dawn (Rani Kamala, 10, 1-11), when the Sun-God descends from his golden chariot and, taking his bath in the sea, scatters the golden particles from its wheels as he commences his journey of the day, is glowing in its primitive simplicity and is as grand as the Riks, addressed to the Goddess Ushā in the Vedas. It shows the noble conception of a poetic soul face to face with Nature, and is entirely free from the trammels of rhetorical convention.

Munshi Jasimuddin has sent me another version of the ballad of Rani Kamala, which gives a different account of the preliminary portion of this story.

In the version published herein the queen requests the Raja to excavate a pond, as a token of his love for her, which would be of the size of the whole length of a *takua* of thread to be spun by her in seven days.

In the version supplied by Jasimuddin we find the Raja and the Rani engaged in playing dice—the condition being that should the Raja win, the Rani must induce her parents to give her sister in marriage to the Raja. As polygamy was the fashion of the day, and marrying a sister-in-law, unlike the custom in some western countries, is sanctioned by society in India, there was nothing unusual or unfair in this condition. On the other side, if the Rani would win, the Raja was to excavate a pond in her name. Its size was to be determined by the range of the sound of a drum to be beaten by the drummer attached to the palace with his utmost strength.

The Rani won the play. At that particular moment the accumulated revenue of the Raj due to the Imperial treasury of Delhi was outstanding for some years, and it had to be paid without delay. The sound of the drum, if the drummer would beat with his utmost power, might be heard from a distance of two miles. To excavate a pond of such a vast dimension would involve an expenditure that could not be met from the funds at the Raja's disposal at that hour of financial stress. So he privately ordered the drummer to beat his drum low, so that the sound might not go very far.

Another point of difference between the two versions is that instead of the Raja dreaming the dream which made his consort to sacrifice her life, the dream was dreamt by the Rani herself in the unpublished ballad. This takes away the stigma of cruelty that might be attributed to the Raja for unfolding his dream to the Rani.

The version secured by Jasimuddin thus gives a more rational account of the story. But the present version is more poetical and possesses a higher literary value. The historian may give credit to Jasimuddin's version, but the literary public will enjoy the one that is published here much better.

I must, however, speak apologetically of the poor quality of my translation. The refined emotional language of the Bengali people, in its niceties of expression, is hardly capable of felicitous translation into a language which, inspite of its unmatched richness, does not seem to me to be equally tender. Besides this, the translator is keenly aware of his limitations in regard to English language. The short ballad of Lila is full of niceties of tender expression, and adequate language could not be found for preserving the beauty of the original. The long poem of Bhelua is comparatively dull, but occasionally rises to a lyrical excellence by dint of the country-dialect, which, divested of its original garb, has become poor in my translation.

Great difficulties have been experienced by me in translating the emotional poetry of Bengal and I may be permitted to refer to some of them here. There is no equivalent word in English for the Bengali word মান. The indescribable sweetness attached to the Bengali word, which under the thin veneer of anger tries to attract rather than repel, is not conveyed by any word that I know of even in the other Indian Vernaculars, not to speak of English. The words রঙ্গিণী and অনুরাগিণী lose all their sweetness in translation. It is vain to expect an equivalent for the extremely tender Bengali word সোহাগ. Climatic conditions of Bengal give a peculiar charm to some words here which is missed in translation. For instance the word শীতল bears more than its face-value and implies the tenderness of a healing balm in this tropical climate of ours. How can the extreme tenderness of the word in such lines as "শীতল তছু অঙ্গ পরশ রস-লালসে" (Jnan Das) and "এস প্রেমময়ি, পরাশিয়ে অঙ্গ শীতল হই।" (Krishna Kamal) be conveyed in English. The English word 'cooling' hardly gives an adequate idea. The word 'জুড়ানু' is another such word. Then in a tropical country mere names of the months 'ভাদর' and 'শাঙণ' recall to the mind picturesque landscape-scenes with the vividness of a kaleidoscopic show and this can be ill brought out by such words as September and October. The word রাঙ্গা in "রাঙ্গা পা দুখানি," conveying to the Bengali mind the associations of the red dye আল্তা or the colour of the lotus with which the feet are generally compared, loses all its sweetness, nay verges on the grotesque if we translate it by the English word "red." There are hundreds of such words in the field of emotional poetry over which the translators will halt. They will vainly strive to find suitable equivalents for these in English. And added to this is my own imperfect knowledge of English which has, as I have already said, been a great hindrance.

There are four kinds of ballads that we could lay our hands upon from the countryside.

The first kind of these is of the nature of Mainămati songs. Superstitious beliefs in miracles, rustic and crude conventions, grotesque scenes and incongruities and faith in the Siddhās, who, like the Druids, could accomplish extraordinary feats of jugglery, form the essential features of this school of ballads. Tantrikism is the underlying principle of these. And the Buddhist Tantriks, when accepting Islam, could not shake off their belief in the miraculous power of Tantrik action. We have got many Tantrik-works written by Muhammadans in Bengali from Chittagong. This kind of ballads may be compared to the Gaelic songs. An element of intense poetry is not, however, altogether lacking in this class of popular songs, though such instances are few and far between. In the present volume, the ballad of Nizam Dacoit belongs to this school. I have found a long printed poem on the dacoit who latterly turned a saint, composed by a rustic poet anxious to display his pedantry. This poem lacks the beauty of simple and direct expression, which forms the *forte* of all genuine Bengali ballads. The present one is fresh from countryside and though comparatively dull, it has not been spoiled or distorted by unskilled hands, trying to improve the diction. Though written by a Muhammadan it has all the characteristics of the ballads of this kind composed by the Hindus about their own saints. There is, however, one thing in it, which shows its difference of conception from the Hindu standpoint. The dacoit is said to have shortened the period of his trial by two murders. Though the Gītā would support such an idea, the Hindus of rural Bengal would never extol a murder, however laudable the purpose may be. I do not say that the Moslem ethical point of view is wrong or that the teachings of the Gītā should be discarded, as regards the merits of a martial deed in a noble cause. But my belief is that an unprejudiced Hindu writer of Bengal during the last five or six centuries of the growth and development of Vaisnava ideas in the country, would never advocate assassination even for the best of purposes. The ballad of Nizam Dacoit shows indifferent poetry, though it is extensively popular among the Muhammadans in some parts of Bengal.

The ballads of the second class are historical. I have given three of them in this volume and the small ballad on Santal insurrection may also be classed under this head. It records an event which caused considerable local consternation in the western frontier of Bengal more than half a century ago. It is not, however, a very important ballad. I must say here that through inadvertence this little poem, though belonging to western Bengal, has found a place in this volume which bears the name of "Eastern Bengal Ballads."

The third class, which is by far the best of all, is represented by the love-ballads of the romantic school, of which we have spoken at some length. Though I have found scraps of verses from this kind of ballads—sometimes only a few lines of them—from other districts of Bengal, the best and the most complete ones are to be found in Eastern Mymensingh alone. Brahminic Renaissance drove away these gems of rustic literature from all other parts of Bengal, because the spirit of romantic love propagated in them ran counter to the strict conservatism of the later school of Hinduism, which totally curbed the liberty of women. These songs were allowed to linger in Eastern Mymensingh, where Brahminic Renaissance could not assert itself for some centuries. In other parts of Bengal, ballads like those of Mahuā, Maluā and Washer-maiden lost favour and were suppressed, and in their places, the stories of Sita and Savitri, of Prahlad and Dhruva, of Nala and Damayanti and the heroic Pandavas, claimed high favour in popular estimation, due to the stress, put upon '*Bhakti*' or devotion in later times, and to the dissemination of orthodox Brahminic ideas, curbing the liberty of the fair sex. But as we have found mere unconnected, scraps of romantic love-songs, (now lost) belonging to a preceding age, still lingering in the memory of the rustics of all districts of Bengal, we are convinced that they had once flourished throughout the province, previous to Brahminic renaissance. The most striking of the ballads of this school in some points, though decidedly not one of the very best of them, is the ballad "The Adventurous career of a young Dacoit." It gives a fresh account of country-life on the banks of the great rivers of Eastern Bengal, of a love-romance, full of the freedom and flavour of rural scenes—with much quaint humour and varied scenes of action, giving us glimpses into the social history and family-life of the cottagers of Bengal, as was to be found two centuries ago. Though it does not possess that appeal to higher emotions, which the best ones of this kind of ballads do, it possesses a singular charm for the variety of scenes of thrilling interest introduced, and the valorous, resourceful character of the heroine, unfortunately stranded midway, as a complete version of this remarkable ballad has not been found. Its archaic language will be of great interest to the students of philology.

The fourth kind of ballads is to be found in the numerous printed books, which form the bulk of Moslem rustic literature. These publications are generally found to give distorted versions of popular ballads. The writers, anxious to make a show of their little learning, change the simple words of original ballads and thus spoil their pristine grace and beauty. They introduce moreover absurd pedantries and erotic descriptions,—the characteristics of eighteenth century Bengali literature,—converting the simple narrations of unassuming rural poets into absurd artificialities and conventional forms of a school of poetry that has justly lost all favour with our people, and is now quite out of fashion.

5. *A description of the ships referred to in the ballads—Pictures and illustrations.*[1]

In the literature of the ballads there are good many references to country boats and ships on board of which the enterprising people of the district of Chittagong make sea-voyages for trading purposes. Ship-building in Chittagong is an art of great antiquity. Bangsidas, the celebrated poet of the Manasa cult, who wrote his poem in 1575 A.D., gives a graphic description as to how the great sea-going vessels were constructed in Bengal in olden times. The poet was a native of Mymemsingh,

[1] Babu Asutosh Choudhury, one of our ballad-collectors has supplied me with elaborate notes on the ships and country-boats of Chittagong, which have materially helped me in writing this account. The photographs of sloops and ships given here have been supplied by him.

the land of great rivers like the Brahmaputra, the Kangsa, the Dhanu, and the Bhairab. The old ships of Chittagong once carried the wealthy merchants of Bengal to China, Ceylon, Maladives, Lacadives, Java, Balli, Cochin and to the coasts of the Arabian Sea. There were many architects and sculptors of Bengal who co-operated with the Kalingas in carrying out the artistic designs of the great Buddhist sanctuary known as the Barabodar Temple of Java and of the sublime Hindu figures in the Prahmva-banam in the Island of Balli. Earliest of these works carry us to the 3rd and 4th centuries A.D. These travellers of the high seas assuredly marched on board the ships constructed by the Balamis on the banks of the Karnafuli in Chittagong. The descendants of these Hindu architects still follow the avocation of ship-building, though the glorious achievements of their fore-fathers are now reduced to mere day-dreams;—the humble avocation of the present-day Balamis is to build large and small country boats and ships of ordinary dimensions and workmanship which still carry the merchants of Bengal to the small Islands of the Bay for trading purposes. At one time the Sultan of Turkey, dissatisfied with the method of ship-building in Alexandrian dock-yards, used to give order for ships to the builders of Chittagong. This we learn on the authority of the Chinese traveller Mahunda. The celebrated Arabian writer Edris who flourished in the twelfth century called Chittagong by the name of 'Karnabul.' This word is no doubt a corruption of the Karnafuli on the banks of which the Balamis constructed ships and so popularised the name of their river among foreigners as to make them call the whole district after it. De Burrarghs, the celebrated Portuguese writer alludes to the commercial transactions carried on between Chittagong and Arabia in ancient times. Many Arabian Dervishes and Pirs came to Chittagong on board the vessels built in that country. In 1405 Cheng Ho, the Chinese minister, was sent to the port of Chittagong by his king for the settlement of some commercial disputes, and in 1443 the Arabian traveller Ebn Batatu came to Chittagong and travelled on board one of her ships to Java and thence to China. In 1553 Nanu de Chona, the Governor of Goa, sent one of his generals, De Manna, at the head of two hundred men and five ships for establishing a trading centre at Chittagong. Shipbuilding in Chittagong has had thus a glorious record since a remote point of antiquity till only recent times. Hunter says that the great art of the country was ousted, failing in competition with European vessels conducted by steam-engine on scientific methods, from after 1875.

The tradition of some of the wealthy and enterprising merchants of Chittagong, who flourished during the declining days of Moslem supremacy, has been preserved in the country. We have heard of the famous merchants Rangya Basir, Gumani Malum, Madan Kerani, Dataram Chaudhuri and others who lived in that period,—some of them owning a hundred ships. When the Portuguese pirates carried on marauding expeditions in Chittagong, the merchants of the place created a defence force by means of their sloops which heroically resisted the attack of the pirates. This united body of sloops went by the name of 'Sloop Bahar' and a port of that name still exists near the town of Chittagong. The hero who distinguished himself in this defence was called the 'Bahardār.' In the early part of the 19th century many merchants owned a good number of ships in Chittagong. Piru Saudagar, Nasu Malum and Ram Mohun Daroga were the most eminent of these. One of the ships of the last named person once went for trade up to the port of the Tweed in Scotland.

I have already stated that the ballads are full of references about these ships and country-boats of Chittagong. In the ballad of the Washer maiden, there is an interesting description of the ships of Tamasā Gazi, carrying an extensive trade in rice. The ballad of Bhelua literally bristles with accounts of ships. Among the many interesting things described in it are to be found accounts of a peculiar custom among a section of local merchants—of the bride and bridegroom elect being married on board the great merchant-vessels in the high seas. The ballad of the Herdsman Lover refers to the voyages of Meghua, the wicked merchant of Chittagong. We have had accounts of the unfortunate prince Shah Suja in the ballad of Mannoor Khan. Shah Suja, it is well-known in Burma, fled from Araccan on board a Balam ship of Chittagong. In the small ballad of (গৌরমণি মাঝির ভাসান) (the voyages of Gourmani, the boatman), there is a description of a fishing excursion in the Bay of Bengal on a Godhu boat, and in the ballad of স্বরূপ জেলের বারমাসী[1] (Accounts of twelve months on the sea of Svarup, the fisherman) there is a similar description.

As, therefore, in the ballad literature—nay in the whole of the old Bengali literature—there are numerous references to sea-voyages, and as the Chittagong ships and country boats were pre-eminently the best of the lot and have up to now preserved the old tradition, though in an humble scale, I take the liberty of giving a detailed account of these ships and country boats with illustrations.

1. The *Balam* and the *Godhu* boats are by far the most common in Chittagong in the present day. Their pattern has remained unaltered from a great antiquity and though they are mere boats of an humble size, not

[1] These two ballads have not yet been published.

furnished with any modern scientific equipments, they are not afraid of running abreast the high seas sometimes for five or six months together. The Balam boats are built by Balamis who have also lent their name to a particular kind of rice in which they traded. These boats even now go to Araccan, Kaikfu and other ports of Burma, their principal article being rice (see Fig. XI). The biggest of the Balam boats of the present day have the capacity to carry 200-250 tons of goods. They are, however, granted license for only 50 tons of goods when journeying in the Bay. In olden times their capacity and size were of course immensely greater. The Balam has sixteen oars attached it, but it chiefly depends on the sail.

2. *The Godhu boats.*[1]—these also like the Balams are very ancient. A full-shaped Godhu complete in all its parts, is to be found in the Bay up to March and April of the year. The parts of the boat are disjointed after April, when the keels are separated from the upper parts and kept safe in the dock. The parts are jointed again in October when the boats are floated once more in water The fishing excursions referred to in the ballads are carried on in the Godhu boats. The Godhu generally speaking carries 25-30 men and goes for fishing to various Islands in the Bay such as সোনা দিয়া (The Golden Island), লাল দিয়া (The Red Island), রাঙ্গা বালী (Red Sands) and other small Islands which are completely submerged under saline water when the flood comes. Hence the soil is not fit for purposes of cultivation but becomes a resort of a rich variety of fish. The dried fish which are carried on a Godhu, go by various names such as '*Badarer Chhuri*, *Ghoanrā*, *Phaisā*, *Laittā*, *Rishyā*, *Palkā*, *Chagaichhā*, etc.,

[1] They are called "Huri boats" in Maldwip and "Fatemari boats" in some places.

In April and March a large number of Godhus return to the Karnaphuli with their rich cargo of dried fish, and then it presents a spectacle which is never to be forgotten by the observer. The friends and relations of these fishermen who come back on their Godhus with the goods offer them a hearty reception, beating drums and tabors and playing on the shrill pipe, called the *Sanai* and the Karnaphuli becomes stirred all on a sudden with a dense concourse of people on her banks and with bristling activities of hundreds of Godhus, receiving a noisy ovation from the kith and kin of the enterprising fishermen. After the business-season of the Godhus is over, the parts are disjointed and kept in safe custody.

The construction of the Godhu is very simple. The keel is carved out of a long huge tree in the form of the crescent moon. Its breadth is very small. With this keel are jointed what the local people call *chāps*,—being pieces of timber not exactly like planks but concave-shaped thin wooden pieces, twenty to twenty five feet long, two or two and a half inches in thickness, and eighteen inches in breadth, which exactly fit in with the keel and with one and another. Nails are not used in joining the wooden pieces. Small holes called "*shama*" are made both ways and a strong kind of cane locally called "*gallāk*" is used for the purpose. The little space between two *chāps* are filled with straws of *ulu* species twisted like cords. They become so tight that not a particle of water can enter the boat though it is dashed by strong current. The *shamas* or the holes, after the cane has been made to enter through them, are filled up with jute, cotton and resin. The roofs of the Balam as well as the Godhu are called *pong*. The prow of the Godhu of old type was made to look like the head of a crocodile. The boatmen used to adorn it with vermilion and floral wreaths.

3. The "Sloop" is like the Balam in many respects, changed into its present form by the influence of the Portuguese (Figs. III, IV, V, VI).

4. *The Sarenga.*—This kind of boat has lent its name to the Captain of a ship; a "*sareng*" means a Captain in the Bengali dialect. It is like a canoe, being carved out from a long tree, and there is no joining or patchwork in it. It seldom ventures on a sea-journey. Its scope of movement is limited to rivers.

5. *The Shampan.*—The shape of this class of boats is like that of a swan. It is a Chinese type with a slight variation, due to Burmese influence.

6. *The Kondha.*—It is made by carving out a huge tree of the Chittagong hills. If is carried with the help of bamboo-poles called the '*lagi*' and never travels in the sea. It hardly dares to face the turbulent waves of a river, having no sail or oar.

A new activity has been in evidence since 1916. Many ships have since been constructed in Chittagong in European style. The great war gave a stimulus to the activities of the Chittagong dockyards, and from the official reports of the ports we find that no less than forty ships were built by the Balamis during the period 1916-21. Mr. Williams and Lt. Wilson took great pains in teaching the Balamis to construct ships in approved scientific methods of the west. Inspite of the defects of the old style, Lt. Wilson was struck with the remarkable skill of the Balamis in ship-building. Their trained hands could build the whole and its parts, joining pieces of timber and going through other details with almost scientific precision, without making any plan or design beforehand. The Balamis belong to the Jogi caste and are called Bāheriās, a local name indicating that the water touched by them may not be drunk by higher castes. This proves that they were probably Buddhists and did not believe in the restrictions imposed on us by later Hindu jurisprudence as regards sea-voyage. In olden times there were docks in Halisahar, Patenga, Doble Mobing and various other places on the Karnafuli. Fig. II shows the congestion of a great number of smaller boats at the Chāktai ghāt of Chittagong port.

At the present day Madhab, Kalikumar and Dwarika Nath have achieved distinction as ship-builders. Dwarika Nath is by far the best of the three men. Madhab is now engaged in building a steam-launch. He has nearly completed the wooden structure by timbers of the Chittagong Hill-tracts. The engine will be placed in due course. Most of the sloops and ships of which pictures are given in this book were constructed by Kali Kumar, and Dwarika Nath is now engaged in executing some orders for ships at Rangoon.

It may be interesting to note here the local names given to parts of a ship in the Chittagong dialect. They call the ship's 'Rib'—*bāk*, its Floor—*Kahana*, Keel—*erāk*, Keelson—*Shukankila*, Stern-post—*Gudasta*, Stem—*Rad*, Mast—*Mastul*, Rake of the mast—*Mastuler chaluta* and Batten—*Ishka.*

The famous 'Kosha' boats used to be made in the district of Dacca. We have got an exaggerated description of Kosha in the ballad of Isha Khan.

In conclusion I beg to offer my thanks to Mr. Jogesh Chandra Chakravartty, M.A., Assistant Registrar, Calcutta University, for making arrangements for the speedy publication of this volume. Dr. John Van Manen of the Asiatic Society of Bengal was kind enough to lend me two blocks containing pictures of cannon of Ishā

Khan and Sher Shaha published in the Journal of that Society for 1910. He has also kindly given me permission to reprint the picture of a cannon of the illustrious Moslem Chief of Jangalbari with a Bengali inscription also published in the Journal of the Society for 1910.

My thanks are due to Babu Biswapati Chaudhury, M.A.—the well-known Bengali writer and artist for the excellent pen and ink sketches that he has drawn of some of the characters described in the ballads of this volume. He did the work with the utmost quickness, though he was suffering at the time from ophthalmia—I am pleased with his work, though I am sorry he disregarded his health in his eagerness to finish the work in the shortest time.

My young friend, Mr. Janardan Chakrabartty, M.A., appointed by the Calcutta University to help me in the compilation of the ballads, rendered me some service in March last when owing to my hard and unsparing labour in connection with the ballads I fell seriously ill. Mr. Chakrabartty translated small portions of the Bengali texts into English for me in that month.

My friend Miss Rowlands, B.A., Lady Principal of the Darjeeling Missionary College, was kind enough to revise a portion of my translations.

Munshi Jasimuddin, one of our ballad collectors, has supplied photographs of the old capital of Laksman Hazra, now reduced to a swamp and of the ruins of the palace and the mosque built by the immediate descendants of Ishā Khan.

Inspite of my great labour in connection with the ballads I am sorry to say that there are many errors in the book. I do not blame anybody but myself for this fault. I am not at all a good proof-reader.

And though I have been writing books for these forty years, I have not at all improved in this direction. This makes me believe in the saying that a proof-reader is born and not made.

7, Biswakosh Lane,
Bagbazar. Calcutta : } DINESH CHANDRA SEN.
The 15th July, 1926.

THE LOVE OF THE WASHER-MAIDEN

PREFACE

The song of the Washer-maiden is one of the typical love-ballads of Eastern Bengal, rich in the musical rhythm of its limpid verses and in the mystic suggestions of its all-absorbing and resigned surrender of self.

The maiden Kanchanmala, a low-caste handsome girl, receives attention from the young prince of her native city. While feeling in her heart romantic sentiments, verging on worship, she knows full well the difference between her own social status and that of the prince. She is, therefore, full of hesitancy in the beginning. The gay light-hearted young prince once passionately seizes her by the hand, when she is all alone on the landing steps of a tank. She is surprised, she is pleased. She struggles to free herself, she makes false promises and trembles in fear. But all in vain. Her mind is filled with his image; she is almost frenzied by the sweet attraction. All the struggle on her part, however, is set at rest by the bold ways of the prince, who takes a vow to court any danger for her sake and speaks many things which one says to another, when Cupid, for the first time, aims his dart at young hearts. The poet describes, with great power, the aggressions of a self-willed capricious but loving youth on her modesty, on the one hand, and the timorous approaches of the maiden, afraid of scandal, and nervously conscious of her low status, on the other. Then, when in the language of worldly men she has actually sinned, she stops with a sigh to reflect, when she sees the Khorāi flowing by, "Whence dost thou come, O stream, and knowing not whither thou wilt go, why art thou in such a mad hurry ?" (Canto III,

Lines 1-2). This little speech indicates an anxious thought about her own mad course and uncertain future.

Here we find her, indulging in reveries, which, shrouded in obscure and suggestive poetry, verge on mysticism. She has loved one, whom neither heaven nor earth meant for her. Providence has made him high and her low. He is a treasure, too big for her heaven and too great for her little world. Neither heaven nor earth will sanction her so great a gift. But what of that? She cannot now give up what, in the estimation of the world, she is not justified to possess, though she obtained the treasure by sheer chance. This is indicated by her mystic reflections (Canto III, Lines 3-6). Often when the prince sleeps on a bed of leaves, she sighs to think that for her poor sake, he has left his golden couches and laid himself so low. When they pass the whole night without a wink of sleep, she feels a pain in her heart to see that the prince is compelled to forego the sweet attractions of rest and go away, with eyes heavy-laden with sleep, at the break of the dawn. (Canto III, Lines 7-10).

The prince treacherously abandons her. She is stunned by the blow. She cannot speak out her grief to others, for they have been already condemning her conduct as stupidly bold. She speaks her sorrows to the river, to the boats and to the trees. It is mute Nature to whom the mute soul finds a solace in appealing. (Canto IX, Lines 35-38.)

Sometimes she madly thinks that he may yet come. She has not yet obtained any proof of his treachery. She is elated by the foolish hope that he may return to her, full of love, and with gifts for her. "He will bring with him ornaments, studded with diamonds and pearls and I will pay the price with two drops of my tears." (Canto IX, Lines 40-42).

But when twelve months and thirteen days passed, from the day of his leaving her, "she blows out the candle of her room with her own breath and creeps into the dark to hide herself." (Canto IX, Lines 32-34.)

It is from the time of the departure of the prince that Kanchan rises to the majesty of a sublime character and becomes the true heroine of the ballad. The pathos of her last appeal to the inanimate objects of Nature shows her intense desire to hide herself from the world, particularly from the prince. He is happy with Rukmini, the princess. She is sincerely afraid, lest that happiness be disturbed. She puts her finger to her lips, enjoining silence. She sees the spot, where she used to make a bed of leaves for him, she remembers how they made garlands of flowers for each other and how, in the depth of night, she used to run away from home at a signal from his flute. She prays that all this may be blotted out from the memory of the prince, lest these should cause him pain. The river will be her silent grave. She prays to her that "not even the little tailor-bird, that drinks a sip from her water, might know of her death." (Canto XIII, 31-32.)

Secretly she has suffered; let her secretly pass away, leaving no sign behind, to cause pain to the prince, whom she found happy, with his new consort, the day before. She asks the waves "to carry her with them, floating into the boundless unknown." (Canto XIII, 47-48.)

One of the striking features of these rustic song-makers is a sense of decency, that pervades their poems. I believe that it is the court-poets who, in the medieval age, used to prostitute their genius by pandering to the erotic humour of princes and potentates—their patrons. The rustic mind breathes a purer moral air, just as these country people enjoy a freer air in the physical world.

We find in these poems situations which give great opportunities to the bards for revelling in indecency, but they instinctively know how far they should proceed and where they should stop. Everyone will admit that the poems override all conventions and canons of conservatism and orthodoxy. They are fresh and vigorous, with Nature's strength; but there is caution in their guarded language, proving their plain life to be a fountain of all that is wholesome and noble. These lyrical poems show the heart of the peasant, sweet as a field-flower and full of flavour as the fruits he grows in his garden.

Of the characters, next to the heroine, is the hero in importance. In these ballads the hero is generally less heroic than the heroine and more or less serves the purpose of a background. We have found several cases, where the hero has taken more wives than one. The custom of the country favoured this practice, and though the extraordinary man may always rise above the level of average people, we cannot condemn a person for yielding to a prevailing social custom. But the prince here is not only weak but treacherous. He takes no notice of a simple-minded and loving village woman, whom he has ruined with high promises.

The poet cleverly introduces many situations with an admirable artistic skill. Tamsā Gazi's description of the old washerman in the concluding part of the account of his interesting travel, undoubtedly creates a new situation. So does the love-letter of princess Rukmini. The plot is formed by a quick succession of well conceived array of incidents, which invest the poem with all the sweetness and effect of a superior melo drama.

The Song of the Washer-maiden was collected by Chandra Kumar from several sources. He owes the main portion of it to one Babu Rajanikanta Bhadra of the village

Shakuāi Bāttā in the district of Mymensingh. Of the rest a part was secured, on his way home from that village, from a milkman named Dinagopa of Char Sambhugunj. An old man of Kirtankhola, who is known by the name of *Madhur Bāp* (father of Madhu), added some songs and the remaining portion he got from Kulpur, Sankāṇḍā, and the neighbouring localities. He sent the ballad to me on the 15th of November, 1924.

The ballad contains 469 lines. I have divided it into 13 cantos. We can give no definite information as regards the time when the ballad was composed, nor any clue as to who its author was. Judging from the language and the spirit of the songs, I believe it to belong to that age when the country-people delighted in topics, showing absolute freedom in love. We have it on the authority of Chandidās that during his times love by mutual selection, untrammelled by, and triumphing over, all social barriers, was favoured by young men, and that many of them fell victims at the altar of the presiding deity of Sahajiya-love.

The lyrical element, the brevity and compactness of the plot, the never-failing relevancy of the topics and the dramatic character of the incidents, described in the poem, indicate that it is one of the oldest ballads that have been brought in to our possession; for, the later the age of composition, the more verbose and pedantic are the verses. The later ballads, besides, often deviate from the main subject in order to pander to some conventional forms or the need for propaganda. The freshness of country-life breathed in this poem, belongs to an age, when Chandidās, the gay bard of Nanoor, sang his immortal songs. Indeed this ballad has so many lines, to be found almost *verbatim* in Chandidās' poetry that we are inclined to suggest a common age for both. There are many points in Chandidās' poems for which no precedent is to be found in classical Sanskrit poetry. The sports of Krishna with the *Gopis* on a ferry-boat, and a hundred other manœvres with which the divine lover seeks the favour of the beauteous milk-maid of Jabat are not to be found in any earlier Sanskrit poem. They have no doubt been incorporated into the love tales of Rādhā-Krishna being gleaned from materials, supplied by ballads like these. This pastoral country was once full of love-tales, of which a refined ideal was conceived and developed in the country-side and subsequently spiritualised in the Vaishnava poems; and our old rural ballads had already perfected a felicitous language of emotion, which became familiar throughout the province and latterly served as a tool in the hands of the Vaishnavas. It is for this reason that many common lines occur in the poems of the Vaishnava poets and in these ballads. The latter point to an age, when Bengal,—a rural country, resonant with the sound of the cowherd's reed-flute and warblings of a thousand singing bards, the land of sweet pastoral occupations and of murmuring rivers and swamps, overgrown with lotuses and screw-plants was, so to speak, Love's own resort. The people were free from the struggles of life owing to the rich fertility of the soil and indulged in songs, of which the one theme was love.

What the age of the poem is I cannot definitely say, but it is one of the sweetest love-poems in our language and both by the testimony of its language and the freedom from all conventions, it seems to me, as I have already said, to be one of the earliest of the ballads that we have yet come across. I shall not be surprised if some contemporary evidence proves it beyond all doubt to be a production of the 14th century.

25th March, 1925. D. C. S.

The Love of the Washer-maiden.

CHORUS—The pain of separation burns me like a flame. I loved but not a day have I been happy.

(1)

Kānchanmālā.

"The Champa-flowers have bloomed on all sides of this beautiful tank. Let me off, my love, I will comb my hair and adorn it with these.

"A soft bed of leaves have I prepared on the side of the tank. There, my love come in the night, and in night, depart. For God's sake, friend! do not visit me in day-time.

"The neighbours delight in spreading scandal. Cruel are they. They would do nothing else, if they find a topic for scandal. If they see us together at such an hour, they will speak unkind things of us.

"My father and mother live in the house. How shall I explain my conduct to them? The topic of our love will be like a rich feast to the village folk at our cost.

"Leave my hands, my beloved. Allow me to go home. I cannot tarry more. Just see, my pitcher is going to be drifted away by the stream.

"From yonder banana-groves, give me the signal by your flute in the night and we shall meet there when it will be dark."

The Prince.

"It is evening. You are going alone to fill your pitcher. Stand for a moment, so that I may exchange a word with you.

"Your long flowing curly hair has come down to your knees. Youth has given you new charms and a fullness of limbs. I will speak to you for a little while. Give me a hearing, dear maiden. Your eyes are blue and dark like the *aparājitā*-flower and your tender body bears all the glow of the *champā*. Know, fair maiden, that it is the beauty of your curly hair, above all, that has driven me mad.

"I will ask of my father his kingdom and riches, and these will be my dowry to you at our marriage.

"Like the bird *Chil*, that hovers high in the air, my mind wanders forth day and night in the region of fancy delighting in your love.

"Stand a little longer and listen to my words, which come from the heart and are sincere."

Kānchanmālā.

"Leave my hands beloved youth. I am but half-dead with shame. At day-time, if they see us together, ours will be a name of shame for ever.

"What will my father and mother say, if they hear a report of our love? Don't you remember that your parents are the sovereigns of this country and my father is your royal father's poor washerman and his humblest subject? All this you seem to have forgotten.

"You are like the Moon and high is your status. Why should you stretch your hands to reach this low earth? What will people say if they hear of this? You are like a golden bee, who should seek a lotus. It is not becoming of you to seek such humble ones as myself.

"Leave my hands and allow me to depart. Sober down your mind and act sensibly."

Prince.

"You wash my clothes, dear maiden, with tenderest care. I trace, with a sigh, the sign of your five soft

The Washer-maiden

"Leave my hands, beloved youth." P. 10.

fingers on them. They bear the scent of flowers, you weave into a garland for me. I feel in my heart that you love me dearly

"Now take the oath that in the night-time you will come to this spot with all the treasure of your youth, sweet as a blooming flower.

"Here on this spot shall I take my stand and signal you by my flute. Here on this spot shall I spread a bed of leaves for you and here on this spot, shall we spend the night together. Here will be realised all the dreams of my youth in your sweet company."

Kānchanmālā.

"How can I, my charming friend, give you the promise you want. My parents always stay at home. Now on my life, be gracious and accede to my request. Be pleased to leave my hands.

"True, there is a surging emotion, which overflows my heart, like a river, overflowing its bank in August. True my heart has run out of all control. When I sleep, I dream of your sweet face. That is all my happiness in this world. If Providence would give an opportunity, even this day, this hour, I would leave my parents for your sake.. This is my oath. Sun and moon, be witness to it; and you, my chief witness, have heard what has fallen from my lips. Doubt not my sincerity." (Ll. 1-53.)

(2)

TIME—NIGHT.

Kānchan hums a tune in her room.

"My oath is broken, O prince. By no means can I come out. My parents I find awake each time I attempt to come out. My home seems to me strange and unwelcome, and the sides of the tank, sweet and familiar, and dear as home. Fear of society and of what the people would say stand in my way.

"But what is this fear for society ? What do I care for honour ? For God's sake, young friend, do not sing any more that song with your flute. It makes me mad. It drives me like a storm, making me a slave to your wishes.

"But do not despair. Wait a little more. Sleep has just crept into the eyes of my parents. Erelong they will fall into deep sleep.

"Lo ! the black clouds are roaring in the sky. O, what a pity ! Providence, I fear, will not allow us to meet to-night.

"I hear the showers falling around. Pray my beloved, do not expose yourself to rain. The esculent plant *Mān* has spread its large leaves behind our house. Cut off one of these from the stalk and protect your head.

"Alas friend I imagine from here, your fair figure to be wet with rain. I am not near you in this depth of night. With what care would I not wipe away water from your body, brushing the drops with my flowing hair !"

TIME—MID-NIGHT.

Kānchanmālā.

"The whole world is asleep. A deep silence pervades all. Only the maddening flute sings that one tune. Now I am coming out of my house. Which is the path that I shall follow in this dark hour ?

"There is no cloud in the sky. The moon shines. If I go by this path at such an hour, I may be caught and exposed to shame.

"There is a tree, which has no branches and no leaves. It bears the treasure of one solitary flower. It is the tree of love.* If I get my beloved near me, what do I care for society, its praise and protection ?" (Ll. 1-20.)

(3)

PLACE—RIVER-BANK.

Kānchanmālā.

"O River, which way dost thou follow? Whence hast thou come and whither art thou bound? Without knowing thy destination, thou seemest, in a mad hurry to go.

"The morning is golden. In the sky wander forth the dispersed clouds. What is this bird that has come down from the sky with its golden wings? If the bird is to be given a space in this Earth, it seems that the Earth is too small for it. If it flies up neither does it find space there that can hold it. Where may I find a cage to keep thee O bird of my heart? How can I keep thee, and where?" †

* * * *

"My beloved has gone away in the morning. Why did the blessed night pass away? I was with him for the whole night.

"Ah a moment he could not sleep in the night (gaily talking with me)! His eyelids were heavy with sleep in the morning. Yet he had to depart in all haste!

"Ever accustomed to sleep on a stately couch, he made the bare ground his bed for my sake!

* The tree of Love does not give protection as society does, but still it has the power to charm the soul, (that is its one flower).

† She is filled with the idea that she has loved one who is too high for her. There is no space, here below in society, none in heaven either, where this love may have a sanction and a place assigned to it.

"When one, in his position, loves a woman of low birth, one becomes the subject of ridicule of all. And this he will have to suffer for my sake!

"I am like the dwarf, aspiring to catch the Moon. Alas, why have I taken this mad course? You seek an answer? I myself do not know, why! My mind has lost all control.

"O my pitcher, sink here in this water, like a drop (no path for escape will you see). I am lost like you in the boundless sea by loving him. Here is the pitcher; I have raised it again from the water. But who will raise me from the sea into which I have been drowned? People whisper all kind of things when they see me. Fain would I tie this pitcher with a rope around my neck and drown myself for the sake of my love. If you come to night, my beloved, I will keep a box of betels, ready for you. I will place at your feet, my youth, my life, my honour and my all! I will leave my parents and my home and seek a shelter in the forest." (Ll. 1-28.)

(4)

The Reporter.

"O lord, your son has been addicted to a washer-woman and become mad for her love. Your Highness seems to be unaware of this fact. He is your own washerman and his daughter washes the clothes of the palace. For such a wretch has the prince run mad. Her name is Kānchan. Her colour is bright and fair. Your son has fallen into her snares. The union is like that of the Moon and the demon Rāhu. It is all the work of that wicked and treacherous old washerman."

The king burnt with rage and looked like flaming fire at this report and commanded the washerman to be brought to his presence at once.

On his shoulders was a bundle of washed clothes and on his hand, he carried a staff. Godhā, the washerman, came trembling to the rich one's mansion.

The Raja was holding his *durbar*, surrounded by his courtiers and body-guards. Godhā folded his palms before his lordship and delivered himself thus:—

"For two days, there have been incessant rain and storm, and the Sun did not even peep into our lands. I could not dry the clothes, O mighty lord, for this reason there has been a delay."

The Raja was trembling in rage, for a time, his voice was choked and then he angrily spoke to the miscreant Godhā thus:—

"Your daughter has come of age and you have not yet given her in marriage. My son, I hear, has taken a fancy to her. If, by to-night, you do not marry her to some one, my constables will go in the morning and bring her to the palace forcibly, dragging her by her locks through the public streets."

Godhā.

"At the dawn of day, to-morrow, I will marry her to Bāguā, the gardener, who works as day-labourer in this town."

Resting the weight of his person on his staff, the old man slowly approached his home. For the whole night the washerman and his wife had not a wink of sleep and cried in bitter grief.

But where is the Prince gone and where is Kānchanmālā? The drums beat through the streets, announcing reward for their arrest. Here ends a chapter of the song. (Ll. 1-30.)

(5)

A Meadow Land.

Kānchanmālā.

"Helpless woman that I am, I cannot see the path in darkness. I am unfamiliar with this place. Look how beautifully the flowers of the screw-plant have bloomed on the bank of yonder river. Clasp me by my hand, my beloved, and take me there. I cannot walk any further. My limbs seem heavy. I cannot carry them any further. Wait, dear love, let us sleep here and take rest for the remaining hours of the night."

The Prince.

"Fair maiden, do not stop here. We must go a little further and cross the jurisdiction of the King, my father.

"Streaks of light seem to issue from the East. I think, it will be dawn erelong.

"Let us go, seeking shelter at the abode of some well-to-do householder. If we fail in this, we shall have to wander about in this forest like two banished souls. There, in your sweet company, shall I walk in the jungle, and when we shall feel hungry, the fruits of the wilderness will appease our hunger. Under the shade of trees, we will spread leaves, and this will be our bed, and the tiger and buffaloes will be our kindred."

Kānchanmālā.

"The night, my friend, seems wellnigh over. The last struggling moonbeams have spread a sparkle on the western sky. I think, we have crossed the jurisdiction of your father, the King.

"My father will mourn my loss in the morning and my mother will strike her head against the wall for grief. You have left your great palace and I have given up all considerations of society and family-life. Though tender by nature, being a woman, I have become hard as stone.

"See the day is dawning over the fair world. But no more shall we see the dear landing-ghat of the Khorāi and no more those fair fields, filled with the golden *sāli*-harvest! The night is taking leave, but no more shall we see our home, our good neighbours, our kinsmen—men and women amongst whom we have lived so long! When the night will pass, no more shall we hear the gay songs of the birds of our Motherland, nor see that sky of morning, through scenes so familiar to the eyes. Alas, the fair flowers of our garden! Never more will they bloom for us. For our whole life have we separated ourselves from the society of our friends and kinsmen."

The Prince.

"Weep not, fair maiden, grieve no more. Henceforward shall we have no home but become dwellers of the forest.

"Weep no more, fair maiden, set your mind at ease. We, two, like two flowers, are strung garland-like, by fate.

"What is that the people are speaking there on the bank of the river? Whose jurisdiction may this be and what is the country called?" (Ll. 1-36.)

(6)

THEY MEET A WASHERMAN.

The Prince.

"Listen to me, O washerman, you are surely a servant of the Raja and wash the clothes of the palace. Can you give a lodging to us two? I have fallen in evil times and my companion is greatly suffering from fatigue. My father has driven us both away. We had to leave home in extreme sorrow."

The washerman, with his eyes wide-open, gazed at them. One looked like the sun and the other like the moon,—both of them as if fallen from the sky. He wonderingly eyed them from head to foot, and overpowered by emotion, could not speak for a time. He took them for a prince and a princess.

The Washerman.

"I have no son, no daughter. You be my children. Come and live with me. My wife Aduna will be a mother unto you. You two will rule my house, like the angels, presiding over its fortune. I earn my livelihood by washing the clothes of the Rājā's palace."

The Prince.

"I take you for my foster-father. Know me to be the son of a washerman. I will wash the clothes of the palace for you. I know how to do that. Your household work will be done by this maiden. We shall be like children unto you, and you like our father. We will stay at your house, so long as we live." (Ll. 1-19.)

(7)

Princess Rukmini.

"How is it that the clothes have been washed so well this time? Never did the old man show such cleverness before."

The maid-servant came to Rukmini and said:—

"A young washerman has come, it is he that washes your clothes. He is handsome and bright as the moon.

and looks like a prince in disguise. With him there is a maiden, whose beauty is wonderful. Her hair falls on her back with many a lovely curl, and her colour is of the *Atasi*-flower or like molten gold. Youth has just dawned on her. She is a wonderful thing to behold."

On having the report, Rukmini, the princess, sent for the washerwoman.

The Princess.

"My maid-servant has given me strange news. I hear you have a daughter and a son-in-law by chance. This maiden, who has brought our clothes to-day to my apartment is young and handsome. I should like to make friends with her."

Days passed, and Kānchanmālā paid her visits to the princess often. The latter liked her for her beauty and became greatly attached to her. How often did they embrace each other, declaring sincere friendship! They opened their heart freely in conversation, and three months passed in this way. (Ll. 1-22.)

(8)

One day Rukmini said to her friend :—

"Where is your home? Who are your parents? Why have you come to this city and where do you intend to go afterwards? How is it that you have left your parents and home, and for what fault? The young man, your companion, is exceedingly handsome. Has he brought you here by force, or was it love for him, which made you give up home-connections and choose this life of an exile? Tell me, dear friend, your whole history, without hiding anything from me."

Kānchanmālā, a girl known for her self-control and prudence, in an evil moment, lost both, and related to the princess her whole story.

The Princess, alone.

"This youth, so handsome, comes often to the palace. It is not fit that he should do the mean work of a washerman. He is not so by birth. He is a prince. It is his evil luck that has doomed him to this life of sorrow. When he comes to the palace with clothes, my thirsty eyes gaze at him through the window. Ah, my bee! Your place should be in the bosom of a lotus. You have turned to be a worm of dung. This daughter of a washerman has reduced you to this plight, turning your head by her wily love. The princess, otherwise so good and sober, yielded to a weakness in an evil moment and sent a letter covertly through the clothes to the youth."

Letter.

"O my love, I do not know who you are. Your handsome figure has charmed me. You are the play of evil stars and have given a false report of yourself to my father, the King. Like the bee, you are a wanderer in the garden, now enjoying yourself lightly over stray flowers.

"The month of April is in sight. The spring has already entered into Nature's fair fields. The cuckoo's gay notes are heard everywhere and the flowers show their full bloom. The women of the city are gaily playing with the red powder *ābir*. Is it the season to come to the inner apartments of the Raja with a load of clothes on the head? Fie! If I could find you for a moment to speak to you in private, I could open my heart freely. Now you may know the pain of Rukmini's heart from this letter, which I cannot make too plain." (Ll. 1-32.)

(9)

O man, inconstant and fickle like the bee, leaving the faded flower and running to a fresh one! Untrustworthy and treacherous is your heart!

One day the prince said to Kānchanmālā, "Permit me leave for three months. Remain here in this washerman's house. I want to travel abroad. After three months, I will meet you again."

She did not suspect anything, she dreamt nothing foul. Her simple soul took the matter lightly and she complied with her lover's request in all sincerity.

Three months passed. In the city was heard the sound of drums. There were great merry-makings, festivities and rejoicings in the king's mansion. Kānchan asked Adunā, her foster-mother, "What is all this festivity, mother, in the palace, for? Why are the drums beaten and why do the pipes sound?"

Adunā returned from the palace and said. "A prince from an unknown country has come to marry Rukmini."

These three months he has gone—the fourth is passing; yet he has not returned. It is the fifth month now, but poor Kānchan still hoped that he would return. In the sixth month, she lost all taste for food, and passed her nights, troubled with dreams. In the seventh she could not close her eyes for a moment in sleep. In the ninth, she began to feel those pangs of the heart, which, like worms eating into the green bamboos, sap the vitality of youthful lovers. She now gave up the last hope. In the tenth month, like unto the arithmetical figure ten, a cipher was put against her luck. In the eleventh month, Kānchan tried to compose her mind knowing for certain that she was doomed to lasting sorrow. On the night of the thirteenth day after the lapse of full twelve months, she blew out the candle of her room with her own breath and wept, creeping into the dark, which she now liked better than light.

She wandered about the bank of the river and cried alone. She addressed the river and said, "I know not whence you have come, O river, and whither you are bound? Perchance you may meet him. And if you ever do so, kindly remind him of me. Ye boats, that come from afar with sails unfurled, does any of your crew know anything of my beloved and can he give me any tidings of him? You have wandered across rivers and through the deep and visited many a land. Did you not come across any place, from which you could get any message about the treasure I have lost?

"O happy day when he will return and bring for me, prince as he is, ornaments studded with diamonds and pearls. Alas, poor as I am, I will accept them from him paying two drops of tears as their price.

"To-day has also past. My hope will rest on the morrow, and when to-morrow will pass, I will place my hope on the day after. Thus will my life end. O my friend, O my love, I was doomed to sorrow by fate and bear a life of scorn for ever." (Ll. 1-44.)

(10)

The Collector of revenues of the Rājā called the washerman, one day, to his presence and said to him in private in a menacing tone, "In your house lives a young maiden. I will pay you for her Rs. 500 in cash, besides a new house and lands with it. You know my power. The calf dies in the womb of a cow, if I give it an angry look. If you do not agree, know it for certain that you will be a ruined man in no time. You are to send her immediately to me."

The washerman returned home and told everything to his wife Adunā and added. "The Collector will ruin me. My house and things will be burnt down. Why should we suffer all these for one, who is nobody to us?"

Adunā to Kānchan.

"O beautiful one, listen to my advice. You have now spent a whole year with us. You are a virtuous girl and I am like your mother. On my life, I ask you to promise me one thing. You will leave our house this very night. The wicked Collector has turned our enemy. Somehow or other, he has seen you in our house. If you stay here any more, we are sure to be the victims of his ire. Our life will be at stake. Our house and things will be burnt to ashes. Now my advice to you is this. Be the true woman that you are and leave our house at once, to save yourself and us from the danger that hangs overhead." (Ll. 1-20.)

(11)

In a village, called Pirer Kānda, lived Tamsā Gāzi, a wholesale trader in rice. He had five ships, with which he used to go abroad, for purchasing rice. He was coming from northern districts, having purchased a large quantity of rice and got them husked there. His five ships were moored on the bank of the river 'Khorāi'; and one of his partners reported to him that a beautiful woman was crying on the river-bank.

Tamsā Gāzi had no child in his house. He had grown old and had no hope of getting any, in the future. He felt compassion for Kānchan and brought her to his home.

At the house of the Gāzi, Kānchan began to do all household duties. When she sat to cook her own meals, incessant tears fell from her eyes. When she dusted the floor, the ground became wet with her tears. She went with the pitcher to bring water from the river There her tears looked like a garland without string. The Gāzi and his wife showed her tender affection but could not guess at the cause of her sorrow.

The Gāzi.

"I am bound on a tour for trade. Tell me what I shall bring for you, dear daughter, you are now a child to us. We had no child to adorn our house. By the grace of God, we have got one in you."

As she heard him speak, she began to cry. "What should I ask of him?" she thought, "I have no desire for anything."

She could not say, for shame, what she wanted with all the longings of her soul.

Three months and thirteen days passed. The Gāzi has returned with many valuable goods. He has brought a pearl-necklace of rare value for Kānchan and a box, full of shell-flowerets to adorn her hair. He has, besides, brought a *sari* for her, of the colour of flame, a belt of beautiful pendants and ornaments for feet and nose. He has brought for her a bee-hive from the forest, full of sweet honey. In a basket he has brought dried fish and other articles of food. His boats are, in fact, stored with many edibles and articles of luxury.

The Gāzi is giving an account of voyage to his wife in detail.

"I saw a country where people built their roofs with straw of the *ulu* species, and another strange country, where water is to be found on the tree-tops.*

* The cocoanut tree, the fruits of which contain sweet water inside.

"In another place, I found men cooking the meals and serving them too, and the women driving the plough in the fields. It is the latter who do the marketing there, and in the public streets and bazars, one may see women, flocking by hundreds. There I found buffaloes, grazing in pastures on river-banks and the deer drinking water from the fountains. I saw many hills and many strange lands, as I was touring in different districts. Through many a river did I pass—big rivers which overflowed their banks and many merchant-vessels tossed on them. I passed through the domains of many Rājās." Then followed other detailed descriptions. He concluded by saying, "In one place I saw a sight, which cannot be forgotten. It was the capital of a Rājā. I saw his big palace from afar; and close to the river-bank, I saw a washerman, busy with washing. He was advanced in years. His eyes looked dim, without much of sight left in them and he did not hear if any one spoke in a low voice. I took him for a deaf man. On enquiry I learnt that he did the washing for the palace, but so feeble had he grown that he took seven days to wash a single piece of cloth. I pitied his condition, and called him to me. He had no son or male heir he said; but he had then, a daughter, who absconded with her lover to his infinite sorrow and shame. She turned unchaste and left her poor parents for ever. He has lost his eyesight and power of hearing by constantly grieving over her. For he cannot forget his daughter for all she had done. At intervals, he stopped and resumed his work, and covering his eyes with his hands, cried at the recollection of the girl, broken down and thoroughly unmanned by grief. His condition excited my pity and has left a deep impression on my mind. If one has no son or daughter, it is far better,

One can bear it; but unbearable is it to suffer the loss of a born child.

When Kānchanmālā heard this, she began to cry aloud for her father.

Kānchan.

"Hear my sorrowful tale, O my foster-father. Take me immediately to my father. I am that woman for whom he grieves. I was born in the family of a washerman, but, as ill luck would have it, I lost my virtuous life, owing to my evil stars or to some acts of my prior birth, I do not know. You cannot conceive, what a smouldering fire I have suppressed all this time in my heart. An object of public scandal, I bear a life of great misery. In this country, I can hardly expect to get my heart soothed." (Ll. 1-77.)

(12)

Kānchan comes back to her Father's House.

Kānchanmālā's Father.

"You fell a victim to evil desire, my daughter and made this house a place of shame. For you, though living, I have become like one dead. My life has been blasted owing to my evil luck. Where was it heard that the high ever loved the low with constancy? One climbs a tall tree, courting the chance of death by falling down. One who tries to place one's feet on the air, despising the ground that one treads, finds no support. And you have known it by the experience of your own life that though you may cut a portion of your heart for another, that one is not likely to be your own. One does not always get, in return, what one gives, however great the sacrifice may be. The bee hums a tune of love and the flower cannot judge the depths of his sincerity at the outset. But the flower knows the truth, when the bee breaks his empty promise and flies to another. The cloud and the moon seem to be fast friends for a time. But the next moment the cloud darkens the moon. If one contracts love with a bad person, the end is sure to be bitter. Just see the teeth and the tongue. They seem to live together in amity, but the former scarcely lose an opportunity to bite the latter. O unfortunate one, without knowing all this, like a baby you put your hands into the fire. Owing to the fault of some unknown deed in a past life, you have now lost all happiness of life.

"Love, dear daughter, is a good thing. To some, it proves life-giving nectar; to others, mortal like poison. Who should seek that love, which brings in scandal and disgrace in its train? The collyrium that adorns the eyes becomes black ink, when placed in an ink-pot. Love, which should have adorned your life, has become like worm-wood, being placed on a wrong person."

The daughter clung to the neck of the father and cried aloud. They both shed tears over their sad lot. The people of that city, however, never knew that the washerman's daughter had returned. (Ll. 1-38.)

(13)

They thought that she was a mad woman and had come there from some distant country. Nobody could know or recognise her, as she had grown so emaciated. Like the spirit of the air, she is for a moment here and then disappears. Like a whirlwind that runs and carries the dust before it, she moves about the city without staying at any spot for a minute. Here is she seen under the shade of a tree; but the moment after, there she wanders by the river-bank. She sometimes sings an unmeaning song or bursts into unmeaning laughter. At one moment, she sits quietly and at the next, she is seen weeping.

Kānchan in the Palace.

Princess Rukmini is seated on a couch in an inner apartment in the palace. Suddenly like a gust of wind, the mad woman of the street enters the Rājā's palace. She saw the prince, seated in the audience-hall, looking resplendent like the moon. People said, "Lo, there goes the mad woman by this path."

For a few months, she had wandered through the streets of the city in that way. But from the day she saw the prince and the princess Rukmini in the palace, Kānchan was seen no more.

The moon and the stars had fallen into the hands of the clouds and were sometimes allowed to peep through the sky, and were obscured a moment after. In the dark night, no path was visible. It was the month of August and the river Khorāi was full. Kānchanmālā, like the very spirit of emotion that she was, maddened by love, came running to the river-ghat. The clouds were roaring and the rain falling in large drops. She came running in that dark night to the banks of the Khorāi.

Kānchan.

"All my sorrows are gone, my hopes have been fulfilled to-day. I have seen his dear face, for a sight of which I was longing all these days. May you, beloved, live long with the new bride! May you for ever enjoy her sweet company! Do not, I pray you, recollect poor unfortunate Kānchan. I bow a hundred times at your feet from here. The trace of the bed of green leaves, we used to make here, on this green bank of the river, may still be seen. But, dear friend, do not recollect the dreams we dreamt in those days. Do not, also, O my beloved, recollect how we once made garlands of flowers for each other here. In the depth of night, at a signal from your flute, I used to come running here. Do not remember those days. Blot out all memory of unfortunate Kānchan from your mind.

"O river, do not divulge the story of my death. Let not even the little tailor-bird, that drinks a sip from your water know of my death. O ye, trees of the river-side, I pray thee, do not give out the news of my death and I pray you, O moon and stars, do not give out the report of my death to my beloved, lest it should cause him pain. I bow to you, my father, from here. Your daughter's last request to you is :—Do not say to any one that I returned home.

"O wind, you are my sole friend; I will whisper to you the tale of my heart. You are the witness of all—of everything that happens by day and everything that happens by night. You are ever present in this world. The scandal about this unfortunate one is so widespread that even the beasts of the forest and the birds of the air have heard of it. Kindly do not disclose to any one that I returned home. Say not a word of my death to my beloved lest he should feel a pain in his heart. I am sure, my own people will not know that I am going to die here.

"O waves, from where have you come and whither are you bound for? Take me along with you, floating into the unknown regions of the sea from which I may never come back to these sad shores.

The stars grew dim at that deep and still hour of the night.

Kānchan threw herself into the river and was lost. (Ll. 1-50.)

THE END.

THE YOUNG HERDSMAN.

(The First Version).

PREFACE

The 'Mahishāl Bandhu' (Lit. 'the friend, in charge of buffaloes,' which I have rendered into a simpler form and called the Young Herdsman) was once very popular in the eastern parts of Mymensingh. Indeed the spirit of romance, pervading the song and its deep heart-stirring pathos have a great appeal. We annex two versions of the ballad. The first one ends where Sujāti, the beautiful bride of Dingādhar, is forcibly carried away by Meghuā, the merchant. The second one repeats the story told in the first, with some material points of difference and carries it to where Raja Fengu of Chittagong holds his Court and passes the sentence of death by impalement on Dingādhar.

Both the versions, of which texts are given in this volume, are evidently incomplete. Babu Chandra Kumar tried his best to secure the last portions but could not. I have not, however, lost all hopes of recovering them.

The reason why so popular a song is on the verge of running into oblivion will not be far to seek. Hindu orthodoxy must have tried to suppress it in later times, just as it did in the case of the ballad of Mahuā. The songs of Bheluā and of the Washer-Maiden, which are also published here, breathe the same air of free love and sexuel romance, which could not be evidently tolerated by the Brahminic school. Hence it is that though in subject-matter and in spirit, these ballads are essentially Hindu, describing tales of pure Hindu life, their singing is now restricted amongst Muhamadan rustics, and these once favourite songs of pastoral love are running out of fashion.

We may now easily find in these songs echoes of those tender emotions, which, in a later epoch, became the distinctive characteristic of the Vaishnava school of poetry. Chronological data should not be used as tests for ascertaining the school, to which they belong. These songs, as we have said elsewhere, represent, whatever the date of their composition may be, the prevailing features of a school of poetry that preceded the one of the melodious bards, who followed Chandidas and made Bengal "a nest of singing birds." The dashing courage of Sujāti, Bheluā and the washer-maiden Kanchan, the exquisite emotions that invest their nature with an indescribable sweetness, their idealistic renunciation and intensity of love and sufferings forebode the coming epoch of emotioned felicity, full of mystic import and spiritual love, which marked the Vaishnava lyrics. In fact in the literature of this rustic poetry, one sometimes comes across, though in a somewhat crude form, the very words and phrases, which have lent supreme interest to Vaishnava poetry. This shows that the essentials of Vaishnava emotional poetry were already in the air, and that the poets, like Chandidās, Jnāna Das and Govinda Das, derived much of their exquisite ideas and inspiration from the soil in which they were born. They only embellished them, whereas the ballad-makers gave them in their original crude form. This literature of the ballads has, therefore, shown us the link, which binds the old school with the new, proving the homogeneity of the Bengal aesthetic culture.

The two versions, as I have already stated, while founded on the same story and showing their likeness in the essentials of the plot, differ materially in respect of some of the details. The first version evidently bears the trace of an interpolator's hands. The story of the love of Dingādhar with the maiden Sujāti, of course, constitute the central plot of the ballad. But the first version appends to the poem the early career of Dingādhar, which is not quite relevant to the point and also brings Balarām on the scene unnecessarily introducing ramifications to complicate the plot. It also shows a little pedantry in describing the beauty of Sujāti and gives, here and there, philosophical reflections, which do not fit in well with the spirit of the simple love-tale that it is. (Cantos I, L 36-40 and II, L 30-36.) But if the interpolator has handled the story and added to its length, it must be admitted to his credit that he is not an unbearable pedant like Abdul Karim of Galāchipā who has recast some of the historical ballads on Isa Khan and his descendants. The poet who has added some passages here seems to be also a rustic bard and gives his added tales with almost the same unvarnished simplicity that we find in the original poem. The second version has none of these superfluities, which have been unnecessarily engrafted upon the main story. Dingādhar is not afflicted here by the loss of his parents, nor is he embarrassed by his father's death and obliged to bear a galling servitude. The ballad-maker leaves no margin, even for the sake of humour, for the advent of Asharia Mandal on the scene. Had such a Shylock actually existed in the original ballad it would not be easy for a later recensionist to do away with it. Though we miss much of the humour and poetry of the added cantos, in the second version, yet we find in it a greater compactness, a keener eye to relevancy, and a homogeneity, which undoubtedly prove it to be the original ballad. It is a pity that the entire poem could not be secured. From the concluding lines of the second version, we are led to believe that Sujāti did some wonderful heroic act, which probably redeemed the fate of her lover and raised her to the status of a real heroine. But the reader's curiosity will be nipped in the bud on coming to the last passage of the text, which closes abruptly, leaving the reader's imagination to grovel in the dark as to the fate of the lovers. One thing strikes me as somewhat anomalous in the second version. It is difficult to understand why Dingādhar married Maynā. But in some of the ballads and folk-tales, we have already found the hero of the tales taking more than one wife—a practice not at all condemned by the social ethics of the Asiatic races. It is hinted (by line 22, Canto 7) that Dingādhar had also married Sujāti. But as we have found the ballad in an incomplete form, we would not like to risk any further comment on the point.

The special charm of the song lies in its description of the dawn of love on the pair. The lines "লাজেতে হইল কন্যার রক্তজবা মুখ। পর্‌থম যৌবন কন্যার এই পর্‌থম সুখ॥" (Canto Lines) are exquisite—indicating, as they do, the precious experience of first youth—the first happiness in woman's bosom, which, without any sense of guilt, makes her shy, suffusing her face with red colour. Unlike all that is known of our girls, given to husbands at an age when they have no power to choose, here is the value of marriage, based on mutual selection, so beautifully emphasised in the line, "সব চেয়ে অধিক শীতল মনোবাঞ্ছার পতি" (Canto 4, Lines 95-96). "There can be no joy, greater in the mind of a bride, than that of getting a youth for her husband whom she has chosen for herself." Let the orthodox Pandits, who have curtailed all freedom of our womankind learn from this that they have no power over the minds of their victims, and let them feel the force of this free expression of the rustic mind, which quotes no other authority than that which nature has stamped on the human soul.

The integrity of the people finds illustrations throughout the narrative in the first version in a clear and forcible manner. Balarām contracted a debt of five hundred rupees—"ধর্ম্ম সাক্ষী করি" by a mere oath in the name of Virtue, and though Ashāriā Mandal, the money-lender, is an exceedingly stingy and exacting man, he accepts this oath as a conclusive surety for the money he lends. Unless a people were extremely God-fearing and honest, such a Shylock as he would not be satisfied by a mere oath of this nature. Loans were not barred by limitation, nor were the pleas of insolvency urged in defence. For Dingādhar had no property which could be seized by the money-lender, Balarām. He came to recover the money, thirteen years after the death of the boy's father. So great was the fear in the popular mind of keeping a debt, contracted by one's father unliquidated, lest the father should visit hell, that Dingādhar was overcome with a great despair, when he found it impossible for him to satisfy the creditor. He went to Balarām and offered his services in the pasture-ground, so long as the debt might remain undischarged. Balarām agreed to the offer but stated that it would take him six years to clear the debt by serving in that capacity. "বড় দুখে ডিঙ্গাধরের হাসি আইল মুখে।" Six years' thraldom was no joke! It was a disaster to spend the most precious part of one's youth in such humiliating servitude. But Dingādhar was happy at the thought that his father's debt would at last be cleared, and forgetting all his distress, he smiled with a sense of relief. This smile illuminates the characteristic honesty of the Bengal peasantry of the olden days.

The picture of agricultural Bengal—the Bengal of marshes, swamps and large rivers—of rustic huts and large ships laden with merchandise, showing the great commercial activities of the people,—of purity of rustic life, and above all, of the sweet emotions of abiding love, which makes the mind ready for martyrdom and great renunciation—is mirrored in this poem in all its true colours and vivid grandeur. At the same time, the autocratic, cruel and arbitrary nature of the men in power, which is proved in other ballads also, is in clear evidence here in the account of Fengu Raja of Chittagong and of the perfidious merchant Meghuā.

We cannot make any guess as to the time when this ballad was composed. The original might have been composed before the advent of the Mahomedans, as throughout this long poem, there is no mention of any Mahomedan men or women. The accounts show that the ballad belonged to a country ruled by the Hindus and inhabited by these people alone. The few Urdu words that have crept into the song were probably later interpolations. In most of the ballads, there are clear proofs of the existence of Mahomedan elements in the incidents described. But neither in the poem of Bheluā, nor in this one, there is anything suggesting such an element. The evidence of vocabulary is not important, since, in the course of recitation of the songs, through long generations, foreign words would inevitably find their way into the body of the songs. The ballads were generally sung by low-class Hindus, and also by Mahomedans. The present Mahomedan rustics, as I have said elsewhere, were mostly recruited from the Hindu community. It is no rare phenomenon to trace the modern Mahomedan singers, to be mostly the descendants of Hindu ancestors, who had originally composed or sung a particular ballad. Hence Persian and Arabic words gradually entered into these songs, in later times.

It appears that the story had some foundation on facts. Apart from the local geographical accounts, given in both the versions, which breathe an air of truth, the incidents of both practically agree in giving a villainous character to Meghuā and in describing the vicissitudes in the lives of Dingādhar and Sujāti. It seems, therefore, that the story is to be traced to some unknown historical source of olden times, to which local bards gave colourings, according to their choice, introducing some new features and omitting or changing the old narrative in some points. But the characters, as originally conceived, have remained true to the old historic tradition, though the ballad-makers have recast the story from age to age.

The town of Singāpur and Rangchāpur, where some of the principal incidents are said to have taken place, and the canal Singakhali, on the bank of which stood the home of Dingādhar may be pointed on the maps of Mymensingh and of the neighbouring districts. It appears from the description that the merchants used to have commercial transactions with the Burmese by means of ships. They also went, far beyond the northern part of Mymensingh, to countries, inhabited by Gāros and Kukis. When in the first version, we find mention of the woman folk, taking lead in the traffic of the market and as fond of dried fish, we are naturally reminded of the Burmese. The "Kamoonir Desh" referred to in the second part, seems to be Kāmākhya or Prāgjyotishpur (Assam).

The description of a storm on the courses of the river Surmāi, given in the second version, is an animated and picturesque one. It is interesting to note that when a rustic poet describes a scene, he reproduces his impressions based on personal observation—without trying to remember, and mostly without any knowledge of, what the earlier poets wrote on the subject. It is for this reason that the account the poet gives here is so life-like and graphic. I quote an extract here, to single out, from the ballad, a passage of rare force of style. It brings a scene of solemn grandeur to the mind's eye.

"শিবের জটা পিঙ্গল মেঘ আকাশেতে খেলে।
কুন্দিয়া তুফান আসে দরিয়ার জলে॥
পাড় পর্ব্বত ভাঙ্গ্যা ঢেউ ফলকিয়া উঠিল।
কে জানে দুষ্মণ্ মেঘুয়া কইবা ভাইস্যা গেল॥
তের দাড়িএ ডাক দিয়া কইল মইষালেরে।
উজান ধরিতে দায় চল যাই ঘরে॥
কাঁড়াল ভাঙ্গিয়া যায় পালের ছিড়ে দঁড়ি।
সামলাইয়া রাখিতে নাও আর নাহি পারি॥"

The rural phraseology of the boatmen of the country-side, the words of East Bengal dialect, such as কাঁড়াল, কুন্দিয়া, ফল্‌কিয়া, etc., conjure up a scene of wild storm, which are now and then witnessed on the big rivers of Eastern Bengal.

Chandra Kumar De was informed, about the middle of January, 1923, that the Ballad of the Herdsman was known to one Golak Viswas of Gopalgrām. By the last week of October, he collected the first version from three persons, *viz.* (1) Chandra Kumar Sarkar of Sutrakona (P. O., Fatehpur), (2) Kullār Abbās, a Mahomedan cart-driver of Rayer Bazar and (3) Nidhu Byapari a jute-merchant of the village Sohāgi. Hs sent me the first version on the 7th of November, 1923. He got information about a second from one Mahesh Ch. Sarkar of the village Māydulā and secured it from three sources:—(1) Gayā, a Namasudra by caste a native of the village Uchhigrām (Perg. Bhowal), (2) Mahajia Shaik, a Mahomedan of the same village and (3) Gāchhuni Shaik, a Mahomedan peasant of the village Kātgharā. Babu Chandra Kumar sent me this poem on the 7th of January, 1924.

The first version contains 494 lines and the second version 346 lines.

It is probable that the whole ballad may be secured from Jagaddal, a village in the Kishoregunj Subdivision of the district of Mymensingh.

3. 5. 12 D. C. SEN.

The Young Herdsman

(1)

There flows the river Singākhāli, whose greedy waves devoured the crops on her bend, last October. Here dwelt once an honest householder, whose story I am going to relate to you to-day.

He tilled thirteen *ārhās* of land with the help of his buffaloes and every season he stored his granaries with rice of fine quality. He had an only son, fair and bright as the full moon. The parents endearingly called him by the name of Dingādhar or Master of the ships. In his tenth year, when, a mere lad, he whistled and wandered about the village-paths with a gladsome heart. His mother died suddenly. Other calamities also overtook the house. The large house of his father, divided into three spacious compartments, caught fire and was burnt to ashes. It seemed that the goddess of luck deserted the family. The buffaloes in the pastures and the cows in the shed died of infectious diseases and the flood of October * washed away the ripe crops on the banks of the Singākhāli. None was there to sympathise with them in their distress. The old man had not a *cowrie* left to him and he was at his wit's end as to how he would find means to plough his lands on the river-bend.

After much hard and oppressing thought, he at last made up his mind. And one day, carrying a small bundle of some fried rice, as provision for his journey,

* I have roughly given English names for the corresponding Bengali months.

he set out for the city of Singapur. There lived a rich money-lender named Balarām, who used to lend money to the needy people on interest. He had become well off by this avocation. Thirteen festivities he performed during the twelve months of the year, especially the Doorgā Pujā with great éclat. In the month of November, he worshipped the god Kārtikeya, and in December, he performed the Puja of the harvest-goddess Lakshmi, with offerings of the new rice of the season. He was, in fact, a very prince among the peasantry of the village. Dingādhar's old father applied for help to this money-lender. He said, "I am in great distress, my lord. My fertile lands, which yield golden crops each season, are lying fallow. I have no plough, no bull. If you kindly lend me some money, regularly shall I pay you the interest. This help will save me from ruin."

He got a loan of Rs. 100, and after executing a bond, returned home with a cheerful heart. He now built one or two houses as the old ones had been burnt down and bought a pair of buffaloes for ploughing the fields. In the month of March, he tilled the land and sowed seeds. April and May rolled by. In June his rice was ripe, but just when he had begun to reap the harvest, the poor man caught fever and suddenly died. This is the course of this world. When after many days' hopes, the prospect of fulfilment comes, alas, one is taken off from his scene of action, showing how frail are human expectations. (Ll. 1-44.)

(2)

Dingādhar, the young lad, lamented wildly. "Alas," said he, "My mother died only the other day and you, my father, you, too, have left me thus! Who is there now to look after me? I have no friend, no kinsman in this village, on whose help I may count." The neighbours came and said, "No one lives with his parents for ever" and spoke many a word of sweet consolation, but he would not be consoled. Again and again he cried and said, "Alas, who will now help me? I am utterly helpless, and an orphan in the fullest sense of the word."

He sold the buffaloes and performed the funeral rites of his father with the money. Thirteen years he lived in his village, earning his bread, with difficulty, by stray occupations. He was a mere child when his father died, and knew nothing of the debt his father had contracted. All on a sudden, after thirteen long years, Balarām, the money-lender, paid him a visit and said, "Your father was a good man with a religious turn of mind. He was a man of character. I was extremely pained at the news of his death." He then produced the document and said that falling into distress, Dingādhar's father had taken a loan of hundred rupees from him. "Here is the document," he said, "and all the people of our village know about this loan. Now tell me if you are willing to pay your father's debt."

As if a thunderbolt had fallen on Dingādhar's head! He prayed for two month's time, which Balarām readily granted.

Dingādhar now wept day and night, without being able to devise means to pay the money on the promised day. The scriptures say, if a man dies without clearing his debt, he finds no place in heaven but straightway goes to hell. If such a man is reborn in this earth as a tree, the loan pursues him as a wild creeper and holds him tight in its grip, giving him no rest. No escape there is from the hands of the man, to whom one is in debt. The pursuit goes on through all future lives.

Often the debtor is born as a bull and drives the plough on his creditor's rice-fields. Loan is worse than fever or headache. Its pain increases day by day. The money-lenders are, as a class, heartless. They do not remit a single *cowrie* of interest. Just as a man, passing by a bee-hive and stung by the bees, becomes mad with pain, even so is the debtor, and he considers the pain of debt the worst of all other ills of life.

His father, before his death, had disposed of most of his lands, hard pressed by want. His houses were now at the point of crumbling down, the roofs out of repair and the posts in a half-shattered condition. The buffaloes were sold long ago to meet the expenses of the father's *sradh*. How could he now clear the debt, swollen into a large amount with interest? What would Dingādhar do under the circumstances? Seeing no way out from his growing anxieties, he left his home and went to Singāpur and one afternoon presented himself before Balarām. (Ll. 1-40.)

(3)

Dingādhar had not bathed, nor had he any meals that day. In great distress he appeared before the money-lender. He found Balarām, seated in his out-house, and approaching him, humbly laid his hands upon his creditor's feet and said, "I have come to clear my father's debt—if only you would kindly help me to do so. A father's debt is the son's; and I do not wish to shirk my responsibility." Balarām was moved. He said, "What amount have you brought with you, my child? Let me find out what the dues are, from the account? Give me the sum I lent. I will not charge any interest."

Dingādhar stretched forth his empty hands and began to cry. "Just see," he said, "I have nothing with me. I am a beggar. Know me to be your slave. I have come with great hopes. Kindly engage me as a servant in this house and thus release me from my father's debt."

Then Balarām thought over the matter for a while and said, "I have need of a young servant. All right. I give you the charge of my buffaloes. If you can do this work for six years, I will release you from your father's debt and tear off the bond."

Though distressed to think of his long years of servitude, a smile still broke upon the lips of young Dingādhar at the thought that he would at last be able to clear his father's debt at a future time. (Ll. 1-20.)

(4)

Let us, for a time, pass from the topic of Balarām and Dingādhar to that of the maiden Sujāti.

Balarām had a youthful daughter in his house, beautiful as the evening-star. She looked like the very lamp of the house and spread a halo of light around like the moonbeams. The crow is dark, the cuckoo, a shade darker. And darker still is the water of the river Singākhāli. But the fine hair of the damsel was praised as the darkest of them all. Her figure was symmetrical and fair; and fair was the smile on her lips. Indescribable was the beauty of that sweet face. Its only comparison was the full moon. Balarām was anxious to find a bridegroom for Sujāti the only child of the house. The best flowers from the garden were plucked every day and with them his wife daily worshipped the goddess, Mangal Chandi, praying for a suitable husband for her daughter.

Now, hear what took place next by a mere accident.

Sujāti one day, went to the bathing-ghat of the river for taking her bath. The perfumed oil from her head spread its soft fragrance, and with a pitcher of water in her arms, she slowly went to *ghat* all alone.

The black clouds were broken and dispersed on all sides by the wild gusts of wind, which madly ran through the summer sky. Alone she stood on the landing steps, gazing at them. The waves of the river violently struck against the banks in their mad fury. There was no passer-by, no traveller, in that lonely region. So freely did she come down to knee-deep water and there washed her fair limbs. She descended still deeper into the river and washed her fair body. Then going down still deeper, with her neck outstretched, she looked on all sides with curious eyes. Just then she perceived that her pitcher of bell-metal was carried away by the waves into the mid-river. "Who will bring back to me my pitcher? Whom should I ask for it?" she thought, "There is no friend, none to help me here." The waves carried the pitcher far away from her. "Alas who will help me to get my pitcher back? I do not know how to swim. It was my fault that I came alone and this is the penalty I have paid. I have lost my pitcher. My parents will blame me. It is now high time to return. They will find fault with me for having come alone and lost the pitcher. How shall I return home with empty hands? O the winds, and the gods of heaven, may you graciously make the current blow to the contrary course, so that I may get my pitcher back."

The Herdsman.

"The winds, O fair girl, will not obey your order. But here is one, who will. I am getting back your pitcher for you. So return home and think no more of it."

Herdsman Lover

"Why does that sound forcibly capture my heart to-day." P. 47.

She was alone there and now they became a pair. On the landing-ghat of the river, four eyes met for the first time. She recognised the youth to be in charge of the buffaloes in her father's pastures, and then analysed her own feelings in secret. The colour of the Jabā flower reddened her face. This was her first youth and the dawning of the first happiness on her maidenly soul.

The young man brought the pitcher back and she carried it home, filling it with water.

He played on a reed-flute eight inches long, with pores at intervals; the burden of his song was, "O my own dear Rādhā, the abused one." Singing the song through his flute, the young shepherd returned to the pastures, after handing over the pitcher. Why is it that the maiden turned her head, again and again, to cast a glance at him to-day?

"I have seen you often. But to-day I discover graces in you, which are altogether new. Why does your flute like an enemy, seems to call me away from the duties of home to-day, to dazzling heights of pleasurable thoughts? Day after day have I seen you. But how is it that to-day the sight of you overpowers me with a strong emotion, as if my life would be unsupportable without you?"

In a room on the second floor of the three-storeyed house did she now enter to change her wet clothes, but her mind knew no rest at the sound of the flute.

"Many a time and oft have I heard the young herdsman sound his flute. But why does that sound forcibly capture my heart to-day? Is it not the same flute? But the tune to-day seems to be a new one. O my helpless lad, do you also bear a death-like pain in your heart in that lonely pasture-field as I do here, in this hall of my father? O my friend, let your buffaloes graze freely in the pastures on the banks of the yonder stream.

Be alone for a moment and hear me. Your flute has captivated a poor woman's heart. Why do you, my poor friend, expose your bare head to the scorching rays of the sun? Why do you allow yourself to be wet with rain? In yonder swamp grows many a lotus-plant. Get one of its large leaves and protect your head. Difficult it is to have a friend—a lover after one's mind. When such a one is found, many a trouble may have to be borne. One bears hurts from the thorns, when one stretches one's hands to pluck a lovely flower. A helpless woman am I, bearing a pain in my heart which cannot be expressed. Like unto a shoal, formed out of the sands of the bank, but unconnected with it, I live unattached to my family, though I was once part and parcel of it. For shame I cannot open my lips to express what I feel. I would have torn out my heart, if it were possible to show you its deep wound. I cannot express my pain to my parents either. A feeling of shame holds my tongue. From the day we first met on the landing-ghat, your flute has maddened me. How can I meet you, being a woman of the harem, always caring for society and its restrictions? The secret pain is unbearable. I try to advise my heart to reason and dissuade it from this mad attachment. But the mind's course cannot be stopped. My youth alas is waning away in deep anguish. No friend of mine knows my innermost thought; not a fly, not a worm has a knowledge of it. Reservedly do I keep my feelings confined to my heart. Were I a bird, how happy would I be, to see your face, sitting on a bough or flying in the air? Fain would I cut off all the ties of the family and would be near you, ministering to your comforts. How gladly would I wander with you, wherever you would go! And if the sun sent its burning rays, I would hold up a lotus-leaf to protect your head. How long shall I deceive others and deceive myself in this way! My parents discuss the question of my marriage. Ah me! they do not know what is in my mind. If one's mind becomes madly devoted, what will social considerations do? Sweet is the cool water of the river, sweeter still the air, that gently blows over it. The milk of green cocoanuts is even sweeter than that air. Greater than these and immeasurably sweet is the first love in woman's heart. But the sweetness of getting a husband after one's own choice, one whom the heart elects, surpasses all other good fortunes of life. Just as the river sends sprays up in the air and in the blue azure these white little things shiningly play together, even so, above this dark human life do such a pair enjoy their blissful love. There is a plant of Champā, on which hang flowers, looking like a garland or like the smile of a sweet face. They are in full bloom and neither decay nor drop from the stalks. My heart yearns to prepare a wreath with them to be presented to you as a symbol of my constancy and love. Alas, I am reminded that I am not allowed to go out of this house! It is then that I feel how helpless I am."

These are some of the stray thoughts—the secret laments of the maiden's heart. (Ll. 1-102.)

(5)

Now let us see what the youth is doing in the pastures with the buffaloes in his charge.

When the clouds are rent by gusts of winds and the stars appear growing brightly from their midst, the young man thinks that they are beautiful like the eyes of the maiden.

The dark clouds fly above, spreading themselves rapidly over the azure,—the young herdsman imagines the maiden to be going to the river-*ghat*, covered with her dark *sāri*.

The winds raise waves over the river in quick succession,—the youth is reminded of the wavy dance of the long flowing hair on the fair damsel's head.

The lotuses are in full bloom on the waters,—the young man imagines that the face of the girl is made of their soft blossoms.

Thus indulging in mad reveries, he became careless about his duties and did not watch the buffaloes in his charge.

Now hear what happened one day.

These beasts ate up the crops of the river-bank. The watchman reported to the Raja that Balarām's buffaloes had eaten up all the crops of the river-bank, belonging to His Highness.

The constables with long bamboo-clubs in their hands appeared before Balarām and wanted him peremptorily to present himself before the Raja's court. Balarām, with tears in his eyes, approached the palace of the Lord of the village in slow steps, while his wife and beautiful Sujāti trembled in fear as to what punishment Balarām would receive at the hands of the infuriated Zemindar.

Balarām now came near the gate-way of the court, where many soldiers, with their loin-cloths bound tight round their waists, brandished their long sticks and swords. They put him into a dungeon and there he remained for some time. Meanwhile Dingādharā approached the Raja with joined palms and thus submitted his prayer, " Do not, O lord, punish my master. In the name of God, I ask you not to take any violent steps against him. Be pleased to have me arrested in his stead, and I will make up for the loss Your Lordship has sustained, by serving you for full six years."

The buffaloes were confiscated to the State and Dingādhar's services were transferred to the Raja's pastures. The compensation being thus paid, Balarām was released, by the order of the Raja.

The maiden secretly lamented in her lonely apartment. "Alas, my friend, you have left our house for good! Helpless as I am, what can I do to save you? If it were possible, I would sell my nose-ornament and make up for the loss, caused by the buffaloes."

When called to dinner, she scarcely ate anything, and when retiring to sleep, she could scarcely close her eyelids. The soft cushions she did not like, but spread the long flowing ends of her *sāri* and lay herself down on the bare floor. The father did not know her anguish; nor even her mother. Like fire smouldering in the saw-dust, grief burnt her heart slowly, unseen by others. This fire was not to be extinguished by water. "Else, my constant tears would have done it. Like the flow-tide is this youth of woman. If either crosses its limits, there is that general whisper and alarm." She thought.

(Ll. 1-44.)

(6)

Asharia Mandal is a notorious miser. When he sat to dine, he used to chain his cat, lest it should come too near and steal a morsel. His wife was almost in a state of nudity, yet he would not buy new clothes for her. His brother, in rage, would often slap him on the face for his extreme stinginess, and his son would abuse him and call him a contemptible mad fellow. But his character was not reformed. He slept on the bare floor and would not buy a mat. He wore a ragged loin-cloth and day and night counted his interest. He was a very "crocodile of wealth," * and when he gave a loan to anybody, he would not remit a farthing of the interest. If any one came to him to clear his dues, he looked intensely into his account-books and calculated the interest minutely and exacted every farthing. He scarcely ate two meals; one was sufficient for him. No one saw him spend money for oil. When night came, he gathered a heap of dry leaves and made a fire to serve the purpose of a lamp.

After thinking wildly over his distressed condition, Balarām saw no way out of his difficulty, and applied for a loan to Ashāria, who gave him Rs. 500, making him swear, on his honour, to fulfil his strict conditions in due time.

Balarām paid a compensation to the Raja with the money and thus got his buffaloes released.

Out of kindness, the Raja granted a release to Dingādhara, after he had served for six months. But the youth had not the courage to return to Balarām's house. (Ll. 1-17.)

(7)

The river, in June, presented a wild spectacle of furious waves. Knowing not what course to follow, Dingādhar wandered about the bank with tearful eyes. He had no father, no mother, not even a brother, and his home on the Singākhāli lay deserted, there being none there to light the evening lamp.

He attempted to cross the river by swimming. But a great storm overtook him in the mid-river, and he was knocked at the head by the dashing waves and rendered unconscious. The river was very deep there and he was about to be drowned hopelessly. Fortunately, however,

* One who has hoarded great riches is generally called in this country a "crocodile of wealth."

a merchant from the east was passing that way with seven ships, laden with salt, molasses, rice, mustard, chilly, pepper, ginger and other agricultural products. His ship was manned by 22 oarsmen. He espied the struggling youth about to be drowned in the Surmā river and out of kindness, offered him help in time. He was brought to the ship. The merchant found his breath almost gone, and he was for sometime in doubt as to whether there was life in him. But the youth slowly rallied.

Dingādhar spent a year with the merchant, who treated him with great affection. In fact he enjoyed the position of the merchant's son in that house. The merchant one day told him, "This house, my boy, is yours. I have no children, nor any landed estate. These seven ships are all my property. And you have seen that I live by trade in countries, far and near."

Not long after, the merchant caught fever, due to exposure to northern breeze, and died. Dingādhar now became the master of the seven ships.

With these he made a voyage through the river Surmā and after many days, returned to his own native village on the bank of the Singākhāli. He constructed many goodly houses there, with doors open to the south. After being thus settled at home he remembered the beloved maiden Sujāti, whom he had not seen for the last five years. "How is she doing?" He asked to himself, "Has she been married by this time? Does she still think of me, after the lapse of so many years?"

He took a bag on his shoulders and a staff in his hand and thus disguised as a Fakir, went to Singāpur, the native place of Balarām.

The big houses he saw there on the point of collapsing. Balarām was dead and his home looked desolate and deserted. From the unprotected roof the thieves stole straw, and the hedges and walls were broken by trespassers. The mother and the daughter occupied a corner of the house and lived in great fear, crying day and night. Dingādhar saw their miserable condition and his heart bled in sympathy.

He shouted like a beggar, asking for charity. Alas! they had not even a handful of rice to offer to the seeming Fakir. The maiden looked at him with tears in her eyes. She was herself a beggar, how could she help a beggar? There were a hundred patches in her '*sāri*' and she looked pale, like fire half hid in ashes. Dingādhar's heart broke at the sight. A silent cry rose in his heart, like when a spark of fire touches the store of gunpowder. (Ll. 1-50.)

(8)

He returned home, convinced that Sujāti was still unmarried. He sent a match-maker to Balarām's house. The mother offered him a wooden seat and received him with respect. He addressed her and said, "Your daughter, I see, has stepped into her youth. She is exceedingly handsome. In fact, I have not seen a girl so beautiful in the locality. I am a match-maker and travel far and near in quest of brides. If you wish, I may try to secure a bridegroom for your daughter. Now tell me your views. I have, on my list, a score of suitable youths, ready for engagement. Say what conditions would you like to propose."

The poor mother's eyes were almost blinded with tears. She saw darkness all around her. Slowly did she say. "The merchant Balarām died, leaving a debt of Rs. 500; a marriage-proposal has been forced upon us on account of his debt. All the buffaloes and our pastures have been mortgaged to the money-lender. We have thus been able to clear half of our debts and prayed for a little extention of time. Six months was granted, during which the remaining money must be paid. Should we fail to do so, Ashāria would seize our house and property and forcibly get my daughter married to his son. Thus the poor girl is to be given away in lieu of her father's debt. Ashāria belongs to a low-caste Urumbariā community. He is resolved to ruin our social status in this way. But know, my dear sir, before I agree to this dishonourable proposal, I will cut my daughter to pieces with my own hand and float the corpse in the river, and then drown myself there. There is only one week in hand; so the time has nearly expired. We do not know what will befall us in the interval.

The Match-maker.

"I will get your house and property released by clearing your debt. Within seven days you will see it all done."

The match-maker returned on the fourth day and cleared the debt with interest to the last farthing. The property was released and the house thoroughly repaired.

The match-maker raised again the question of marriage, but did not disclose the name of Dingādhar. The maiden Sujāti now thought over the matter. The date of marriage could no longer be put off. She took recourse to a pretext and said to the match-maker, "There was a young man in charge of the buffaloes of our house in my father's time. He was appointed for six years, but having served us only for six months, left this house. I do not know his present whereabouts, nor the name of his native village. The condition of my marriage is this. This youth should be found out. Myself and my mother are helpless women. Who will take charge of our buffaloes? We cannot go to the pastures and keep watch over them.

The match-maker went to Dingādhar with the message.

When he heard this, Dingādhar disguised himself as a match-maker, and went to the house of the maiden. He bound his long hair into a knot, after the manner of a match-maker and spread an umbrella of split bamboos over his head. Arriving at Singāpur, he approached the maiden and made a hurried speech to this effect. "I am a brother of the match-maker, who lately called here. We have now heard of your strange condition. You should have told of it beforehand. We have repaired and reconstructed the houses and paid off your debt to Ashāria. The marriage is fixed. The bridegroom has already come here and is staying on his boat in the river. Now what pretexts are these? Where can you expect us to find out your young herdsman? Who is he? We do not know. However, I am prepared to take charge of your buffaloes and serve as your servant from to-day. Now be true to the engagement and consent to the marriage." Saying so, he threw away his false hair and the guise of a match-maker. He became once more the young herdsman he was, by wearing a cap on his head and taking the shepherd's crook in his hand. The maiden looked intently at the youth and now recognised her herdsman-lover. He had the same flute in his hand, and sang a song—that old song, which had captivated Sujāti's mind on the bank of the Surmā.

The drums and tabors were beaten and the music of Sānāi's note was heard from afar. Beautiful Sujāti was thus married to Dingādhar.* (Ll. 1-82.)

* After this we have some lines, composed by the ministrel, who sang this ballad, to this effect :—

"When this part of the poem was sung, the audience became excited with joy. The night is far advanced. Will you give us a '*Silim*' of tobacco? After a little recreation and smoking we will resume the story.

(9)

Meghuā, a merchant of Chittagong, was passing by the river Surmāi with his five ships. The oars were coloured red and blue, and as they struck the waves, a musical note arose, filling the air with the sound. The river, struck by the oars, was in commotion, presenting a spectacle of wild turmoil.

The oarsmen and the Captain asked the fishers, who were throwing nets into the river, "Will you tell us, friends, the name of this country?" "Go a little up," said they, "and you will find the landing-steps, known as Dingādhar's '*pāt*,' near the bend of the river."

The landing-steps were made of stone. Here the young wife Sujāti was bathing. She looked beautiful as the full-moon. She was dressed in her blue '*sāri*,' through which the lustre of her body shone forth in bright contrast. There, sitting on the landing-steps, she opened the five-fold braids of her chignon and with the end of her '*sāri*' wiped away the red dye from her feet.

Staying in the mid-river, Meghuā looked at her beauty and was charmed. She looked like a fairy with her blue '*sāri*,' her moon-like face and the curling hair which fell loosely round her head. She was busy with her toilet-articles on the landing-*ghai*, but when she saw foreign people coming on a ship, she hastily took the pitcher in her arm and in slow steps walked towards her home.

She went all alone. Meghuā ordered his ships to cast anchor there and, for sometime, sat musing, forgetful of himself. When evening came, he set out for Dingādhar's house.

In a pleasure-house, raised in the midst of a tank, Dingādhar sat in a happy mood, when Meghuā paid him a visit and offered himself as a guest of the house for the night. On pretext of friendship, he spent the night there. He incidentally talked over many matters, concerning the prospects of his trade and said, "In the north there is a place called Arang. I am going there for trade. It is a strange place. In exchange of rice, they give us large quantities of gold. They are greatly fond of dried fish, which is not available in that country. For some quantity of dried fish, they would give us a golden cup. For shaddock they would offer precious stones. In their country there are no betels or nuts. If they get these, they would gladly give oyster-pearls. They accept banana, cocoanut and other fruits in exchange of gold-leaves."

These accounts inflamed the imagination of Dingādhar and he started for that northern city for trade with his false friend. He took leave of his wife Sujāti and in great speed, in six days, he performed a journey, which, in usual course, would take six long months.

It was evening and the sun was setting with glittering rays. The ships were going fast over the waters, aided by the playful winds. At a certain place, Meghuā ordered his boatmen to cast anchor with a foul motive. Dingādhar entered his friend's ship for the purpose of playing at dice. There after playing for hours, Dingādhar fell asleep in his friend's cabin.

Now the wicked Meghuā cut off the ropes of his ship which went straight to the sea with Dingādhar, carried by the current; and the oarsmen and others on Dingādhar's ship lay unconscious in deep sleep and the people of Meghuā, at a signal from their master, led the other ship against the tide, which, aided by favourable winds, marched off, with sails unfurled. (Ll. 1-60.)

(10)

In the morning Sujāti was taking rest in her own compartment, accompanied by her female attendants. Buddhu, a servant of the house came with the report that a rumour ran in the city to the effect that the master of the house was coming back.

Sujāti, when she heard it, went to her toilet-room and wore a '*sāri,*' gorgeous like the tail of a peacock. In her arms, she wore bracelets and an armlet. She adorned her chignon with a garland of Champa-flower and over it put some golden bees. Near her forehead, she wore golden stars, and a *besar* adorned her nose. A pair of golden pendants of the pattern of '*Jhumka*' flower hang from her ears; and when she wore the red sign of luck on her forehead, verily did she look like Lakshmi, the harvest-goddess. On her feet sounded her anklets, making a merry jingling sound.

She made ready a flat basket with sacred articles, chiefly blades of grass, a handful of rice and some sacred things, which were first offered to the goddess 'Bana Durga.' Her husband had returned after six months, and she was there to give a due reception to his ships, performing the sacred rites. She came to the river-*ghat* and recognised her husband's ship. She was now to take the goods and treasures from it, observing the usual ceremonies. She came down to the river and first made a sign with vermilion on the prow and placed on it the blades of grass and a few grains of rice. After long days her husband had returned. Her heart was full of joy and a smile adorned her lips. At this stage, the devil of Meghuā appeared there and with the suddenness of a vulture, which swoops down upon a fish, about to be cut by the fisher's knife, seized Sujāti and carried her to the ship. Then at a signal from him, his men immediately started the ships, which being favoured by the strong current, flew off like a flash. The clouds were roaring in the sky and the sails were aided by high winds. The people on the bank stood stupified by the suddenness of the action. In an instant the ship went out of sight so fast that they could not believe that such a thing hat really happened before their eyes. Sujāti was seen last time striking her head with her hands. It was like the Rakshasa carrying off Sita from her sylvan home. (Ll. 1-35.)

INCOMPLETE.

THE YOUNG HERDSMAN.

(A SECOND VERSION.)

The Young Herdsman.

(1)

" O my youthful herdsman, O my friend, my heart weeps for you! From where do you sound your flute? I look on all sides in vain and see you not on the banks of the Surmāi."

" On one side of the Surmāi, I see the bank, risen to great height, all black, and off on the other, it is all white with sands. Between her black and white banks, flows the Surmāi. From where dost thou sound your flute in this region? I cannot see thee. The Hijal-tree stands high there, I ask it, " Will you tell me, my good tree, who sounds the flute so sweetly?"

"The blossoming Champā and the flowers of the screw-plants adorn this bank of the river. Here have I lost all control over my heart at the sound of your flute. My social ties, my family honour have now no meaning for me."

Her pitcher which was full to the brim, she empties and, on pretext of fetching water, she goes to the river-*ghat* and gazes around.

The water, which is emptied from the pitcher, is sucked by the earth and, with it, the tears that fall from her eyes. She cannot see the path through her tears and says, " O my bee, why do you not come to the flower, which has bloomed for you." (Ll. 1-16.)

(2)

So indifferent was she to everything else, while listening to the flute, that she knew not that her pitcher had been carried away by the current and floated far off. The sound of the flute captured her heart completely. She sat on the landing-steps and opened the five braids from her chignon. From under her wet *sāri*, her dazzling beauty appeared like a flash. With the help of a *gilla* (seed of scandres), she cleansed her body and wiped away the dirt with the end of her flowing *sāri*. The red dye of her feet was washed away by the waves of the river. She came down to knee-deep water and washed her fair feet; she descended still down and washed her fair limbs and then coming down still deeper, her body fully merged in water,—with her neck stretched out,—she cast her glance, full of curiosity, on all sides. From the other bank of the river, came floating at this moment the sound of the youngman's flute. The air was sporting and became resonant with the sweet music. The girl found her senses completely subdued by the flute's appeal. The black clouds were moving wildly, driven by the winds. From what depth of the forest was the flute singing so sweetly?

"Day by day have I heard the sound of this flute. But never felt its maddening effect as greatly as to-day. Ye, bees, that are flying from one flower to another in the grove of the screw-plants, in quest of honey, will you tell me, who it is that plays on the flute? Show me the path, so that I may find him at last. My eyes are nearly blinded with tears. Every day I come to the *ghat* in quest of him. I came yesterday, and have come to-day. But in vain goes my search for the player of the flute. Had I known how to swim, fain would I cross the river and catch him on the other bank."

The western clouds went flying to the eastern sky. The pitcher of bell-metal was carried by the current far off. Her day-dream vanished, and coming back to her senses, she perceived the helplessness of her situation. Who would help her to bring the pitcher back? It danced on the waves and went far away. She did not know how to swim. What should she do now?

"At an evil hour did I come to the *ghat*. My pitcher is lost. My parents will take me to task. It is high time to return. I shall be rebuked for coming to the river all alone and losing the pitcher in this way. How shall I return home with empty hands? O the winds, and the gods of the sky, order the current to take the contrary course, so that it may bring my pitcher back to me. O river, so cruelly sportive have you been; flow with favourable tide to get me back my lost thing."

The Herdsman.

"The winds will not obey your orders, nor the river. But here is one who will. I will get for you the pitcher back, you may return home quite at ease."

It was midday. He came to me with a cap on his head and a shepherd's crook in his hand—a perfect stranger to me. I had been alone, but now we became a pair. This meeting was ordained by Providence, and so we met."

A sense of shame coloured her face with the scarlet hue of the Javā flower. This was her first youth and this was the dawning of the first happiness on her maidenly soul. The bee imprints a kiss on the flower and leaves a sign. The impression of this meeting, likewise, made a sign on her heart, never to be effaced.

The youth brought her back the pitcher. And she filled it with water, and carrying it on her arms, she was about to return home, when she softly said, "Who are you, handsome youth? I never saw you before, nor heard of you. You have really offered me a great help to-day, when I needed it most. The sound of your flute and the sweetness of your smile have such a charming effect on my mind! I cannot resist it."

The Herdsman.

"I tend my cattle on the other bank of the river. My buffaloes graze in yonder pasture. In that unprotected land, scorching rays of the sun burn me, and when rain comes, I become drenched with it. So do I sing a song of my sorrows through this flute to assuage the pain of my heart—not that others would hear it. From to-day I will wait in yonder avenue of *hijal* trees and you will come with your pitcher for water here. I will stay on the other bank and you will be here. It will be only for a sight of your face—nothing more."

He carried with him a reed-flute, eight inches long, with holes at interval. On other days, he used to sing the name of Rādhā through his flute. But how is it that a strange tune sounds from his flute to-day?

The Maiden's Soliloquy.

"Why to-day has such a change come over your spirit, my friend? Your flute, it seems, is pursuing me like an enemy, calling me away from home, to an uncertain life of danger. From day to day have I heard the sound of your flute, but its music comes to-day with a strange message for me. It seems, a great trouble it will bring to my life."

When she was robing herself after her bath in her pleasure-house, rich with floral wreaths, she listened with all-absorbing attention to the music of the flute, that came from the far-off groves of screw-plants.

"How plaintive is the sound! Is it the same flute on which he used to play before or another? The pathos of the sweet music fills the mind with alarm; is the poor youth going to die of despair?

"Leave your buffaloes, dear lad, in the pastures on the bank of the milky river. Do you know that your flute has charmed the soul of a helpless woman? Why, my beloved, why do you expose yourself to the alternate freaks of the season—to the burning rays of the sun, or to the incessant rain, that drenches your body? Why not secure a leafy branch from yonder tree and thereby protect your head? How helpless am I! Fain would I wipe away the drops of sweat on your brow, caused by the sun and minister to your comforts!"

Thus did she lament in a wild manner in her lonely chamber. Now hear what happened to the herdsman in the pastures. (Ll. 1-84.)

(3)

The bright stars peeped through the clouds, torn by the gusts of wind in the azure, the youth looked at them and became reminded of the soft eyes of the maiden. And when the dark clouds flew in sportive ways, spreading themselves over the sky, the youth thought of his love, clad in her dark-blue *sāri*, sportively going to the river-side. The playful winds created an array of flowing waves on the river and this reminded him of the wavy dance of the long curling hair, that fell on her back. The beautiful lotuses, that bloomed in the water made him think of the maiden's sweet face, which he fancied to be made of soft petals of lotus.

Thus thinking always of the maiden he became indifferent to everything else and forgot his duties to watch and tend the buffaloes. Now hear what took place one day.

The buffaloes, uncared for, in the pasture made a raid in the corn-field near the bend of the river and ate up the crops. The field belonged to the Rājā of the place and his men reported to him of the damage.

The constables and peons, with long bamboo-clubs in their hands, marched to the place, bound the youth, hand and foot, and brought him to the Rājā, who took possession of all his buffaloes and ordered him to be banished from his country.

The river Surmāi looked menacingly in June and flowed in its mad course. The young herdsman wandered about its banks in despair. No mother, no father had he, nor even a brother or friend. Whither he was to go, he knew not. He was like a bird, flying in the infinite sky without aim or destination.

"O river, your course is towards the southern places ; tell my love, if ever she happens to come to your banks, that her friend, the youth has drowned himself. Ye, black bees, that hover in the sky, tell her that the herdsman is no more. Ye, kites, that fly above the tops of the bamboo-groves and ye, crows that croak, sitting on the boughs of yonder tree, tell the maiden that her beloved friend has died of unbearable grief."

The herdsman tied his clothes like a rope round his neck and jumped into the river. The waves came on, furiously dashing and well nigh drowned him. The river was very deep at this spot. But providence wished it otherwise. A merchant from the east was going by that river with seven ships, which were laden with rice, chilly, salt, ginger and other agricultural products. The merchant's residential ship, which was the biggest, was plied by 22 oarsmen. From the water, they picked up the half-dead youth.

Thus saved from death, he stayed with the merchant and learned from him the secrets of his trade. The merchant gave him the name of Dingādhar or master of the ships. After a time Dingādhar was sent by his master to the Garo Hills for trade. When he was returning, he saw on the way large bamboo-groves. He cut a bamboo and made a flute with it. (Ll. 1-48.)

(4)

Let me here revert to the story of the maiden's love. Separated from her young lover her beauty faded away. Her rich hair became knotted and wild like jute. Careless of her apparel, she ate little and had scarcely any desire for toilets.

The parents tried to assuage the pain of her heart, not knowing what it was, but all in vain. The very beasts of the forest and birds of the air seemed to feel a sympathy for her; while all alone, she lamented thus.

"I am a feeble maiden, O my friend! and feel as if my heart is on fire. Like a shoal, produced by the sands of the bank but owned neither by the river nor by the bank, I find myself cut off from all. Alas, I began to love as a child but felt its pain at the threshold of youth."

"How difficult it is to select the object of one's love! If one wishes to get a lovely flower, one should be prepared to encounter thorns. I feel shame in expressing my sentiments. To whom may I open the doors of my heart and show my innermost thoughts?

"The sportive winds play with the flower and tear its petals. Even so has Fate rent my heart. It is a great pity that I cannot tell my sad tale to my parents.

"I cannot go out of my house, lest people should blame me, but like a bird, sickened in the cage, my mind distressed by its environment, fancies itself flying in the free air.

"How sincerely do I try to dissuade my mind from this mad course, but in vain. The pitcher of my life, once full, is gradually losing its liquid treasure. The beasts of the forest know it not, nor do the birds of the air know what my grief is. Insupportable is this grief of mine unshared by others.

"Had I been a bird, I would have sat on a bough of the tree and seen your face, day and night, to my heart's content. No more can I thus deceive myself. My parents are discussing the question of my marriage.

Sweet is the air that blows over the waters. Sweeter still is the milk in a cocoanut. But sweeter than that is the first love in the dawn of youth. Sweeter than all these and immeasurably sweet is to a woman the husband of her own choice.

The playful waves rise high, driven by the winds. They send forth white sprays in the dark azure, which look like white flowers in the midst of dark ones. Verily are the lovers like these white sprays, living in bliss in the midst of dark evils attending life.

Look at the blooming Champā flowers! From whose neck has a garland dropped on the plants? Whose smile is it that shows itself in these full-blown flowers? They do not drop from the stalks, nor do they fade. When I go to the garden to pluck these, my eyes grow tearful. When I sleep in the night, I see in my dreams a figure sweet as yours,—my young friend."

Thus did the beautiful maiden lament day and night.

(Ll. 1-44.)

(5)

Now my topic will be the story of a merchant, named Meghuā, a native of Chittagong. He was going by the river in a pinnace plied by sixteen oars. Meghuā heard the sweet sound of a flute, when he was near a bend of the river. It was so sweet that the very current seemed to flow in a contrary direction, in order to listen to the music.

Dingādhar and Meghuā met there and both were pleased with one another. The merchant said to the youth, "My home is at Chittagong. Let us both go there. I would ask you to stay at my home for a full year. Then both of us will set out for some foreign country for trade."

(6)

From the bough of a tree, the cuckoo's note was heard and the night bade its farewell at this sweet signal. On the floor of her room the maiden laid herself down, lamenting her separation from the youthful herdsman.

"Why is it, O cuckoo, that your note has lost its usual charm? And who is it, O sky, that has robbed thee of the glory of moonbeams? He went away long ago. Meantime, many a flower bloomed and faded away. Just as the honey of a blooming flower dries within itself, the well of my happiness has become dry within."

One night she rose up from her sleep—all startled. It was the sound of *his* flute, no doubt of it, that she heard.

She did not say anything to her father, nor to her mother. She had become completely fearless and cared not what the consequences of her action would be. In the morning the parents would fill the air with their laments and the neighbours would abuse her as an unchaste woman. But she thought neither of this nor of that. As soon as she heard the sound of the flute, she straightway made for the landing *ghat*. The sky was covered with clouds and the night wore the hue of collyrium. The moon had completely disappeared behind the clouds. To the river she went, following the sound of the flute. Yea, the neighbours would call her a bad woman and revile her. The parents would be overwhelmed with grief. But she thought neither of this, nor of that. With her herdsman on the boat of his friend, she left the country.

It was like a bird, cutting by its beak the bars of its cage. She thought of the frantic sorrow it would cause to her mother and of the grief of her father. She shed a few drops of tear at the recollection. When the neighbours would call her a bad woman, what would be the feelings of her poor mother? How will she bear it?

With sixteen oars the pinnace of Meghuā flew like a bird over the river. They shortly reached Chittagong, the native place of the merchant.

One full year rolled by. The maiden could not be traced by her parents. Her beauty smote Meghuā with love. She was neither tall nor short-statured. Her hair was soft and curling. Meghuā became mad as he gazed on her beautiful figure. (Ll. 1-47.)

(7)

Meghuā (to the Herdsman).

"Hear me, O friend, how long shall we pass our time at home in this idle manner? I engaged carpenters to repair my ship. They have made it ready for a sea-voyage. Let us go to the north for trade. You are not probably aware of the prospects of trade in those regions.

I will tell you something of them, which will be interesting to you. The womenfolk there earn money by hard work. The males are lazy fellows and sit idly at home. In the public market, you will see women only as sellers and purchasers. In their rivers, pearls and precious stones are found in abundance. These they secure by nets. So great is their number that they store them without counting. In exchange of very ordinary goods, they give very large quantities of gold. If you can supply dried fish, they will give you hoards of money, measuring in the scales. They are madly fond of tortoise and goat. If we take with us some of these animals, we are sure to get countless gold and silver in return. Let us secure these and try our luck. If a person goes to trade to that country but once, he will hoard up so much wealth that his sons and grandsons will not be in need of going abroad for trade. The money acquired by a merchant, will make the family well-off for at least three generations."

After having made the head of his friend Dingādhar giddy with this false and exaggerated report, Meghuā went into the inner apartments of his house and saw his sister Maynā.

Meghuā.

"Hear me, my dear sister, I am going to the North for trade. The moon-faced maiden, we have secured, I leave to your care. Cover her with your flowing *sari* just as you would do a dearly prized treasure. Keep her in close custody—shut up within the walls of this house, so that even the sun or the moon, not to speak of any outsider, may not have a peep at her. I will return after six months and then shall I find a suitable bridegroom for her and think of her marriage. I will make for her a gold necklace and purchase a *sari* as white as the waves of the Ganges. She will, moreover, have nose ornaments, and gold bracelets for her arms, and anklets for her feet."

With these allurements, he tried to please the maiden, and set out on his voyage, accompanied by his friend.

The boat of Meghuā was plied by sixteen oarsmen, and that of Dingādhar by thirteen. Meghuā's boat went ahead, and the latter's behind.

In the North there is a large tract of land, inhabited by the Garos and the Kookis. These men are fierce like the Rākshasas and eat human flesh. No one, who travels there, has a chance of returning to his native country. Meghuā determined to send his friend thither on some pretext. After crossing thirteen bends of the river 'Surmāi' they came near a junction, and Meghuā here addressed his friend and said, "There are two courses of the river here. Yonder dark and furious stream leads to the land of the *Kāmunis* (Kamaksya). You had better proceed by it, against the tide. You will reach a place, full of fabulous wealth. I will go by the other stream, which leads to the country of Bharais. Now let us try our luck in two opposite directions for a period of six months. If you happen to come earlier, let your boat be moored here at this junction and please wait for me. If I come earlier, you will find me waiting. Both of us will go home together from here."

Thus they followed the two different streams. Now hear of the misfortune, brought on by Providence.

The clouds which had the look of the brownish knotted locks of Siva, the God of Destruction, rolled on menacingly in the sky. The winds with the furious voice of a challenge blew over the river. The turbulent waves broke the banks as high as hills and jumped like wrestlers. Who knows where wicked Meghuā was carried away, dashed by the waves? Dingādhar thought "Meghuā, like a traitor, has certainly led me astray."

The thirteen oarsmen cried out in one voice, "Master, it is impossible to go against the tide. Shall we return home? Kindly give us order to do so." The ropes of the sail were all torn and the helm was on the point of breaking. They could no longer control the boat. At this crisis, Dingādhar complied with the wishes of his men, and ordered them to ply homewards. It would take six months in going ahead against the tide. But the same distance could be traversed in thirteen days, if the boat followed the current.

He went to Meghuā's native country in quest of the maiden. Meantime, a rumour spread there that Meghuā's boat was capsized by storm. Three years passed and Dingādhar stayed at Meghuā's home, waiting for his return. But as he did not turn up within this long time, Dingādhar felt sure that he must have died. So after some waverings and hesitancy, he married Maynā, the merchant's sister. (Ll. 1-72.)

(7)

There was a Raja in Chittagong whose name was Kengu. He was a tyrant and oppressed his subjects. He had seven hundred good-looking women in his harem. But even this number did not appease his desire for the fair sex. He was always in lookout for handsome women, and ready to marry any number of them.

Four years rolled by, and the fifth was also going to expire, when Meghuā returned home, a wreck of his former self. His body looked like a thin piece of wood, and his beard had grown grey. On returning home after these long years, Meghuā saw what had happened in his family during his absence. He was inflamed like a blazing fire, fed by butter. He called all his neighbours and friends to his house and wanted an explanation. They all said that their information was that he had been drowned. Most of them failed even to recognise him. His hair, which had been jet-black, was now grey. Some of them thought that Meghuā had died and that it was his ghost that they saw before them. So they tried to drive him away from the village. Some wanted to have him arrested for false personation. Others advised patience and a full consideration of the matter before taking any steps. Those, who had borne him a grudge, now availed themselves of this opportunity and gave him some blows.

Being dealt at home in this rough manner, Meghuā went to Raja Kengu and lodged a complaint that his friend had played false with him. He had left his wife at home and gone for trade. This friend now turned into an enemy and took possession of his wife. He besides, married his sister Maynā. With the two women, the wicked man was enjoying himself in his home. He drove him away by force on his return. With this complaint Meghuā stood before the Raja, supplicant for justice.

Now I am going to describe to you how the Raja disposed of this case. He took a great interest when he heard of the two women. It was reported that they were exquisitely handsome ; so he forthwith sent constables to bring them up before him. They were now presented before the Raja, who passed the order of death by impalement on Dingādhar. At this stage, listen to what Sujāti, the maiden did.

* * * *

"He is my brother but has become my enemy."—cried Maynā and her laments made even the beasts of forest and birds of the air sad. (Ll. 1-34.)

KANCHANMĀLĀ

THE BRIDE OF A BLIND BABY.

PREFACE.

The song of Kānchanmālā, or the bride of a blind baby, is a *Gītikathā*.

The *Gītikathās*, as I have defined them in my 'Folk Literature of Bengal,' are tales, narrated in prose, interspersed with songs. The prose-portions are sometimes less genuine, as the singers have simplified the archaic forms of the language in course of reciting them through generations. The chief interest of this class of tales lies in the poetical portions, which are full of the unadorned simplicity of rustic life, though the language is oftentimes crude.

The tale of Kānchanmālā was collected by Babu Chandra Kumar from two men chiefly. The major portion he secured from one Hara Chandra Barmā of Marichali (P. O. Daubakhola) and the remaining part he got from Ramkumar Mistri of Aithor (P. O. Kendua). The two versions do not seem exactly to fit each other. In the first version, it is indicated that Kānchanmālā left her father's palace with her blind husband, disgusted with her father's capricious conduct. While, in the concluding portion of a second version that we have secured, it is distinctly stated that she was banished to the forest, owing to the wily contrivance of her step-mother. There is, however, no mention of a step-mother of the unfortunate girl in the first version of the tale.

It seems that many of these Gītikathās had several versions, which, though agreeing in the main with one another, differred in minor details.

I am sorry to find that the Gītikathā, as given in the following pages, does not appear to have retained its genuineness in all parts. We have always found, in these ballads and songs, instances of spirited women, whose minds are untrammelled by tradition or conventional ideas. The heroine has suffered all that a human being can endure for the sake of love; but we scarcely find in these tales a trumpeting of Brahminical canons in regard to wifely duties and devotion. Here, however (LC 31-44, Canto 10) there is that distinct ring of propagandic ideas of the later artificial school. The stereotyped phrases of Brahminic wisdom, such as "আসমানে সবুজ যেমন রাত্রিকালের বাতি। সেই মত ঘরের মধ্যে সতী নারীর পতি॥" (LC 39-40, Canto 10) "সতীর না পতি যেমন সাপের মাথার মণি" (LC 31, Canto 10) are here and there preached in long speeches, sounding a discordant note in a field, which is full of the warblings of Nature's glee birds. These sentiments seem particularly sickening and irrelevant, when a girl of fourteen is found to lament in that style over the loss of her husband, only six years old. The minstrel, who sang this song before an assembly of men, imbued with the new ideas of the Brahminic school, must have tried to introduce some wise sayings, current in the air at his time, however ill-suited they might be to the occasion, in order to humour his audience.

But though the minstrel's interpolations contain some burlesque elements, marring the naïve simplicity of the song, it is only occasionally that we find this to be the case; the general spirit of the whole has remained true to the characteristic charm of rural life. It is interesting to notice the vivid accounts of the forests of Mymensingh—full of 'Dāruk'-trees and the swamps, abounding with lotuses. Graphic are the descriptions of the wanderings of Kānchan, parted from her husband, through countries full of *sundhā methi*—sweet-smelling shrubs, whose leaves yield the red dye for decorating a woman's feet,—through wild tracts, with scarce human habitations, where men live in the company of serpents, bears and tigers, often dying in the hands of these enemies in the forest,—and through the chilly regions of the north, where the Kookis, the Gāros and other hill-tribes live in a state of perfect nudity and eat human flesh. The simple portraiture of his native land by the peasant-poet is really charming; it is so life-like that the reader occasionally hears, as it were, the roarings of clouds, and sees the landscape, lit up by lightning—vividly, brought before the eye, by a poet, in whose simple soul Nature seems to be mirrored in her true colours.

The account of the forest-life and of the joyful days that the Prince spent with Kānchan, given by him in a somewhat veiled language, lest it should hurt his wife's feelings, and the clever manner in which Kunjalatā drew from him, unawares, the story of his childhood, bring out, by contrast, the psychological phenomenon of two struggling hearts, not actuated by candour but by a motive to suppress facts from each other. The subsequent events, happening by the agency of the green-eyed monster jealousy, are drawn with exceedingly subtle hands, showing that our unlettered poet was no mean artist but an adept in all matters relating to the tender susceptibilities of the human heart. When Kānchan slept, stealthily did the prince stand by her, and looking on all sides with watchful eyes, lest he should be discovered, would gently fan her. But he could not hide his action from the ever-wakeful and vigilant eyes of the princess. At times the princess perceived that through the apertures of doors, he was intensely gazing at the sweet face of Kānchan. It was the cruellest cut of all, however, when the Prince, while going on a hunting excursion, one day, took leave of Kānchan but forgot to say a parting word to his wife. Such omissions, however regrettable, are but natural, when the mind yields to a new fascination. (Canto 15, Prose, Line 7.)

During the absence of the Prince from home, at a deep hour of night when the inmates of the palace were all asleep, and the clouds were roaring and the rain falling in incessant streams, Kānchan, requested by the princess Kunjalatā, with her voice choked with tears, told her the story of her forest-life,—how in the huts of reeds, covered with creepers and flowers, she lived with the old man and his wife,—how her boy-husband blossomed like a wild flower in the fresh air and light of the solitude and she delighted in him as the greatest treasure of her heart, till at last he was carried away forcibly by the King (Canto 17, Lines 15-38). In all this simple narration there is an appreciation of rural life with its simple pathos which we miss in our modern artificial poetry.

The most elevating portion of the tale is that in which the great renunciation of Kānchan is described. She wanted that her husband should be cured of his blindness. She offered the Sanyasi all that he might demand of her, for this great favour. She was ready to give up her kingdom and riches and would fain wander with her lord in the forest, as she once did, living upon fruits and vegetable roots. "Cure him of his blindness at any cost, and if all that I have offered is not enough, take out my eyes. I will prefer to remain blind all my days but let my husband have his eyes restored." (Canto 24, Lines 13-16.)

She was turned out from the palace by the plottings of her co-wife Kunjalatā. This had no doubt sharpened her bitter feelings towards her. The Sannyasi knew it and hit at her weak point. He said, "All right. Here is a fruit, give it to your co-wife and with it, give your husband and your kingdom to *her*. You will never be permitted to see your husband any more. He will be hers for ever."'

"There is another condition besides: when offering the fruit and, with it, your husband and kingdom to the co-wife, you are not to feel any pang in your heart. You will neither sigh nor sob, nor drop a tear. If you can pass through this ordeal with a tranquil mind, eyesight will be restored to your husband. But if you feel the least tremor in your heart he will remain stone-blind as he is."

What a trial! Here see the Hindu woman in all her towering strength and firmness, evoked by love. Turn over the pages of these ballads and songs and again and again behold the superb spectacle of renunciation and sacrifice, which are only possible by means of superhuman love—a patience, which only a statue may show, but not a creature of flesh and blood.

In a moment she collected herself, like the great prince Rāma, on the eve of giving up his kingdom,—"ধারয়ন্ মনসা দুঃখং ইন্দ্রিয়াণি নিগৃহ্য চ." For a moment she felt herself to be dedicated at the altar of love. She had no right to weep, no right to sigh,—lest her husband should lose this great chance. She rendered herself into a stone, nay more, she even felt elated at the thought that by her supreme sacrifice, her husband would be saved. Inwardly feeling a contentment that her husband would again see the smiling face of Nature, she turned herself away and never looked again at him, surrendering a privilege, which was prized by her more than paradise. Is this not a sight for gods to see?

How could these peasants conceive such a noble ideal of love? Is it not really wonderful that crude minds without any culture, driving the plough through fields and tending the cattle all their life, could conceive and appreciate these wonderful virtues in womankind ?

It appears that the Buddhist ideal of noble self-abnegation and suppression of animal-passions gradually filtered down to the lowest stratum of our society and rendered this world of ours into a paradise of the highest virtues of the soul.

In the following epoch of our history, when the Buddhist ideas passed away and stress was laid upon Bhakti or devotion, we begin to see another side of the picture. The tendencies of the age favoured abstract virtues, soaring above the secular plain. Prayers, fasts, vigils, ecstasies and esoteric joys became the craze of the spiritually-awakened soul. And in the place of a Maluā, a Lila, a Madinā and a Kanchanmālā, we have had other types, such as Dhruba, Prahlad, and many other heroes of faith, described in the Puranas. With the age of the ballads and songs, we have lost the period of the secular school, elevated by its romantic ideas of love, and gained access to a new world, of which the characteristics are spiritual bliss and abstract devotion.

D. C. SEN.

KĀNCHANMĀLĀ

The Bride of a Blind Baby.

Prologue.

O my audience, pray accept my salutes. Be kind to hear this account of Kānchanmālā with patience.

I have no knowledge of the science of music and may not always keep time with the instruments. My only hope is that my master, who taught me the art of singing, has blessed me. His blessings, I hope, will carry me safe through all trials.

The sky is square-shaped and is lighted by stars. There the spirits and fairies wander in the air. Their palaces are made of clouds, shining like mica. Without any lamp there is light there. On the walls of their mansions illuminations are fixed. The doors are all made of gold, and bolts are of the same metal. On all sides, gold glitters and illuminates the background of deep purple. In such palaces live the spirits and fairies. On bedsteads, made of mica, they enjoy sound sleep.

I shall relate to you incidents of one particular day.

Kānchanmālā is dancing before an assembly of spirits and fairies. The cymbals are being played by a musician, who sits close by her.

The spectators are beholding the sight with breathless interest. She is dancing, standing on and lightly touching a clay vessel.[1]

[1] The Indian dancing girl of yore used to dance, lightly touching a clay vessel with her toes. This unburnt vessel was naturally so brittle, that a slight pressure was enough to break it. The girl rested her whole weight on the air barely touching the vessel with her feet by a peculiar occult training. If the vessel broke under the pressure of the feet, she was branded as unsuccessful.

Small bells are ringing from her waist-belt and the anklets are jingling, keeping time with the music. Her toes scarcely touch the clay-vessel; so agile is her motion that she seems to rest her whole weight on the air.

She was playing her part excellently well. But evil was in her luck. Suddenly, the clay-vessel broke, touched by her feet.

The king of the fairy-land was angry at this and cursed Kanchanmala. His first word of curse made her braids all loose. The second word made her ornaments drop from her tender body; but there it did not end. As he pronounced the third word, a death-like pallor spread on her face and her eyes lost the power of sight.

King.

"Though you are a free spirit—a fairy, be thou born in the mortal land—in the house of mortals. For twenty years thou shalt remain a mortal and, on the expiry of that time, return to our fairy land."

Now let us leave these topics of spirits and fairies and begin a tale of the sublunary stage—this world of ours. (Ll. 1-40.)

(1)

In a city called Bharai, there lived a merchant, who owned fourteen splendid ships. With these he traded over seas and became a master of immense wealth. He made a house with profuse decorations of gold, but lived there with a sad heart, as he had no child. The house glittered like a show-thing, but the mind of its owner was ever-darkened with despair, for he considered all the wealth he had amassed to be of no purpose without an heir. His heart was sad and he bemoaned his lot in silence.

"Providence is against me," he thought, "what is the good of being near a dry canal having not a drop of water to quench one's thirst? What is the good of having a house which has no light and is covered with perpetual darkness? Even a monkey will not care to climb a tree that bears no fruit. The flower which has no honey, does not attract the bees. This my house without an heir, is joyless to me."

Thinking sadly in this strain, he came out one day for a walk in the public streets and saw a *sādhu*, going by the way. With his heart charged with sorrow, he prostrated himself at the feet of the holy man and said with tears in his eyes, "I am a miserable wretch, O master, without a child. People hate me because I am so. They turn their face to avoid looking at me.[1] Often do I wish to drown myself. It may be that this my meeting with a saint like you is due to God's grace. Can you, revered Sir, help me in my distress?" (Ll. 1-20.)

(2)

The heart of the holy man melted with compassion at the appeal of the merchant. He gave him a fruit and said, "Go home with this fruit. Let your wife eat it on a Tuesday or a Saturday. She will bear you a child,—a girl—of such exquisite beauty that the whole palace will be lighted by her presence. Through her you will have all joy and your sorrow will come to an end. But take care of one point. You must give her in marriage in her ninth year. If you foolishly allow this period to pass even by a moment, all your fourteen ships will be wrecked, your city will be destroyed by fire and the

[1] The childless man used to be called an '*atkuria*'—a wretch, and people would not like to see his face in the morning lest his whole day would go joyless, for the sight of an "*atkuria*" according to popular belief was inauspicious.

planet, Saturn, will be annoyed and burn your riches with his angry look." (Ll. 1-12.)

(3)

The merchant returned home with the fruit in his hand. The first two hours of Saturday, held inauspicious, passed away. During this time the merchant took care to wash the fruit. A quarter of an hour later, he entered the inner apartment and after another hour, he interviewed his wife. When it was about ten 'dandas' (about 9 A.M.), he placed the fruit in her hand and a quarter of an hour later, she ate the fruit, after having offered her prayers to the goddess Nava-Durga.[1]

A month passed and the lady spent the time thinking all the while if really something would come out of this. The second month she felt weak and lay mostly on her bed. In the third month, she knew that she was *enciente.* In the fifth month, the ceremony of *Pancha-mrita* was held in the palace. In the seventh month, her relations and kinsmen gave her feasts and clothes, by a ceremony called the *sadh.* In the eighth, she felt very uneasy in her mind and in the ninth, she was so unwell that she could not move. On the expiry of ten months and ten days, a beautiful girl was born of her. So resplendently handsome was the baby that the whole palace seemed to be lighted by her smile. (Ll. 1-20.)

(4)

Time rolled on. The baby grew to be a girl of nine years. Only three quarters of an hour remained to complete her ninth year.

[1] This dilatory procedure in handing over the fruit to the wife is probably due to waiting for the auspicious moment.

Her hair was flowing and long, it aspired to touch her feet and was so profuse that she seemed to feel its weight, when she walked. Her eyes were like two stars on the blue azure. Her lips were deep purple and looked as if perpetually dyed with a red paint. Her appearance looked bright like a figure of molten gold. On her breast, hang a string of pearls of rare worth and beauty.

The merchant was suddenly reminded of the words of the *Sādhu*. Only three quarters of an hour remained to complete her ninth year.

It was all their destiny. Alas, what woe was reserved for the girl! She was like a star, born in the sky but by evil luck thrown into the earth. The merciful God has no mercy for the unfortunate.

Suddenly the merchant recollected the words of the *Sādhu* and he made up his mind. Perchance the curse of the holy man might really be fulfilled. Only three quarters of an hour remained. She must either be married within this time, or his fourteen splendid ships would be all sunk in the sea and his palace destroyed by fire. As he thought over the matter, he grew firm in his resolve, "Whomsoever I happen to meet first within this time, to him shall I offer my daughter." This was his decision. What is written in one's destiny must happen. No one can wipe out the decree of one's fate, not even one's parents. (Ll. 1-24.)

(5)

At this time a Brahmin-beggar came to the merchant's door.

He was worn out with care and bent under the weight of his years. He supported himself by a stick and carried a baby in his arms. The baby was six months old and blind. With this child the old man stood at the gate for a handful of alms. Shortly after the birth of this child, the Brahmin's wife had died. Though blind, the baby was fair to see and looked bright as a flaming fire. The old man spent his days in utmost distress, continually thinking as to how he should prepare himself for the next world. After much distressing thoughts he had come to the merchant. He said, "Be pleased, Sir, to give shelter to this baby. I will leave it to you and being released of all anxieties, start for the holy shrines of Gaya and Benares. I have spent all my life, begging from door to door. What little time I may have before death, I want to devote to making myself prepared for it—living in one of the holy cities. To add to my innumerable miseries, as if they were not already enough, God has given me this blind baby. If I can trust it to your care, I shall feel myself quite free, having no attachment for this world."

The merchant thought over the matter for a while and then took the baby from the Brahmin and carried it to his daughter. Very little time now remained. The merchant stood before his daughter with the baby in his arms. Tears fell down from his eyes, as he stood silent for a time. (Ll. 1-18.)

(6)

She was sorry to see the merchant in that condition. She addressed him with tearful eyes and said:

"Why is it, father, that you are weeping in this way? What have I done to wound your feelings thus? My mother died when I was born and you have nourished me all this time with the affection of both a father and mother. Like a cloud, pouring out rain and causing rivers and canals to overflow, your tears are flooding my mind with grief. Tell me whence you have obtained this blind child, beautiful as flaming fire. Did its cruel mother leave it on the wayside, whence have you picked it up? Oh, what monsters must have been its parents, to leave it thus uncared for! The poor baby, alas, has no eyes to see the Sun and the Moon! How miserable is this child from birth! Its whole life will indeed be like one long night." (Ll. 1-20.)

(7)

The merchant began to sob aloud as he heard his daughter's words. It was not a thing to be spoken out. Yet it must be spoken. The merchant wept and thus related the whole story:

"I was childless and people called me names and hated me for being so. By chance I met a Sannyasi, who gave me a fruit. Your mother ate it and as a result, we have got you, darling, our best treasure. But woe to my luck! Well it is that your mother is dead. Had she lived to-day, she would not be able to bear the insupportable grief of this hour. It was settled that at your ninth year, you must be given in marriage. If the ninth year was allowed to pass and you remained unmarried, evil luck would pursue me. My fourteen ships would be lost in the sea with their cargo and my palace destroyed. This was the oracle delivered by the Sannyasi. Think not that I have remained idle all these nine years. All along I have sought for a suitable bridegroom, but none could I find, to my choice.[1] There remain only a few minutes for

[1] In Canto IV, it is stated that the merchant had forgotten all about the prophecy of the Sannyasi and was suddenly reminded of it in the eleventh hour. But here he gives a different story. These anomalies are due to the faulty narrations of the rustic folk who not infrequently miss the proper links in their narratives and give accounts of an inconsistent nature. It should be remembered that these ballads and songs were not written, and the errors and inconsistencies have occurred owing to faulty memory.

you to complete the ninth year. How can I now keep you in this house as an unmarried girl? Strange to say, at this critical moment, a Brahmin beggar came to my house and leaving this blind child to my care, has gone to visit the holy shrines of Gaya and Benares. Now take over the child to your custody. It was ordained by luck that you should have a blind baby for your husband. How could this be helped?" (Ll. 1-24.)

(8)

The roaring of the clouds filled the whole expanse of the sky. The deep sound was like the call of sympathy from heaven. On the boughs of trees sat the forest-birds and sang a note of wailing. She wept and reflected, "Alas, my father has turned my enemy. God is against me. The path before me is dark, not illumined by a single star or moonbeams. In this stream of life, I have not a ferry-boat to help me in crossing it. A brother's affection is a great treasure. I have unhappily no brother born here. Here in this very room, my mother used to comb my hair. Alas! This unfortunate one will never see her any more, nor feel that tender embrace. There is nothing so sweet as the morning-breeze, and one's mother's call of affection in childhood. Alas! that sweet voice will never cool my burning heart. Had she been living, surely she would not have given me this blind baby for a husband. How can I blame my father? It is all the work of my evil luck. O Sun and Moon, bear witness; and you, little baby in my arms, bear witness, too. I elect you as my husband, as my father has wished. From to-day Kānchanmālā is lost to him and lost to all happiness."

For a long time she bewailed her lot and then when night drew her dark veil over the world, she left the

Kanchanmala

"I will try to read your future to-morrow and offer you what help I can." P. 93.

palace and the city of her father—Bharainagar. As she wandered forth in the forest, she called its fierce dwellers—the bears and tigers—and asked them to eat her up, sparing her little husband. "It rent my heart," she said, "in twain, to leave the city of Bharainagar and my father's palace." The strange and unknown path faded in the depth of darkness. The sun shone like a mark of the red paint, vermilion, on the brow of the firmament—so dense was the forest. The day gave a glamour, not brighter than the evening, so dense was the forest. The wilderness, dark as it was, grew terrible in the night—her only companion, a small blind child. There she came near a large and ancient fig-tree. It was there since the Age of Truth (Satya Yuga). She approached the tree with the prayer that it might afford her a shelter for the night. "Lord of the forest art thou, O noble tree, save this little child. Be like a parent to this unfortunate one." Praying in this manner, she gave three gentle strokes at the tree, which instantly opened itself and showed a cavity inside.

(Ll. 1-36.)

(9)

From this hollow of the tree, came out a *Sannyasi* and asked Kānchanmālā as to whence she came and whither she was going in that dark night, whereupon she related to him her whole story.

The Sannyāsi.

"I leave my seat in this cavity. Sleep here with the baby for this night. I will try to read your future to-morrow and offer you what help I can."

The clouds glistened in the eastern sky, which glowed with a yellowish light. The Sannyasi stood near Kānchanmālā at the dawn of the day and said:

"You were once in great happiness, being born in the family of a rich man. But great sufferings await you. These are due to your evil luck and there is no remedy for them.

"I give you this fruit. Let the babe eat it. He will gain his eyesight. As you will proceed on the way, you will meet with woodsmen. Follow them and live in their company. There your husband will grow into his youth. If you ever happen to fall into a danger, remember me, and I will try to help you." (Ll. 1-13.)

(10)

Kānchanmālā gave the fruit to the child to eat. As soon as he had tasted of it, his eye-lids opened. He was a cripple from birth, but his body became straight and well-proportioned. It was as if a corpse came back to life, at the touch of a magician's wand, so did the baby thrive, tasting of that divine fruit.

Proceeding on his way, she espied the huts of woodsmen, as the Sannyasi had told her.

An old woodman and his good wife had founded there a small colony of their kinsmen. The small huts were built with creepers and wild plants which looked fresh and beautiful. The woodsmen carried wood and fuel on their heads to market-places and sold them to customers and thus earned their living. The women had smiling faces, pleasant to look at, like the full moon. They lived there happily with their husbands and children. Their hair was curly and they wore bark-dresses. They all came to see Kānchanmālā, as she approached their huts.

"Where is your home, dear girl? What is the village called? Why have you come to this wilderness of ours? How cruel must be your parents to have the heart to send you thus away. Tell us all the facts, without hiding anything. Your villagemen must be hard-hearted people to send you to this wild land. You are so beautiful! You look like a fairy. And they had the heart to send one of your tender age all alone! If you have done any wrong, what could be the fault of this baby, bright as the moon. How could they bear to send the sweet child in this way? It seems, your parents are void of all tenderness and affection. How are they bearing their life without you?"

Kānchanmālā.

"No father, no mother have I. Like a weed, carried by the current, I wander about helplessly, driven by Fate. That I am here in this forest is neither the fault of my parents nor of the people of my village. It is all due to my ill-luck."

In that place, the old woodsman and his good wife had no children. They welcomed the girl and the baby in their house. Kānchanmālā went with the woods-women and cut trees. The very path she trod became lit up with her graceful presence, so beautiful did she look. The woodsmen and their wives wondered as to who this little Queen of beauty was.

Some said, she was a fairy, others held her to be a princess. One admirer said, she must be the spirit of the moon, dropped from the sky; and a fourth swore that she was Lakshmi herself, the Goddess of harvest. She had come thither to taste the joys of forest-life. But all agreed in believing that she was vouchsafed to that forest to remove the sorrows of poor woodsmen. They bowed their head down to her secretly, paying the whole-hearted and grateful respects of their soul.

Four years passed in this way. The woodsmen, during all this time, sold their goods at fourfold their usual price. They were firmly convinced that they owned their extraordinary good luck to her grace and that she was a goddess in disguise.

The little baby now grew to be a lad of six years.

(Ll. 1-32.)

(10)

One day it so happened that the prince of a neighbouring country came to that forest-land for hunting. The women of the poor people took Kānchanmālā there in their company, and while they themselves carried loads of wood, presented fruits gathered there, to her, as a token of their love. She tied these in the flowing end of her *sari* and cheerfully walked about with them.

The prince saw the lad Phulkumar, who was hunting birds in the company of the children of woodsmen.

He was barely six and strikingly handsome. The prince looked at him with eyes of curiosity. He was convinced that such a child could not be a woodsman's son. He called the child to his presence and looked intently at him. He was surprised to mark, on the forehead of the boy, signs of noble birth. The unique sign of royalty—the *raj tika* shone from his brows. The prince was surprised and pleased and ordered his men to carry the child to his palace. "If he does not agree to go, of his own accord, bind him by force and carry him to my city." This was his order.

As soon as the order was passed, his soldiers laid siege to the whole tract, inhabited by the peaceful woodsmen and destroyed their huts, even as wicked boys break the nests of birds, built on tree-tops. The wood-boys ran away to their homes. All lamented the loss, done by the prince's soldiers. Their small money was looted by these robbers. They sat in despair, reflecting sadly on their heavy loss. Some of them cried and sobbed aloud and others wept in silence.

But poor Kānchanmālā was maddened with grief, losing her little husband. Like the fabled jewel on the hood of a serpent, which if taken away, it dies, was the lad a dear treasure of the chaste wife's heart. Parted, for a moment, from him, she felt her life unsupportable.

Alas, the grief of a true wife! As a boat sinks in a muddy pool without a man to steer it, what woe befalls the lot of a wife, deserted by her husband! What is left of a woman, whose husband has left her? She looks like a house, of which the lights have been put out. She may possess wealth, high rank and a retinue of servants and dependants. What will all these avail her? The stars cannot illuminate the sky, though they are many, if there is no moon. Like the sun in the sky and lamp in the house is the husband prized by a woman, who is chaste.

This life, alas, is unbearable without a husband. A woman, deserted by her husband, becomes an object of ridicule by all. Some abuse her openly, and others do so behind her back.

Thus did Kānchanmālā lament and her wild cries and piteous wail made even the beasts of the forest and the birds of the air cry in sympathy and grief. (Ll. 1-46.)

(11)

Kānchanmālā wandered about like a mad woman, seeking her husband, in the company of the old woodsman, her foster-father.

In the Sundhā-methi-Valley, where men were like monsters and lived upon human flesh—in the far-off Jigâ-hills, where men lived together with serpents, and where tigers and bears killed them every year by hundreds—in the Gāro hills, where the Kookis and Garos lived, a set of wicked savages of the North, who had acquired great physical strength by eating human flesh and wandered about, in a state of complete nudity in the forests—Kānchanmālā travelled like a mad soul, searching her little husband. She often slipped her foot on the stones of the hilly country and got severe hurt and she sobbed aloud in pain. No one came to solace her by sympathetic words. In the deserts, where the sands were so hot as if they were fried on fire, uncomplainingly did she go on foot, which burnt and became full of sores. But she heeded not all these sufferings. For six years, she searched her husband through hills and dales, through deserts and plains and at last reached a city, named Soomāi. (Ll. 1-20.)

(12)

The name of the Raja there was Vidyādhara. He had a very handsome daughter, named Kunjalatā. When Kānchanmālā arrived at that city, she heard the drummers beating drums, with the proclamation that a maid-servant was required in the palace for the princess Kunjalatā.

When Kānchan heard this proclamation, she saw the woodman and his wife, who had all along travelled with her, and requested their permission to offer her services as maid-servant to the princess Kunjalatā, saying, "O my mother of the woods, I am fatigued and can no longer travel. Your daughter bids you farewell. O my foster-father, you have been ever kind to this girl for all these years. Forgive and forget all the faults of this child. Do not, I pray you, be unhappy on my account, remembering the past and the sweet affection that has bound me to you all this time. I never remember to have seen my mother. But you have been tender to me in our forest-home and shown me a truly paternal affection. To-day I am going to start my life anew; my tale of sorrows, the thousand things of our forest life, will remain untold for ever. From to-day, think that your Kānchanmālā is no more in this world, and no more feel any anxiety for my sake."

The woodman's wife began to sob aloud at this and said, "The pain, dear girl, I feel at parting with you can not be expressed in words. We had no children, but got a child in you. You have been, to us, like a treasure, unexpectedly found by a poor man. The cool shade of our fig trees and the fresh water of the hill stream have, alas, no more any charm for you! If you would leave us in this way, why did you allow our affection to grow thus!"

It was by a mere chance that they had become united in affection. The girl and her foster-mother embraced each other and wept. (Ll. 1-14.)

(13)

Kānchanmālā laid her hands on the drum of the public drummer. As soon as she did so, the soldiers of the Raja approached and looked up for the person, who was her guardian. She was selected and they found out the woodman and satisfied him by offering a lakh of rupees as the price of the girl.

Then did the people of the Raja take Kānchanmālā to his inner court.

Now I am going to relate what happened next.

The same lad—once the baby husband of Kānchan,—had married the princess Kunjalatā in due course. The young bridegroom and Kunja spent their life in great happiness in a lovely bower, attached to the palace. Like a peacock, with its mate in a rich man's garden, did they happily reside in their apartments. Like the pigeon, which gently touches the beak of his mate with his, and sweetly spends the time, did the happy pair remain together without knowing any sorrow.

One day Kunjalatā asked her lord to relate to her in full the story of his forest-life.

Kunjalatā.

"When a mere child, you were nursed in a woodland; how could you live in the forest, infested with tigers and bears? Who are your parents? What place was your native land? What made you come to the forest and live there? You are so handsome that kings take fancy for you. How is it that you were banished in the forest? What makes you sad on occasions and sigh like one, who hides a deep wound in his heart?"

Phulkumār.

"No father, no mother, had I. Your father carried me away from the forest, taking pity on my forlorn condition.

"Our forest-life, dear lady, was a very happy one."

Saying this, he seemed to hesitate and hide something. The princess, perceiving this, said with great eagerness.

Kunjalatā.

"Tell me all facts of your forest-life. How do I wish to hear the account from your own lips? Do not hide anything from me. I am your wife—your beloved; why should you not open your mind freely to me?"

Phulkumār.

"In the depths of the forest did we live. Our days passed happily. A beautiful maiden looked after me. She was handsome beyond all description. I remember her faintly and even now feel a great pain in my heart, when I think of her. She was my sole companion and friend in the forest. She was like a woodland goddess—a mother, whom the forest gave me in the days of great sorrow. It was she, who nourished me from infancy up. I still remember her with the load of woods on her head,—the tropical sun burning overhead and making her perspire all the while. She would approach me with sweet forest-fruits and hand them to me with great affection. At times, she carried me in her arms and walked over the forest-path. If she would miss me for a moment, she would search me madly. Your father carried me from the forest, separating me from her. I do not know how she is bearing her life, parted from me." (L.l 1-44.)

(14)

Kunjalatā.

"What a tale of sorrow have you told me, dear lord! The maiden must have felt a great pain, parted from you. Wherefrom did the unfortunate girl come to live in that wild region? Was there nobody there, whom she could call her own? Has she no parents, no brother, no kinsmen in that forest? She must be wonderfully beautiful, as you praise her so much. I am eager to see a likeness of her handsome figure. Can you not draw her picture and give me an idea of her beautiful face?"

The prince hesitated for a moment and then sat in that nuptial bower to draw the picture of the maiden of the forest. He drew her as he remembered—with her long flowing hair, touching her very anklets. Slowly did he draw her eyes and fine eye-brows, her fair limbs and slender waist, and her breasts soft as the buds of Kadamba flowers.

When Kunjalatā saw the picture of the handsome woman, she spoke thus to her lord, * * * (some lines not found here). (Ll. 1-16.)

(15)

Then did she see her father, the Raja and said to him, "Here is the picture of a woman. I want a maid-servant, like her, so far as possible."

The Raja ordered it to be announced by a beat of drums.

People said that the girl, whom the Raja had appointed as maid-servant for Kunjalatā must be some princess in disguise, so beautiful she was. Some misfortune must have reduced her to this plight. The princess found that the woman was the very forest-maid her husband had painted.

Now her mind became disturbed by conflicting thoughts. "I have perchance brought a crocodile by digging a canal myself. I am to blame for it. She seems to be my natural enemy. Better it was that she lived in the forest. Why have I brought her to the palace?"

I will tell you the reason of her sorrow. She was at first moved by a spirit of compassion. But now she felt very differently. From the day of her marriage, she was happy with her husband. But now what a change! Phulkumār slept in the nuptial chamber that night and slowly Kunjalatā approached him. On other days, they talked and laughed together and felt like one soul. But to-day it seemed as if a cloud had covered the moonbeams. The prince looked at Kunja and yet did not glance in the same sweet way. His smiles on other days were always on his lips, but to-day they disappeared too quickly like a flower that bloomed only to fade away. Perceiving this change in him, the princess became sad in her heart and did not know what she should do.

But Kānchanmālā was happy beyond measure. It was like the acquisition of a great wealth by a poor man, or like the recovery, by a serpent, of the jewel, dropped from its hood.[1] Such was the great joy of Kānchanmālā on getting her husband back. They lived happily, satisfied with a sight of each other, like a pigeon and its mate, living in the same nest—like the cuckoo and its consort, singing the same song of love. If they did not see each other for an hour, they felt pain. They felt this strong bond of love secretly in their hearts.

It so happened afterwards that the prince would not relish any food, unless it was served by Kānchan. He would not be lulled to sleep, if she would not be fanning him. She became indispensable to him in his daily life. The princess perceived that Kānchanmālā had become her *husband's* maid-servant and not *hers*. She was at her wits' end to find out a remedy. More than this, she perceived that when Kānchan slept, the prince stealthily fanned her. Sometimes he secretly peeped through the doorway and intently gazed at her beauty. The princess' heart burnt with anger and jealousy. Now, one day the prince was going on a hunting excursion. He took leave of Kānchanmālā but forgot to say a word of farewell to the princess. (Ll. 1-12.)

(17)

Kunjalatā called Kānchan privately and told her that as her husband had gone away for hunting, she would not like to sleep in her chamber alone but would

[1] It is a tradition in this country that if the serpent with the fabled jewel on its hood, loses it by some chance, it dies of grief.

have her as companion in her room. "We will spend the night happily in sweet conversation and sleep comfortably on our couches."

It was midnight and the stars shone on the sky brightly. Kunjalatā at that still hour of night asked Kānchan to give an account of her past life.

Kunjalatā.

"Your life, dear girl, is shrouded in a mystery. You lived in the forest like a wood-nymph. Who were your parents? Have you no brother? It seems that you are the most unfortunate girl in the world. I feel a curiosity every day to know your past life. But my husband would neither tell anything himself about you, nor allow me to ask of you. He is to-day absent from the house and this is an opportune moment. Please tell me all facts, relating to your birth and past life."

Kānchanmālā was hitherto known to be a prudent girl. But imprudence prompted her to-day and she gave a full account of herself from the very beginning.

She first related her life at Bharāinagar. When she spoke of her parents, often did she wipe away her tears with the edge of her *Sāri.* At this time the clouds roared in the sky and rain fell in heavy drops. The girl could not proceed owing to overwhelming emotions that made her voice choked with tears. Often did she lift her hands to wipe away the growing tears. Anyhow she managed to give an account of her mother and of the mysterious Sanyāsi, who gave her a fruit to eat. Then she related the story of her marriage and how she became the wife of a blind boy at her father's command. Then with tears, which she could not check but fell incessantly like rain, she told what she had sufferred in the forest. She then referred to the kindness and hospitality with which the woodman and his wife had received her in their home. And last of all, she spoke of the misfortune that befell her. She had gone deep into the recesses of the forest for wood, but on her return did not find her husband at home. For six months had she travelled in quest of him but in vain. Then by the dispensation of Providence, she came to that city. Here she ended her story with a sigh. (Ll. 1-38.)

(18)

She spoke sincerely but her words produced an effect which poisoned her life.

Kunjalatā privately spoke to her mother thus, "O my mother, from you alone I can expect sympathy. Hear what an woe I am suffering from. I felt a great pain in my heart last night. It seems as if a sharp arrow pierced my breast right through." Then she related to her mother the whole story of Kānchanmālā, and ended by saying "A co-wife has come to our house to destroy all my happiness. It is like living in the same house with a venomous snake. Was it ever heard that a woman, living with her co-wife could ever be happy? Even if she sleeps on a soft milkwhite bed a thorn seems to prick her body and though she lives in the midst of the greatest happiness in all other matters, she scarcely feels happy for a moment. Just as the house is burnt to ashes by fire, it is even so by a co-wife. She takes away all the good luck, which otherwise would be her partner's.

Then the mother and daughter laid their heads together to devise means to banish Kānchanmālā to the forest.

At this time, the Raja of that city, Kunjalatā's father, died. Within a few days, the royal elephant, the pride of the stall, also died suddenly. All this had happened before the prince Phulkumār returned from hunting. A report was somehow in the air before his arrival that a witch had come to that city and all this mischief was her doing.

The prince came back but did not give credit to the rumour. Then the old queen secretly formed plans with her advisers and had the finest horse, belonging to the royal stable, killed one night and besmeared the bed and floor of Kānchanmālā with the blood of the animal. This was shown to the prince as evidence.

Then the report spread rapidly that the King had brought a witch to his palace, who was eating the elephants and horses of the stable. The people were frightened and resolved to leave the city for fear of being devoured by the witch. Thus the prince was compelled to banish the unfortunate Kānchan from the palace.

(Ll. 1-16.)

(19)

A moment's happiness is followed by continued sorrow. This life of ours, alas, is a sad mixture of weal and woe. Now the bright moonbeams light up the sky, but a moment hence, it is darkened by clouds. Like the water-drop on a lotus-leaf, the fortune of a man is unsteady and fickle. For a moment, the drop seems to stand firm on the leaf, but a moment afterwards, it tremulously glides down. To-day a prince, in the height of pomp and power—to-morrow a beggar of the street. To-day a millionaire, to-morrow a pauper. To-day the royal umbrella is spread overhead, to-morrow, a houseless vagabond, he seeks shelter for his head under the branches of a tree. To-day a father of seven children, to-morrow childless, he laments the death of his dear ones. A queen the day before, but an exile in forest to-day.

Be not too proud of your good fortune. One's luck shows the flow and ebb tides, like a river, and constantly changes.

Kānchanmālā.

"Oh my luck, tell me which way I will follow in this forest. Ill-starred am I from my birth. My father drove me away, when a mere child, taking me for an unlucky wretch,[1] and my God, who created me, joined my hands with those of a blind lad. My mother died untimely and I had no brother born. My lot has ever been to wander in the forest, weeping, helpless. If one is doomed to sorrow by Providence, who will, alas, help that one? Queen Sita, when *enceinte*, had to spend her days in the forest, banished from her palace. Ye tigers, that roam in the forest seeking prey, eat me up and get strong by eating human flesh. Ye serpents, that wander in this wild region, relieve me from my misery, once for all, by biting me with your venomous teeth. Death is like life unto me and life, to me, is bitter as death."

So did the unfortunate damsel wander weeping and lamenting in the depths of the forest, but she did not seek out the woodman, her foster-father, lest it should cause him pain to see her condition. Like the river in August, impelled by a strong emotion, she wandered from forest to forest and knew not when the day dawned or when it closed. (Ll. 1-34.)

(20)

Wandering in this way for six months she suddenly recollected the Sanyāsi, who had promised her help at the hour of danger.

[1] This is another instance of anomalous statements. In the beginning of the story it is stated that she left her home of her own accord, disgusted with the flagrant injustice of her father.

She sought the fig-tree for some days and then by chance found it out.

She gently knocked thrice at the tree. The Sanyāsi came out of its cavity.

She was still beautiful and bright as a flame. The holy man instantly recognised her. Kānchan fell at his feet and related her whole story, as to how the mother and the daughter had conspired to banish her to the forest. It was all her own fault as she had sincerely confided the story of her life to her co-wife. That sincerity caused her ruin.

The Sanyāsi promised his help, but asked her to wait there for a few days.

She lived in the hollow of the tree for three days. Once when the night was far advanced, she heard a sound like that of the strokes of hundreds of axes and felt as if many hands were employed in cutting down the woods of the forest. Each night she heard the sound and once in the depth of night, she came out of the cavity and saw ploughs made of gold and of silver. Bears and tigers were yoked together for driving the plough. Unnumbered labourers had assembled there and were constructing a city in the wood. A large number of palaces and houses were built there.

Nine days and nine nights passed in this way, after which the Sanyāsi called Kānchanmālā to his presence and showed her the city that was built there. She was surprised to see the city, which not only surpassed, in grandeur, Bharāinagar, the home of her father, but the one that belonged to Kunjalatā's father. She had travelled through many places in search of her husband, but nowhere had she seen a city like that.

The Sanyāsi proclaimed, by beat of drum, that a new city was built, of which the mistress was beautiful as a golden statue. "She will herself elect her husband at a public Durbar and desires princes to come and become suitors for her hand." Through seven big cities, the proclamation was made by beat of drums. Seven young princes of the seven cities came to sue her hand, with their retinue and attendants. But none of them could satisfy her conditions and win her.

The princess Kānchanmālā, the mistress of the city, knew a song. Half of it she would sing. The other half must be recited by the person, who wished her hand. This was her condition. The seven princes returned home disappointed. (Ll. 1-20).

(21)

Then came a blind beggar. He was so weak that he had to walk with the help of a stick. He stood at the gate of Kānchan's new palace and begged alms, saying "O princess of the new city, I have heard a good deal about your wealth and liberality." So saying, he stood at the gate.

The princess saw the beggar from her balcony. Though blind, the beauty of his person was dazzling to the eyes. She filled a golden plate with alms and herself came there to offer it to the beggar. He had long hair and his beard had grown, as he had not shaved it for many days.

"Where do you live, poor man, and where would you go at the end of the day?" asked Kānchanmālā.

The Beggar.

"I have heard your proclamation. I am not here for begging alms. That was a mere pretext for having an opportunity of talking with you. But, maiden, will you sing the song, of which the remaining portion you want your suitor to complete. And I ask you this question, if I can satisfy your condition, will you be ready to marry me?"

Kānchan had to sing her song. She sang of her early life,—how she was born, and how she had to marry a blind boy, how, by the grace of a Sanyāsi, the boy gained his sight and how she passed her life in the forest in the house of a wood-cutter—how that husband was carried away and how, after long wanderings, she at last found him and how the princess, with her mother, plotted against her and had her banished as a witch.

Here she stopped and said that so far she knew the story. He who will be able to relate events that occurred after this, shall win her for a wife, according to her vow.

The beggar said, "I will, with your permission, sing the rest of the song." (Ll. 1-34).

(22)

"Having banished his forest-queen, the prince became mad with grief. He had no desire for food or drink and one night left his palace. He cared not for his kingdom—nor for his throne. He cared not for Kunjalatā, his beloved wife, nor for the golden couch on which he slept. He left his army, retinues and escorts and wandered about in quest of Kānchanmālā, like a mad man. He is still wandering and his eyes are now blind with constant weeping." (Ll. 1-10.)

(23)

The blind beggar was none other than Prince Phulkumār himself. They recognised each other and Kānchan offered her whole-hearted services to her blind husband. She washed his feet and wiped them with her own dishevelled hair. Thus did she pass her days in great sorrow.

Six months passed and Kānchan had not seen the Sanyāsi all this time. He returned after six months and Kānchan told him her sad tale. She said, "Once you helped me at a critical hour of my life. Now be pleased again to restore sight to my husband." Saying this with a look of entreaty and appeal, did she clasp the feet of the Sanyāsi.

"Once you cured my husband's blindness. I am grateful to you. You can sympathise with a wife's grief. My happiness of life entirely depends on my husband. I do not care for my own self. I seek no other boon at your hands than what will promote my husband's happiness. Restore him his eyesight. I do not care for this kingdom, nor for wealth and pomp. Once I lived with my husband in the forest and I am prepared to do so again."

The Sanyāsi said, "I once cured your husband of his blindness. Why should you again and again trouble me in this way?"

The girl said weeping, "It is because you held out the promise that whenever I would be in distress, I should come to you for help. And what misfortune, revered Sir, can be greater than mine? Where is a woman whose sufferings are greater than mine? I do not crave wealth or kingdom. Take away my own eyes, if you will. I shall be glad to bear the life of the blind. But restore sight to my husband." (Ll. 1-16.)

(24)

The Sanyāsi.

"Then accept my condition, and swear that you will act accordingly, whatever it may be.

"You will have to leave this city this very night. You will have to leave your husband for ever. No more in life will you be permitted to see him. Then and then only shall your husband be restored once more to his vision. You should not, moreover, leave him with a sigh. With a perfectly tranquil mind, you will have to make this renunciation. On this condition alone, I can cure your husband. But hear something more. The princess Kunjalatā is here. She is a wanderer in this forest in quest of her husband. Now make a gift of this lovely city and your husband to the co-wife, with a mind not at all disturbed."

When Kānchan heard this, she burst into loud sobs.

It is the garden which adorns a house. The woman looks lovely when she has a child in her arms. The lotus adorns a tank and the land is beautiful, when flowers bloom on it. The flourishing kingdom gladdens the heart of a king and the store, which is full of wealth, becomes a coveted treasure. It is the lamp that illuminates the dark spot and it is the crown that adorns the head of a prince. Like all these and even more, is the husband prized by a devoted and chaste wife. If a boat is left by the helmsman, it sinks into the whirlpool of a river. The parents do not care for the daughter after her marriage and if the man, with whose hands she joins hers, gives her up what would her beauty avail her? Who will, alas, preserve the honour of a woman, deserted by her lord? To her, death and life are the same.

She lamented in this way and then wiped her tears away. Then she said in a calm and firm tone, "Yes, cure my husband's blindness. I will go away from him and from this place for ever." (Ll. 1-34.)

(25)

Then the Sanyāsi asked Kānchan to follow him till she reached anothor fig-tree. He gave three strokes to the tree with his fingers and from the cavity of it, came out a woman. Kānchan saw that she was the princess Kunjalatā, her co-wife. The Sanyāsi gave a fruit to Kānchan, saying that her husband would be cured of his blindness on eating the fruit, but ordered her first to offer the fruit to the princess.

The Sanyasi.

"Though painful the condition, make yourself ready to fulfil it, without feeling any pain. With this fruit give your husband to Kunjalata. Make your mind firm, so that you may not feel any pain in this act of renunciation. If, however, you give this fruit, with the least sorrow in your heart, your husband will not be cured."

Then did Kānchanmālā with a great effort rise above the level of ordinary human beings and forget all about her own happiness and sorrow. With the fruit in her hand, she stopped a moment to collect herself and then she gave it to her co-wife, together with her husband and kingdom. No one saw a tear in her eyes. Nor did her heart beat but once in sorrow. She left her husband with a tranquil mind. Lest her tears should, in the least, interfere with her husband's cure, she gave up all sorrowful thoughts, and unmoved in her mind, she made the great gift.

It is the hardest of all trials, from which she came out a victor. Though she was a feeble woman, she could do so. Even the strongest of men could hardly cope with a situation like this.* (Ll. 1-18.)

* A friend is telling me that Kānchan's renunciation resembles that of Gilliatt in Victor Hugo's 'Toilers of the Sea' where the hero made a sacrifice worthy of the Bengali ballad's heroine. But I cannot agree to this. With my great respect for the high character and devotion of Gilliatt, I should say that he did nothing wonderful by giving up his claims on Déruchette. She had no love for Gilliatt,—not only so, Gilliatt found positive proof of her great dislike for him and actually saw her in the arms of Caudray whom she loved with her whole heart. What sane man would care to marry such a girl? Here in the Bengali ballad love is mutual and genuine and this makes the renunciation glorious and real. Gilliatt certainly suffered greatly for love, but his renunciation was forced, and cannot therefore be compared to the sacrifice made by Kānchan who gave her husband to her co-wife, knowing that he was attached to her and not to her co-wife. She thus performed an act of great sacrifice, simply wishing the good of her husband—a sacrifice which showed the greatness of her love, no less than the high ethical sense which inspired her action.

Another Version.

(26)

When Kanchan was about to depart, the Sanyasi said, "Go to your father's city. You were banished from Bharāinagar at the contrivance of your step-mother. She is a witch. Take this magic-rod with you. She has devoured many men and women of your father's city. As soon as you will arrive at your father's palace with this rod, she will fly away in terror, and your father will be free from her charms."

Kānchan did as she was directed and released her father from the influence of the witch. Then the ministers and other officers of her father advised him to look after a suitable bridegroom for Kānchan.

But there was a hindrance to this proposal. In the countryside they talked about Kānchan's absence from the palace for a long time. How could it be known that she had led a chaste and virtuous life? The wise heads assembled in the palace and expressed an opinion that there should be an ordeal to test her chastity.

A long cobweb should be thrown up in the air and Kānchan must steadily hang in the sky, catching hold of it. If she succeeds, it will then be known that Kānchan is a chaste woman. The report of the coming ordeal was trumpeted out all over the country and princes and potentates from the neighbouring cities came there to behold it. In this assemblage of noble men was Phulkumār, her husband, who had come there with Kunjalatā.

Kānchanmālā.

"I bid adieu to you, my esteemed father. Your unfortunate girl would no more be a source of trouble to you; and O my father's ministers and officers, to you, also, I bid a farewell. No more will you have to counsel my father as to the right path about his daughter. I call upon you to be witnesses, O sun and moon, night and day, as to what sort of woman I am. I do not know what is right or wrong, what is vice and what is virtue.

Now farewell, O Kunjalatā, my dear sister. I leave, in your custody, my own husband, far dearer than life.

And you, my dear husband, the true lord of my heart are you. I bid adieu to you. Return to your city with Kunjalatā. Do not, I pray, feel any pain for me. A hundred times do I bow to you, before final separation. Try to forget me in your whole-hearted love for Kunjalatā.

O princes and kings, who have assembled here, I pay my respects to you, before I depart. The period of curse is over. I have passed my twentieth year."

So saying, she slowly caught hold of the fine thread of cobweb, which her father's men had thrown up in the sky and began to climb up till she completely disappeared from the sight of all.

Like a room, where the light is put out, the whole palace became dark for a time at her disappearance. The citizens of Bharāinagar lamented for one, who had been born of a heavenly spark and disappeared like a heavenly spark. (Ll. 1-32.)

SANTI

PREFACE

The ballad 'Santi' was collected by Munshi Jasimuddin in February, 1925, from an illiterate Mahomedan, named Esem Khan, aged 50, of Pearpur in the district of Faridpur (E. B. R.).

It contains a hundred and fifty lines and the rules of rhyme are disregarded in many of them, though the metre of the ballad seems to approach the 'Payar'—the familiar measure of versification, generally adopted by our country-bards.

Though the song has been preserved by Muhammadan rhapsodists for some generations past. It is essentially a Hindu-tale, originally composed by a Hindu poet.

The author's name is Jaidhar Bania. We have found several versions of this ballad and in some of them the name of the poet is given in the colophon. In one version the name of the heroine is given as Lila, instead of Santi. But as there is a general agreement in the details of treatment, these various varsions seem to be the offshoots of the one and the same Ballad, changed in places by the village-singers.

It is an exquisite ballad, inspite of its rugged and irregular rhyming. The old ballad-makers may be at times crude but never verbose. This ballad, in the form of a dialogue, is more suggestive than elaborate, and oftentimes leaves gaps which the reader must fill up by the suggestions of the stanzas, for appreciating the consistent beauty of the tale as a whole. He must, for instance, discover, closely reading between the lines, that the husband of Santi, who makes bis appearance at the end of the ballad, is none other than the person who tried to entice her away during all the twelve months of the year by temptations and threats. If this is not understood, the interest and the beauty of the ballad will be considerably missed. It is clear from the dialogue that the husband of Santi married her years ago and went abroad for trading purposes. She was a mere child at the time of marriage. Her husband returned when she grew up and became a woman. Like most of the Hindoo wives, she instinctively felt the sacredness of marriage-vow and knew that her life was dedicated to her husband, even before she could have any opportunity of forming an intimacy with him. The usual custom with a young married girl in this country is that after the night of marriage, she spends eight, or sometimes ten days, called *Astamangal* or *Dasamangal*, as the case may be, in her husband's home and then returns to her father's home, where she remains until she comes of age. The husband of Santi returned after many years. The girl had merely vague memories about the marriage and could not recognise her husband. He wanted to put her character to a test and, disguising himself as a stranger, tempted her during each of the twelve months of the year in various ways. She was modest and courteous, but strongly rejected his overtures. She did not strut and fret at the insult of this offer of love, as a loyal woman of a more violent temper would do. But her replies, couched in clever words, oftentimes bordering on pleasant humour, showed the unrelenting strength of her character that raised her far above the level of ordinary women. Though outwardly she showed a bit of coquettishness, it only served to show the lovely spirit in her of being able to enjoy pleasantries, without affecting the dignity of her character in the least.

Then after the long and protracted trial of twelve months comes the stranger's profession that he is no other than her husband. She is staggered at the report suspecting foul play again. She hangs down her head, not fully knowing what she should do. She puts to him question after question as she has no distinct memory about her husband and his parentage. But when, on a reference to her own parents she is fully satisfied, then does the glow return to her cheek, and she sits with her toilet-box, robing herself in the best of her bridal attire to receive her husband.

We have had many occasions to remark that each of the twelve months of Bengal has some distinctive feature, peculiar to its own. Some particular flower that blooms, some gay bird that sends its high notes to the skies, not to speak of the festivities bearing pleasant associations, mark out the passing away of a particular month and the advent of the next. These Bāramasi songs are peculiarly Bengali, as the clearly defined climatic features of a particular season and its parts are scarcely found so distinctly anywhere in India outside Bengal. They lift up the veil from the face of Nature, showing her sometimes as smiling with sunshine or blooming flowers, and at others, casting her angry looks through her lightnings and clouds. The joyous flood, the *shāli* rice, the boat-race, the bloom of *Mallikā* and *Keoā* flowers, the Durga Puja, the Manasā Puja and other festivities, the gay note of the cuckoo and the shrill song of the *Papia*, the mists that shroud the early mornings or the genial sun-light that brightens them, are associated with particular months, and the *Bāramashis* have an exclusive Bengali charm, which the country-poets are never weary of describing. This ballad will recall some of the passages of Shakespeare's Venus and Adonis. It may be held in contrast with the famous Spanish ballad, "The ill-married Lady," which gives the tempter a nobler character than the husband. The sacredness of conjugal love carries a great weight with the rural-poets of Bengal and it would be inconceivable to them how adultery and libertinism could be elevated to an æsthetic plane in the name of art, as we find it to be the case in the Spanish ballad. The art that makes attempts at brushing aside the claims of the husband, elected by the woman herself, and sketching on the canvas a second figure, her next choice, cannot carry a high value, æsthetic or artistic, in the soil of India; where true love is another name of life-long devotion. "La bella mal maridada," the favourite Spanish ballad in Sepulveda's collection, will appear shocking to Bengal peasantry, inspite of the appeal it bears in its concluding lines. Yet this Bengali ballad is as fresh as a flower just blown, without any conventional element in it. The date of the ballad is unknown; but it carries the stamp of the age when the school of free love flourished in Bengal—when the spirit of Sahajiya had a strong hold on Bengali youths—before the austere Brahminic renaissance doomed our womankind to stern ordinances, declaring that a young woman's path was not one of rosy dalliance but the secluded domestic chamber, where music was forbidden and where she was not even privileged to listen to a song of the cuckoo, lest it gave rise to some unholy thought. Another version of this ballad is published in Part II in which the heroine is named Lila. It bears in the colophon the name of Jaidhar Baniya as its author. I have got from Sylhet a quite different version published by one Md. Ashraf Hossain who calls Jaidhar a native of Sylhet. Jaidhar Baniya does not seem to be the original poet; he may be a mere recensionist.

Santi

"False ! It is the virtuous King who has dug the tank and made its landing ghat for public use." P. 123.

Santi

(1)

"Sweet October has come, sweet is the milk in unripe *āman* rice. My mind is restless, O Sānti, as I behold thy youthful charms."

"Calm thy restless heart and quiet thy soul, O lad, to-morrow at dawn shall I go to yonder landing-ghat all alone and meet you there."

"Neither am I a physician, lad, nor versed in the sacred lore; a simple village-girl, daughter of Guno of the Baniya-caste am I. If indeed you suffer from a malady, how can I cure it?"

(2)

"You are filling your pitcher, girl, go on doing so. But know that I am in charge of the tank and guard it here."

"False! It is the virtuous king who has dug the tank and made its landing-ghat of stone for public use. I, the girl Santi, am filling my pitcher from the tank. I do not believe thee and care not for any guard."

"You have deceived me, O Santi, all these days of November by your glib tongue. My hopes have evermore remained unfulfilled. Behold with new charms on the landscape, November has made its appearance."

(3)

"In this sweet November thou lookest like a silvery streak of moon-beams; O, do not vanish away, but allow me, a stranger, to be revived by a sight of thee."

"Night is coming. I must take care that my mother-in-law may sleep in comfort. Know me, O youth, to be the darling of my husband. I hold a stranger like you in the light of a father or brother."

"This month, too, thou hast deceived me by your glib tongue. Behold the change on the fair face of Nature, announcing the advent of December."

(4)

"It is December now and hear my vow. I will enter your sleeping room at the end of the night and get by stealth what I cannot get as a gift."

"A hundred candles will I keep burning in my room to-night, and at the gate our elephant, Gajamati, will keep watch."

"I will blow out all your hundred candles, and the elephant Gajamati will I kill at your gate by the force of my arms."

"I will cover my bracelets with the edge of my *saḍi* lest they jingle, and, sword in hand, shall I keep watch all night. If, at the end of night, the thief is caught, this is my vow that I shall sacrifice him at the altar of the goddess Chandi."

"This month too, Santi, you have deceived me with your glib tongue. With a change in the landscape has January made its appearance."

(5)

"It is January. Look, dear one, the *saḍi* you wear is too short. Spread its flowing end as far as you can and receive the humble present of sweet betels and nuts that I have brought for you."

"Take away these presents, I do not want them, lad. You have an elder sister at your house, present these to her, if you like."

"Cruel words hast thou spoken, O Santi. The presents I mean for *you*, and you wish them to be given to my sister! You cause pain to my heart by saying so. Now for all these days of January you have played cunningly with me, deferring my hopes from day to day. Behold February shows itself with all its new and beauteous colours in Nature."

(6)

"It is February. The nights are long. If on such a night a guest comes to your door, what will you do to receive him?"

"A couch and sofa will be spread for him in the outer room; soft pillows will be given to make his sleep easy and sound. He will have fine rice and pulses for his meals and a blanket will be given him to make the wintry night warm."

"You have beguiled me, dear girl, with your glib tongue this month also. My hopes remain unfulfilled evermore. Behold the approach of March, bringing an array of fresh charms to the landscapes around."

(7)

"It is March. The heat is scorching. Thy beauteous and youthful figure, O Santi, burns my heart with a desire, which I know not how to allay."

"A bad mother gave birth to you, wicked youth, and your father was a wretched eunuch. If there is heat in your body, why not jump down into yonder river and cool your body's heat therein."

"This month is also gone, O Santi. You have deceived me by your glib tongue and withheld the fulfilment of my hopes. On the fair face of Nature have bloomed forth new beauties announcing April."

(8)

"It is April now. Like the sweet layer of cream over milk is your lovely youth, O Santi! but what purpose does it serve, if like a miser, you guard your treasure from others."

"My youth is not a water-melon to be cut to pieces for distribution at dinner. Nor is it the milk of a woman's breast for feeding her babe."

"O cunning one, this month is also gone and you have beguiled me by your glib tongue. I pine with unfulfilled hopes. Behold the new charms of the landscape, indicating the approach of May."

(9)

"It is May. The mangoes are ripe in yonder grove; plenty of these fruits, besides jacks and black-berries, have I brought as my humble present for you."

"Keep these aside, lad, I do not want them. Go home and present them to your sister."

"Cruel are your words, O Santi, these presents are made to you and you cause pain to my heart by your refusal. This month has also gone and my hopes are ever-more deferred. Look at the change of landscape, announcing June."

(10)

"It is June, O Santi, behold the flood in rivers. Near Kanchanpur in the swelling stream has your husband been drowned on his way home."

"False! Had my husband died in the swelling stream near Kanchanpur, the chignon on my head would have been unloose of itself. The pearl-necklace on my breast would have been unstrung, the shell-bracelets in my hands, known by their pet names, *Ram and Lakshman* would have been broken and the brightness of the red sign of luck on my forehead would have slowly faded away. I believe in these signs and not in your reports, O false lad."

"This month, also, hast thou beguiled me by thy glib tongue. My hopes are unfulfilled and I am joyless.

Behold, on all sides, July's advent is proclaimed by a change in the landscape."

(11)

"It is July. The muddy knee-deep water is seen everywhere. When passing from one house to another through this watery path, you will be served with some gentle strokes from my stick of twigs as punishment."

"Beat me as hard as you can with your stick, O lad. Kill me and float my body in the river. But know, still I will not go to a stranger's house."

"This month, also, hast thou beguiled me by your glib tongue, and my hopes remain unrealised. Behold Nature wears a new apparel at the advent of August.

(12)

"It is August. The rivers are full. I will give you a boat, rowed by sixteen men for playing race in this pleasing season."

"Give your boat to your sister or to your mother, or to those who care for your presents. I do not value them."

"This month, too, you have beguiled me by your cunning words. Nature now has changed her scenes and announces September."

(13)

It is September. In every house the divine mother Durga is worshipped.

"Look at me closely, O Santi, I am here, thy own dear husband, returned home after long days. Don't you know me, dear?"

Santi bowed her head down at these words. "Swear by God," she said, "and speak the truth."

"Which is your native city? What is your name, O youth? And who are your parents?"

"I am a native of Bāhātiā. There I own a house of my own. My father is a Kalpataru and my mother's name is Ganeswari. I married you, O Santi, years ago, on the fifteenth of an October. The pet name, by which I am called, is Killan Sadāgar."

"If really art thou the dear one of my heart, be pleased to stay here a while. I will return instantly after enquiring of my parents if your account is true."

(14)

"O, my old father and O, my dear mother, what are you busy with, at this moment? Will you tell me to whom you gave me, your daughter, taking the due sum of money?"

"You have passed your twelfth year, and now stand on the threshhold of youth. Is it the inclination, natural to your age, that makes you discover a husband at the gate?"

With a lamp in hand and a *toka* on his head, the old man walks in slow pace to see if really the son-in-law has come.

"It is he, O Santi, no doubt, it is he. Go, receive him. He, the jewel of your heart, has been found at last. Now open the chest, containing your dresses and ornaments. Find out your hair-comb of mica and articles of toilet."

Santi divided her hair into two lovely rows and made a chignon, over which she spread garlands of *champā* and *parul* flowers. She put a *tiara* on her head and wore the *chandrahar* and a waist-belt of the moon-pattern. From her neck hung a lovely necklace. She wore armlets on her arms and bracelets on her wrist. Anklets jingled on her feet and a string of the largest pearls she wore on her breast. Her eyes she beautified with the black *kajjal*-dye, and to finish all, she put, on her forehead, the red mark of luck.

See how bright and lovely she looks to-night, as she softly treads the ground to go to the nuptial room to receive the husband of her heart.

THE TALE OF BHELUA, THE BEAUTIFUL ONE.

PREFACE.

The Ballad of Bheluā is complete in five parts. The first part describes the journey of Madan, the young merchant of Sankhapur, to Kanchannagar by ship for trade. There he falls in love with Bheluā, daughter of Manik, a rich merchant of that place. This love develops into an intrigue and Madan returns home in a very distressed state of mind, owing to separation from his beloved. He communicates the story of the love to his friends, so that his father gradually comes to know of this affair. He sends a match-maker to Kanchannagar, proposing the marriage of his son with Bheluā. Her father, however, rejects the proposal, on the ground of Madan's inferior social status.

The second part deals with another visit of Madan to Kanchannagar and his absconding with Bheluā. He returns to Sankhapur with her, but Murāri, his father, gets angry at his misbehaviour and turns him out from his palace. Madan goes with Bheluā to Rangchāpur on Sylhet-border and settles there, securing, for the time being, the good will of Abu Raja, a cruel tyrant who reigns supreme at the place.

In the third and fourth parts, we find Abu Raja plotting against Madan and sending him away to a foreign country on some pretext. He carries away Bheluā to his palace by force. Bheluā flies to the Jaintia hills, in obedience to her husband's wishes, expressed at the time of parting, and seeks shelter at the hands of the merchant Hiran, a friend of Madan. But the friend becomes enamoured of Bheluā and woos her hands. She escapes from his city with the help of Hiran's sister, Menakā, and meets Madan, while journeying by river. But being pursued, on all sides, by the ships of Raja Abu and of her own kinsmen, Bheluā finds no other way of escape than by throwing herself into the river. Menakā, the sister of Hiran, who was on another ship, sees this and follows her friend, with a view to save her life. They are about to be drowned. Madan, also, shares a similar fate, trying to rescue them.

An old merchant discovers the fair ladies, with their lives almost extinct, on a shoal in the Chou Gangā (*lit.* the junction of four rivers). By his care they are restored to life, but the good old merchant while trying to find out the city of Bheluā's parents, falls at the hands of the marauding pirate, Abu Raja, who sieges the girls and carries them home, sending away the old man in a shattered boat from Rangchāpur, after having robbed him of his fourteen ships, laden with merchandise.

In the last part, the adventurous expedition of Madan, aided by the ingenuous contrivances of Bheluā and her friend, Menakā, is described in detail, ending in Bheluā's happy union with Madan, who marries her with the consent of her father and inflicts an adequate punishment on the wicked Abu Raja, by leaving him on a wild and desolate shore, bound hand and foot, to be starved to death. Madan not only marries Bheluā but also Menakā, both having been, from the beginning, bound by vows of sisterhood and love for Madan.

This Abu Raja might have been a real historical figure, though the folk-tales of the country have evidently contributed a good deal to the development of this story in its present shape.

Though the poetical value of this ballad is not much, there are many points which would make up for the scholar's toil, if he could patiently read the whole. The origin of the tale must be traced to some incident, which occurred in a remote period, when the Bengalis were celebrated for their commercial activities overseas. The account of profuse gold and jewels, employed in decorating houses and ships, to be found in this poem, gives us glimpses, through much exaggerations and crude rustic conventions, into the condition of our country, which literally teemed, at the time, with untold wealth. No doubt it was a report of such proverbial riches of the Orient spread afar in the West, which made Milton sneeringly refer to the 'barbaric' gold and pearls of the East in his Paradise Lost.

On the treacherous banks of the great rivers of Eastern Bengal, it was not safe to undertake masonry works on a large scale, but wealthy people built artistic bungalows, spending fortunes over their decorations. To this point I drew attention in my introduction to the first volume of the Ballads. In this ballad very graphic descriptions are given of such bungalows, with four and sometimes eight slanting roofs. The houses were so spacious that often a hall contained fifty-two doors (Text, page 143, Ll. 3-4). The beams and rafters were plated with gold (Text p. 1, L. 2) and the bottom of the roofs were covered with the feathers of kingfishers and peacocks. The upper part used to be decorated with artistic designs of mica, inlaid with leaves of gold, from which shone forth jewels and pearls, elegantly studded therein. Merchants, who went to trade overseas, had sometimes a fleet of a thousand ships. We need not place much reliance upon this description of the rustic poet. But the humble figure of fourteen ships, generally mentioned in such accounts, seems to be a more rational number which we may believe.

With much margin left for the excesses of popular fancy, one cannot but be struck with an impression of the great wealth and grandeur of the Bengali merchants of those days, while perusing these ballads. A rich merchant's daughter always enjoyed the status of a princess. She had usually twelve maiden-escorts to attend her, when she went to the bathing ghat (Text, page 145, L. 1). She carried soap-berries and other toilet-articles in golden boxes (Text, page 145, L. 4). Food was generally served to the rich people in golden plates. The infatuated chief would buy the favour of his lady-love by giving her landed estates, yielding seven lakhs a year (Text, page 175, L. 71). The mast of big merchant-vessels were plated with gold and the ensigns in which there were rich golden embroidery works, shone high up in the sky, reflecting the dazzling rays of the sun.

When a merchant reached his native shore after a successful sea-voyage, the elderly ladies used to come to the river-ghats to welcome the ships with due rites. The details of these rites are to be found in the Gitikathās, published by Mr. D. R. Mitra Mazumdar and called the 'Thakurdadar-Jhuli' and referred to in my work "The Folk Literature of Bengal" (pp. 65-68).

Though not marked by much pastoral poetry—the characteristic of the ballads of this class,—there are situations in this song, which are quite dramatic. The interest of the reader never flags and is even raised to a high intensity by a rapid succession of events, especially towards the end. The freshness of river-breeze, the wild life in turbulent waters, with ships, tossed by dashing waves, and the constant alarm caused by the pirates are everywhere in evidence, reminding the reader that the scene of the ballads is laid in the wild river-districts of Eastern Bengal,—a country of swamps, marshes and great water-courses, where the roarings of clouds above are sometimes responded to by the clappings of a thousand waves, deafening the ears and where, every now and then, Nature assumes an awe-inspiring aspect in her sky and vast watery expanses.

The last scene where Abu Raja meets with the allied fleet of four great adversaries on the limitless waters of Chou Gangā takes us by a sublime dramatic surprise and this would be a fit theme for a thrilling cinematographic show, if it could be properly reproduced.

This ballad, in its original form, must have been very old, for it seems to trample down all the canons of Brahminic social system. The ideas were no doubt anterior to the foundation of the modern social life in Bengal. Both Bheluā and Menakā are seventeen years old when they themselves chose their bridegrooms (Text, p. 144, L. 33). The daughters are given perfectly free scope in love matters and their conduct is not called in question, even when they intrigue with strangers before their marriage. Society hardly condemns them. A woman, who lives with her elected lord as his wife, is sought after by another lover, who offers to marry her (not merely to pay her attentions as a mistress), with the full consent of his father and other elderly relations (Text, page 177, Ll. 13-16). When, after all kinds of adventurous love-makings, the woman returns home, she is accepted in a generous spirit of forgiveness so that throughout the whole of the poem, there are events and incidents, which seem to be subversive of all law and order of our present-day social fabric. I cannot say if these represent the conditions of an alien society of the Burmese and

Tibetans in particular, imbibed by the Rāja-Vaṃshis and Kāṃbojis, among whom the ballad was originally current,—or they show a state of things that existed in Hindu society itself prior to the priestly Renaissance. One, who is at all conversant with the modern Hindu society, I mean, the society which is about seven hundred years old, could not have possibly conceived the incidents of the plot and it is for this reason that Bheluā is now mostly sung by Mahomedans, and the Hindus, even of the depraved castes, have given it up. The Brahmin is hardly mentioned in the ballad ; even when the merchant is distributing money at a religious function, the poet refers to the poor people as recipients of such charities and curiously here also the Brahmin has no place. (Text, page 206, L. 103). For such purposes in our society, the Brahmin would stand as the foremost claimant.

The one redeeming feature of the tale is that though the accounts do not show any respect for social or priestly conventions, the rustic mind that gave shape to it was conscious of that superior law in the sphere of tender emotions, which makes a woman adhere to a single object by her life-long devotion, and though surrounded and tempted by many suitors, retains her constancy in all her trials and would never break her vow of honour and chastity. Though she cares not for marriage-laws, made by men, she has the heart of the chaste and the devoted ones, clinging steadfastly to the lord of her heart, elected by herself.

The rhyme is very irregular and rugged. The metre halts in many places. This also shows that the original poem was composed in a remote age,—may be, in the pre-Muhammadan period, though it has undergone many changes in its language and spirit, during the long ages that have intervened.

This ballad was once very popular and used to be sung, throughout the vast tract of country, from the Soorma Valley on the Assam-borders to the sea-shores of Chittagong. I saw a printed edition of a ballad, called "Bhelua" a long time ago, to which I referred in my 'Banga Bhāshā-O-Sāhitya' in the year 1897. I drew the attention of my readers to the intermixture of Hindu and Moslem spirit, which found place in that version, published by a Muhammadan of Chittagong. I need scarcely say that the present version is quite unlike that one. I have presently noticed the awkward distortions of the simple country-ballads at the hands of the enterprizing Hindu and Moslem publishers. They invariably recast the ballads, introducing into them not only erotic scenes and gross things, but by thoroughly changing the style and making it approach more or less a classical model—not at all dignified, as the recensionists are not scholars at all but assume a false air of pedantry, which is very repellant. This takes away from the published editions the flavour of country life and the simple charm of rustic songs. The ballads in their hands look like the very tombs of the poetical ideas, with which the simple rustic had built his temple.

The Tale of Bhelua, the Beautiful One.

Canto I.

(1)

On the banks of the river Ujāni, there lived a merchant, named Murāi, in the village of Sankhapur. Hear, my learned audience, the tale of this merchant.

This merchant of Sankhapur was the lord of several towns. His wealth was immense. He worshipped Saturn, the planet, and by the grace of his deity, became the very prince of merchants. In fact, in the surrounding locality, there was none, who was his equal. So immense was his wealth that he measured his gold, like rice, in large scales. The story of his riches became proverbial in the countryside. His big houses had four, sometimes eight, slanting roofs. These were plated with gold, at the top. The beams were made of silver and the roofs were covered with gold-leaves, in place of straw. The rafters were ornamented with jewels and stones. His fleet consisted of a thousand merchant-vessels and it was a wonderful sight to behold the array of his ships, as they marched over the high seas, bound for trade. Their prows were plated with gold, the helms and the oars were of solid gold and the masts of gold raised their heads high up in the sky and the golden flags fluttered in the air, making a gorgeous show. In the landing-ghat of the river, adjoining the merchant's city, these ships lay anchored, awaiting his command.

Marching with the help of ebb-tide, and at times, struggling against the current, the merchant once arrived at a stream, near the Jaintā-Hills. I will tell you what the object of his travel was.

Murāi had, by the grace of Saturn, got a son, bright as the moon. The lad was twenty years old and shone with the lustre of gold or the morning-sun. He was called Madan, after the name of the god of Love. When the lad had passed his twentieth year, his parents became anxious to get a suitable bride for him.

Murāi was touring in different countries, not for trade, but in quest of a handsome and accomplished bride for his son.

I am going to leave the topic of Murāi here and make a little digression. My audience should now be ready to hear the story of Bheluā,—of her birth and other incidents of her life, of her beauty and accomplishments. (Ll. 1-43.)

(2)

I am going to relate to you the story of Bheluā. It is a wonderful story, divided into five parts. I crave the patient attention of my audience.

In the city of Kānchannagore there was a merchant named Manik, who, also, possessed immense wealth. His palace was divided into five large apartments, in which the audience-hall particularly, bore profuse decorations of gold. This hall had fifty-two doors; its roofs were covered with mica, adorned with jewels and pearls. The whole palace sparkled like the beams of the moon on the ripples of a river. Whoever beheld it admired the merchant's æsthetic taste. There were many large tanks inside the palace, with their landing-steps of solid silver. Inside one of these, was a temple, dedicated to

Lakshmi, the goddess of Fortune. Manik was descended from the illustrious merchant Chānd and had the status of a 'Kulin' in his community. Proud of his pedigree, the merchant held others in contempt. He had a daughter, handsome as Rati, the consort of Kāma, the god of Love. The beauty of Bheluā was a marvel. It shone like a flame, and there was nothing to be compared to it, in the whole world. Her hair was thick and black as cloud and her eyes were bright as stars. Youth had just dawned on her. Her slender figure had the brightness of gold and her eye-brows had the graceful curve of the rainbow. Her gait was so lovely that she seemed to spread a charm around her, as she walked. Her face was lovelier far than the moon. When she walked, her hair seemed to touch her feet; the maids held it up behind her back. When her curling hair fell over her lovely face, it seemed as if cloud covered the moon, for the time. Her father had given her jewels and ornaments, which, as it were, vied with one another in adorning her fair limbs.

The parents had given her the pet name of Bheluā, the beautiful. She had passed her sixteenth year and stepped into the seventeenth. The merchant was anxious for securing a bridegroom for her. He went about visiting different countries for trade and sought for a suitable groom everywhere. The suitors were not after his liking. He at first seemed to choose some one, but a little flaw was discovered, later on. In some cases the social status was not equal, so he could not agree to lower his prestige. "She is lovely as the moon," he reflected, "the man who will be given her hands must be bright as the sun." Day and night he had no other thought than that of the marriage of the daughter.

Then he settled a plan. He sent his five sons to fiv different countries to seek a bridegroom for Bheluā. He himself marched on board a ship and visited different countries with the same object in view.

"What will the success of my trade avail me and what good will my palace and wealth bring, if my daughter is kept unmarried?" Thus did he think day and night. (Ll. 1-46.)

(3)

Bheluā goes to the bathing-ghat and meets Madan, the young merchant.

She held in her hand a golden plate, containing soap-berry fruits, and also a silver one, containing betel, and proceeded towards the bathing-ghat, beaming like a flame of fire. The wives of the five brothers followed her, the twelve maids of Bheluā following in the train. The winds sported with her scented hair and the sweet smell of her perfumed body attracted the bees more than a flower-garden in the spring-season. Thus did Bheluā, the beautiful one, arrive at the landing steps of the river.

Now listen to what took place next, as recorded for her in the unalterable Book of Fate.

Young Madan just at the time, with fourteen ships, was going by the river, near Kānchannagar. He saw the beautiful town on the bank of the river and, being attracted by it, ordered his ships to be anchored there. There, on the landing-ghat, was Bheluā, with her maids, for a bath. The five sisters-in-law and Bheluā all came down and were in the mid-stream in an instant; they pleasantly laughed aloud and sported in the river. The five wives all swam till they came up to a great way in the stream, but Bheluā stopped and stood near the bank and cast her curious eyes towards the approaching ships. She was attracted by the sight of the ships. "Who is this merchant? Whence has he come to our city? Which country will he visit for trade and where did he spend the last night?" Thoughts like this occurred to her. Her sisters-in-law saw that she was in a serious mood. For she did not swim with them, nor smiled and laughed, as usual. She hid her feelings from them and they wondered as to what produced this change in her mind. "A stranger he is certainly," she thought, as she adjusted her clothes to hide her charms. She was in knee-deep water and came further down and opened the braids of her hair, which floated on the water like clouds in the sky, and hid her moon-like face. At this moment, the young merchant came out of his cabin. "Is the morning-sun himself the captain of the ships?" She asked herself as she glanced at the young merchant, "or is it the moon that has fallen in the waves?"

Thus they saw each other for the first time in the river and the merchant's son at once felt the charm of her beauty. Both fell in love at first sight. It was like a meeting between the Sun and the Moon. What they had to tell one another was communicated by their eyes. She could not walk, so depressed she was; her feet, it seemed, refused to carry her back home. When she came up to the bank, she cast her glance on all sides to see if others had marked the change in her mind. Alas, her feet advanced slowly, but her mind wished to stay. Again they cast their eyes on one another and spoke everything by those silent messages which heart sends to heart. The message was understood by them and by none other. On board the ship, the youth peeped this way and that, his eyes seemed to say to her, "I am conquered." They bade adieu to one another by means of their stolen glances. With the full weight of her long flowing hair, now wet, she seemed to walk heavily. The maids came to her rescue and held her tresses up. Then did she adjust her clothes once again and with slow steps, returned home.

Now what did the beautiful merchant do? He let his trained bird, the 'Suka' go in the air. The bird followed the girl and entered her compartment.

(Ll. 1-62.)

(4)

"Whence have you come, Oh bird, where is your house? By what name did the merchant use to call you? From what country has the merchant come and whither would he go? Oh the moment, when our eyes met first in the bathing-ghat! How handsome is he, like the moon! What dear name has been given him by his parents? He is surely going for trade, but on the way, he has acted like a thief and stolen my mind! He has taken my mind, my life and all that my youth yearns for. But wicked is he, not to have taken *me* with him! He smiles often, but his mind is not frank; with a glance, cast carelessly, he has caused me all this pain. I find no peace of mind at my home; it seems, my youth is struggling against the tide. If you know it, dear bird, tell me, like an informer, when will the dear merchant be coming back to our country, after he will have left it now?"

"On the banks of the river Ujāni is a village, named Sankhapur. There lives a merchant, named Murari. The youth is his son and his name is Madan. He has given me the name of Hiraman. The young merchant is going to foreign lands for trade. Wait, maiden, he will return and meet you again, at the bathing-ghat."

Madan had taught the bird this message and nothing more could the poor forest-bird, devoid of sense, say.

In slow whispers did the maiden again ask the bird question after question. But the bird made the same answer over and over again. For, beyond this, his master had not taught him anything.

The nights were bitter as poison. The charm of youth lost its lustre, owing to unhappy thoughts. She felt no rest either in pacing the courtyard or in lying in her bed. All the time, she felt an emptiness in her heart, which nothing could fill up. She brought a mate for the bird and looked at the pair, wishing ardently that she might meet the merchant in the same way.

Alas, to what country has he gone! Night and day she looks at the river and pursues with her eyes the course by which he would return. One day passed and she recorded it. Then the second, and then the third. In this way, unnumbered days came and went. She could not give up her hopes but lay expectant of his return all these long long days.

She took no care of her apparels, nor braided her flowing hair. Indifferent to everything, she looked like a girl, insane. The golden lustre of her form slowly faded away. What unnumbered tears did she not shed for the beloved merchant? The dark colour of her noble hair which had the look of summer-clouds, assumed a greyish tint without oil. She never combed it. Uncared-for, it grew matted. It was the freshliest period of youth. Yet she looked like a stern ascetic. People began to whisper as to what had become of her. She shut the doors of her bed-room and lying in her bed, on which smiled a hundred flowers, she smiled not, but spent her night in deep mental agony. Her floral couch became to her a bed of thorns.

She leaves the couches, and spreading a part of her *sadi*, lies down on the bare floor. There she sleeps and dreams that her young merchant has returned. Often does she awake with a start.

There she approaches the bird of her lover and says, "Go, dear friend, where the merchant has gone and tell him how I suffer." She asks the bird a hundred questions, alas, all in vain!

The attending maids whisper among themselves, "Alas, her head has gone wrong." (Ll. 1-60.)

(5)

Now listen, oh my audience, to what transpired on a particular day.

The young merchant returned from his voyage in the sea. There behold the red flag over a mast, glittering with golden embroidery. "A great merchant is coming this way," people say amongst themselves; and the report comes to all. The bank of the river receives the dash of the waves, stirred by the ship, and the villagers assemble on the bank to have a sight of the merchant.

The report is heard by Bheluā. She thinks within herself, "What should I do now? If my own merchant has come to this city in quest of me, how can I go to the bathing-ghat? Who will accompany me? Where shall I go,—to what country, with my beloved, if he will agree to take me with him?" She indulges in all kinds of wild thoughts, like one who sleeps and dreams. Then she resumes her thought and goes on with her reveries. 'Many are the merchants who come and go by the river adjoining our city. Many have come and gone, but my sorrows have not come to an end. Who knows that this ship belongs to my beloved? My hopes and wishes are like day-dreams? Who will tell me that they will be fulfilled and assure me that it is *he*, that is coming? Alas, this ship may belong to some one else!" At this thought her moon-like face became pale. The girl clasped the bird *Suka* with her arms and weepingly asked it question after question, "Tell me, O *Suka*, has your master come back in this ship?"

Alas, the ignorant, the senseless bird repeated what it had said on the first day; it gave an account of the merchant's parentage and home,—the only thing it had been trained to say.

* * * *

The great merchant Manik sat in his court, surrounded by his friends and officers. There our young hero, Madan, approached him with a present of some precious stones. The merchant said to the youth, "Who may you be, my young friend, possessed of such handsome features, shining as the moon? What is the mission of your visit to this city of ours? To what illustrious family do your father and mother belong? Give me a full account of yourself."

Madan.

"My father is called Murari. He is a merchant. Our home is at a place called the Sankhapur on the Ujāni. I wander about in foreign lands for trade. My parents have given me the name of Madan. I am in some trouble and have come to you for help. I have made the sea my home, as most part of my life I spend in sea. The sea has swallowed my fourteen ships, with all my treasure. But most bitterly mourned has been the loss of my bird *Suka*, which I held dear, even as my life itself. During the hours of night, it flew away from me and I have become like one mad to miss it. I sent people far and near in search of the bird, and only the other day the informer has given me the news that a bird, of the *Suka* species, has come over to your palace and that your daughter, Bheluā has taken a fancy for it and kept it concealed in her apartments."

Manik, the merchant, immediately sent a servant to the inner apartments, ordering that if such a bird actually was with his fair daughter she should at once give it up. The young merchant was right glad at this order. The servant brought the bird in a cage ; but before delivering it to Madan, the master of the city asked him to give proof that the bird belonged to him. Madan said, "I need not do that. The bird itself will do it." The trained bird sang that one song, which it had learnt to sing, namely, "There is a city named Sankhapur on the river Ujāni. There lives a merchant, named Murari. He has an only son and he is called Madan. He has given me the name Hiraman."

Manik, the merchant, was astonished at the account thus given by the bird, and made it over to young Madan with the cage. In return for the presents received, he bestowed jewels and precious stones on Madan as a mark of his favour. He came to his ship with the bird, and after having travelled a bend of the river, ordered the ship to be brought back to the station from which it had started. It was now night and he anchored his ship near the landing-ghat. Then he trained his Suka to recite the following words:

"Arise, O beautiful one, how long will you sleep? It is I, Suka, who wants to speak to you. Behold, a thief has entered your garden of flower-plants. He has robbed it of all its treasure. Awake, arise, and see the night has advanced."

After having trained the bird in this way, he set it free at midnight to fly towards Bheluā's apartments.

The bird flew away, and reaching the palace of Bheluā, repeated what it had learnt in the evening.

The maiden rose up with a start, for she had hardly any sound sleep for many months. She opened the door and came out of her room.

In the sky, a star met her eyes,—floating in the blue. In the mid-firmament shone the moon and it was just past midnight. She sat a while, resting her head on her hands, and meditated as to how she could get free from her environment.

She did not raise her maids from sleep nor spoke to anyone else, but entered the flower-garden, all alone. She held in her hand the female-bird *Sāri* and lo, in an instant, her mate, the *Suka*, flew to her side. She caught hold of a branch of a flower-tree, that stood near by, and bent it low in order to pluck flowers. Now, what is it that she sees at a short distance? Has the moon come down from the sky to her flower-garden? They met in the depth of night and they retired to a lonely place and sat near one another.

Bheluā.

"Whence have you come here? Who showed you the way? Don't you know, dear, how miserable I have been for you? I have become mad. Is it a fair act on your part, a respectable merchant as you are, to come to one's flower-garden without permission and steal its flower?"

Madan.

"From the day I have seen you, fair maiden, I have become maddened by your beauty. No longer do I care for trade. My mind dreams of the fairy I saw first near the landing-ghat and thinks of nothing else."

He took out the diamond-ring, which adorned his finger and put it on the finger of the maiden. She, on her part, took away the garland of Mālati-flowers from her neck and hung it on the breast of her own Madan.

He said in murmurs, "Now, my sweetheart, farewell. The moon is on the wane. Let me depart hence and go home, before any one rises up and knows of my adventure."

"But how can I live, dear, without you? Come to my apartment and there I will cover you with my long flowing tresses. I will wander with you to lands, far and near. Upon my life, I tell you, I will leave my parents, my five brothers and this palace, in order to accompany you wherever you will lead me to. I cannot bear the idea of separation from you, now having tasted this sweet union. I fear, I may turn mad, if you leave me in this condition. Take me to your ship and with you I will go. But don't, for the sake of my life, leave me here to pine away alone! I will surely chew the diamond-ring [1] and die, if you desert me cruelly." Madan caressed her endearingly and said, "I am planning how to marry you. I must first go to my father and tell him everything. Meantime, have patience, my darling, I promise, you will not have many days to wait."

"If indeed you are to leave me, kindly make me a gift of your bird, Suka." He smiled and said good humouredly, "My bird is worth a lakh of rupees. What price are you going to offer for it, my dear?" She said, "Yes, I shall give its price. I have a female-bird of the species; it is my *Sāri*. Let us make an exchange." "That is not enough," said the merchant, "what else

[1] There is a tradition in this country that the diamond is poisonous and that many people have committed suicide by chewing their rings.

will you give me?" "That I have already given. That is my own self," murmured the beautiful one.

So he bade her farewell. The night was nearly over. The humming of the bees was heard in the garden. He came back to his ship and started homewards. It usually takes one six months to reach Sankhanagar from that place. But the young merchant hurried on and his native shores were reached in one month. The ladies of his palace, as soon as the report of his return was received, came to the banks of the river and after usual rites, carried home what treasure he had got by trade. The captain helped in unloading the ships. The women welcomed him with cries of "Victory" and the father asked his son many questions regarding his voyage abroad. (Ll. 1-150.)

(6)

But the thought of Bheluā was now uppermost in his mind. He looked pale like morning, covered by a thin cloud. It was an ailment, which made him sick at heart—a disease, which no doctor could correctly diagnose. The parents did not understand what their dear son suffered from. His friends talked among themselves and tried to find out the cause of his depression in spirits, but could not hit at the reason. But such a thing could not be long suppressed. Unable to keep his feelings secret, he divulged it to a comrade. A second one also came to know of it, so that, after a time, many of his friends knew the whole thing, and last of all the father himself heard of it one day from one of the intimate friends of Madan.

As soon as Murari, the merchant-prince, learnt of the desire of his son, he ordered fourteen ships to be prepared. They were laden with various goods. A match-maker was called in. Together with the goods, the merchant sent a few diamonds and precious stones, to be presented to the merchant, Manik, of Kanchannagar. He sent the match-maker in order to propose the marriage.

The match-maker arrived at Kanchannagar and duly communicated the message to Manik, the merchant-prince of Kanchannagar, in the following words:

"We have learnt that you have a daughter of surpassing beauty. I have come to propose a match for her. On the banks of the river Ujani, there is a town, named Sankhapur. This town belongs to the merchant-prince, Murari. His only son is Madan. The old merchant has sent me here for proposing his son's marriage with your fair daughter. Young Madan is handsome as the god Kartikeya. His accomplishments and handsome appearance make him truly worthy of your daughter's hands."

For a moment Manik sat still, meditating within himself, and then addressed the match-maker and said before his court :—

"I must tell you something about my lineage. My great ancestor was Chand, the merchant of world-wide repute, whose son Likshindara was killed by snake-bite. I enjoy the highest social honour in my community. If I offer my daughter to one of inferior status, I shall be humbled in the eyes of my community. When any social function takes place, the merchants assembled do me a distinct honour by offering me food on a golden plate; a special seat is reserved for me there. In point of honour, social status and wealth, my family occupies the highest position and my community admits it in every social function. How can I lower myself by offering the hands of my daughter to one, who has not acquired the status of a Kulin. If it were my son, the case would have been different. A daughter, you know well, cannot be given away to a family, less respectable than mine. My family shines bright like the moon. It will be spotted with dishonour, should I accede to your proposal. Many are the proposals that I have hitherto received. But I cannot entertain them for this reason."

The Ghatak took his leave, and returning to Shankhapur, related the whole story to Murari in private. He became sorry, when he heard it and felt greatly humiliated by the arrogance of Manik, the merchant.

But when young Madan heard of it, it seemed his heart was pierced by a spear or as if a thunderbolt fell on his head. Home became like a hell to him and he took leave of his parents, saying that he would go abroad for trade. The astrologer fixed an auspicious date and with fourteen ships, he started on sea-voyage with various commodities.

He took the bird *Sāri*, the present of his beloved in his hand; and bade adieu to his parents requesting them to allow the maid Saluka to accompany him. On the day fixed, he started for distant countries with Saluka, the maid, as his companion and confidante. The ships went through the high seas and at last Kanchannagar was in sight. When there were yet a few bends to cross, the ship marching by the flow-tide, the young man told the maid Saluka all about the pain of his heart. He concluded by saying, "Jewels and precious stones I will present to you to your heart's content. Now you must save my life at this crisis. Take this *Sāri* with you and go about the town on the pretext of selling it there. She who will set no price to it but demand it as a matter of right, to be sure, that one you must know to be Bheluā, the beautiful one. Have a private conversation with her and give her the *Sāri*, which, in reality, belongs to her and which she loves dearly. Tell her, if there be really no chance of my being united with her, I swear by this ebb-tide, I will fling myself into the river and drown myself. Tell her privately that if she has any love for me, let her meet me in the flower-garden."

She took the cage in hand, containing the bird and paid a visit to the town. She went to the palace of the merchant-prince and sought a purchaser for the bird. But none came forward to buy it. She then entered the apartments of Bheluā. She was lying on a rich couch, her profuse hair lay dishevelled on all sides. Saluka stopped there and laid down the cage. Bheluā instantly recognised her own bird and asked in a tone of entreaty, "Tell me, maiden, where you got this bird."

"My profession," said Saluka, "is to sell birds. I wander, in quest of purchasers, from town to town. Now I will tell you the story of this *Sāri*. This Sāri and her mate lived in a great forest, where there were big fig trees. These were blown down by a storm all on a sudden and the bird Suka flew away to a distant country, leaving his consort forlorn and in great distress. This little thing flew on and on and at last, all tired, allowed herself to be caught by me and I have since put it in this cage and have been trying to get a purchaser." "I will reward you," said Bheluā, "with precious stones and jewels, if you can give tidings about him. For I am sure, you know all the facts. Tell me, without reserve, if you have pity for my life." Saying so, she took the golden necklace from her breast and presented it to Saluka.

"What is the price you want for the *Sāri*," she said again, "Tell me the truth and do not deceive me."

Saluka said, "Listen to me, O beautiful one, one who will set no price to it but demand it as a matter of right, to her may I give it,—to none else."

She gently drew Bheluā with her soft hands to the shade of a tree. It was a lonely place and there did she sweetly murmur to her ears. "At a distance of fourteen bends from this city, where the ebb-tide flows, your lover waits with fourteen ships. Hear what tidings he has sent for you. If you have any love for him, meet him in the flower-garden, adjoining your compartment."

With these words, Saluka took leave of her and went to where the merchant was waiting when there was an ebb-tide in the river at the distance of fourteen bends from the city.

* * * * *

Her day does not come to an end, so cruelly tedious seems the march of time; nor does the night come. There was no pleasure in taking the meals, nor does she comb her hair.

The evening at last came to an end and the night presented itself to the palace of the old merchant. She lay on a couch in her room and thought random thoughts, all alone.

Then as the night advanced, she began to comb her hair and bind it into a chignon. She wove a garland of Mālati-flowers and hung it on her neck. She took a betel, the purple hue of which adorned her sweet lips. It seemed as if the ebb-tide had passed, giving place to flow-tide; she seemed to revive with the fullness of youth, her handsome face became doubly so. When it was about 10 o'clock, her toilet and dressing were finished. The next three hours she spent, sometimes awake, sometimes sleeping, till it was the last part of the night, when she left her bed and came to the flower-garden. There in the garden, touched by the gentle air of the latter part of the night, Mallikā, Mālati, Gandharāj,

Tagar, and Jessamine bloomed in splendid array, making the spot one of the loveliest in the palace. She plucked the flowers, and seated in a lovely place, wove a beautiful garland with them.

There the rustling of leaves was heard. She spread her *Sāri* and slept. But suddenly opening her eyes, she saw some one, sleeping in the shade of a tree. She slowly approached and at once recognised him. She called him aloud, "How long will you sleep, my beloved! awake and see, before you, your own wretched Bheluā. Just look towards the East. Does not the sky there show the glamour of the rising sun? If night comes to an end, danger may befall us."

He heard her voice as if in a dream and then opened his eyes, from which the illusion of a dream had not yet passed away. He embraced her and said sweetly, "What is it fair maiden, that you have resolved to do? For me, I assure you, I have given up all hopes. If I cannot get you, I will throw myself into the river and die. My fourteen ships will I sink thither, so that there may be no trace left of me. Now be quick, we have no time to lose. If you will make up your mind to leave your parents and go with me, there is not a single moment to lose. The night is nearly over, no time for vain talk. If you agree, come with me, and I will immediately start with you, with my fourteen ships, for my native land."

Bheluā.

"O Sun, that is rising and O Moon, that is setting, be my witness. O creepers and trees of the forest, be my witness. I leave my father and mother and five brothers to-day. I leave my dear native city of Kānchannagar. I leave my companions, my dear maidens all. I am desperately in love. For his sake I go to a distant country. Now adieu to you, O ye birds, that wander in the sky, and the plants and trees that abound in this city. Hide from my mother the tale of my scandal. If she asks you all as to where I have gone, tell her, "Your Bheluā, dear as your life, has been drowned in yonder river." I have not sought permission from my father or brothers. I have put the shame of scandal on their brows for ever. For the sake of my love, I have become like one, that has gone mad. O my friends of Kānchannagar, I bid you farewell in this solitude, in this depth of the night. I leave you all, all who were dear to me up to now, for the sake of one, who is now the dearest."

With fourteen ships and with Bheluā as the richest treasure of them, did the young merchant return to Sankhapur. The voice of welcome was heard in the town. First of all came the mother, and then the aunts of Madan, to give him reception with their blessings of *Dhān* and *Durbā* (rice and grass). Now, all on a sudden, a rumour spread in the country that the young merchant had brought in his ship a wonderfully beautiful woman. "He must have stolen her," whispered the citizens, "from some unknown place. Her hair in its curly and wavy dance almost touches her feet. There is no maiden as beautiful as this girl in our city." When the report reached the old merchant Murari, he called Madan to his presence and asked him what truth was there in the public rumour. "What has been your profit by the last voyage and where did you get the beautiful girl?"

Madan hid nothing from his father but made a clean breast of the whole affair and related the story of his love in full.

Murari was wroth. He knit his brows and said in a harsh tone, "Get out of my city. I had sent a match-maker with the proposal, but he returned insulted. And you have, like a thief, stolen that maiden and brought her to my house. This will blacken the fair name of my family in the eyes of people for ever. Better I had no son than a son like you. You have destroyed the honour of an honoured house. I am resolved that I shall have nothing to do with you in future. I would have called an executioner and had your head cut off, but that would be going too far. Go, and return the maiden to her parents and never venture to come back to Sankhapur."

The mother cried and the sisters cried. There was a shadow of great grief all over the city. Madan came to a ship with Bheluā and went by the sea for some days till he reached Ranchapur, the city of Raja Abu.

Raja Abu was a pirate,—a disgrace and shame to his noble family. With what wealth and goods he had, Madan approached the Raja, seeking shelter. Abu was pleased with the precious stones that the young merchant presented him and gave him a good house to live in.

Here lived Madan with Bheluā for some time. I am now going to relate to you what followed.

Oh my audience, I have now finished two parts of the poem, I shall relate to you the incidents of the third part. (Ll. 1-202.)

PART III.

(7)

I will now speak, in detail, about Raja Abu of Ranchapur. His wealth and power were unlimited. He was a demon incarnate and every one held him in awe. The tiger and buffalo drank from the same fountain without quarelling with each other,—such was the dread in which he was held in his dominion. He had as many as five hundred beautiful wives in his harem. But unsatisfied still, he was always on the lookout for fair damsels of respectable houses. The spies were ever ready, giving him information about handsome women, and as soon as he got the report, he carried them by force to his palace. He was an enemy to the people and cared not at all for the gods. Women and wealth he plundered from everywhere. It was at the city of such a vicious chief that Madan built a house and lived for some time. Now hear what followed next.

There was a barber-woman named Kausalyā, who went to the house of our young merchant one day to help Bheluā in her toilet. She was struck with the splendid-looking house with its rich furniture and decorations, which bore ample signs of wealth in every room. But the most valuable of all the wealth of the house was the fair-looking Bheluā herself. The barber-woman admired her beauty and thought that she had never before seen a woman, handsome as that one. She looked glorious in her youth like the moon with a halo round her. The barber-woman came home and told her husband that the young merchant possessed a diamond which was worth all the riches of seven kings. "Her beauty is wonderful," she said, "her face is like the moon. I saw her lying on her couch with hair dishevelled. Youth has just dawned on her and the profuse curly hair, I saw, touched her feet playfully. I never saw any woman, whose hair is so wonderfully long. The hue of gold emanates from her body and her eyes are soft and sparkling as stars. If you happen to go to the palace of Raja Abu, give him this piece of information. I am sure, as soon as he will get this report, gladly will he reward you with gold in profusion."

The barber.—"It is a clever bait that you have laid before me, my good wife. There is a little danger, however, in the matter. If our story proves untrue, he will have me beheaded forthwith. You say that her hair is very long and that you never saw any hair of the human head with such a curling grace. Now I will give the information to the Raja, if you will secure for me a hair from her head, so that I may show it to His Majesty."

Now, on some pretext or other, the barber-woman again paid a visit to the house of our young merchant. She saw Bheluā, lying on her couch and looking handsome as Rati, wife of the god of Love. She openly praised her beauty, which surpassed that of all other women. She gently touched her body and pressed her beautiful feet with her hands and said, "Even the nails of your toes have the lustre of the moon. Rarely fine must have been the stuff with which the Creator made this angelic form of yours. I never saw the hair of human head so luxuriantly long and curling. The moon seems to be stricken by shame at the sight of your beauty. The hue of gold is seen in your body and your eyes are soft and sparkling like stars. Really, I never saw a woman, so beautiful. There are five hundred fair women in the harem of Raja Abu and none of them is worthy even of being your maid-servant. Your husband, fair lady, is one of the most handsome youg men that I have ever seen, and you are fully worthy of him."

She gently touched the fair maiden, pressing her hands and feet softly and fanned her at times with a fan, decorated with mica, while she went on saying "Had you been the consort of an Emperor, he would have adorned your body with diamonds; he would have been your very slave, carrying out your least wishes with the obedience of a menial." She continued babbling in this way and Bheluā, under the cooling influence of the fan, closed her eyes in sleep. And now the barber-woman watched her for a moment, and with the help of a grain of rice, gently plucked one of the hairs from her head, and thus gaining her object, tied the hair in the edge of her *Sāri* and went straightway to her home. She presented the hair to her husband. The beauty and length of that single hair filled the mind of the barber with astonishment and he exclaimed, "In my early days, I heard a fairy tale. The dream of my childhood is fulfilled to-day. Whence has the young merchant obtained this fairy?"

The barber went to the palace, as usual, and with a razor in hand, was about to ply his task. But the king said, "I cannot spare time to-day for shaving. You have come without notice."

The barber.—"Really it is not for shaving that I am here to-day. I have dreamt a dream, which I would like to communicate to Your Majesty."

"What is it?" asked the Raja.

The barber.—"It is a private matter. Not here."

They went to a private chamber, where the barber spoke to him all about the beauty of the merchant's wife and then he handed over the long hair.

The Raja felt a thrill in his heart, as he touched the soft thing of wondrous length and then discussed with the barber as to how he could secure Bheluā. He sent for Madan, and when the latter appeared in his presence, he said, "You are aware, my young friend, that I have five hundred queens in my harem. But woe to me, not one of them is fit to be the chief Queen! I want a lady whose colour will be like that of a golden beetle. Go forth in search of such a lady. A friend of mine, a merchant living in a distant country, has given me information about such a lady and has sent me a hair from her head. It is here. Take it with you and find the girl out. You must report to me of any girl whose hair is as glossy and long as this one. Be satisfied that the lady has the colour of a true gold beetle and hair of the length of this one (he hands over the hair to the merchant). If you can get for me such a lady, I will make her my chief Queen. If, through your kind help, I can have such a one for my harem, I will reward you with a palatial house, which will glitter with its gold-decorations and you will, besides, have the gift of twenty *purahs* of rent-free land from me. I will also find an exceedingly beautiful girl and get her married to you."

Sad at heart, with the hair in his hand, did the young merchant return home that day. (Ll. 1-110.)

Madan.

"O Bheluā, dear as life, hear the sad tale. A thunder-bolt will shortly fall on my head. We were enjoying the flow-tide of fortune all this time, but the ebb-tide has set in from to-day. Our fourteen noble ships will sink down in the sea to-day. The full moon will be covered with clouds and fire will break out in this house of pleasure, that we have built here. We came floating like stars in the stream of distress and hoped to find refuge in this land of a demon. Here we are destined to meet a miserable end. From my own dear native land, I have been banished for your sake. But I bore this banishment with a gladsome heart since you are by far more valuable to me than anything else. Your beauty is now a source of eternal trouble to you and your youth is your enemy to-day. Now, my sweetheart, cut off your long flowing hair and besmear your golden colour with soot. The wicked king has ordered that I shall go to distant lands, leaving you here."

When she heard this, Bheluā felt as if a thunderbolt had fallen on her head; the hair of her body stood at their ends in fright.

They both set their wits together, planning means of escape. The merchant said, "In course of this day, I shall have to start from here. This is the order on me. It is for securing you, dear Bheluā, that the king sends me to distant lands. So if I take you with me, there will be no escape. A female spy has given him information about your beauty and he sends me away to make his way clear. Now listen to my plan. Near the Jaintia hills, there lives a merchant, named Hiran, a particular friend of mine. There you will have to go from here. I leave a boat in the river made of light "*man pavan*" wood; the oars thereof are made by the famous artisans of Maldah. This boat will be your only hope in this dangerous night. I will take the bird Suka, leaving the female Sāri with you. If, by the grace of Mother Durga, you may flee from this land with the help of this boat, then go straightway to Jaiteswar, where my friend lives, and wait there for me. If you cannot effect your escape, I need not remind you of the diamond-ring on your finger, the refuge of all chaste women in their distress. If the situation be a desperate one chew it and die. For myself, if such a thing happens, I will drown myself in the sea with my fourteen ships and will never show my face to any mortal."

Early in the morning the merchant started with fourteen ships.

Abu Raja's generals and soldiers now proceeded to the merchant's house and surrounded it like ants. The Raja entered the inner apartments and there saw Bheluā, whose beauty at once charmed him. With the flowing tresses, long and glossy, with the colour that shone bright as that of the golden beetle, she stood in front of him, like the moon descended on the earth. The Raja said, "Come to my palace, dear lady, I will be a slave to your wishes. I have five hundred queens in my harem; they will all be your slaves." Bheluā said, "I pray for justice, O mighty monarch. I have a complaint to lodge before Your Majesty. Madan, the young merchant, played wickedly with me; he carried me away from my father's palace, while I was sleeping, all alone, in my garden-house. My sleep was to me the source of the great danger that followed. He carried me into the ship and came up here to escape the wrath of my parents and five brothers. I have been cut off from my kith and kin and am leading this deplorable life. No more shall I see my parents, nor my five brothers. No more shall I have the privilege of talking gaily with the wives of my brothers. People are spreading all sorts of scandals, and I am weary of life. I shall chew my diamond-ring and die of the poison." As she said so, she was about to act up to her threat, when the Raja intervened and said, "What are you doing, fair girl? Do not rashly chew the diamond-ring. I will make you a gift of landed estates, yielding seven lakhs a year, and I shall, as I have said, be a slave to your wishes. Near the temple of Kāli, in my palace, I have made a new altar; there shall I sacrifice Madan as soon as he comes back. Come to my palace; there the couches and sofas have been softly spread for you. I will make you happy by all means. You will be the owner of immense wealth, of hoards of jewels and diamonds, and to crown your happiness, I will make you my chief Queen."

Bheluā.

"I have my parents and brothers at my home. How can I marry without their consent? My father lives at Kanchannagar, and he is known as Manik, the merchant. There send information at once. My parents and brothers will all come up here, and in the presence of them all, the marriage will take place. Wait these few days and do not pay a visit to my chambers. Stay at your palace these few days. If, however, you do not agree to my wishes, I will end my life by chewing this diamond-ring.

The Raja was right glad and sent a messenger to Kanchannagar. In the meantime, Bheluā began to discuss with Saluka as to how she could proceed to the city of Jaiteswar. Just as a wild bird, put in a cage, cuts with its beak the wooden rods, and tries to break the chain of its feet by constant biting, it was even so with Bheluā who constantly tried to effect her escape from the city of Abu Raja. Three days passed and on the fourth, Bheluā came to the river-ghat on the pretext of floating lights in the water,—a rite which Hindu women perform in some special months of the year. She took with her the maid Saluka and also her dear bird *Sāri* and went into the boat of *man pavan.* They both plied the oars, made by Maldah carpenters. The night was dark and the waves roared menacingly, and over them floated the small boat of *man pavan.* The wind was trembling and the sail was backed by strong wind, and the boat crossed rivers with the speed of a shooting star. Even without knowing the way, they plied the oars in unknown regions, and the boat reached the shore in half a day, which, in usual course, would take three days to reach. The city of Rangchapur. the abode of Raja Abu, lay at a great distance and the boat of *man pavan* approached the city of Jayanta.

(Ll. 1-106.)

(9)

When they reached the city of Jaintā, Bheluā, with her maid Saluka, went to the palace of the merchant Hiran. She introduced herself as the wife of his friend Madan. But Hiran, as soon as he saw Bheluā, became enamoured of her. Strange that the flower itself came flying to the bee, so unexpected it was. What if the hedge, raised around the field to protect its corn, itself took to eating up its protegé, the corn ? It was a case like that,—all this being the result of evil destiny.

" How unfortunate am I," cried Bheluā. " Whenever I catch a branch for shelter, it breaks at my touch. Alas, my beauty has become my enemy and my youth the cause of my ruin."

A few days passed. The girl remained at Jaiteswar without finding any means of escape.

Meantime the merchant Hiran discussed with his people as to how he could win the hands of Bheluā and marry her himself. At last he confided the secret of his heart to his old father. The old man thought over the question for a moment, but at last being swayed by an undue affection for his son, yielded and gave his consent to Hiran's marriage with his friend's wife.

The whole thing was so secretly arranged that Bheluā could have no inkling of it at the outset.

Now Hiran had a sister named Menakā. Youth had just dawned on her; she was a paragon of beauty. She was in fact considered to be the most valuable treasure of that family. The stars of heaven looked pale before her bright eyes, when she gazed upwards, and the moon was stricken with shame at the lustre of her face. She had just completed her sixteenth year and stepped into the seventeenth.

Some years ago, Madan had paid a visit to his friend Hiran's house and there they both saw one another. Menakā fell in love with him and began to brood over her feelings in solitude. Madan and she met privately and both seemed to exchange words of love.[1] There was a whisper in the city about the marriage of the pair. Meantime, Bheluā came there and the matter grew complicated. The proposal of Menakā's marriage with Madan could not be seriously entertained, as the time was declared to be inauspicious by astrologers.

From the first day of her arrival at the city of Jaiteswar, Bheluā and Menakā became fast friends. Menakā now learnt everything and felt that she would surely meet Madan soon. The snake had left the jewel of its head there, and it was sure to come in search of its treasure. Both confided to one another their love for Madan and felt a relief by unloading their sorrows to one

[1] This had been, of course, before Madan saw and loved Bheluā.

another.[1] They both became one soul, one mind. At dinner, in the sleeping bed and everywhere they kept inseparable company. They bathed from the same landing-ghat of the river; they slept together on the same bed. They ate from the same plate. In fact they became as one body and soul.

The day of marriage (of Hiran with Bheluā) approached, and drums were beaten in the city. The flute-players of Jaita merrily played on their pipes.

Menakā one day privately said to Bheluā, "My wicked brother, O sister, is enamoured of your beauty and will marry you. My father, who, owing to his dotage and foolish affection for my brother, has lost his sense, has given his consent to such an unholy thing."

Bheluā felt stupefied by the dire news and could not speak for sometime. She then lamented her fate in this way, "I came to a friend's house in great distress, just as a traveller comes to the shade of a tree for protection from the sun. Alas! the powerful sun sends its burning rays through the leaves and allows him no relief. I prepared a bed for taking rest and laid myself thereon. Alas, the house caught fire and burnt it, owing to my evil luck."[2]

Menakā.

"Do not lament, sister, call my brother to your presence and ask him to grant you three months' time before consenting to this marriage. If your husband still lives, he will not go to Rangchapur but come to our city. If within these three months he does not turn up, both of us will drown ourselves in a pond.

[1] As a man often took more than one wife in those days, there was generally no sting of jealousy in a woman's heart, when her husband married a second woman. She often took the matter lightly and even graciously.

[2] *Cf.* "সুখের লাগিয়ে, এঘর বাঁধিনু, অনলে পুড়িয়ে গেল"—Chandidas.

Bheluā took the advice and sought an interview with Hiran. She said to Hiran, "You want to marry me; that is all right. But you must give me three months' time for deciding my course. My husband has gone out for trade. I do not know if he is still alive or not. Marry me after three months. You must wait till this time and should not proceed further in your attempt to win me. If you do not agree to my request, I will chew the diamond-ring and put an end to my life."

Hiran very privately discussed the matter with his people and made up his mind to follow this project, namely, that he would start from home on the pretext of trade and find out his quondam friend Madan, now an enemy. If he can meet him on the way, he will assassinate him. He matured this plan, and before setting out, saw Bheluā and said, "It is for your sake, dear girl, that I am going to distant lands, in quest of my dear friend, your husband. If I can find him out, rest assured that I will bring him up here with me. I start after two days hence; I have come to take leave of you."

Honey was in his mouth but poison in his heart, when he told this to Bheluā and bade her farewell.

Menakā overheard all that passed between Hiran and his friends. She divulged the secret intentions of her brother to Bheluā. Bheluā became mad with grief at the report, but controlling herself as best as she could, taught her parrot, the *sāri*, her little tale of woe. Briefly she recited to the *sāri* the story as to how she came from Abu Raja's city to Jaiteswar, how Hiran consulted his friends and developed the plan of murdering him, and the sorrows she had been suffering so long. "You are to shun the company of your friend and fly away from him with the utmost speed. He goes to kill you. I am like a bird, put into the cage in this city. Do not think of your unfortunate Bheluā any more. I will throw myself into fire and die, or cut my throat with a knife. If you still live, never come to this city of Jaiteśwar. If you do, death will be sure. Alas! my beauty has become my bane and my youth the cause of my ruin."

When the *sāri* was trained, Bheluā sent for Hiran and insisted, in tender words, on his taking the bird with him. She said, "Go to distant lands with this *sāri* of mine. Take care that you do not lose this bird. Whatever country you may happen to visit, you should bring from it some new thing, some curiosity, after my choice, as a present for me. This *sāri* knows well the things I like and it will let you know by signs what I would prize. You are to purchase those things and bring them for me in your ship."

Right glad was Hiran at this request from the fair one and considered himself as a crowned king, being favoured with this command from the lady.

He took the bird with him and set out for distant lands.

Following the ebb-tide, he proceeded, and after seven days met Madan. He had laid anchor to his ship and was bathing in the river, where Hiran met him with the bird in his hand. They embraced each other, having met after such a long time. All the time Hiran was bent upon devising some place to kill his friend. At this stage, the bird *sāri* was seen by Madan, who at once recognised it. He naturally took a great interest in the pet bird of his wife and enquired of his friend as to where he could have got it. He caught it and kept it near him with his friend's permission.

At the still hour of night Madan brought the bird near him and said, "You must have been sent here by Bheluā. Please recite to me the words that she might have taught you at the time of parting." Then did the bird deliver its message in the following way, without understanding it: "She escaped from the city of Abu Raja by the help of the boat of *man pavan* and came to the palace of Hiran, the merchant. This young man got enamoured of her. He has planned to kill you." "Fly, my lord, fly in all haste to your own country. Do not tarry a moment to brood over my fate. Like a wild bird, put in the cage, I am here in this city. Do not think of your unfortunate Bheluā any more. I will throw myself into fire and die or cut my throat with a knife. If you are alive, my friend, do not come to this city of Jaiteswar. Here death will be sure. Alas, my beauty has become my bane and my youth the cause of my ruin."

Big drops fell from Madan's eyes, as he thought over the condition of his beloved wife. Two-thirds of the night passed and only one-third remained. Hiran, the merchant, was enjoying deep sleep in his ship. He would put poison in a betel and with that kill Madan the next day. This he had planned. Madan, who had not slept at all, rose from his bed at the dead of night. He cut the chain of his ship, which was moored there, and set sail to it. Taking advantage of the ebb-tide and the favourable winds, the ship marched on, and in four days, the city of Jaiteswar came into sight. In usual course, it would take a month to reach the place. He laid anchor to the ship at a bend of the river and in the disguise of a hawker came to the city with the bird in his hand. He cried out for a purchaser of the bird, and travelling through the paths of the city, arrived at the house of Hiran Sadāgar. The report reached the inner apartments of his house and Bheluā at once recognised the bird. She offered a price in the shape of her finger-ring to the seller and purchased her own *ṣāri*.

"Oh my *sāri*, O my pet bird, dear as my life, tell me now where my husband is. You must have travelled a good deal. Tell me now what countries you saw. Have you met my dear husband and has he taught you any message for me?"

The *sāri* had learnt a song, which it began to sing.

"Yes, yes, dear lady, I have seen your dear husband. He wanders about in the guise of a hawker in quest of you. He has become mad for you. He spends his days without meals and nights without sleep. At the bend of the river, where flows the ebb-tide, he is waiting for you with his ship. Manage anyhow to escape from this palace and meet him there."

Bheluā now took leave of Menakā with tears in her eyes. They both wept at the hour of parting. In the dead hour of night, she left Hiran's house with the bird *sāri* in her hand. She reached the bend of the river, where the ship of the merchant lay anchored. Nobody knew of her flight except Menakā in that large city.

The merchant cut the ropes and set sail to the ship, which swiftly ran through the waters in the ebb-tide. After a short journey, the flow-tide set in and the ship went against the current, aided by the wind. Madan felt as if he had obtained the moon in his hands. He embraced his consort, and both were blinded by tears of joy, so that they could not see one another for some time. They had met at last, but were afraid lest they should again be separated by cruel destiny. The day passed and the night came. The night also passed and another day dawned. They saw, in their front, a shoal, known as *Kaichar bāk*. Who is it whom they see coming in that direction? From what country does he come, raising a flag over his ship? At the sight of this, Madan became pale with fear. There the merchant Manik, the father of

Bheluā, is coming with her five brothers. Madan recognised the ship and, turning to the contrary course, went in the direction of the current. But after going some distance, he saw another flag, in front of him, and again became pale with fear. It was the flag of Abu Raja's ship. He again turned to the contrary direction and took another course. With the speed of a shooting star did his ship steer on, but there was yet another ship, which nearly overtook him. It was the ship of Dhananjaya, the merchant, who was advancing with his fourteen ships, with a large number of men and amongst the crew was there the beautiful Menakā. Three bends of the river Madan crossed but in front he could recognise from the flag that the young merchant Hiran was approaching towards him. It was on the vast watery expanse of *Chougangā*, the confluence of four rivers, where Madan felt his position a critical one, surrounded as he was by enemies on all sides. There was no escape this time. Providence was against him.

Her hair was all dishevelled and her face was bright, this being the dawn of her youth. Bheluā ran like a mad woman through the deck of the ship and threw herself into the water. Slowly did the black hair of her head, like clouds strewn over the river, sink in it. Menakā, who observed her from another ship, also, threw herself into the river and caught hold of the hair of her head. They were both seen struggling in the river and at this point Madan, also, threw himself into the waters. "Oh my Bheluā, oh dearer than life, what is it that you have done?" were the words that he had uttered before he jumped into the river.

At this time the sky became menacingly black and underneath, the great river swelled, till the whole region seemed to be swallowed by waters. The sails of the ships were rent by storm and the rivers roared, rising far above her banks. The ships all capsized. In the four directions, the ships of the four merchants all went straight into the bottom of the river with the crew. They passed through a death-struggle in the vast expense of *Chougangā*. None could help the others in that critical situation. Alas! who would help his comrades to step into the shore, helplessly scattered as they were. Where, alas, was Madan, the merchant? Where was Abu Raja? Hiran, the merchant, was, also, punished by Providence, as he deserved.

The ships capsized and were carried far away. Alas! where was the beautiful Bheluā gone, dearer to Madan far than his life? (Ll. 1-258.)

(10)

A grave-looking old merchant of saintly character was passing by the river against the current in that region. His ship was plated with gold and the flag bore the embroidery of mica. It was loaded with gold and precious stones. The flag was seen far above in the sky. The ship, as already stated, was going against the current. She suddenly stuck into the shoal. The sail was pulled down and the helmsman and those, who plied the oars, exhausted their strength in their attempt to make the ship free. But she would not move in the least and the merchant in that dangerous situation felt as if some one had struck him with an axe on the head,—so stupefied he was at this crisis. Four days passed in this way and now listen to me, oh brethren, what transpired next. The oarsmen were striding over that lovely shoal and they espied, at some distance, two figures, bright as the sun and the moon, lying with their swan-like necks on the sand. They looked more like dead than living. Alas, what unfortunate man had lost his best treasures on these sandy banks?

The old merchant had dreamt a dream last night. Was that fair dream going to be fulfilled to-day? The oarsmen came to him and said, "Look here, Oh master, the sun and the moon are lying on yonder sandy bank." What did the merchant do at this report? He hied to the banks. He found the sun and the moon, dropped from the sky and lying on the sands. He brought them to his ship.

He gave them fine apparel and jewels to wear; they were, besides, served with rich meals. The ship went against the tide and in a few days, they reached the shore of the merchant's country. When the ships came to the landing-ghat, the women of the city accorded the merchant a hearty reception by singing songs of welcome. With rice and tufts of *Durva*-grass, the female members of the merchant's house came to the *ghat* in order to welcome the treasures brought. They first placed flowers and sandal-paste on the prow of the ships, and then invoked hymns in honour of Padmā (Manasā Devi) and bent their heads in obeisance to that deity. They carried the vessels, in which were stored up the treasures of the ships, one by one, and then suddenly they saw the two beautiful girls of exceeding beauty. The citizens assembled there and were astonished at the sight. They said, in low murmurs, "We never saw such women, nor ever heard of such exquisite beauty. Whence has our merchant brought them?" The wife of the merchant said, "What country did you travel during the voyage and from where have you secured this wonderful treasure? We have no children; our house is dark. From what golden city have you brought these darlings? I take them as gifts from God; lucky is the day indeed."

She assigned to them two rooms, in which a pair of lights, fed by butter, burnt the whole night. She took great care for the girls.

The merchant brought from his treasure the best jewels, precious stones and gold ornaments and with great taste, adorned the girls, just as people adorn the figure of the goddess Durgā during the month of October.

Three months passed, during which no question was asked as to who the girls were.

But at the expiry of the third month, when they had grown sufficiently familiar in the house, the merchant one day asked them, "You are here, my girls, at my house and looked upon as my daughters. May I ask you kindly to give me some account of yourselves. Where is your house? I travel in different countries and may perchance give you some clue to trace your parents. It is surely your cruel husband, who banished you in the lonely shoal in the mid-river.

The girls could not suppress their feeling but began to weep at the question. They then related through their sobs and tears their whole history without reserve. They gave an account of their parents,—how Bheluā met the young merchant and fell in love, how they both fled and went to the young merchant's house, where her father-in-law would not allow the couple to reside any more, owing to their scandalous flight from her father's palace. Then she described in heart-rending words the story of Abu Raja,—how that wicked man sent her husband away from his city on some pretext, how she marched to Jaiteswar in a boat of *man pavan* and at last how they drowned themselves in the midday at the confluence of four rivers, known as *Chougangā.*

The merchant wept, as he heard their sad story and all the people of his town expressed their great sympathy for the girls. The old merchant and his wife put their wits together to decide what should be done for the girls. At last he settled to go on sea-voyage. He took the girls with him. He would first go to Kanchanpur (Bheluā's father's home). From there he would go to the city of Jaita, where Dhananjaya, the merchant, father of Menakā lived. He would make over the charge of the two girls to their respective parents. He took with him merchandise of various kinds, and thought that after having placed the girls under proper custody, he would go abroad for trading purposes. This was his programme. At an auspicious hour, he bowed low to the goddess Padma and set sail to his ships. So bound for Kanchannagar, he set out from his own home.

(Ll. 1-102.)

Now listen to what transpired next.

The wicked Abu Raja did not die, though his ship capsized. He returned to his city after having suffered much on the way. He discussed with his ministers as to what should be done. Then he appointed guards to watch over the ships that passed by the great river, on which his city stood. The ships of merchants, who went by that river for trade took fright and fled away, before Abu Raja's guards overtook them. But all could not escape. Woe to the ship, which fell at the hands of the guards. On pretext of a search, they plundered everything belonging to the ship. There our saintly old merchant approached the landing-ghat, unaware of the danger. The guards and informers, who kept watch, cried out, "Stop, Oh merchant, do not go. For if you move an inch from where you are, we will, according to the king's commands, take possession of your fourteen ships and sink them in the river." The merchant laid anchor there in order to save himself.

The guards came on board the ships and plundered everything that was there. Then they espied the two girls, bright as the sun and the moon and in great joy, they gave information to the Raja. Abu at once hied to the banks of the river with his ministers and other officers. He saw Bheluā and said, "What luck! I have not only obtained a gift but also a fee. I was madly searching for my lost lady and here she is with another, equally welcome. Now these two ladies will be the ladies of my heart. One will adorn the right side of my sleeping couch and another its left. Ah me! What have I not suffered these six painful months for that pair of star-like eyes and that treasure of black hair, profuse as the clouds? How many nights, have I not spent, dreaming of our joyous union? So long my wealth—nay the whole of my kingdom—was like poison to me, bereft as I was of my greatest fortune. Now God has at last been propitious to me." Saying so, he seized the girls by force and brought them to the palace of Rangchapur. The fourteen ships of the good merchant were taken away forcibly and he was placed in a half-shattered boat and ordered to leave the city. Just see the condition of the old merchant. He is now helpless as a straw in the stream as the reward of a pious wish to help others!

(Ll. 1-46.)

(12)

Now I shall, for a time, stop the narration of this part of the story and resume the account of the young merchant, Madan.

The skilful oarsmen of Madan, who steered the boat of *man pavan*, tried their best, at the risk of their own lives, and saved Madan, the merchant, at the junction of *Chougangā*. In that boat Madan carried the birds

Suka and *Sāri* and was accompanied by the trusted maid-servant, Salukā. The young merchant travelled in that boat from place to place in quest of Bheluā, maddened by grief. Then as he went in his boat, one day he espied the old merchant passing along the river in a shattered boat, supplied him by Abu Raja. The boat could no longer stand the gusts of wind and the waves rose over its sides till the leaky barge was about to sink.

Madan saw the sad predicament of the old merchant and hastened, with his own boat, to the shattered one, belonging to the merchant. On his asking the oarsmen about the whereabouts of the old man, they gave him some account. Just at that moment, the boat was about to sink; the old man came out and took shelter in the boat of Madan with his people. Meantime, his boat was carried away by the winds and sank in the waters, near the next bend of the river. The old man gave a full account of the dangers he passed through—as to how he happened to save two girls of exceeding beauty from perishing on a lonely shoal near the junction of *Chougangā*. "The eyes of the girls were star-like and their hair as profuse and black as clouds." When he was thus giving a full description of the beautiful ones, Madan felt a sudden thrill in his heart and he eagerly asked the old man many questions about them. "Where did you take them? Why did you come in a shattered boat? Have they been drowned in the vast expanse of waters?"

"No, no, my young friend," replied the merchant, "they were not drowned, I took them to my own country. Myself and my wife took care of them as if they were our own daughters. For six months they lived at our house. But evil fate betook us afterwards. I wanted to do good to them, but did them harm instead, owing to the inscrutable will of Providence. I took the right course but fell in a great danger. One day the girls gave me an account of their respective parents and began to weep and wished me to take them to their paternal homes. I ordered my fourteen ships to be ready and planned to go first to Kānchannagar (where the parents of Bheluā lived). On the way lay that Tiger of men, Abu Raja, and as I was passing along the river, which flows by the city of Rangchapur, he fell upon me, plundered all my treasures and forcibly carried the two girls. A thunderbolt, as it were, fell on my head. All my ships were seized by that Rakshasa and the two girls are now living as prisoners in his palace."

Madan, with the old merchant, first went to his city in the boat of *man pavan*. Now when the saintly man was safe at his own home, the young man with Saluka set out for Rangchapur, the city of Abu Raja. Near a bend of the river, where the current was strong, he anchored his boat and discussed with Saluka as to the ways and means he would now adopt.

Saluka disguised herself as a *Dom* girl, selling fans and cane-baskets. She visited the palace of Abu Raja. She dyed her hair yellow, and bound them into a knot straight above the head in the fashion of a *Dom*-woman. She tied round her waist the flowing ends of her *saḍi* and went into the inner apartments of the Raja's house. She said, "My husband's name is Sankar. My profession is to sell these fans and cane-baskets." This was how she introduced herself to the queens of Abu Raja. They purchased her goods according to their choice. Last of all, she paid a visit to Bheluā's room. She saw Bheluā, sitting with her friend Menakā. From her eyes streamed incessant tears, as she privately talked with Menakā. There was none in that big palace to feel sympathy for her except Menakā. When Menakā wept, Bheluā, with the flowing folds of her *sadi*, wiped away her tears and when Bheluā wept, Menakā tried to offer her solace. Thus both of them lived in great sympathy for each other, sorrowing over their lot, like poor Sitā in the prison of Rāvan, the Rākshasa-chief. When Bheluā saw Salukā, she felt like one, restored to life. She at once asked her information about her lord. But Menakā put her fingers on her lips, signing her to stop. Menakā asked Salukā, "What is the name of your husband, O *Dom*-woman? To which country do you belong? What is your mission here?" Salukā smiled at these queries and then introduced herself thus in a loud voice, "Our village is called Ujāni. I am the wife of Sankar, a *dom* by caste. I have come to this palace to sell my cane-baskets. You see how artistically these have been made. Rich men vie with one another to possess these fine baskets. If you want some, please purchase them without delay." Menakā took the gold necklace from her breast and gave it as price of several baskets and fans, that she purchased. She ordered the *dom*-woman to bring two fans more on her next visit. Salukā took leave of them, after having received a present from the betel-box; but she had already handed over a letter to Menakā along with the fan, which she pretended to sell to her. Menakā read the letter. The merchant said in it that he was living in that city with Salukā and requested Bheluā to let him know, through the maid-servant, what means she would now devise for escaping from the hands of the Rakshasa-chief. (Ll. 1-94.)

Now I will tell you of an incident that took place shortly afterwards. One day Menakā had a private talk with Bheluā, in the course of which she said, "Promise to me, girl, that you will marry the man, whom I shall elect as my husband. If you will make this promise to me, all your dangers will pass away." Bheluā thought for a little time over the matter and then consented. Menakā then addressed her and said, "I have settled to marry this Abu Raja. He is handsome in features and possesses great powers and immense riches. In fact, there is scarcely to be found another man like him in the whole world. His riches are unbounded; his name is honoured and dreaded all over this vast country. I shall wear diamonds and jewels, being his queen, and you will be my dear companion."

Bheluā began to cry as she heard this and abused Menakā, saying that she was a vile and unchaste woman. "If you like," she said, "you may marry Abu Raja. For myself, I will drown myself in the river before I consent to marry the wicked Raja. There is that sharp steel-weapon in the house. I will put an end to my life with it. No more shall I go to the dancing hall." Saying so, she cried incessantly and wiped away her tears with the flowing end of her *saḍi*.

Menakā said, "My friend, set your heart at ease and follow my advice. Try to be conciliatory to this Raja, however bad he may be. Tell him the next time he comes that you are willing to marry him and call him endearingly as the lord of your heart."

In the depth of night Abu Raja paid a visit to her chamber and said, "Come to my embrace, my lost treasure, found again. Hear me, dear lady of my heart, have some affection for me. I have already appointed an astrologer to settle an auspicious day. Know that within a short time, the marriage will take place. Do not kindly put off the date on some pretext or other, as you have been doing these many months. I have ordered a valuable string of pearls for you. I will spend my night with you in the pleasure-house, which I have raised in the midst of our tank. How fine is your curling hair and how pleasing are your silvery eyes! I have six hundred wives in my harem. They will all be slaves to your wishes and you will reign supreme in the palace."

Bheluā.

"But before I consent to be your wife, I have some religious rites to perform. If you violate my vows, it will cause me great pain. I hope you will not do so. My friend Menakā knows all about my vows. She is here and you may know from her what they are. I am a merchant's daughter and our custom is to meet the bridegroom in the great sea. Wherever there is a marriage amongst our kinsmen, the bride and bridegroom go to the sea on board their merchant-vessels.

"So you are to marry me in the sea. There shall I offer you the present of the customary string of flowers, due to the bridegroom."

The auspicious day of marriage was fixed by Abu Raja and he left the chamber of Bheluā, thus settling all points.

"Hear me, Oh Salukā; last night Abu Raja called on me. I have given him word, agreeing to marry him. I have, besides, made a vow to the *Pirs*, promising to make them presents, if my object is fulfilled. To-morrow it will be announced in the public streets by a beat of drum that *Suka* and *Sāri* (male and female birds of the parrot-species) will be married and that two birds, thus to be united, will be purchased at a high price. The Raja's men will go forth in the country in quest of the birds. Tell my lord to come with our *Suka* and *Sāri* to the city. Let him demand the fourteen ships and the treasure of a merchant, lately looted. Our enemy, the Raja, will not mind the price but, in order to please me, purchase the birds, paying down the price demanded.

"On receipt of the treasure and the ships, you are to go at once to the city of that saintly man, who has suffered so much and lost so much for the sake of us, unfortunate women. Give him back the fourteen ships and the treasure that he lost.

"Next proceed to the city of Kānchannagar. Let my lord stay near a bend of the river, where the strong current flows and yourself go alone to my father and deliver this message to him, 'Your daughter Bheluā, Oh old merchant, is in the deep sea, alone and in great distress. Separated from her parents, she is in a dire calamity and helplessly she floats like a straw on the waters. She has asked me to convey this news to you, crying all the time that she spoke. She has asked you to go and save her.'

"Next you are to go to Sankhapur, your own city and approaching the father of my lord, acquaint him with all facts. Tell him, 'Your dear son, Oh master, is in the milk-white sea, helpless and about to be drowned.' It is sure that the parents, however strict and relentless they may be, bear a secret pain in their hearts for their only son. They have not surely been able to give up their affection. Tell him, 'Go forth to save your son. In the milk-white sea his shattered boat is without a sail, without oarsmen; it floats like a straw and your only son is at the mercy of the waves. This city of yours is dark without him. The queen is shedding incessant tears and these hang on her eyes like a cob-web. She has, as it were, lost the most valuable necklace of her heart. If you do not go and save him at once your son will be drowned.'

"Next go to the cities, where our friends are living. Issue invitation-cards, stating that the marriage of Madan and Bheluā will take place in the milk-white sea. Let them all attend the function. Invite all our friends and kinsmen in fitting language. Go everywhere," said Menakā, "but do not go to Jaiteswar. Go not to my brother. If he gets the least inkling of the matter, great danger may befall us. Alas, he fell into the great junction of four rivers, called the *Chouganga.* I do not know if he is alive. If he lives still, we may hope to see each other on some future day."

Salukā took leave of Menakā and Bheluā and went to the young merchant Madan and told him all that she was instructed to convey to him. (Ll. 1-107.)

(13)

When the auspicious time came at last, the Raja set out with his ministers and other officers. He took with him fourteen ships, manned by a promiscuous crew of musicians and drummers. One of the ships was manned exclusively by soldiers, who were in charge of magazine. Bonfires, rockets, squibs and fireworks of various kinds were taken in plenty. Large kettle-drums were beaten incessantly and people cried, "Victory to the Raja" on the eve of his marriage, which was to take place in the milk-white sea.

But the Raja, as he was about to start, saw evil omens on all sides. A blind fly sat on one of his eyes. Sneezes were heard in front; the women, while rejoicing on the happy occasion, found their voices choked for some mysterious reason. The people's words of exultation sounded like laments. A vulture came hovering in the sky and sat on the top of the mast of the flag-ship. The ropes of the ships were torn by a sudden gust of wind. The ship which carried the auspicious articles of marriage suddenly capsized in the landing-ghat. Those things were lost in the river. The queens apprehended danger, and dissuaded the Raja from undertaking the trip that day, but he listened not to their good advice. In one of the ships, the Raja went with his ministerial officers and in another, Bheluā started with Menakā as her companion. The barber, the barber's wife, the priest and other people, whose services would be required at the function, started, too, in one of the ships. But the inauspicious signs on the eve of this happy occasion cast a shadow of fear and unrest on the minds of all.

Meantime what did Madan, the young merchant do? He started with fourteen ships and their treasure (got as price of the birds *Suka* and *Sāri*) and went to the city of the kind-hearted old merchant. The ships and all that belonged to him were returned and he was, besides, formally invited by Madan to attend his marriage with Bheluā.

Thence Madan went to the city of Kanchannagar. He remained in the ship, hiding himself from the citizens and sent Salukā to the palace of Bheluā's father. Salukā, with tears in her eyes, related the story of Bheluā's misfortunes to the inmates of the house. She tenderly appealed to the feelings of the parents, whose hearts, notwithstanding all outward indifference, were burning in grief for their dear girl. To the five brothers Salukā made a most pathetic appeal. "My heart breaks," she said, "at the thought that when you are living in all prosperity here, your sister is about to die in the milk-white sea. She, the beautiful one, the beloved of all, is in the utmost distress."

The message had its effect and the old merchant, with his five sons, immediately started for the milk-white sea.

Then did Madan go to his own city of Sankhapur. The young fellow hid himself as before and sent Salukā to his father. She gave this message to him, "Your only son, revered sir, is about to be drowned in the milk-white sea. He is wandering in the vast waters in a shattered boat. I cannot tell you if he is still alive or all is over with him. You should try to save him, if he is not already lost for good."

Thence speedily did Madan go to other cities, the homes of his friends and kinsmen and distributed invitation-letters, wishing them all to be present at his marriage, which would take place in the milk-white sea.

Only two days were in hand; on the third day the marriage comes off. The merchants in all speed started for the milk-white sea. There all the chief men of the mercantile community met in a short time.

Raja Abu wonderingly saw ships on all sides, huge as mountains. "I never sent any invitation. The whole thing has been managed as privately as possible. I have brought Bheluā to this milk-white sea, without notice. Whence are all these ships assembled here?" thought he and became puzzled.

Then did Madan pass orders on his people to arrest Abu Raja with all his men. The barber and the barber's wife and the rest of the crew, who came to help in the marriage, were bound hand and foot. The Raja's ships were sunk in the sea and he, with his men, were brought to the great shoal, called the *Alangher char*.

The sandy land covered a space of 160 miles. There no trees, no plants grew; it was a waste land without habitation of men or even wild animals. If one happened to be in that vast area of sands, he could not find his way out. With the clothes they wore,—the long *dhuties*,—the men of the Raja were bound. The barber and the barber's wife (who had shown the long hair of Bheluā to Raja Abu) were bound with the ropes of the ship. The Raja himself shared the same fate. As he lay helpless and bound, with his face downwards, Madan approached him and said, "Now, Raja Bahadur, come and marry." In that condition he was left there.

Then with all humility, Madan described his misfortunes to the people of his community, assembled there. He took all of them, with imploring words to Sankhapur. His kinsmen and the father of Bheluā were pleased with him and the pride of high social status of Bheluā's father, which was the cause of all these unfortunate events, was now removed. He now consulted the astrologers for an auspicious day, as to when Bheluā should be formally given in marriage to Madan, the merchant.

The prow of the ship looked bright with its workmanship in gold and the sail, raised aloft, caused it to move with the speed of the winds. Maladhar was the head of the oarsmen. The young merchant ordered him to go swiftly to the city of Dhananjaya and there present him an invitation-letter.

Maladhar's boat went as speedily as an arrow. Dhananjaya, the father of Menakā and his kinsmen, all assembled at Sankhapur. Madan was to marry both the girls, Bheluā and Menakā. The loud music announced the happy event and the women sang festive songs. The merchant distributed gold and silver to the poor people. Thus was the marriage celebrated. Young Madan was pleased with both his wives and spent his days in great happiness. The three were like one soul, one body. Salukā was rewarded with many valuable gifts. The kinsmen and friends went to their respective homes. Here ends the tale of Bheluā.

The Minstrel's Apology.

This is my humble prayer to the audience. May the president of to-night's congregation pardon me for my faults. For I am untrained and have surely committed many errors in music. The story of Bheluā is a long one, complete in five parts, and I am quite unfit to sing it. I am unacquainted with musical airs and modes. So I bow down at the feet of all and crave their pardon. Accept, sir, my humble *salaam.* Now, Oh brother host, give us some betels and tobacco and let us go back to our homes with thankful hearts. (Ll. 1-120.)

THE BALLAD OF RĀNI KAMALĀ DEVI

BY

ADHAR CHANDRA.

PREFACE.

The ballad of Rāni Kamalā Devi could not be recovered in full. Babu Chandrakumar De sent me, on August 30, 1925, a short summary of the contents of the two missing cantos from memory. The tradition, widely prevalent in the district of Mymensingh, is that as no supply of water came to the tank Kamalāsāgar, though it had been dug deep, the queen Kamalā Devi of Susang Durgapur, in conformity with a dream, dreamt by her husband, Raja Janakinath Mallik, descended to the bottom of the tank and gave up her life by performing some rites there. When these were performed, a rush of water came all on a sudden from underground, not only sweeping away the queen, whose body was irrecoverably lost, but also flooding the sides of the tank with its overflow.

The tradition, so far as the death of the queen is concerned, may be accepted as a historical fact. In those days, unnumbered were the instances of people, high and low, in this country, who sacrificed their lives as a result of prevailing superstitions—the most striking examples being supplied by the well-known *Sati*-rites. In the present case when the tradition is so widespread there can be no question as to the authenticity of the fact that the queen became a willing victim to superstition. We have heard innumerable stories in the countryside of poor coolies being sacrificed for propitiating the gods, when no supply of water was obtained from the underground in a newly excavated tank. The Kamalā Dighi exists to this day. Whether the rush of water, described in the ballad, was due to some cunning priestly device or some natural cause, brought on at a later stage, by the persistent attempts of those engaged in the excavation of the tank, cannot be ascertained at this distance of time. The gods can only say if the water of Kamalāsāgar was produced by their grace.

Babu Chandrakumar De approached Mr. Saurendrakishore Raychaudhury, Zemindar of Ramgopalpur, Mymensingh, for being illuminated as regards the historical questions involved in this ballad. Mr. Raychaudhury supplied him with the following piece of information in his letter, dated the 3rd of April, 1925 :

" Kamalā Devi, about whom you want to know was a contemporary of Jehangir. She was the mother of Raghunath Singh, who got from that monarch the decoration of the title of Raja. She was the wife of Mallik Janakinath, an ancestor of the Susung Durgapur Raj family. The tradition of the place is that Mallik Janakinath heard an oracle in his dream, in conformity with which Kamalā Devi gave up her life. A part of the Kamalāsāgar still exists, the rest having been swallowed up by the river Someswari. Janakinath was a contemporary of Akbar. He lived towards the end of the sixteenth century. The baby referred to in the tradition is the son of Rani Kamalā Devi, who afterwards grew to be the illustrious Raja Raghunath Singh of Susung Durgapur. All noteworthy historical facts relating to Raja Raghunath are embodied in the 2nd part of my history of Varendra Brahmin Zemindars of Mymensingh."

Mr. Lethbridge furnishes the following account of him in his book, called the "Golden Book of India": " Mallik Janakinath was succeeded by his son Raghunath. The fragrant wood, produced largely in the Garo Hills, called *aguru*, was in request at the Court of Delhi and Raghunath agreed to supply a quantity of *aguru* to Delhi yearly as a tribute, in return for the help of an Imperial Force, which enabled him to subdue his turbulent Garo subjects and for the title of Raja. The Emperor further conferred on Raja Raghunath the title of *Garo Tambi Munsavi* or Commander of Five Thousand."

The first canto, which is missing, contained a description of the marriage of Raja Janakinath with Kamalā Devi. The subject-matter of the first portion of the second canto may be thus summarised. The king and the queen lived happily for some years. One day she asked her husband as to what he would do for setting up a memorial for her in case she died earlier—in order to show that all his professions of love were true. The Raja said, "I promise to carry out your wishes, whatever they may be. Tell me what you would wish me to do." The queen said, "I will spin a *takuā* of thread in seven days and seven nights. You must have a tank excavated in my name, which will be of the size of the entire space covered by the length of the thread."

The queen, working night and day for the whole week, spun the same *takuā* of thread and the Raja ordered a tank of that size to be excavated at his town, to be called after her, the Kamalāsāgar. But the tank, dug at so much pain and cost, had no supply of water. The popular belief on this point was well-known, *viz.*, the ancestors of a man up to his fourteenth generation were doomed to hell, if the tank, dug by him, yielded no water.

Unlike most of the other historical ballads of Mymensingh, this one has a mythical and legendary element in it, which cannot obtain any credence. But we find in the ballad itself that the Raja had grown a maniac after the death of his wife. The subsequent developments of the story may be taken as illusions, conjured up by his excited fantasy. The story is told in a graphic manner and with a candour, characteristic of the rustic poets. The legends, interspersed in this tale, have an old-world charm of rustic-poetry. The poet, Adhar Chandra, who composed this ballad, cleverly touches the delicate point as to how the queen met with her death. The Raja is described as having simply related the dream to his wife. He had not the heart to wish her to act up to it, he seems to have yielded to a superstitious faith in the dream, but even this he did not speak out to any one. He can by no means be accused of any deliberate act of cruelty. The ballad-maker does not even hint that he wished in the least that the queen should sacrifice herself. She herself became a willing victim. The Raja's great love for her is clearly in evidence in the succeeding events that transpired. If he did not actually come forward to stand in the way of his wife sacrificing herself, it was due to a lurking fear in his heart of incurring divine wrath for offering obstruction to what he considered to be an act of religious merit. This weakness on his part should not be severely judged, as we ought to make some allowance for the faiths and superstitions of the 16th Century. The queen believed that if no supply of water came to the tank, her husband's ancestors would all go to hell. Hence there was no other alternative on her part than to sacrifice her life in that tragic manner. Inspite of history and myth being blended together in this rustic song, it is a very enjoyable piece of popular poetry and I am not sure whether I should like its historical portion or its beautiful myth more. The latter adds a fascination to the tale and is as beautiful as the Idylls of the King, particularly the Mort de Arthur of Tennyson.

We have no information about Adhar Chandra, who composed this ballad. There is no doubt that it was composed in the beginning of the seventeenth century, since all such ballads, in commemoration of acts of local heroism, are composed immediately after their occurrence. In many cases the language of the original is gradually changed in course of their recitations through long generations. In the present case, however, the language is crude and rustic and does not seem to have undergone any substantial change.

In the Ballads such as Mahua, Dewan Bhabna and the Washer-maiden, the art of the rustic poets seems to be perfect in as much as superfluities find no place in them. The ballad-makers show an instinctive power of stringing together the essentials of the plot, leaving aside all irrelevant topics. In the present ballad, however, there is an element of rustic pedantry (as in Canto 7, Ll. 9-12, Canto 6, Ll. 17-20, 27-34) which has marred, to some extent, the compactness of the plot. The laments especially are monotonous and wearisome (Canto 6, Ll. 1-10), the ballad-maker's fondness for metaphorical phraseology, current in his rural districts seems to be often tinged with affectation, making his descriptions sink into dullness. This element, which does not strike so much in the original text, becomes apparent in my translation. In the Bengali original there is a grace and finish in the style which is missed when put in the garb of a foreign tongue. Inspite of this shortcoming the ballad has an irresistible fascination about it, due to the noble sacrifice of the queen, though inspired by superstition, and also to the romantic nature of the legend, described in it, which, like the Holy Grail of Tennyson, leaves an edifying effect on the mind.

The ballad of Rāni Kamalā Devi, so far as we have obtained it, is complete in 342 lines. I have divided it into 10 cantos.

I learn from various sources that this ballad was once very popular. I have not lost all hopes of recovering it in full.

The Ballad of Rani Kamala Devi.

(1)

In his big bungalow with twelve doorways, the Raja was having a quiet sleep, when, in the depth of night, he dreamt a dream.

The dream disclosed to his wondering eyes a land, resplendent with diamonds and pearls,—from which came floating an odoriferous and sportive breeze,—a land where it dawned at the glee cooings of the gold-winged cuckoo,—and where at the deep hours of night the birds sat on the boughs of trees and sang. And he dreamt of many wild things, besides.

He called the queen from her sleep and said, "Awake, my beloved, how long will you sleep? I am here, calling you. Open your eyes and see me.

"What a horrible dream have I dreamt, O queen! I cannot forget it for a moment.

"In the still and deep hours of night it seemed to me that all the stars were sunk in the sky and that the world was filled with an impenetrable darkness.

"Alas, why is it that the tank I have excavated in your name yields no water! I have dreamt a strange dream, which I am going presently to relate to you."

The queen lay in her bed,—bright and lovely as the full moon,—lost in deep slumber and the Rājā called her aloud sitting by the pillow, on which her head reposed. It was the last part of the night. The little lovely baby slept soundly by the side of its mother and the Raja's eyes now rested on the child and now on the mother. (Ll. 1-18).

(2)

The queen awoke with a start and found the lord of her heart, sitting by her side. The quiet rest of the deep hours of night was broken and her eye-lids were still heavy with sleep. She said to her husband in sweet broken words,—"What is it, lord, that troubles you at such an hour as this? Strange, I see your eyes, full of tears. Tell me, my lord, what may be the cause?"

The Raja.

"A strange dream have I dreamt. It is about the tank, newly excavated in my city. That tank, O queen, may, after all, turn out to be a cause of our ruin. Though deep it was dug, no water has come out of it. I heard an oracle in my dream, saying that should you, my beloved, go to the bottom of the tank, water would come out of itself. I dreamt also as if, on hearing my words you descended to the bottom of the tank in slow steps. Scraps of unconnected scenes then presented themselves to my wondering eyes. I saw that all on a sudden there came a flood which swept you far away into the dark nether lands; as if the great flood from the underground came furiously rushing with foam at its mouth and inundated all the four sides of the tank. Then rose a terrible uproar as splashes were thrown up from some mysterious regions. I do not know, Oh queen, what evil spirit induced me to have this tank dug—to worry us all in this manner! My heart trembles in fear. Oh my dear queen, I do not wish my empire, nor my wealth, what pleasure will these yield to me if I lose you? (Ll. 1-22.)

Rani Kamala

" Some maids took sacred grass and rice for worshipping the gods and the others carried the queen's toilet articles on their head." P. 199.

(3)

The queen rose from her bed and slowly approached the big outer bungalow with twelve doorways. Her maid-servants were sleeping there. She called them out from sleep and ordered them to accompany her to the river-*ghat*. Some took golden pitchers, others cups of the same metal. Some carried towels, prepared by the artists of *Mecha*-country, others took valuable blue-coloured apparels. One maiden carried cups filled with incensed oil, the fragrance of which spread miles and miles afar. Some of them took the powdered *Gila*-fruit for cleansing the queen's body, others beautiful baskets, full of blooming flowers. Some maids took sacred grass and rice for worshipping the gods and others carried the queen's toilet-articles on their head. In that dark and dead hour of night they all went to the river-*ghat*. Above their head was the blue expanse of sky, which showed the stars, beautiful as the *Champa*-buds of golden hue.

Neither the sun nor the moon could have a peep into the face of the queen, which was then like an angel's, nor the people of the city who lay in profound sleep at that dark still hour before the dawn of the day. The maid-servants helped in washing her body with the *Gila*-fruit. Her hair was anointed with scented oil. The queen got down into the river for bathing. The maidens gently wiped the dirt off her body with the towels of *Mech*. When bathing was finished, they gave her a flame-coloured *Saḍi* to wear. Seated on the bank of the Somai, she worshipped the gods with offerings of flowers, sacred grass and rice. And then she prayed. " Be witness, O river Somai; and O my husband, rest assured that I am going to obey the oracle you have heard and am prepared to give up my life. Be witness, ye trees, standing still on the sides of the tank, and ye sun and moon, and O ye gods presiding over the world, bear witness too! whom else may I call at such a crisis of my life? For keeping the pledge of my lord, I am going to sacrifice my life. Strange that though dug so deep, the tank has yielded no water! The ancestors of this house up to to the fourteenth degree in ascent will visit hell. O, what a horror! O gods, I pray unto you all, save us from this danger. Save this glorious house but take my life, if indeed that is needed for it." With tearful eyes did this queen offer the sacred *bel*-leaves and flowers at the feet of the unseen powers. She repeatedly prayed that they might be propitiated and graciously inclined towards her lord.

After having offered the *Puja*, she returned home. No one, in that vast city,—outside her palace—knew of her holy bath in that deep hour of night. The night was fast wearing away and the gleam of morning was seen.

After return home, what did she do? The little baby was sleeping on a couch. She took it in her arms and gently kissed its sweet face a hundred times, shedding incessant tears all the while. "O my dear son," she cried, "You are to me what the prop is to a blind man. From to-day we shall never more see each other again." She suckled the child and, with a choked voice, said again, "Your beautiful face, dear child, which is like the moon, I will see no more." She then silently wept without uttering a word. Her heart was, as it were, pierced by a spear, but she bore her cruel pain mutely. (Ll. 1-53.)

(4)

From the depths of her heart, rose a plaintive appeal all secretly, "O lord of my heart, I leave this poor baby of mine to your care." Inaudibly murmuring this, she addressed the old and trusted maid Suā and said, "To you, maid, I leave this baby—this treasure of my heart." She looked up to the birds, *Suka* and *Sāri*, whom she had brought from her father's house and asked them to teach the baby the sweet word 'mamma,' which they had learnt to recite. To all the servants of the house her silent request was that they might take care of one, who was far dearer to her than all the treasure of her palace. "That I leave this empire and the throne," she said with a sigh, "is not at all a matter of sorrow to me. But I feel a pain, which pierces my heart like a shaft, at parting with this child."

After weeping long, her eyes became dry. And then she made over the baby to Suā, the maid-servant. The attendants, male and female, stood aghast and did not know what would happen. A feeling of awe struck them and they cried in silence.

Then did the queen take a golden pitcher in her hand. In the flowing end of her *saḍi*, she tied some sacred grass and rice. And then she hied to the side of that ill-fated tank. She, who had never been seen before outside the harem, was seen to-day by hundreds of men and women, assembled there to see the woeful sight of the hour. It was very early in the morning when the chief queen approach ed the tank. The morning-clouds above were tinged with a red colour and crows were cawing, seated on dry boughs of trees. The wind was blowing forcibly at times. A crow seemed to say to its mate, "What a pity! we shall never more see the face of the Queen-mother. The whole kingdom will, as it were, lose its eyes to-day and the throne will be void. Let us depart from this cursed land." Signifying some such resolve by their cawing, the crows hovered in the sky for a time, and then flew far away. The people, assembled there, saw, with eyes uplifted, the strange spectacle. Some men said, "Alas, what a misfortune!" Others remarked that the virtuous king had lost his head. One man observed how foolish it was for the king to send the queen to that cursed tank for such a purpose. "It may be that he is going to lose her for ever. What good will the tank serve him? What, if there be no water in it? Let not the queen descend to the bottom of this tank." (Ll. 1-36.)

(5)

The queen, now in firm steps and with a calm majestic look, descended to the bottom of the tank. As she went down, she threw the sacred grass and rice on all sides from the flowing end of her *sadi*. The people were crying, "Alas, alas!" all the while. Then did she offer this prayer publicly. "If I am a chaste woman, and have lived true to the will of God, then may water spring up from the bottom of this dry tank. If I am chaste and have lived true to the will of God, may the water of the tank overflow its sides and may my people see this sight. If I am chaste, then fulfil, O God, the desire of my lord, the king. This object attained, it will not at all cause me pain, if I be swept away by a stream to the nether world." She sprinkled water from her golden pitcher on all sides. What an inexhaustible quantity of water did the pitcher hold! It seemed as if it would never get empty. Then did water gush out from the bottom of the tank and drench it gently together with the queen's beautiful feet. She continued sprinkling water and the water of the tank became knee-deep. She went on throwing water from her pitcher and the water of the tank swelled up to her neck. She raised her hands up and still continued sprinkling water and her noble figure became gradually and totally submerged under water. Her dishevelled hair now floated over the ripples of the surface like the stream of the Ganges, flowing from the matted locks of the great God, Siva. Look there and see the flowing ends of her flame-coloured *saḍi*, carried by the flood. The water of the tank rose higher and higher and inundated the sides of the tank, foaming in furious rage. The people who stood there began to lament loudly, saying "Alas, alas!" Whence came that great flood, no one could say. All the four sides of the tank were now flooded over. A roaring sound, which inspired awe rose from underground. Alas, to what land the queen had gone, nobody could know. (Ll. 1-27.)

(6)

Then did the Raja throw himself on the ground, overwhelmed with grief, and begin to cry wildly like a mad man. The very trees, on the sides of the tank, deeply affected by the king's sorrows, seemed to shed their leaves in sympathy. The cows, in their sheds, and the birds, in their cages, were seen to drop silent tears. The cowherds, the horses of the stable and the elephants, men and beasts, all seemed to be alike stricken with grief. The pigeons of the palace and wild birds of the air stopped their chirpings and showed their grief, remaining mute all the while. The ministers, officers, the servants and maid-servants did not speak but shrank into a corner of their houses, overwhelmed with the general sense of grief. The mothers of that city did not care to suckle their babies but silently wept, leaving their dear ones aside. The good wives did not care for their toilet but, with dishevelled hair, wept, forgetful of the presence of their husbands. In the gardens the flowers bloomed not but strangely faded away. Weep, weep, O river Somai, and sing the sad tale of how the goddess of the city left it for ever. O flood, roar out the tragic tale of how she was swept away for ever from the land of the living. The citizens cried, saying "To-day is the *Dasami*-day [1] for us, when our goddess has been taken away from the temple, to be drowned in the water."

The sky shines brightly with the moon and stars,—the house with its flower-garden and the river with her sailing-boats. The dark night is illuminated by a lamp; one's home, likewise, is brightened by the presence of the wife. The Raja saw everything dark before him, losing his beloved queen. "Ah my bird, where hast thou flown away, leaving thy golden cage." He cried day and night.

The Raja turned nearly mad with grief. He wandered night and day by the side of the tank, sometimes lying there, stretching his body like a dead man,—silently shedding tears. The ministers and officers met him often and advised him not to indulge in grief. He listened to their advice but, at the end, simply said, "Alas, alas!"

What becomes of the house, when the lights are out! What is the value of a twig deprived of its floral treasure? What good is served by a tank, in which there is no supply of water? What is the value of the body without life? And how does the hole look when its pigeon has fled away? Like all these and worse than all, is a man's house, deserted by his wife.

[1] On the Dasami day the image of Durga is thrown into a river or some adjacent ank.

"Am I not like a bird, whose mate has been killed by the arrow of a hunter ? Alas, who has taken away the diamond of my heart, worth seven times the value of this my kingdom ? What shall I do with it and with my riches ?" Thus did the king lament day and night. He would not touch food, nor drink water.

Adhar Chandra sings this song of sorrow. The grief of the Raja was so great that the very stone melted at the sight.

The Raja walked by the sides of the tank, and sometimes with vacant look entered the deep jungly land of Durgapur, foolishly believing that he might perchance meet his queen there. But days and weeks rolled by ; she no more appeared before him. " What is the good of this nice hall with twelve doorways, that I have built ? Woe be to my pleasure-house, built in the midst of a tank, where we enjoyed each other's company in summer ! That house saddens my heart with the sight of its forlornness and desertion."

One month passed in this way. The waters of the tank Kamalāsāgar looked dark and transparent, as on the day when the queen was carried away by the flood. Suddenly an idea came to the king's mind. He called all the divers of the land and ordered them to get down and bale out the water of the tank. " Some evil spirit made me exacavate this tank, which has caused my ruin. O my good men, bale out the entire water with *seyat* (a vessel) so that I may make a last attempt to find her out. Six thousand and four hundred men were employed to empty the tank of its liquid contents. For nine days and nine nights they applied their whole strength to carry out the king's command. But though they employed their whole might, not a hair-breadth of water decreased. The tank remained full as ever. The coolies in terror fled away. The vast body of water, baled out of the tank, flooded the shoals of the river Somāi. All the neighbouring land was drowned and the houses of the poor ryots were swept away. They fled to distant lands in fear. But still the dark waters of that ominous tank did not decrease by an inch. The current of the Somāi flew in a contrary course and the foaming flood reached the very tree-tops. (Ll. 66.)

(7)

Now listen to what transpired next, to add to the wonders of this wonderful tale.

The Raja again dreamt a dream.

There, in the great hall, with twelve doorways, the king was sleeping. In the depth of night, he dreamt a dream. He was half-awake and half-asleep ; and in that semi-conscious condition it appeared that he vividly saw his queen slowly approach him and take her seat by the side of the pillow, on which rested his head. The queen spoke :—

" O my dear lord, listen to my sad tale. I am passing my days in the nether world in great sorrow.

A sound sleep in the night gives refreshment to the soul. I never enjoy the blessings of such a sleep.

When one's baby is near its mother, how happy she is!

How cool is a sweet mat in the summer and how happy one feels, when, in a dark room, light comes suddenly to dispel the darkness!

Sweeter than all this is the company of a husband to a woman!

I have lost both my husband and my child. How miserable am I! I am maddened with grief, like a wild bird, desiring to break open the bars of its cage, I yearn to break through my present environment and have my child once more near my bosom! How can I live without him!

Now, my beloved, kindly fulfil my wishes, of which I am going to tell you. Build a house on a side of the tank. Let the maid-servant Suā spend the night in that house with my child, mentally wishing for my return. Let not even the tailor-bird, nor a fly, know of this. Everything should be done secretly. Let not the citizens have any inkling of this. I will come to see the child in the deep hour of the night if this is done. For one full year you must not shed a single drop of tear for me. I will come every night and suckle the child. After one full year both of us will meet again, and if, for this one year, I can suckle the child every night, it will grow to be as powerful as Indra, the god of heaven."

There she stood before him, — not a whit stouter, not a whit thinner, exactly as she was before. Her complexion shone with the same lovely grace; — the same flame-coloured *saḍi* she wore; the very ornaments that once adorned the body of the chief queen added the same lustre to her graceful figure. Her flowing *saḍi* waved in the air, playing with her dishevelled hair as before, and her eyes bore the mild light of stars, as before. The same sweet voice — the perennial delight of the king's ears, — sounded like the musical note of the cuckoo.

The Raja awoke from his sleep wiih a start and looked around. He had already become half-mad for grief. But from that day it appeared that he completely lost his senses. The interview was in the land of dreams. Could it ever be brought within the range of realisation?

(Ll. 1-38.)

(8)

When the morning dawned, he gave orders to his men to build a spacious house on one side of the tank. The architects prepared strong posts of the *sāl*-wood and the roof was covered with straw of the *ulu*-species. They built the house in one day, as the order of the king was to have it done with the utmost promptitude. The walls were covered with fine mats and were so thick that even a fly could not enter. There was not a pore left, through which an ant could pass, though it was a straw-bungalow. In the day-time not a streak of light could penetrate into the hall, nor the wind had any access there by night. Thus was the house made, packed like a box. In the centre of the hall was a bedstead of ivory. A valuable mat was spread over it, with a goodly curtain and a number of pillows. A fan of mica and a pitcher, full of water, were placed by the side of the bed. The bungalow was furnished with all necessary things, required for a sleeping room. In a corner, burnt a lamp, fed by butter.

The Raja sent the nurse Suā there with the child on the very first night. A betel-box was supplied her. There was, besides, a supply of sandal and sweet-scented *chua* and the bed was milk-white. Many a night came and passed away ; and one day the Raja asked the maid-servant, " Have you, O nurse, observed anytning happen any of these nights ?" The maid-servant replied in slow accents, " Strange sight I see my lord every night, the queen comes and suckles the child at the deep hour of night. The figure is exactly the same, not a whit stouter, not a whit thinner is she. The same bright and lovely colour,—the same curly hair, waved by air, the same ornaments, adorning her person, and the same flame-coloured *saḍi* which she used to wear. She spends the whole night with the child and suckles it. It is she, I solemnly avow to you, my lord,—your wife, our gracious queen, and none other. The doors are bolted, the windows are shut. In the morning she goes away. Strange, and mysterious are her appearance and disappearance. I cannot find out how she comes and goes. (Ll. 1-38.)

(9)

The Raja, who had been known for his wisdom, acted foolishly that day. He asked the nurse to come to the new house with the child that day before nightfall. Only a day had remained to complete the year and the Raja missed a great opportunity, losing his patience for that one day.

In a golden box were preserved betels, scented *aguru*, *chuā* and sandal. The nurse came to the room with the child, rather early that day. She shut all the windows and doors. On the bed she slept with the baby.

In the midnight the Raja did not find any peace of mind. He had not a wink of sleep that night. Slowly did he come out of his great hall and wandered about the side of the tank. The moon and the stars glanced at him from the sky. He slowly approached the new bungalow. There he saw flower-plants, standing still with their soft-petalled treasure and not gaily playing with the air. People all around were merged in deep sleep. The citizens slept soundly in that vast town, but its lord had no sleep in his eyes. He bemoaned his lot, walking to and fro like a mad man.

The cuckoo suddenly sent a shriek through the sky and left its nest. At that hour the Raja lost his sense. (Ll. 1-22.)

(10)

Who ever saw a stone at the top of a mountain, which could illuminate, by its brilliance, all the fourteen regions of this universe? Who ever saw a lamp, so bright, that, lighted in one house, it could dispel the darkness of all the houses in the world? The sun is that brilliant stone and that great lamp. He, the Lord of the day, bathed in the Eastern Sea and found a chariot ready for him. He would presently ascend the chariot and begin his journey through the world. The horses of that chariot were milk-white and their wings were fire-red. The speed of the horses surpassed that of the winds. So quick it was that they could scarcely be seen. The palaces of the great luminary were made of mica, which sparkled like fire. The god of the day was about to ascend his chariot—he was going to meet his consort, the Dawn.

At that hour of junction of day and night, the Raja stood at the gate of the new house with his hair loose and wild. He cried hoarsely, "O nurse, open the door and show me but once my queen." At the sound of his foot-step, the queen herself came out, opened the door and stood before him.

"O my life!"—more the king could not say but clasped the queen to his breast.

The Queen.

"O my beloved, O my king! Allow me to depart and leave my hands. The period of my curse is over. I must go back to the abode of the gods, from where I came."

Saying so, the queen freed herself from his embrace and disappeared. The Raja, when he rose from his stupor, found a fragment of her flame-coloured *saḍi* in his hand,—this was torn in his attempts to keep her.

Adhar Chand, the poet, is sorry and laments thus :—
"Why, Oh Raja, did you become impatient? Else, your son, the prince would have been as powerful as Indra, the God of heaven." (Ll. 1-22.)

THE END.

THE ADVENTUROUS CAREER OF A YOUNG DACOIT.

PREFACE.

"The adventurous life of a young dacoit" was collected by Babu Behari Lal Ray from Mymensing and sent to me on the 22nd of September, 1925. The ballad is called "Maniktārā" in some localities, after the name of its heroine. Babu Behari Lal Ray wrote to me that he took infinite pains to collect it from different places of the district. It is complete in three parts, of which the first part only was secured by him. "The remaining two parts," wrote Behari Lal on the 22nd of September, 1925, "will take some time to collect, as it will involve journeys of a difficult nature; for the minstrels who know it live in widely distant localities." Two days after, on the 25th of September, Behari Lal died of failure of heart all on a sudden. He had been suffering for a long time from chronic fever, and the task to which the University appointed him required him to tour in unhealthy places of mofussil in his very delicate state of health. He died in harness, as it were, having worked till the last day of his life in the cause of the collection of old Bengali ballads.

It is very doubtful if the remaining parts of this ballad will ever be collected in future. I do not know from what villages Behari Lal had collected the first part. I expected that, as usual, he would furnish me with such information, later on. But there is no means, now available, to ascertain the localities where this ballad is sung. I will, of course, try my best to collect the remaining parts.

This ballad does not seem to be a very old one. Though it is composed in a colloquial language, spoken by the rustics of the backward villages of Eastern Bengal, and there is no attempt at embellishing it by felicitous classical words, yet the rhyme seems to be more regular than that of our earlier ballads. The words here are rugged and coarse, befitting the illiterate peasantry of Eastern Bengal; but the lines conform to the regular cæsura and pauses of the *Payār* metre, though they do not always follow the canon of 14 letters a line. The classic influence had reached the masses at the time of the composition of this ballad so far as to produce a rough impression of the developed *Payār*-metre on the rustic poet,—which accounts for the somewhat crude regularity of its measured metrical sound. But the ballad was composed certainly before the advent of the English. There is no indication of any European influence in it and no trace of western ideas in the description of village-life. Trade was carried on, at the time, chiefly by a system of barter and we find the currency of a very large number of *cowries* in ordinary transactions of life. A ferry-boat, for instance, sometimes charged as much as 12,800 *cowries* from each passenger, which shows scanty or no use of coins in those days in our villages (Canto I, Ll. 37-43). This state of things existed before the country passed into the hands of the British. The villages of Bengal and her rivers, in those days, were haunted by gangs and the passengers feared the pirates more than the wild storm that raged in the waters of the dreaded Brahmaputra. All this takes us to the declining days of the Muhammadan rule, when the Imperial power was not adequate to cope with the revolting chiefs or even the marauding gangs, who oppressed the people, unchecked and fearless. This ballad was composed not later than the middle of the 18th century.

Women of those days were sometimes expert archers; nay, they even learnt wrestling and other masculine games—a fact which we find proved not only by evidences of the ballads but also from various other circumstances. We have found in the ballad of Feroz Khan how Sakhina fought in the field of Kella Tazpur against the Imperial Army in the 17th century.

There are very many other curious facts on which the ballad throws light. The mode of operation of the robbers,—how they killed innocent wayfarers,—how, with the help of ropes, tied secretly to the ferry-boats, they made escapes with their booty after the boats were made to capsize in the big rivers with passengers and how the booty was buried underground,—all these are vividly drawn in interesting sketches.

We have found names of two poets in the colophons of the ballads—*viz.*, Amir and Jamait Ulla. Both of them write in the same strain and it is difficult to find any special feature by which the composition of the one may be distinguished from that of the other. By far the greater portion of the ballad is the composition of Jamait Ulla, and Amir has so wonderfully adapted his composition to the style of the other poet that the ballad, as a whole, shows a compactness and homogeneity in style and diction. I am at times led to believe that Amir is the name of the minstrel, who sang the ballad at one time. We find it on occasions that the rhapsodists sometimes put their names in the colophon claiming the dignity of authorship. It is rather difficult to say anything definite on the point, until we get some more recensions of the ballad.

The chief excellence of this ballad does not lie in its poetry, though occasionally we meet with passages of much ingenuity; nor is the ballad noted for any dramatic quality. It is more like a narrative, giving details of the life of some of its chief characters,—the main compliment being due to the graphic domestic and social sketches with which the ballad abounds. Though the accounts of particular episodes are long, they are not wearisome or verbose, so that there is a sustained interest, preserved from the beginning to the end. The poets display a good deal of humour in many passages. The portraiture of the physician Tinkari (Canto IV, Ll. 80-96) is drawn with considerable skill. The quaintness of the country-dialect, with its pointed and forcible words, sometimes verging on the slang, gives to the figure of the village-quack an amusing interest, hardly conveyed in my translation. The much-vaunted efficacy of the three pills, one blue, one red and one white,—the ingredients with which they are to be swallowed, the physician's diagnosis and the almost immediate failure of his prognostications are meant to hold the physicians as a class up to ridicule. During the Muhammadan times, all references to physicians in our literature are ungracious and even acrimonious. I do not know how to account for this sarcastic treatment of physicians as a class. In the Chaitanya Bhagavata, written towards the end of the 16th century, Chaitanya Deva is represented as satirising the physician Murari Gupta over his knowledge of drugs and pills, though the latter was a profound scholar. Kavikankan about this time gives a sketch of physicians which is far from complimentary. His great European contemporary, Bacon, wrote in his essays, "Physicians cure diseases as the sailors bring wind by whistling." The thing is that in good old days the countrypeople-believed more in the rules of diet and habit for preserving their robust health than in the physician and in his patents. In the present case, the use of tamarind as a sequel to swallowing pills prescribed by the physician is significant. It suggests the conclusion that the village-doctor often used poisonous drugs and it is well-known that tamarind is an antidote to poison. The village-people would not wait patiently for their cure for a reasonable time. When they paid something to the doctor, they wanted instantaneous cure. I know a physician, who was once assaulted by the illiterate relations of a patient in a distant village of Tipperah, because he had taken a rupee but could not effect the remission of fever in three days. On my asking how his predecessor in the profession was so popular with the village-folk, the physician said, "He was a quack, sir. He used *mitha bish* (poisonous drug), the result of which was immediate remission of fever. In order to prevent the patient's temperature coming down to a sub-normal point or his succumbing to the effect of poison, tamarind and other antidotes were prescribed. If the patient died in spite of them, the good name of the physician still remained intact. The village-people would say that the treatment was all right, that the doctor caused a remission of fever by his potent drug, but that the fellow died of sheer weakness, as he was destined to die. These villages do not require a physician, sir, they want quacks."

The poet Jamait Ulla sometimes aims his humorous attack at some vulnerable points of Hindu rituals with considerable effect (Canto VI, Ll. 24-30).

The love-scene introduced in Canto V (Ll. 36-108) breathes an air of vigorous country-spirit and freedom without showing any trait of undignified coquetry or lack of feminine modesty in the heroine. Life, in the lower stratum of society in Bengal is even now sometimes healthier than in the upper grades. This will be evident from many passages of the ballads. The characters are bold, natural and full of the vigour of life. There is of course wickedness rampant in the incidents of the story ; the hero himself is a notorious robber-chief and the heroine, too, so far as we can guess from this part of the ballad, is one of his accessories. While taking recourse to stratagems and manœuvres for achieving wicked ends or engaged in a piece of daring and downright robbery, Kanu and Vashu are undaunted figures, whose actions are characterised by a superabundance of masculine energy, untrammelled by any hesitancy or wavering. Maniktārā's character is just rising into prominence in this part, indicating the future achievement of some superb point of glory; but we have not yet secured material to see its flowering point. As the ballad is sometimes called by the name of Maniktārā, we believe that the heroine cut a prominent figure towards the end.

While the accounts of villainous deeds, perpetrated by the hero and his colleagues become sickening to a degree, the character of Vashu's mother, sketched in a few lines, redeems the atmosphere and shows what spiritual grace and moral apprehensions adorn the character of our country-women. Vashu was dearer to her than life; yet when she heard of his wicked adventure, she sighed and said that it would have given her a greater relief to behold the corpse of her son than to see him turn a robber (Canto 4, Ll. 71-72). Her great grief at the discovery of her son's villainy blasted her life and she died of a broken heart.

This ballad has many points in common with a modern romance, though its authors were thoroughly illiterate and belonged to an age when romantic narratives of this kind were not generally composed.

This ballad is complete in 832 lines. I have divided it into ten cantos.

16th November, 1925. D. C. S.

The Adventurous Life of a Young Dacoit.

(1)

Direct to the north from here is a river. But 'river' is a poor name for this vast reservoir of water—looking like seven (mythical) seas, blended together. This vast sheet of water is called the Brahmaputra. It seems as if a Brahmadaitya (the fabled goblin) roars night and day from the bottom of the river. How grand is the river to behold !

One may see its bank from the *Ganja-ghat*, but the other bank is beyond the range of human ken. It seems that the river has one boundary-line, but has none to indicate the other side.

When storm blows over it, the ordinary boatman dares not steer his boat across the river. The waves, high as house-tops, fall and break, foaming furiously.

The little tailor-birds leave their nests and scream over it, struck with fear. Many a tree is observed floating down the stream, drifting towards the eastern hills.

But this turbulent temper is set at rest, when no storm blows over the stream. Then one may see it running a quiet course, without sound,—smoothly flowing from bend to bend—when through its transparent water the boatmen and rowers are seen merrily plying their boats and pinnaces. When the air is still, the river has scarcely a ripple on its surface but looks plain like a flat can.

On the bank of the river is a landing-place named *Ganjer-ghat*, and close to this, there is a mart, known as the *Ganjer-hāt*, held regularly thrice a week. The mart is a flourishing one, astir with brisk traffic. People every day assembled there, having crossed the river by the help of ferry-boats. They came to the mart in the morning, hired a house for the day and after making purchases, cooked their meals and passed the night in the house and departed the next morning. Hundreds of such ferry-boats and small fishing canoe-shaped vessels might be seen day and night, carrying men to the mart.

These boatmen are recklessly bold—they do not care a fig for storm or wind. When the river is furious, they face it like bold soldiers and when, as ill luck would have it, their boats capsize, they do not fear at all to meet with a watery grave.

They charge heavily from passengers. Heaps of cowries—regular hills of them—the passengers have to pay to the boatmen, in return for the risky service, rendered by the latter, namely, carrying them across the river. I will calculate the charge in detail. One *pan* is equal to 80 *cowries*, and a *kahan* is equal to 16 *pans*. A passenger is required to pay 10 *kahans* (12,800 cowries) per trip. Even after this heavy charge is met, their lives are not secure in the boats. Some are carried safe to the other bank of Sherpur by the grace of God, but instances are not few when passengers get drowned. From *Ganjer-hāt* to Sherpur, as already stated, the ferry-charge is 10 *kahans*. Hence this port of the river is called *Dashakahaniā*.

The ferry-boats have also other dangers to face. Thieves often rob the passengers of their money and jewels, and before they can reach Sherpur, they are sometimes cruelly murdered by wicked gangs. Among these boatmen, however, all are not dishonest; but many of them feel no scruple whatsoever in thrusting their knives into the breasts of people and seizing their property, even in broad daylight. Sometimes they forcibly plunder all jewels and other valuables of the passengers; they take them to the very heart of some dark and shady jungle, and leave their poor victims there, all naked and in abject forlornness. Sometimes these dacoits cut the throats of these people by sharp swords, sometimes they rend their skulls by strokes of axe and fling their body into the river, binding them, hand and foot, with ropes. They seize the valuables and ornaments from the persons of their victims and loot their property by breaking open their trunks and baskets. All these are duly made over to the leader of the gang. (Ll. 1-56.)

(2)

Close to the *Ganjer-hāt* lived a barber, named Vishu, who had, at one time, pursued the avocation of a boatman. He had his wife and five children. So poor was he that he had not a cowrie in his hand, to provide his family with food and raiments. He could not secure a bundle of straw for repairing the roof of his little house or wooden posts for fixing the thatch-walls.

Vishu, in his distress, had no other resource, left to him, than to live by begging. But even though his wife, too, became a beggar, their joint earnings were quite inadequate. Of the five sons, Vashu was the eldest, aged twelve, but he had not yet learnt any trade. Then came disaster upon disaster on the poor family. The second son Kushai unfortunately got drowned in the Brahmaputra. The third Dāshu was one day carried off by a crocodile from near the landing-ghat. The fourth one, in his attempt to climb a tree, fell down on the earth and died of a mortal wound that he had got by his fall. The youngest suffered long from infantile diseases, till he, too, was finally relieved of all trouble by the hands of death.

Vishu became almost blind with tears. Many a time he blamed his Maker for creating him and found fault with His dispensation.

"You have made me a poor wretch without a cowrie in my hand. We starve for want of diet—which no doubt you can see. You were gracious enough to grant me a valued treasure in my children. When the five children would talk, their merry voices would make me forget, for the time, the stings and anguishes of poverty. Now all the lights you have put out, save only one. I do not know when that one, also, you will take away. This Vashu of mine is the only lamp of the house. If this, too, is blown out, it will be all over with me.

"Alas, thou cruel Sporter, why dost thou play with human heart in this manner? If thou gavest them out of thy grace, why hast thou taken them away again? Thou hast no regard for the feelings of the old parents. I cannot bear my grief. Why dost not thou, O God, take me away from this world, to heal my bruised heart for ever?"

Often would he sit on the bank of the river and lament in this way. He became so absorbed in grief that he forgot that it was a treacherous bank, which, yielding to the force of the under-current, would sometimes crumble down unwares; and one day while thus grieving, the ground beneath his feet gave way and fell into the bosom of the river with a violent crash. The boatman Vishu was drowned in this way.

Losing her husband after all the bereavements she had already suffered, Vishu's wife became almost insane with grief.

"All the grim sufferings of poverty I bore with patience, picking up strength at the sight of my husband. I have now lost him, too. I will hang myself on a tree in yonder jungle and put an end to all this misery. If I cannot hang myself, there is the cool breast of the river, where I will find rest, as my husband has done."

Grieving in the above manner, she left her home and went towards the neighbouring forest. Vashu, at this time, called "mamma" from behind. She turned her eyes back and saw the lovely face of her son. The sight filled her heart with affection. She forgot the great bereavement and also that she had nothing to eat at home. Amir, the poet, says, "Why should you now give up your life? Return, O mother, to your cot and wipe away your tears."

The widow, with her young son, begged from door to door, and kind-hearted men doled away small gifts in charity. She did not leave her cot, nor her little son. Like a bird, hatching its young one under its wings, she attended to her charge with utmost devotion.

(Ll. 1-58.)

(3)

Near her little cot lived fishermen and Kochas. She had no kinsman, no relation, in the neighbourhood. No parents had she, nor any brother, under whose roof she might expect to live for a few days.

One, who is deprived of all help from outside, receives help from unexpected quarters. From among the Kochas, a woman, whom people called Kanu's mother, came forward, full of compassion at her distress. Vashu's mother and Kanu's mother became bound in fast friendship. Kanu's mother considered this friendship as god-send to her. Kanu and Vashu were nearly of the same age, Kanu being older by three years only. Kanu had stepped into his twentieth year; streaks of thin moustache had just appeared on his chin. He became now Vashu's guide and friend in all matters, leading him sometimes to evil ways. Vashu's mother tried to dissuade him, but he heeded not his mother's advice.

Obliged as she was to Kanu's mother for pecuniary help, rendered now and then, she could not too strongly insist on her son's dissolving all connections with Kanu.

The heart of Kanu's mother was full of kindness for her friend, and Vashu's mother knew this very well.

She prepared almost every day some dainty dishes to entertain Vashu's mother. Seldom did she visit her friend when in her towel she did not tie some pulses or rice for her, nor brought a little cup filled with oil. Fresh brinjals, chillies and fruits of garden—she brought every now and then and presented to Vashu's mother. Behind her house were large pastures, where she used to milk the buffaloes and this she stored in bamboo-cups and brought to Vashu's mother as her little gift from day to day.

Vashu's mother, however, did not sit idle, relying on her friend's help, but worked as best as she could. She spun thread for the nets of fishermen and husked rice; this she did not consider beneath her dignity, though she earned only a little by these stray occupations. Sometimes she got a quantity of rice-dust and at others some small fishes by her own labour.

She spent her days in this way, feeding herself all the while with the hope that her child Vashu would soon grow into manhood and relieve her of all her sufferings. "Then will our wants be removed and we shall once more be blessed with prosperity and happiness," thus did she think within herself.

Now Vashu became a strong lad of twenty. He delighted in sports, jumped and played in the village-paths and woods like a wild horse. Kanu, the *Koch*, became his *guru* and Vashu, the barber, became Kanu's worthy disciple. They two were utterly reckless and feared not men or beasts. They walked about, twisting their moustache in truly gallant fashion.

Behind Vashu's cot there were some fig-trees. The people of the locality said that these trees were haunted and hence no one dared enter the wood land at night for fear of being molested by ghosts.

One midnight when Vashu's mother was enjoying a sound sleep, she became suddenly disturbed by a voice which awoke her from sleep.

"Arise, O Vashu's mother, and look at the sky. You consider that your cot is very secure with its wooden posts and thatches. Not at all. If the storm comes, those will be shattered in no time and your cot will be swept away from the earth, leaving no trace of its existence. Then, O Vashu's mother, where will you put your head and find a refuge?"

The barber-woman became frightened. She caught hold of her sleeping son and held him tightly in her arms. Then gathering a little courage, she addressed the voice, which she believed to be a ghost's and said:—

"In this depth of night you are calling me from behind this house. Who may you be? If my cot is to be swept away by inclement winds, what can I do to prevent it? How can I resist my ill-luck? God has taken away my children, one by one, and I know not if more evils are in store for me. But is it worthy on your part to joke with a woman in her distress, living in this shattered cot?"

"But, aunt, why should you be angry with me? You seem not to have known me. Your son Vashu calls me Kanu Dada. I am his companion and friend and my mother, too, has been bound fast in solemn ties of friendship with you. I expect you to regard me as your son. Why should you be angry with one, who knows and respects you as his mother? I have got some work to do at this dead hour of night. Many ripe fruits are there in the woody-land. I have come to take Vashu with me to gather those and eat them at ease together. Do not fear, aunt. Just look at the sky, the wind has blown away the storm that had filled the sky a little before the black clouds, that had darkened the atmosphere,—have all gone away and left the sky bright and clear. Rouse Vashu, Oh dear aunt, from his sleep and let him accompany me."

The barber-woman was ashamed of her conduct and regretted having used rude words to her friend's son. She changed her tone and said in an apologetic voice, "How could I know, dear Kanu, that you were seated on that haunted tree. I was sleeping and was in a semi-conscious state, when I spoke unkind words to you. Do not, dear Kanu, take offence, and you must also excuse me for not complying with your request. I cannot allow Vashu to go out of the house at this hour of midnight. You know that Vashu is to me what the prop is to a blind man. He is dearer far than a rib of my breast. While I walk in the village-paths, it is his lovely face which I recollect and thus do I gather strength to bear the hard lot of day-time. In the night he is my treasure, and I cannot spare him for a moment. Come in the morning and I will allow him to go with you wherever you may wish to take him."

When she was speaking, Vasu was roused from his sleep by his mother's voice. He said to his mother, "With whom, mother, are you talking in this lonely hour of midnight ?"

Vashu's Mother.

"Kanu has come ; he has climbed up that haunted fig-tree and is talking from there."

At these words of his mother, Vashu at once sprang up from his bed and opening the door of his hut, ran towards Kanu and soon overtook him ; and having embraced Kanu, he asked him in all eagerness, "Why, brother, what is the reason that has made you visit this house of ours at night ? "

Kanu replied, "I came to take you with me, but your mother is not willing to part with you. There is the difficulty."

Vashu said, "Don't, brother Kanu, worry yourself about that. I am presently going with you and what you have got to eat I will share with you."

He said to his mother, "Arise, mother, shut the door. A brother is going with his brother. Why should there be any foolish anxiety over this ? "

Vashu left home with Kanu. Vashu's mother spent the remaining hours of the night in sleepless anxiety.

Struck with fear and anxiety, she lamented thus :

"You came to this cot, Oh cruel boy, like an enemy to steal away the peace of my mind ! Your face is my only consolation. I hide you like a treasure in my breast. But, foolish lad, you have treated me like a beast or a savage and cast me away without any respect for my feeling." "Oh Sylvan deity, I pray unto you, keep my boy safe and secure. I will worship you with fried oat, molasses and rice. My prayer to you, Oh Goddess Subachani,. is to keep my boy safe and I will worship you with betel and betel-nuts."

Just at that moment an owl screamed from an adjacent tree-top. Vashu's mother, in all haste, prayed the bird to stop its ominous moping. "I will roast a *Boâl*-fish for you, Oh black owl, and also burn a *shail*-fish to offer you, if, through your grace, he, the treasure of my heart, returns home all hale and hearty."

Vashu's mother wept all night, lamenting in this strain. I have no adequate words to describe her grief. It was when the raven cawed from the house-top, indicating the advent of morn that her eyes closed, yielding to the influence of sleep. (Ll. 1-100.)

(4)

Walking to a considerable distance, Kanu sat under a tree and disclosed his object to Vashu.

"You know the old Brahmin and his aged wife, who live in a hired house on yonder river-bank. They are going to cross the river. and go to the other bank before it dawns. I shall have to carry them thither in the ferry-boat belonging to Sona, the boatman. You must be my companion in my trip; so hurry up, lad, lest the night should pass away."

Vashu.—"Why should Sona, the boatman, make over the charge of his boat to you? The hire he might enjoy himself? Why should he give up his share?"

Kanu.—"Oh dear boy, you do not know, for these four or five days Sona Majhi has been down with fever; for another four or five days, his boat-hooks will remain fixed to the ground, as there is none to ply it.

"Now hear my plan. I will carry the old Brahmin-couple in the boat, and somehow the boat will capsize near the treacherous sands of the river at Ganjer hāt. I had a peep into his gold mohurs, ornaments and other valuables last evening. They are indeed a tempting sight."

Vashu.—"But, brother, it is all right; when the boat will capsize we two together, with all the valuables, will get drowned, as well, in the mid-river. The sands are treacherous there; no one can escape from them, if one gets plunged. How will you save the things and how will our lives be saved?"

Kanu.—"Do not worry yourself over that. I have thought over the problem and hit upon a solution. I went to the fisherman Sambhu this evening and procured a strong rope from him. One end of the rope will be fixed to the trunk of a *Simul*-tree on the bank and the other end will be fixed to a raft made of banana-plants. I will loosen the rope in the middle and the raft will float behind our boat at some distance without attracting notice. When we shall have done our work, we will return home by means of the raft. We will plunder the jewellery and other things and with them plunge into the river, after having broken open the lower planks of the boat with an axe. The old Brahmin will verily shake his beard like a goat, while bidding adieu to the earth. In the meantime, we will drag the rope of the raft, so that in no time we shall be able to reach the bank. When the old woman and the still older man will breathe their last, who will be left there to help the detection of our deed? I will return the rope to Sambhu to-morrow. Well! there will end all matters and there will be none to whisper the grim tale of the night.

"The much desired-for property we will make over to our mothers; and then, dear Kanu, we shall, be placed far above want, and marry two fairies!"

Vashu and Kanu, in a firm attitude, left for Ganjer ghāt, determined to carry out the plan. They led the Brahmin-couple to the bank of the Brahmaputra. Whatever they had planned, they carried out fearlessly. The tragedy was duly enacted and then they returned home with the booty on the raft, being dragged to the bank by means of the rope.

When they returned home, just at that moment vultures shrieked overhead, ravens croaked and other birds and beasts proclaimed by their confused cries the advent of the morning.

Vashu knocked at the door and called out, "Oh mother, awake; Dawn's light is just peeping in. How long will you sleep? Now our misery is at an end; just come and see what I have got. You may now live at perfect ease. No more, mamma, will you have to shed tears, for having no food in the house for your son. Your days of tears and sorrow are over."

The mother, startled at her son's voice, rose from her bed and opened the door. In the meantime Vashu took the load from his head and handed it over to his mother. Vashu's mother said, "What is it that you have got? The contents, if they are food, cannot last for many days. How is it that you are vaunting about this small basket so much?" Vashu replied, "It is no food, mamma; open the basket and see that in it are stored things, which will supply us with food as long as we live." The old woman wonderingly opened the basket and was astonished to find the whole house, illuminated, as it were, by the riches contained in it. The sight struck her with surprise. There in the basket were a number of *Beshars* (nose-ornaments), *jhumkas* (ear-rings) and various other ornaments of flower and fruit patterns, inlaid with precious stones. There were some precious necklaces, head-ornaments, beautiful gold-flowers for ears, also bracelets, lockets and garlands, strung with gold-flowers. There were nice pins and nose-ornaments, studded with pearls and diamonds. In one corner were observed about a hundred golden amulets and other ornaments of various patterns. There were, besides, belts with gold and silver pendants and beautiful *Gujris* for feet. Besides these, there were a large number of gold coins of the days of old emperors, bars of gold and silver of various sizes and golden cups and hair-combs of mica, of which the handles were solid gold. In a bundle lay valuable flame-coloured *Sadis*, which only ladies of the highest ranks wore.

Vashu's mother was wonder-struck, and, with gaping mouth, looked at her son and said, "What are all these things? How could you secure this property of a monarch?"

Then did Vashu relate the whole story from the beginning to the end, and as she heard it, Vashu's mother began to tremble in fear. She said in a sad tone, "What is it, Vashu, that you have done? You have killed a Brahmin, and know for certain that the curse that came out of his lips at the moment of his death will blast away all our future happiness. The lamp of our house will burn no more. There will be no children born in a house, cursed by a Brahmin, to light the evening lamp. If you were dead just after your birth, it would have been much better for me than to see you turn a robber. I sincerely wish now that you be drowned. Your death will indeed give me some relief."

She began to shed incessant tears. In the meantime Vashu took care to bury the treasure under ground. For the whole day Vashu's mother did not eat a single morsel of food, and, in great anger, did not speak to her son. When it dawned, her eyes appeared abnormally dull, sunk in their sockets; and a fever seized her, making her body dark as charcoal. For five or six days, she remained in her bed without any food and without speaking a word. The neighbours were full of sympathy and said, "Your mother has suffered much in her life. Try your best to place her under proper medical treatment."

Tinkari was a great physician in that locality. Vashu walked ten hours and reached his house. Vashu called on him and said in a hurry, "O doctor, my mother is passing through a great crisis. You must accompany me at once to my house." Tinkari, the physician, dressed himself decently and in the corner of his *chudder* tied some medicine. He took his long stick in hand and spread a big umbrella over his head. Before starting, he bowed to the sacred *Tulsi* plant in his house. The physician was of a dark complexion. His body seemed to have been polished by constantly rubbing oil over it. He had a flat nose and his whiskers were cut short. But his feet bore marks of sore on account of his having to walk along the uneven village-paths. His eyes were small and he looked around like a pigeon, as he walked. At times, he stumbled over the hard ground; but anyhow he reached Vashu's house in due time. Reaching the patient's house, the doctor said, "Only three pills, Vashu;—these will cure your mother, I assure you. To-day you are to give her bark of *bel* and *nim*-leaves, well boiled in water, to-morrow give her some spices boiled in hot water. On the third day you are to give her that red pill, mixed with a few drops of country-wine, and the day after, you are to give her that blue pill with cold water, and on the day next, you are to administer the white one. This will bring her round, rest assured. When the fever subsides, give her a hot bath, and then she may be allowed to take rice of a very fine quality. But when you will give her the white pill, you must also give her the broth of tamarind to drink."

Vashu took the pills and the physician said, "Now I must depart." Vashu gave him one *kulá* of rice and a basketful of pulses. From his orchard, he gathered some brinjals, chillies and bananas. He gave him, besides, some turmeric and salt and also a cupful of oil. The doctor was right glad, and smiling, left his house. In the evening of that day, Vashu's mother opened her eyes and looked at her son. That was her last and she left Vashu for ever and went straightway to the other world, whence her call had come.

(Ll. 1-112.)

(5)

Vashu took his mother's dead body on his shoulders and went to the river-ghat. There, in conformity with the usage of the Hindus, he first set fire to his mother's mouth and then floated the corpse in the stream. He then returned home and wept bitterly. In the whole world the barber-lad Vashu had none other than a mother to call his own and she, too, now left him for ever. Many a time did he lament, saying, "In this country, I will live no more. I must go to some foreign land. There I will live by begging from door to door. It is my crime that shocked my mother and thus caused her death. I cannot bear the stings of repentance. Grieving over her, I will give up this sinful body of mine."

For four or five days, he did not stir out but continually wept in his lonely room. Kanu and his mother visited his house frequently and tried to console him. By the healing influence of time, Vashu once more applied himself to his work. His occupation now became definitely settled. He used to kill the wayfarers by the blow of his long club and plunder whatever they possessed. Day and night Vashu and Kanu pursued this avocation, bound in brotherhood, and sometimes in the night, Vashu returned home, cooked his own meal, ate the same and went to bed in that lonely house.

On an auspicious day, fixed by astrologers, Kanu married a suitable bride and Kanu's mother now advised Vashu to be on the look out for a bride. "You burn your hands in cooking your own meals, my lad, and sometimes you have to live upon raw *chira*. You have been reduced to a skeleton and you know no peace of mind. About six miles from this place, there is a village called Mainda. There lives an honest man named Sadhu Sil. I have heard that he has got a real fairy in his daughter. Her name is Māniktārā. She is exquisitely handsome. Why not go to that village one day and open negotiations? And it may be that, by the grace of God, you will be happy by this marriage, if you can win her hands."

Being advised by Kanu's mother in this way, Vashu realised his situation and thought that it was a good advice. He resolved to go to Mainda the next morning. When it was morning, Vashu dressed himself decently. The day was very hot, it being the month of April. He covered his body with a *chudder* to protect it from the Sun, when he reached the village, it was about 2 P.M. He was perspiring and sorely feeling the heat. Close by, flowed a canal with transparent water in rapid course. The women of the village came over there with their pitchers to carry water. On one side of the canal were rows of beautiful houses, but on the other side there was none. So Vashu sat under a *Simul*-tree. He breathed heavily and looked with thirsty eyes at the stream. He felt a desire to drink water, and so came down the landing-steps. Just at the time a maiden came from the other side. On her breast was a fine towel of green-coloured cotton and her hair was dishevelled, which waved playfully at her back. The hair was so long that it nearly touched her ankles. The coy maiden bent her eyes towards the earth and descended to the stream. She was quite unaware that Vashu was on the other side. Vashu, while drinking water, looked at her and felt as if a fairy had come down from the heaven. Vashu himself was a youth of handsome features and he felt love for the maiden at first sight. The girl, as she looked at him, became pleased with his handsome appearance. In her mind for the first time grew that passion, which, to maidenly souls was a novel experience, full of sweetness. Appeasing his thirst, Vashu the barber-lad, went back to the shade of the *Simul*-tree, but with crooked glance, looked again and again at the stream of Bailākhali. He reflected thus, "This girl is assuredly not a human being. She must be a nymph of heaven, I must try to know who she is." Thus resolved he addressed the maiden in a gentle voice and she was right glad at his words, standing on the other bank.

"Who are you, gentle maiden, all alone here, at this hour? Verily is your face like the moon. How beautiful do you look with sweats on your brow. The transparent water of the Bailākhali is playing with the flowing ends of your *Saḍi*. Your lovely figure produces an ebb and flow in my blood. Your black hair is to be compared only with the black tip of the *Kuch*-fruit. Your lovely brows delight my eyes with their gentle curves. Your two black eyes throw their dart by sweet glances, which make a human being tremble as if shot by an arrow. How happy are you, O stream of Baliākhali! you seem to be so cheerful because you have got her sweet embrace. Thanks to this shade of the *Simul*-tree, from where I have obtained a glimpse of you. With sacred blades of grass and rice, I will worship you." Pausing for a few moments he again addressed the maiden, "You are not a fairy, nor a nymph, nor any spirit of the air. I have known you by your moon-like face. I remember to have seen you in the landing-ghat of the mart; and to-day I see you here in the stream of the Bailākhali. It now seems that my good luck has to-day given me my goddess, who is to adorn my house.

"Who are you, maiden, and whose daughter are you? You have cast your sweet glances upon me, which have made my head unsteady. I have lost my parents, I have lost my brothers and thus do I survive, —a wretched vagabond. I remember to have seen you some day in a mart near the *Ganjer-ghat*, and to-day you are here,—a piece of unparalleled good luck for me."

Māniktārā.

"All is done by the will of God. Human agencies are powerless. Though God has put you to a trial, that has not diminished, in the least, your worth in my eyes. Sometime ago, I went with my parents to your house. There I saw you in your room, though you did not notice me. Your mother treated me very kindly. She gave me *phul-bātāsā* (sugar-balls) with fried rice of the *binni*-species. She also served me with curd of excellent quality. She took me kindly in her arms and said, "How happy would I be, if I could have you for my daughter-in-law!" My name is Māniktārā and my father's name is Sādhu Sil. If you are willing to have me, I do not think there will be any difficulty in your way."

Vashu.—"I do not know where your house stands on the other side of the canal. Will you point out the path leading to your house?"

Māniktārā.—"There is a ferry there on the eastern side of the canal. On crossing it, you will find a temple dedicated to the Goddess Chandi. That temple and the lands, adjoining to the same, belong to my father."

Māniktārā remained in the bathing-ghat and Vashu hurried towards her home. Reaching there, he called out, "Who is there in the house? May I come in?" Sādhu Sil had just finished his bath. He came out at the voice of a stranger and young Vashu saluted him, when he came near. Sādhu said, "You do not seem to be known to me. Who are you, young man? Where is your home and what is your father's name?"

"My house," said Vashu, "is at the village Ganjer-ghat. My father was Vishu Sil. But my mother and brothers are all dead." Sādhu recognised him after this introduction. He spread a mat in the temple-compound and showed him a warm hospitality. He entered the inner apartments and said to his wife, "The son of Vishu Sil is at our house. I do not know what may be the object of his visit." The good wife said, "Could you not learn why he has come?" "I have not asked that yet," replied Sādhu.

With a pillow in his hand, meant for the repose of his guest, did Sadhu Sil come near Vashu again and ask him the object of his kind visit to his house.

Vashu bent his eyes towards the ground and in a voice half-choked by shame, delivered himself thus, "You know, Sir, that there is none in my house now. All are dead and gone. This is just the time when I should seek for a suitable bride to look after my household. I have come out in search of one, who would take charge of my household. I have heard that you have got a marriageable daughter. I have made myself bold enough to approach you with the proposal. If you would kindly approve of it, I shall be a slave to you all my life."

Sādhu was right glad at his heart at the proposal and went into the inner apartments to discuss the matter with his wife. He smilingly said to his wife, "Mānik-tārā's bridegroom is there in our temple-compound." She replied, "It is a very good proposal. Now make arrangements to entertain him suitably (*lit.* to kindle the hearth)." Sādhu Sil had three sons, but none of them was present at that time. All of them had gone out for fishing. So the old man was in some difficulty. The mistress of the house ordered her second daughter-in-law to cook and the two others were required to do sundry things. "It is nearly noon-tide, already late. Send him some oil for bath." Saying this, the old woman began to look after other things.

Vashu rubbed oil over his body and went to the river for bathing. The second daughter-in-law was cooking and the other two were helping her in the necessary preparations. Just at this moment the eldest son returned home with a big *Rui*-fish in his hand. The second son also appeared shortly after, with some *koi*, *puthi*, *khalishā* and other small fishes. Next came the third son with a basket, full of vegetables, especially one big *chai*-plant. Vashu now came back from the river-ghat and was served with the kernel of cocoanut, fried rice, molasses, sugar-balls and other confectionaries, such as *chirār-moā* and *tiler lāru*. He was, besides, served with the *doa*-fruit, bananas and a cup, full of sweet milk with some sugar. This was light refreshment, which Vashu partook of with avidity and then took a midday-nap in the temple-compound.

The second daughter-in-law was busy preparing the soup of pulses and the male members of the household grew impatient at the delay in preparation. Her brothers-in-law, the younger and elder ones, went to take their bath; but when they returned home after finishing bath, they could not be pleased with what they saw. For, their sister-in-law was still busy with a fork, trying to dissolve the pulses in the hot water; the soup had not yet been prepared. The eldest son's wife sat over the kitchen-knife, dressing the fish; while the youngest of the three wives hurried to the pond to wash the rice. To add to the confusion, the eldest daughter-in-law sustained a wound in her finger from the prickly bone of a *singi*-fish. The mother-in-law administered pepper-paste to the wound. It was midday; but the soup of pulses was not yet ready, and as such, how could it be offered to the bridegroom-elect? The second daughter-in-law, in utter confusion, diligently applied the fork to the yet unboiled pulse-soup for dissolving the peas; and a sound was thus generated, resembling the rattle of a spinning-wheel. Everybody became impatient with hunger. The elder brother-in-law was grumbling over the delay, the younger one was muttering out his discontent; while the old father-in-law sat in greedy expectation,—spotted, like a tiger, all over his body, with sandal-marks. All were dying in hunger, as it were; the husband (the second son) in a rage, rushed into the kitchen and caught his wife by the forelocks. The mother came to the rescue of the daughter-in-law and delivered her from the rude grip of the infuriated son. She then gave her three sons water to drink. The pulse-soup was ready in the meantime, and so was the fish-curry, too, though prepared in a hurry. Seats were spread on the floor of the spacious dining-chamber. The old man of the house, together with Vashu and the three sons, sat on the seats, assigned to them, to eat their dinner. Five plates were placed before the five men. But Sādhu's eyes waxed red in anger, as he looked at the plate that had been offered to Vashu. The old man howled out his strong disapproval of the conduct of the old mistress and the daughters-in-law. "Being women, you do not know the rules of domestic discipline. By your unworthy conduct you will bring about the ruin of my household. My daughter is matchless, all points considered and every virtue reckoned; and you, ignorant hags, have conspired to blast her fortune. What stupidity, first to offer fried fish to a son-in-law! Have you considered the evil that would follow from your conduct? The effect is that the son-in-law becomes half-dead in his father-in-law's house. (Other) sons-in-law taunt him, the mother-in-law maligns, the sisters-in-law torture, and the brothers-in-law despise the poor fellow." [1]

At these words, the guilty matron took the plate in her hand and removed all fried and roasted items of food. Vashu, however, felt it to be a loss, thus to be deprived of the big fried fishes of the *Koi*-species, roasted brinjals, fried potatoes, sesamum-balls, the toasted *ulkis*, flavoured with the paste of split peas and also the overdone *châpati*.

[1] This superstitious belief is still current among the rustic folk of some districts of Eastern Bengal.

"I got the delicacies," he mused within himself, "exactly to my liking, but have been forbidden to take them This, however, augurs the intended matrimony and makes me glad at heart."

Pulse-soup, prepared in combination with fish-heads and herbs of the Bâlai-species, was next served in a good quantity by the youngest daughter-in-law. She also served the *Suktâ* (a sort of slightly bitter vegetable condiment) and the preparation of gourd. She then gave the dried sauce of *khalisha* and *puthi* fishes and also a cupful of half-boiled pulse-soup, prepared with *Mâsha*-peas. Vashu, however, did not take the last-named item, which remained as it was, full in the cup. But another cup, containing the *muga*-soup, prepared in combination with the flavorous heads and bones of Boāl-fish, Vashu emptied over his plate. Another cup, filled with the soup of Boāl-fish, was also served, but this was not much relished on account of its pungency. The broth of Rui-fish, however, together with five pieces of soft fish, was tasted with good appetite. The *murighanta*—a preparation with the head of Rui-fish beaten into fine pieces with a pestle—Vashu smilingly partook of, and in greedy appreciation of the flavour, he ate up the last grain of rice from his plate. The sour gruel of unripe *āmni* was next served, which Vashu sipped up in the fashion of drinking water. A cupful of sweet milk and another cupful of curd were then relished with fried corn (*khai*).

Sādhu became pleased to witness the appetite with which Vashu relished the dinner. Sadhu became thus resolved, "I will give my daughter in marriage to this youth. This is my intent. May the youth be granted a long life! Let the will of God be fulfilled. But I will not disclose anything now."

Dinner finished, the five men left their seats and went to wash their face. Sādhu then, together with his three sons, repaired to the drawing room adjacent to the temple; and when all had seated themselves at ease, Sādhu Sil spoke to Vashu in a soft and slow voice, "Hear me, Vashu, my girl is possessed of all maidenly virtues. She performs all the household duties, inside and outside, with a neatness and dexterity, which would surprise the male members of any house; and there in the sphere of her activities, she would not brook any intermeddling—she must do everything herself. She is verily a paragon of beauty, and the thought, that is indeed uppermost in my mind now, is that of seeking out a suitable groom for her. Who knows what has been decreed by Providence? You see, the difficulty about you is this, that your parents are, neither of them, alive, and as such, how can we entrust our treasure—the very moon on earth—to your care? Whose help will she count upon in your house and who will be her help-mate in restoring order to your household? When, at night, you may be off, rowing your boats in the river, Māniktārā will be all alone in your house and this thought makes me particularly anxious."

But the three sons of Sādhu Sil had already conceived a liking for the youth. They said to their father, "Why, father, what makes you vacillating still? Our eldest sister Panchā is a widow. She is, besides, perplexed with the problem of procuring her bread." Vashu gladly approved of the idea of taking this lady to his house and promised to maintain her as long as she would live. This assurance from Vashu encouraged the old man and he gave something like a half-assent to the proposal. The three daughters-in-law expressed their consent and the mother, too, could not but approve of the proposed matrimony.

The date of celebrating the marriage was fixed sometime early in *Baisakh*. Fried paddy with sweet milk formed the evening-repast of Vashu. And glad at heart, Vashu then donned his *dhuti* and *chudder* and proceeded homewards. (Ll. 1-250.)

(6)

Astrologers were next consulted by Sādhu and an auspicious date was fixed. As for the rest, namely, the future of the match, they could not have any fore-glimpse of that. Fate alone would determine it. The fifth day of *Baisakh* was fixed and Sādhu Sil, with the help of his three sons, set about preparing themselves for the occasion. A toll of three hundred rupees was exacted by Sādhu Sil from his son-in-law, and the celebration duly took place on the 5th of *Baisakh*. The night of marriage was spent in high glee, amidst the festive songs and merry-makings of the three wives of the three brothers and other girls of the village; and on the day following, the customary social banquet was provided.

Vashu started homewards in company with the bride, Māniktārā. While parting, Māniktārā spoke to her mother, "Do not forget, mother, to send for sister Pancha. Her absence on the occasion of farewell-greetings makes me sad at heart. When she will be here, ask her to go to me." On the eve of their departure, Vashu and Māniktārā stood before their superiors; the ladies of the house blessed them with offerings of sacred grass and paddy. The mother, too, pronounced her benedictions, wishing the couple long life and unbroken happiness. She also said to her daughter, "You will be alone there my child, do not neglect your health." Māniktārā shed silent tears; she had no speech to suit the occasion.

"Grieve not, mother; should God keep me safe and sound, I shall return to your arms," she delivered herself in these few words. The mother then stood before Tārā, and performed certain rites which would have the effect of making her beloved of her husband and then threw away a quantity of dust from the hole of a mouse, an observance which symbolises the daughter's formal absolution from the debt she owed to her mother for her sustenance and upbringing.

The poet Shekh Jamatulla enjoys the fun and smilingly remarks, "What would this formality avail? It is a puerile idea. Every single drop of milk, sucked from the mother's breast, binds the child fast in a profound debt of affection and gratitude, which nobody on earth can repay. The scriptures of the Hindus are authoritative indeed. But is this idea very commendable, namely that parental debt may be repaid by means of the gift of a quantity of dust from a rat's hole?"

(Ll. 1-30.)

(7)

Vashu arrived, with his young bride, at Ganjerghat. Not being attended by any procession or party, they entered their house and seated themselves on a bedstead. In the meantime, Kanu's mother arrived there, and Kanu, himself, came, followed by other relatives and neighbours. The wives of the fishermen, too, came there to have a look at the bride, and their object fulfilled, they went away, remarking that the union of the two was suitable and would prove happy and peaceful.

A day passed; another rolled by and thus a fortnight wore away; and Vashu Sil did not, for a day, stir out of his house, leaving his lovely bride alone. One day finishing his mid-day meal, Vashu retired to the shade of an adjacent tree, oppressed by heat and perspiring profusely. The gentle breeze that blew, shaking the leaves of the tree, cooled him and removed the drops of sweat from his body. Tārā, in the meantime, finished her dinner and retiring to her own room, did not find her husband there. She prepared betels, took some of them herself, and taking some in her hand, began to look for him in every part of the house. While, coming out of the house, she looked around, she found him resting beneath the shade of a tree. She then went up there and said, "Lo! how long have I been seeking for you with betels in my hand and having left me alone, you are staying here, gazing at the sky! what default of mine are you pondering over and what has made me guilty in your eyes? Pray tell me, whose love has turned you mad? But hang me first before anything else."

"What do you mean, Tārā, by all this? Have you gone mad? You are the very ribs of my breast—the collyrium-paint of my eyes. There is sweet drinking water, close beneath my lips, and shall I drink the cup of hemlock, rejecting that ambrosial draught?"

"Tell me, please, what wonder in the sky has caught your vision and what thought has kept you gazing heavenwards?"

"Yes, I am telling you, Tārā, what has kept my eyes fixed towards the sky. I mean to catch the Harikal birds by spreading a trap. Twelve species of birds, during the twelve months of the year, build their nests and roost upon the boughs of this tree. I have conceived to-day a longing for the sweet flesh of Harikal birds."

"I cannot quite understand you; my wit fails me. But I am burning within, with an intense desire—I know not how it will be satisfied. If you had a mind to taste the flesh of Harikal birds, why did you not tell me that?

I might have given you necessary instructions about the contrivance of catching the birds. Go to my father's house and tell him, "I want Tārāmani's[1] bow and missiles before night-fall." Vashu forthwith left for his father-in-law's house, anxious for securing the Harikal birds. Tārāmani here sat in the house, constructing arrows to shoot at the birds. She also made a score of earthen bullets; she looked up, at intervals, towards the nest of Harikal birds.

"Come, O Tārā, make haste and take these missiles of yours. But who will discharge them?"

"My bow and missiles I will wield. Will you be satisfied if I can give you those Harikal birds,—yes, a good number of them?"

"Yes, yes, prove your skill by acts. Just kill two of them first. Give me four daily, afterwards, if you can."

Tārā discharged two bullets at a shot and two Harikal birds were struck down and fell, screaming and writhing on earth.

"Bravo," exclaimed Vashu, "Expert indeed you are! Two birds at one shot!"

Tārā said, "Four shots are sometimes discharged from this quadruple-stringed bow; and five animals are sometimes struck down with a single missile. Two Kochas, Daru and Sumaru, lived in my father's house. Hundreds of unruly animals were sent to Death's region by means of their arrows and missiles. They were my teachers in archery and I have learnt much from them. Even if a hundred enemies confront me, they cannot long hold their own before the volleys of Tārā's arrows."

At these words of Tārā, Vasu thought within himself, "How shall I carry on my trade before Māniktārā? My energy shrinks within me and I feel abashed before her

[1] Māniktārā is sometime endearingly called 'Tārā' and 'Tārāmani.'

superior skill." Tārā beheld this and tenderly put this question, "Why, darling, do I find your lovely face so gloomy and pale? Have my words pained you any way?"

"No, Tārā," replied Vashu. "No sorrow do I feel at heart. But one thing I am hiding from your knowledge—which I dare not disclose."

Māniktārā came closer to Vashu and clasping his hands in her own, said, "If you keep it a secret from me, no more shall I take my meal. The matter will one day come to my knowledge, be it to-day or to-morrow. The household cannot run smoothly unless there is mutual understanding between you and me. So, my lord, tell me your secret. I am bound to obey you in all matters and consider myself to be your trusted servant. Why should you not take me into your confidence! Don't you consider me worthy of your trust?" Vashu said, "Who else, then, is to be trusted with my secrets? After meal, I shall make a full disclosure to you."

Tārā made a delicious preparation of fish-curry and Vashu relished it with good appetite. Finishing supper, both husband and wife entered their bed-chamber. There Vashu dug the earth of the floor and a wooden casket was exposed to their view. Māniktārā started at the find—the casket with its contents of gold mohurs—even as one starts in fright at the sight of a snake. She fixed her wonder-struck eyes upon her husband's face and asked, "Whence have you got this treasure?"

"That is what I am hesitating to tell you. I do not know what you will think of me if I tell you all; the disclosure may hurt your feeling.

"Our neighbour Kanu and his mother are indeed bound to me in deep affection—I regard Kanu as my brother, and his mother is verily my mother too. To them indeed I owe my life. My mother was in abject poverty and lived by begging, till Kanu's mother came to her succour and our sufferings were over. Kanu became my constant associate and guide in all affairs. How many acts of theft have we committed in a sportive spirit! When we came of age and became strong in physique, we took to the game of robbery and thus have we amassed some fortune by committing violence on the persons of way-farers. Only for the last twenty or twenty-two days, I am not stirring out to carry on our felonious pursuit and have, besides, removed all plundered riches from the house—for fear of detection by you, Māniktārā."

Māniktārā said with a smile, "Is this the cause of your fear and hesitancy? Admit me, my lord, into your comradeship. The husband is a woman's all-in-all; implicit obedience to his will is the very essence of womanly virtues. Wherever the husband may live, be it in a lowly hut or at the foot of a tree, the wife should bear him company, even at the risk of her life. No sacrifice is too great, which a good wife should not undergo for her husband's sake; a husband should not be deserted, even when he treads on forbidden paths. Banish, my lord, all your fears and scruples; I shall be your partner, in every sphere of life."

These words of Tārā roused the drooping spirit of her husband. He then made a full and frank confession before Māniktārā.

"Kālu, the notorious thief of Khaiea, is my formidable enemy. I can, by no means, cope with him; even as a snake of the 'Dhora' species is powerless before the poisonous Sankhini (snake), so am I before this rogue. Many a defeat has he inflicted on me and has, only through grace, spared my life. The next scene of his marauding operations will be Naterkhuti, whither he will start to-morrow, crossing the forest. My band will attack them near about the pond named " Rajdighi " and seize their ill-gotten wealth. So I am waiting for the opportune moment. But I am not without my anxiety. You will have to stay alone in the house. How shall I go away, leaving you unguarded in this lonely house ?"

Tārā replied, " What is the meaning of all these foolish apprehensions ? What is the harm if I have to stay alone ? Rest assured, my lord, Tārā single-handed, will be a battalion herself,—she is a match for a hundred. Twenty trained wrestlers I can easily cope with."

Vashu was pleased with her words ; his mind now became free from all anxieties and premonitions of danger. He opened the casket of ornaments and adorned his consort with them—which made her look like a fairy, descended on the earth from her etherial abode.

A husband's presence is like unto a lamp, illuminating a dark mansion. A husband is the very crest-jewel of a woman, even as the fabled gem on the hood of a serpent. To a good wife, he is like the blessing of eyesight, vouchsafed to a blind man. He is indeed the honey of the honey-comb on the tree. The love of husband soothes the heart of the wife ; nothing can make her happier than the affection of her lord. Tārā felt much satisfaction at having worn the ornaments. She gently touched the dust of her husband's feet, and for a time, merry conversation and blithe exchange of jokes went on between the happy pair.

Jamaitulla, the country-bard, now advises you all to retire to bed. (Ll. 1-136.)

(8)

The bandits, twenty in number, led by their two chiefs, started out stealthily on their wicked errand towards even-fall, when the lingering rays of the setting sun glistened over tree-tops. Vashu and Kanu, each took a dagger in his hand and their grim associates armed themselves with spears, clubs and shields. Reaching Palasbari, they reposed for a while. Kanu, pointing to the pond at some distance said to his comrades, "There you can see the pond of the "cowherd-chief," full of clear crystalline water. We shall throw the bodies of our enemies into it, cutting them to pieces. Fortunately for us, the rogue Kālu is off his guard today, and has not got any track of us ; besides, this being Thursday night (*Jummā bār*) the party will not pursue their usual avocation to-night." These and other topics kept the mirthful band engaged there. They spread a worn-out mat on one of the sides of the pond and seated themselves there. They took light refreshment, consisting of sugar, plantain and fried rice. They next drank from the neighbouring pond and felt refreshed. Then they resumed their seat on the mat and began to chew betels, when, on a sudden, the distant rattle of the wheels indicated the approach of a bullock-cart. Kanu whispered to his comrades, "There comes the treasure. Be alert, my freinds, ready to wield the clubs. Prepare your mind ; do not, my friends, slip out from the scene of action."

Kālu's men arrived straightway there, carrying bags of coins on their shoulders, escorted by mounted guards, who formed the frontal array. All on a sudden, heavy blows were struck at the legs of the horses and the riders, too, were, in no time, sent to Death's door, their heads being cut off—their mouth stopped for ever. The six carriers of the purses were also quickly dispatched, their possessions being, as it were, spirited away. The six custodians of the sacks of coins lay dead in the neighbourhood of the pond.

Vashu accompanied Kanu to his house, where the booty was carried. A great hue and cry was raised, in the meantime, in the vicinity of the pond. On receipt of the news, Kālu rushed to the spot but missed Vashu there, who had made good his escape, snatching away the morsel, as it were, from his mouth. In presence of some fifty of his comrades, Kālu felt himself humiliated; he pursued the marauder and overtook him within a few paces. Five robust persons caught hold of Kanu, and Kālu, their chief, seated on the pavement of the bathing-ghat, proclaimed his order, "Here is the miscreant Kanu with his men. Bind him fast to the wooden post inside the boat. You must take care to bind them tight, their legs fettered by strong chords and the hands of two persons, twisted backwards and shackled together. Let the night pass away; when the day dawns, they will be hauled up for trial. We need not return home in this dark night; let us stay here. Those of us, who can find leisure, will, in the meantime, roast fowls and prepare *Khichuri*. Returning home, you must behead these scoundrels or drown them in the river near about the *Ganjer ghat.*" Supper finished, Kālu and his gang fell fast asleep. Who knows what dire fate was awaiting the victims? (Ll. 1-42).

(9)

Vashu carried the sacks of coins to Kanu's house and made them over to Kanu's mother, addressing her as his foster-mother. The old woman said, "What have you done, my child? Leaving my Kanu at the mercy of enemies, you have brought these purses to my house!" Vashu replied, "What makes you afraid, aunt? Kanu is not alone; my band is there. Kanu will come back presently with the rest and then you will be relieved of your apprehensions."

Just at this moment, four or five men of their party came up to the spot, their anxious look betraying their great concern. They delivered themselves thus, "What a melancholy news, brother Kanu, are we bearing to you? Kālu fell upon us, and took away Kanu, together with four or five of our men, bound in ropes. They have moored their boats at the 'canal-ghat,' guarded by a strong array of men. The next morning the rogue Kālu will return home."

Vashu, as he heard this, left the place, and going home, related all that had happened to Māniktārā. Vashu said, "Will you feel yourself secure at home, if you have to stay alone?"

"You need not be anxious on my account; sister Panchā has come."

Relieved by the news, Vashu rallied together his men and hurried towards Kālu's boat, determined to deliver his captive friend. Darkness had now dissipated and the sky was lit up with the silvery rays of the moon. Kālu was sleeping, surrounded by a strong body of guards, who were keeping watch during the night. Vashu, on arriving at the spot, paused and said, "It would be an act of rashness to jump at the point of enemies' weapons. I would rather keep myself concealed in the yonder bush and wait for an opportunity."

(Ll. 1-22.)

10

Tārā, in the meantime, tried to think out some device, whereby she could bring about Kanu's release.

This act alone would satisfy her as releasing her and her husband from the debt of gratitude they owed to Kanu's mother. While engaged with this thought, Tārā's face was suddenly lit up with a flash of joy. She went forthwith into her room and set about dressing Panchā, whom she adorned with ornaments of various colours. She then equipped herself with a bow and arrows and selected some of the picked men from amongst her husband's associates. Coming to the river-side, they got into a picturesque barge. They went past Kanu's house, which stood on the left-hand side of the river, and farther down the stream, at a short distance from the spot, Panchā attired herself as a dancing-girl and Māniktārā in a jovial spirit began to sing a tune in a musical voice. Panchā danced to the accompaniment of the jingle of her anklets and Tārā sang a merry tune; and thus with great pomp, the boat floated down the current, wafted along the ebb-tide. Kālu's house was seen at a distance; but no elderly member was at home at the time. So Kālu's son, Dulu, shouted out to them, "Ho, blithe dancers on the picturesque boat, who may you be? If you have no mind to court evil, give us all details about your whereabouts; remember this is Kālu's house."

At this invitation from Dulu, they moored their boat there; and although a Kazi was seen approaching from a distance on the river-bank, they gave the following false account about their party and their pursuits.

"On occasions, like this, we generally make merry by drink and dances; if, at this moment, we are fortunate enough to secure a lover, we lock him fast in deep embrace and entertain him with our dance. Now we have come to you. Give us some drink, come to the boat and fulfil the desires of our young hearts."

Dulu, the young rogue, jumped into the boat—a dupe to their coquettish charms. They steered the boat homewards, singing and dancing all the while. On reaching home, Tārā first made a display of the warmth of her feelings and provided, for him, a well-furnished bedding, spread out on a brand-new bedstead. But next to that, Dulu was in fetters, bound hand and foot and tied to a pillar. His release was made conditional upon Kanu being set free. If Kanu was to lose his head at Kālu's hands, Dulu, too, was to meet with a similar fate. (Ll. 1-32.)

INCOMPLETE.

SANTAL INSURRECTION

INTRODUCTION

TO

SANTAL INSURRECTION

This short ballad was collected from Suri by Babu Sivaratan Mitra and sent to me on the 8th of September, 1925.

The theme of the ballad, as the title suggests, is the rising of the Santal population, inhabiting the hilly frontier of western Bengal—which presented a great menace to the security of life and property among the people of the frontier districts of West Bengal about the middle of the last century.

A brief preliminary account as to what were the circumstances, leading to an armed insurrection on the part of the Santals may not be out of place here.

The Santals of Birbhum, a branch of the ancient race of aboriginal descent, live in small sequestered hamlets, where they procure a living by hunt, but not unoften follow the avocation of agriculturists by growing paddy and other indigenous crops. In the past they eyed the Hindu lowlanders with suspicion and distrust and shunned, as far as possible, all contact with them. They did not grudge, however, people of the blacksmith caste, dwelling in the outskirts of their villages, as the services of the latter were requisitioned for making arrow-heads and also for fashioning iron-ornaments for Santal women —a fact, to which reference is contained in the text (Ll. 17-18).

The neighbouring lowlanders were not immune from the marauding raids of these hillmen; the latter, after having gathered in their winter-harvest, stirred out on their hunting excursions, in course of which they would often make a sudden descent upon the lowlying tracts and plunder and frighten away the people. Thus, for a long time, the mountaineers remained a terror to the western border of Bengal.

But an important change was wrought on their habits of life by the introduction, in 1790, of Lord Cornwallis' momentous legislation, known as the Permanent Settlement Act, by which the Government became pledge-bound not to make any further assessment of land-tax on reclaimed lands. This resulted in a wide extension of tillage, which made the capitalists seek the aid of labour. So the services of the sturdy Santal were much in demand for reclaiming waste land by clearing jungles and chasing away wild beasts. The Santals, too, earned an easier living by working as day-labourers ; sometimes they were given small grants of land, where they settled down to peaceful habits, turning waste lands into cultivable fields.

But the growing numbers of these Santal immigrants who often turned into restless wandering bands, caused an alarm to the inhabitants of the slopes. To prevent them from relapsing into their old marauding habits, the Government raised a solid fencing of pillars to wall off the Santal territory from the lowland districts. But a vast stretch of land, intervening between the fencing and the actual boundary of the tract occupied by the Santals remained for some time unoccupied, as the low-landers dared not come too close to the enclosures of the Santal territory. Here the Santals flocked in overwhelming numbers, quitting their crowded mountain-home, and were soon blessed with a life of plenty and prosperity. In these fertile slopes, the Santals lived for a considerable length of time, as peaceful neighbours of the lowland people.

But this state of affairs did not long continue. The money-making zeal of the Hindu shop-keepers and tradesmen tended to strain the tranquil relation existing between the two sections. The Santals were simple and straightforward, honest and scrupulous, the Hindu merchants were often found to be crafty and unscrupulous. The dishonourable Hindu merchants practised deception upon the unsuspecting Santals in numerous ways in their daily transactions. The Santals brought rice and other grains and clarified butter for sale, for which they got cloth, oil and salt in exchange. But false weights were used in measuring the Santal's supply. Gradually, however, the Santals came to realise that they were the dupes of the Hindu speculators. Their miseries were further accentuated by usury. Sometimes, after having exhausted their little harvest on festive occasions, the Santals were driven to the need of approaching the Hindu usurer, who gladly advanced them loans.

But this act of kindness practically bound them down to a state of serfdom. The Santals found it difficult to extricate themselves from the liabilities of their debts, and some day they were surprised to find that their kind benefactor had managed, without their knowledge, to obtain a decree against their persons. Thus usury, in a large number of cases, developed slavery. The Santal could not get redress in law courts; the protection of law was hardly of any avail to the ignorant Santal. The administration of the Santal territory was not beyond reproach. Mr. Hunter, in his "Annals of Rural Bengal," while criticising the cheap and practical mode of administration, obtaining in the Santal area, remarks, "In the administration of the Santal settlement, everything that cost money without bringing in a tangible return was avoided."

The Central Government knew nothing of the grievances under which two millions of human people were groaning. The English Superintendent of the Santal territory was busy collecting revenue and took no pains to ascertain the grievances of the people, whom he was deputed to rule. The Divisional Commissioner, too, was approached without any result. This indifference on the part of the authorities upset the balance of mind of the rude mountaineers. They massed together under two Santal leaders, who were brothers and one of whom was probably Subha Babu, mentioned in the opening lines of the text. Emissaries were sent all over the Santal-world; and there was raised among the Santals a general expectation of some mighty event, for which they thought they were called upon to be prepared.

In a few days, a great expedition set out and moved down upon the plains; but so long as food lasted, the expedition retained the character of a peaceful procession. The original intention of the expedition, Mr. Hunter holds, had been to march on to Calcutta with a view to laying the tale of their grievance before the Governor-General. But the danger of undisciplined armed masses, with no provision for food, marching through prosperous cities and villages, soon manifested itself. The character of the expedition changed; slaughter of Hindu usurers, looting of shops and raiding the houses of well-to-do citizens followed in the wake. The local authorities were not at first alive to the gravity of the situation; on the other hand, they seemed to treat the matter lightly, disbelieving that an armed insurrection had really burst forth within their jurisdiction; and we find in the text harrowing details of the sufferings which the blunder of the authorities entailed on the people.

The ballad-maker has given the route, which was followed by the rebellious band and localised the scenes of disturbance. Thus we find in the ballad that the Santals first mustered strong on the bank of the Maurakshi, whence they probably moved to a village, named Bāshkuli. Here they assassinated a money-lender, named Becharam in cold blood. Thence they proceeded towards Sadipur, having created a havoc among the innocent villagers on either side of their route. At Sadipur, they plundered the cloth-shops and then went to a place named Kapistak. From Kapistak, they moved on and burnt down, on the way, the police-station of Langul. They were proceeding towards the east, but on meeting a detachment of sepoys under a commander marching to meet them, the Santals changed their course and turned back towards the west. They stopped at the house of one Gayaram in a village named Pererpur. In the meantime, while engaged in their plundering raids, they found the Sepoys on the opposite bank of the Maurakshi. But neither army dared cross the river. The Santals were beating their drums and making merry on one bank of the river, but the Commander of the Sepoy army was keenly watching the situation from the other bank. All on a sudden, the Commander of the Sepoys ordered his army to beat a strategic retreat.

Unable to comprehend this strategic move, the undisciplined Santals jumped into the river, elate with a sense of their supposed victory, and crossed over to the other side. The Sepoys now turned back and opened firing; a havoc was thus created among the Santal rank. The news reached the Santal head-quarters and caused a general depression of spirit among the mountaineers.

But soon a re-inforcement of twelve thousand hillmen from the Rajmahal hills swelled their rank and, with renewed vigour, they marched on to the neighbouring villages and towns and perpetrated unnumbered atrocities there, details of which are given in the text.

Speedy measures were, however, subsequently taken to reduce the insurgents and peace was soon restored in the affected areas. Compared with what we have known about the Santals from a perusal of historical accounts, the ballad seems to have presented them rather in an unfavourable light. We have seen, however, in the text itself, how the half-armed and undisciplined Santals, quite innocent of military stratagem, were mowed down by the disciplined British troops. The Santals knew not how to surrender. They answered the call for surrender by volleys of arrows, which made their mighty opponents open firing, and thus the poor Santals perished to a man on this spot. Mr. Hunter has, in this connection, quoted the remark of an officer, who took an active part in putting down the insurrection. " It was," said the officer, " no war, but execution."

The ballad-maker subscribes himself as one Krishnadas Ray in the colophon; from the vividness of its descriptive details, the ballad seems to have been composed shortly after the rebellion had been quelled. " In 1262 B. S.," writes Krishnadas, " when the country was inundated by a great flood, innumerable men were slaughtered by the insurgents at Abdurpur." (Text, ll. 126). So the author's own statement brings the date of the insurrection to 1262 B. S., which corresponds to 1855 A.D.; and from this, we may conclude that the ballad was composed sometime towards the latter half of the nineteenth century.

The Ballad on the Santhal Insurrection.

Lend me thy ear, brethren. To thee, my worthy audience, I shall relate the narrative.

The Santhals are up in arms, rallied together at the command of their chief, Subha Babu. They are raising their battle-cry and gathering in thousands. The security of life is at stake. Any moment, they can invade the locality and plunder the citizens. Wailings of widows are rending the sky; a general consternation is being felt everywhere. Even utensils and other small articles of daily use are buried underground by the panic-stricken people, who are always apprehensive of a general raid. The Government, of course, are anxious to devise means for the defence of their realm. Relieved, to a certain extent, on getting correct information about the resources of the insurgents, the people are speaking to one another thus, " Do not run away, leaving behind your properties. Hold on to your home. There, the British soldiers are coming to our rescue, with their bayonets erect, girt in their martial cloak. Their guns are loaded and they are, besides, expert riders themselves."

"Just tell me where the rebels have pitched themselves," some one asks, to which another replies, "Oh, we have just seen them arrayed on the bank of the river Maurakshi, where they are lying in ambuscade, turning towards the east and parading their skill in archery by shooting arrows at trees. Quite a colony of blacksmiths are being maintained on their staff (of armour-makers). Arrow-heads are being supplied on demand and weapons are made to order with a surprising promptness, lest the supply should run short. The rebels are tight—girt in their peculiar uniform, with strings of sacred thread hanging across their breast. They proclaim their approach by the beat of drums; they take delight in slaughtering and revel in meat and drink. Having crossed Bāshkuli, they have stepped into the village-area; and people, at their sight, are flying in hot haste. Somebody, in the meantime, was expressing his deep lament for having to leave behind the big pieces of cooked fish. "Fly away! what a catastrophe!" these were the words on every lip and there was raised in the locality a great hue and cry. The rebels have grown furious,—thirsty of human blood, after having slain Becharam, the money-lender. They set the courts of law at open defiance and overthrow all authority. They are keeping to the forest-track, and arriving at Sadipur, they have looted the cloth-shops. Having looted as many pieces of cloth as they desired, and having made bundles of those, they have departed thence, carrying those bundles on their shoulders. In the course of one night, the bundles have been briskly removed from the spot and they have arrived at Kāpistaka. The drums, which are beaten day and night, have become a regular nuisance. At mealtime, the children of the Santhals come thronging in batches, with these words on their lips, "Brethren, we will gain the kingdom for ourselves and make our fortunes."

After two days, they set fire to the police-station at Langul. On receipt of the report, the sepoys marched with their guns and met Darga Munshi on the way, who promptly retreated to the west in fright. The Munshi's band stopped at the house of Gayāram at Gorerpu They next broke open the locks of all the rice-granaries and looted them ; and hungry as they were for having had no food for several days past, they held a sumptuous feast there.

At once a detachment of sepoys, equipped with their bayonets, arrived at the river-side, commanded by their captain. They studied the situation very carefully and postponed, for the time being, crossing the river Maurakshi. On the other side of the river, the opponents were ready with their bows and arrows, and other equipments, but the fight did not commence yet. The Santhals were beating their drums and dancing in merriment. Nobody would, for life, dare to cross the river at that point; there was danger on either side of the river. The captain held a lance in his hand and closely watched the situation. Calculating the numerical strength of the opponents, two of the commanders held a private consultation between them and ordered the sepoys to keep the guns ready for firing. After a time the *Hāoldar* asked the Subadar to bring him a telescope, which being very promptly supplied, he mounted an elephant, and taking his seat on the back of the animal, fitted the telescope to his eyes. He noticed, from a distance, that the Santhals were staying in bushes and thickets, occupying an area of two to three miles. "Beat a retreat" was the order issued by the Sahib, and he himself led the strategical retirement. The Santhals, at the sight, marched quick almost with the speed of the wind. Elate with a sense of their supposed victory, they jumped into the river and thousands of the Santhals swam over to the other side. Their only cry was, "Ho! catch them and kill. To-day we will plunder the head-quarters of Suri and overthrow the authority there. We will rush into the jail-compound, muster strong there and set the prisoners at liberty. Our Subha Babu will henceforward become our king. The Judge Sahib will be put to death and all authority will be snatched by our chief. We will break open the grog-shop, owned by Krishna Saha, and drink wine to our fill."

In the meantime, the order was shouted forth to the sepoys, "Ready quick. Take arms. No delay." Alas, the Santhals were now brought to bay by the stratagem of the sepoy-force. An un-organised tribe, without any military training and tactics, the Santhals could not apprehend this strategical move on the part of their mighty opponents. All on a sudden, they heard the order, "Fire" thundered out from the enemy's rank. Promptly did the sepoys hold their guns aloft and discharged fifty shots at a time. The bullets flew in all directions like shooting stars, striking the Santhals on their back and piercing them through. Those who survived took to their heels. The rank of the Santhals was thinned by the loss of eight score of lives. The Santhals fled from the field in hot haste, not even daring look behind, and arriving at the Salakh hill, reported the sad news of their defeat to their chief. The report caused a depression of spirit among the Santhals.

The next morning, they all assembled together,—a re-inforcement from the Rajmohul hills was added to their number, their numerical strength now increased to the figure twelve thousand. They were now past all fears of death, always ready to give battle, equipped with bows and arrows. They came as far as the bounds of the town-area and sounded the trumpets. The citizens began to flee in great confusion—all castes and ranks of the towns-people. The people of the milkman caste—the

Sadgopas—fled from the city, not forgetting, while flying away, to take away the pots of delicious preparations. Old and decrepit people struggled to effect their escape, supporting the weight of their body on their sticks. The Mussalmans and Fakeers, with grey beard, fled in great haste, with these words on their lips, "Oh Āllā! how sharp are their arrows! Oh thou great Pir of Truth, save us in this crisis. Alas, alas! we are going to lose our life and all. What a dire calamity has befallen us!" But the mother of one Kālu Sheikh was lamenting only because her hen was missing. Everybody was anxious to make his escape; so there was a great rush—a whole population was on the heels, deserting the city in great consternation.

In the mean-time, two thousand of the Santhals made a forcible entry into the palace of the local Raja. They crowded thick there and looted all the apartments, setting up a great uproar. The number of the victims, killed at their hands that day, exceeded two score and a half. After all this was done, the Santhals, in great exultation, sat there, sharpening their battle-axes. Subsequently they beheaded the bald-headed fellow at Lâujur. Next they marched on to Kuṃrabad and crowded the locality by their overwhelming numbers. This village, too, was devastated by fire. Granaries of rice, sesamum and other seeds were burnt down to ashes. Cows, buffaloes, goats and sheeps were burnt in hundreds in that great conflagration. Just as, in the days of yore, the monkey-hero Hanuman jumped from one house-top to another, burning down the city of Lankā, even so were the Santhals marching from one house to another, setting fire thereto. Sadhu Das, a native of that village, in company with four others, approached the District-Judge and made the following representation to him: "Our lives are insecure. We do not know what steps your lordship is contemplating to take. My paternal homestead has been reduced to ashes, and my brother, too, has lost his life at their hands. So please devise means; punish the rebels and defend the subjects from the horrors. With battle-axes they are devastating the country, which will soon be reduced to a forest-realm." On hearing this, the sepoys held their guns over their shoulders and marched on to Kumrabad before daybreak.

Now the fight that took place there will take a long time to describe; besides my attempt to describe the same vividly is like the dwarf's venture to catch the moon. The rebels took their bows and discharged arrows. They had thousands of trained dogs with them.

The Santhals heard the Sahib shouting forth the command "Fire"; and thousands of their rank were shot dead at once. This put the Santhals to rout and they fled towards the west. Some twelve men were killed that day in the *Boragar*. What untold sufferings and indignities were inflicted on the people by the Santhals! Many a woman, who were *enceinte*, were delivered of child on the way. In this way the Santhals went about looting houses everywhere. What to speak of men, even gods like Gopal had to fly away from their presence! Borne on the head of the temple-priest, the deity fled in haste from the Bhandi-forest.

"Oh mother Kali of Birsingpur, how can I describe your glory? Krishnadas prays only for this, mother. Allow him a place at your feet. Take pity on me, mother, and in your infinite kindness, deliver me from the bondage of the world. In 1262 B.S. when the country was inundated by a great flood, innumerable men were slaughtered by the insurgents at Abdarpur."

Krishna Das Ray says, "The Santhals have achieved a deed. All that I have recounted before you, my audience, are true. Believe me, brethren, my account is not a creation of fancy. Now before we part, let us utter the name of God ; for our days are numbered."

THE END.

THE BALLAD OF NIZAM DACOIT.

PREFACE.

The ballad of Nizam dacoit was collected by Babu Asutosh Chowdhuri, one of our ballad-collectors, from several sources. The greater part was collected by Ashu Babu from a village-rhapsodist named Sadar Ali Gayen of Allah, a village within the jurisdiction of the Police Station of Boalkhali in Chittagong. Sadar Ali, like all other rustic minstrels, follows an agricultural avocation during a major portion of the year, devoting himself to singing songs of this nature in neighbouring localities in December, when he is free from field-work. The remaining part of the ballad was collected from a juggler named Matiar Rahaman.

This ballad is still extensively sung by the village-peasants of Chittagong and is very popular with the Muhammadans.

The date of composition and the name of its author are unknown. The original might have been composed in the fourteenth century or earlier, shortly after the death of Nizam, the robber. But evidently some changes were introduced into it by the rhapsodists of later times.

It has hardly any poetic value. But it should be remembered that the simple village-folk greatly enjoy this class of songs, sung in a melodious voice, accompanied by a chorus—the charm of which is accentuated by the sound of musical instruments. Thus the ballads, which show no intrinsic poetry merely as a piece of literary production, do not lack in the pathos of emotional poetry, when sung by a trained band of singers, and I have heard that the ballad of Nizam, the robber, is much enjoyed by the masses of the countryside when it is sung.

I have already found it to be the case in regard to these ballads that if the topic is social or domestic, the ballad is often found to contain fine lyrical sentiments, enlivened by flashes of true poetry. But when it has for its subject a religious tale, it becomes full of miraculous legends, much on the lines of the well-known Maināmati songs. There is no difference in this respect between a Hindu and a Moslem tale. They bristle with accounts of supernatural and superhuman feats, full of mysticism and wild beliefs. It is borne out by history that there was a Mahomedan dacoit named Nizam and that he latterly became a true saint, after passing through great penances and austerities. But in the legend of all the saints of the world, the element of miracle is a dominant factor; and this is as true on the Northern shores of the Mediterranean as it is on the hilly tracts of Chittagong or other provinces of India. The ballad is important from the point of view that the legend bears affinity to many Hindu tales and shows human psychology working in the same manner in the East and the West, in the account of saints. This ballad holds before us an important phase of popular Moslem belief and we, as neighbours of our brethren professing Islam, ought to be interested in these legends and traditions. When a person, whether a Mahomedan or a Hindu, rises above the level of ordinary men and becomes a saint, he is claimed by all, irrespective of the faith which he might profess in his earlier days. He becomes a friend of the world, fully cosmopolitan in his views; and many are the *Pirs* at whose *Darga* the Hindus offer their *puja* and similarly many are the *Sannyasis* amongst Hindus, who receive a tribute of worship in the hands of the Mahomedans.

It is a curious thing to observe in this ballad that the Muhammadan rustic had a great respect for the Hindu shrines, nay for the Hindu deities, in those days. In the prologue, evidently composed by a Mahomedan, he sings hymns in praise of some of the local Hindu shrines and even pays his tribute of worship to Rādhā Krishna and other Hindu deities. It is a well-known fact that there are still many Muhammadan singers in Bengal, whose avocation is to sing the song of Manasā Devi and even of Kāli. This respectful and sincere recognition of the Hindu gods and goddesses by the Mahomedan rustics of the countryside and the corresponding regard which the Hindus have always shown to Mahomedan *Pirs* and to their *Dargas*, once strengthened the bond of unity between the two communities and caused them to have a genuine regard for the feelings and sentiments of each other. I do not know why, but the Mollahs and orthodox Brahmins are now trying to create and widen a gulf which never existed, and which is so fatal to the cause of our country's welfare.

In the preliminary hymn, we find mention of the Bara Pir Sahib. The mosque of this worthy still exists in the village of Noapara on the Karnafuli, within the jurisdiction of the Police Station Ranjan in the district of Chittagong. This mosque has a great celebrity among the Mahomedans of Eastern Bengal. Pilgrims gather here in particular seasons to pay their respects to Bara Pir Sahib from the remotest parts of Chittagong, Noakhali, Mymensingh and Dacca.

Sheikh Farid is one of the great saints, mentioned in the ballad.

Only five miles to the north of the town of Chittagong, there is a village named Nasirabad within the jurisdiction of the Police Station Panchlish. Here the *Darga* of Sultan Bazed Bostami exists to this day. Close to it is a fountain of transparent waters, which gushes out from a rocky underground and goes by the name of "Farid's Spectacles."

The village Nizampur of Chittagong was, according to some, named after Nizam, the hero of this ballad. Chittagong is held sacred by Mahomedans owing to the fact that this district was a resort of twelve celebrated *Aulias* or Moslem Saints. Iban Ba Tuta, the celebrated Arab traveller, paid a visit to Chittagong in order to see the mosque of Pir Badar.

The meeting of Sheikh Farid with Nizam is described in a legendary tale, which has many points in common with the account of Vālmiki, who had originally been a robber, named Ratnakar and was latterly reclaimed by Nārada, the sage,—as given in the Rāmāyana by Krittivāsa. I will presently make extracts from the two legends and place them side by side in order to show this striking point of agreement.

"পুনঃ বলিলেন পাপ কর কার লাগি।
তোমার এ পাতকের কেহ আছে ভাগী ॥
মুনি বলে আমি যত লয়ে যাই ধন।
মাতা পিতা পত্নী আমি খাই চারিজন ॥
যেবা কিছু বেচি কিনি খাই চারি জনে।
আমার পাপের ভাগী সকলে এক্ষণে ॥
শুনিয়া হাসিয়া ব্রহ্মা কহিলেন তবে।
তোমার পাপের ভাগী তারা কেন হবে ॥

করিয়াছ যত পাপ আপনার কায়।
আপনি করিলে পাপ আপনার দায়॥

কৃত্তিবাসী রামায়ণ, আদিকাণ্ড।

* * * * *

ফকির কহিল—"তুমি কর এক কাম॥
ঘরে তোমার মা জননী স্তিরি পুত্র আছে।
এই টাকা লৈয়া তুমি যাও তারার কাছে॥
রুজি করিয়াছ টাকা অনেক মানুষ কাড়ি।
মাডিদি বানাইয়ে শরীল শেষে হৈব মাড়ি॥
ডাকাতি না করিও যে বুলি তোমার স্তরে।
এবে হন্তে ভালা হৈয়া থাক নিজের ঘরে"॥
এই কথা বলি ফকির হৈয়া গেল চুপ।
হেষ্ট মুখী রৈল ডাকাইত হইল বেকুব॥

নিজাম ডাকাইতের পালা, ৩য় অধ্যায়।

Now a word about the history of Nizamuddin Aulia. According to my friend, Maulavi Sahidulla, M.A., B.L., Lecturer, Dacca University, Nizamuddin flourished in the 13th century and was a native of Delhi. As a robber, he is said to have killed fifty-two men before he had met the celebrated saint Farid and latterly, after having undergone great austerities and penances, he killed the infamous Jabbar. He is said to have exclaimed যাঁহা বায়ান্ন তাঁহা তেপ্পান্ন—a phrase, which has since become a familiar adage in this country. There is this difference between the versions given by my friend and what we find in the ballad, that in the latter we find Nizam first meeting Farid after having killed innumerable men at the rate of ninety-nine men a day, whereas the number of Nizam's victims, as laid down by my friend, is only fifty-two.

But a story very much like the one described in this ballad and in the Krittivāsi Rāmāyana is also related of the saint Fariduddin, who flourished in the 13th century. An account of this is to be found in the "Tazkiratul Aulia."

It is difficult to ascertain whether Krittivāsa, who composed his Rāmāyana in the beginning of the 15th century, attributed a legend prevalent in his times, to Ratnākar (Vālmiki), having taken it from the legends related of the two Mahomedan saints, or it was an ancient legend about some forgotten saints of the past—the original source from which the Hindu and Moslem writers copied it and attributed to their own apostles.

I do not know how Nizam dacoit, who was born in Delhi, could be so popular in Chittagong that even the rustic people there have been singing his praises for long generations with such warmth of admiring devotion.

The description of Nizam, the robber, his awe-inspiring figure and great physical strength, have their parallel in Kenārām, the hero of the ballad of the same name, published in the 1st Volume of this work. One striking point of difference cannot, however, be ignored. Chandrāvati, the poetess, who described Kenārām, was the very soul of candour. She gave the story as she knew it, without trying in the least to heighten the glory of the saint, her father, by attributing to him any miraculous powers for effecting the reformation. Yet the simple pathos of her tale shows the great saintliness and spiritual power of Bangshi Dās and the sincere repentance and devotion of Kenārām in such a powerful way that no legends, full of miraculous tales, could so effectively produce an impression about the power of faith, as her simple narration of facts, in her beautiful poetical style, has done.

Many traditions are related in Persian Literature about Nizamuddin Auliā. Tuzuk-i-Jahangiri relates a story showing the liberal views of the Auliā. On one occasion when he saw a large concourse of Hindu people reciting the name of Siva (Hara—Hara) on the bank of the Jumna, Nizam composed the couplet "Har Kaumarasth Rahe dini Okili Gahe" (Every nation has a straight path to heaven in their religion) upon which his disciple Amir Khasru replied by another couplet "Man Kibla a rasth kardam, bar simal-a-kaj kulahe" (The crooked turban of my Guru is my own straight path). This refers to the slanting turban which Nizam wore. There is a tradition to the effect that the prophetic curse of Nizam, incensed at the oppression of Sultan Muhammad Toghalak, reduced Toghalakabad into a desert inhabited by the savage Gujar tribe.[1]

The ballad of Nizam, the robber, was received by me on the 15th of July, 1925.

D. C. SEN.

---

[1] From an article by Mr. Jadunath Sarkar, C.I.E., in the Anandabazar Patrika 15th Falgun, 1332 B.S.

The Ballad of Nizam Dacoit.

(1)

First of all, I bow down to the Supreme Deity, and secondly to (the same Omnipotent Being conceived as) the Creator; and thirdly to the benign Incarnation of Light. The Koran and other Scriptural texts I regard as revelations—the sacred utterances of the Lord himself.

When the Lord was engrossed in deep meditation, the luminous figure of Mahomet flashed before His mind's eye, and as He gazed and gazed upon the vision, He began to feel a certain softening of the heart. So out of love, He created the prophet Mahomet and sent him down to the earth as the very flower of the *Robikul* (the solar race). He next created the entire universe. Had there been no incarnation of Mahomet, there would not have been established the seat of God in all the three worlds.

All reverence to Abdulla and to Amina; salutations at the feet of her, who bore in the womb Mahomet (the deliverer) of the earth. All honour to the city of Mecca in the west and to the Mahomedan saints; and further west, I do reverence to the city of Medina—the burial place of our Rosul. Bibi Fatemah, daughter of Rosul, honoured of all, was called 'mother' by all excepting Ali.

In the north, I offer my tribute of respects to the Himalayas, beneath whose snowy heights lies the entire universe. I bow down to the rising sun in the east, and also to the shrine of Vrindāvana, together with Lord Krishna, the Eternal Lover of sweet Rādhā. I next do reverence to the milky rivers and the ocean, dashing against the two shores, with sandy shoals in the middle. In all the four directions, I tender my respectful compliments to all the four sects of the Mussalmans. I pay my homage to Mother Earth below and to the heavens above. I bow down to Mother Isāmati in the village of Râunyâ and also to the mosque of the great Pir at Nawapara. I next make my *salaam* to the hill of Kurâlyâmura to the right and the mosque of Hirmai to the left. The great upholder of truth once passed through these tracts. The river Sankha is also sacred,—in the middle of which there are shoals, obstructing its course; so the stream seems to be crying for deliverence from the threatened silting up of its bed. Tendering my regards to all these sacred spots, I proceed onwards and arrive at Sita Ghat, where I offer my tribute of worshipful regards to that ideal of womanly virtues—Sītā Devi,—and also to her lord Raghunātha. But the worthiest object of my worship is my father and mother, to whom I owe this corporeal existence on earth. The ungrateful son, who speaks harsh words to his parents, is first allowed a peep into Heaven and then hurled down into eternal Hell, the horrors of which become thus glaringly presented to him. There the wretch is doomed to rot for ever, surrounded by hell-fire and to cry for deliverance in the agony of his soul.

Finally do I make my obeisance to my teacher and then begin, with your permission, my learned audience, to sing the ballad of Nizam dacoit. (Ll. 1-44.)

(2)

In the eastern hills lived Nizam, the dacoit. He roamed over those tracts, always on the look-out for victims, whom he would dispatch on sight. Early in the morning the dacoit used to rise from his bed and proceed towards the *Dighar*-forest, sword in hand. He had a strong-built physique and a very dark complexion. His eyes were fiery, and red like the *Jabā*-flower. His hair was crisp, and beard and moustuche long. His arms and legs were like wooden pillars, built from the trees of the *Jarail*-species. The grip of his hands was verily like the tiger's paw, his neck being like unto a lion's. His gaze resembled that of a buffalo and his movements could be compared to an elephant's gait.

To the east of the *Digar*-forest, stands a steep hillock, surrounded by thick bamboo-groves and cane-bowers. Tigers and bears, elephants and boars roam over this tract. To the west stand small mounds, overgrown with straw; and between two such mounds, runs a narrow pass. At one extremity of the pass there is a big banian tree, beneath the shade of which Nizam takes his seat. When travellers are seen passing by that tree, the dacoit suddenly makes his appearance before them and snatches away all their possessions. If they do not easily consent to part with their riches, Nizam bursts into rage and terrorises them; and sometimes the heads of his poor victims are blown off. Thus innumerable innocent wayfarers lose their lives in the *Digar*-forest. (Ll. 1-24.)

(3)

There was a Muhammadan saint, named Shaik Farid. In the deep forest he lived in seclusion, absorbed in meditation. He would constantly mutter the sacred formulæ and his eyes knew not a wink of sleep. It so happened on an occasion, that as the Fakir sat steeped in contemplation, his mind was distressed by thinking about this pest of the forest, and by dint of his meditative concentration, he knew at once that the robber killed every night about a hundred wayfarers, in a ruthless manner.

The next morning the Fakir rose, and after thinking a while, assumed the guise of an old man. He filled a bag with plenty of money and having placed the same across his shoulders, proceeded on his way. With an iron stick in his hand, the old man walked slowly, bent with age, his eyes fixed downwards. When he came near the entrance of the narrow pass, he heard from a distance the thundering voice of Nizam dacoit. The dacoit had his sword unsheathed, his eyes reddened with rage. Then did he approach the old man and accost him thus, "Hear me, old man; give me all the money you have with you, or you lose your head." The old man asked, "How much do you demand of me?" "Two hundred rupees paid," replied Nizam, "might save your life." The Fakir, on hearing this, put his hand into the bag, brought out the amount of two hundred rupees and made it over to the robber. When his first demand of two hundred rupees was promptly satisfied, the robber gazed at the Fakir's bag, which still seemed almost full. The dacoit paused a while and then made a further demand of five hundred rupees in the following words: "Be prompt in complying with my demand, or you die." Uttering this threat, he began to brandish his sword. So the Fakir counted another five hundred rupees and handed it over, with great promptness, to the robber. This demand, too, being satisfied, the dacoit gazed somewhat surprisingly at the bag, which remained even then as full as ever. This set him a-thinking and thus did the dacoit muse within himself, "No ordinary mortal this old man seems to be. No drain or diminution has been caused to the contents of the bag even after this rather heavy payment. So he must be some Darwesh or Fakir." He then addressed the old man thus, "Hear me, old man; more money you must give me or your head will be dashed to pieces."

The Fakir, on hearing about this fresh demand, silently opened the bag and coins poured forth in profusion with a jingling noise. Very soon, quite a heap accumulated there, which looked as high as a small hill and Nizam saw this. The Fakir said to him, "Just do one thing. You have your mother, wife and children at home; go to them with this money. A vast wealth have you amassed by making slaughter of men your avocation in life. But this body of yours is composed of earth and into earth will it finally dissolve. So please do not pursue this sinful avocation any longer, I beseech you. Mend your ways from now and return home." With this exhortation the Fakir stopped. The dacoit felt somewhat abashed and hung down his head. A shiver went through Nizam's body, as if an earth quake shook the Digar forest.

Once again the Fakir smilingly remarked, "What benefit do you derive from the slaughter of men? How do you profit by this money? Why do you build up a structure of misdeeds for your future? By your murderous activities, you make yourself guilty before God. When the final crisis will come, nobody will share the evil."

Nizam looked heavenwards first and then towards the ground. He looked vacantly and it seemed as if he saw darkness all around. He stood there motionless, as if transfixed to the spot like one thunderstruck. His grip loosened and the sword dropped on the ground and Nizam, the dacoit, sat there, weeping in distress, supporting his head on his hands. Shedding profuse tears, the robber approached the Fakir and threw himself down at his feet.

"Thousands of people have I slain for the sake of money. But how is it that my heart breaks to-day, as I am proceeding to take this money? Countless murders have I perpetrated for the sake of money, incurring overwhelming demerits thereby. Plenty of money have I earned to-day, but my heart is sinking in dismay."

Nizam wept violently, incessant tears flowing down his cheek. Sheikh Farid drew him close to his breast and asked him in compassionate terms, "Why do you shed tears? You wanted money, which I have given you in plenty." The dacoit replied, "No more craving for money do I entertain now. Accept me as your slave; this is my only desire." (Ll. 1-78.)

(4)

Sheikh Farid took Nizam in his company and wanted him to carry the empty bag in his back. In course of their wanderings, they found themselves in the heart of a dense forest. Nizam looked around in a restless manner and the Fakir now thought of conducting him through a trial. So a plan was devised by the far-sighted Fakir; the stone of the hill was at once transformed into gold. Looking towards the ground below, while walking behind the Fakir, Nizam noticed lumps of gold. He thought that luck had become propitious. A golden hill had greeted his eyes to-day! So he gathered a fairly large quantity of gold and placed it inside the bag. The Fakir, however, though walking ahead, perceived everything, and turning round, noticed, with regret, that the bag was quite full. He then said, "What is there, Nizam, contained in the bag? Just show me the same." At these words of the Fakir, Nizam opened the bag. But what were the contents?

Gold no more, but all trinkets of no value! Shaik Farid demanded, "Oh, where is the gold?" to which stupefied Nizam replied, "gold has been transformed into stone." Then the Fakir said, "Just return home. For, what will you gain by following me?" The dacoit replied, "The world is an illusion and so I have stuck to your company for initiation at your hands into the life of a Fakir." The Fakir stood up and said, "Oh no! You are not meant for that. Robbery and saintliness are quite different things. A vast treasure you have amassed by the slaughter of men. Why, in an advanced career, should your choice fall upon the life of a Fakir? You still cherish in your heart a hankering after wealth. So it is useless professing your choice for Fakirhood." Nizam, as he heard this, burst into tears and threw himself at the feet of the Fakir. His eyes bathed in tears of remorse and he said at last, "No more, I take an oath before you, shall I entertain in my mind any greed for wealth. If you do not take pity on me, I will kill myself in your presence." So saying, the dacoit began to strike his breast against the rock. The rock was flooded with tears from his eyes and blood from the wound in his breast. Shaik Farid hastened there and clasped him in his breast. The Fakir then said, "Y u have your mother, children and wife at home, all in anxious eagerness, looking for the moment of your return." Nizam said, "No, I must not think of them any longer. Certainly they will not share the evils that will befall me as a sequel to my sinful career. Evil company has ruined me. Save me, father, by initiation into the life of a Fakir."

Shaik Farid, on hearing this, fixed his iron stick to the ground in that deep forest and thus addressed Nizam, "Hear me, Nizam, this is the stick of my liking and I prize it much. I would only leave you the following instruction to-day. Hold your gaze steadfastly towards the tip of this stick. Go on reciting the sacred formula with undivided attention, taking no thought for food or sleep, with your eyes rivetted on the tip of the stick. When, after the lapse of twelve years, you will split the point of the stick, a fine creeper will come out therefrom and greet your eyes; and on the very day of this occurrence, I shall make my appearance before you. So saying, the Fakir paced a few steps aimlessly and then went about his own business.

The forest was deep, infested by boars and tigers; but Nizam did not mind anything else. He went on contemplating the sacred formula with a concentration that nothing could perturb. His wife and children were left at home, quite ignorant of what had happened to Nizam. In the meantime, a rumour came floating to their ears that Nizam had been devoured by a tiger.

Six long years rolled by. A very wonderful incident happened in the meantime in the kingdom of one *Jangli Patsah* (the chief of a hilly tribe). (Ll. 1-68.)

(5)

Jangli Patsah was the chief of a hilly tribe. He lived in happiness in his forest-dominion. Riches he possessed in super-abundance. He had a daughter born to him—a wonderful creation of beauty. Her face could only be compared to the full moon; her voice was sweet and musical, resembling the notes of a cuckoo, or some soft tune of Kānu's flute. Her whole frame was comely and bright. She had a very slender waist and her breasts were like the budding growth of the plantain-flower. She was a rare beauty, having scarcely an equal in the world. Lāl Bai was the name given to her by her parents. She had just stepped into her youth and even now, the lustre of her person could scarcely be concealed by her cloth.

Now hear me, my learned audience, what an untoward incident took place in the kingdom of the *Patsah.*

The *Patsah* had a Vizier,—a very good man, held in great esteem. This Vizier had a son named Jabbar, who brought on a great evil by reason of his improper sentiment towards the daughter of the *Patsah.* Jabbar was a rogue and a scoundrel. He tried to think out some device whereby he could abduct the girl.

Being the son of the Vizier, Jabbar had a free access into the Patsah's harem, which he visited frequently. He had already conceived a passion for Lāl Bai, and to achieve his wicked end, he resorted to the following trick. One who is pierced at heart by the dart of the triple-lettered word *Pi-ri-ti* (love) becomes forgetful of his prestige and honour, caste and pedigree. The fruit of love, even if swallowed, does not appease one's hunger; this evil fruit has been sent down to earth by God for the trial of men with an appeal to senses.

It once so happened that in her harem Lāl Bai was training her female-parrot to speak in sweet accents of human speech. She was all alone there. Jabbar Mia seized the opportunity and hastened to the spot. Drawing near Lāl Bai, he caught her by the hand. Shocked at this unexpected incivility she cried out. Jabbar left her at once with a start and took to his heels. Lāl Bai's mother came there and found her daughter weeping. So she asked, "Ah, my Lali, how is it that the golden hue of your face has grown pale and lustreless? Lali replied with tears in her eyes, "The wicked Jabbar came and caught me by the hands, I know not why."

When the matter was reported to the *Patsah*, the Vizier was summoned to his presence. Addressing the Vizier, the *Patsah* said, "Your son Jabbar had the audacity to clasp the hands of my daughter. Bring him here in my presence without delay. I will have both his ears chopped off."

The Vizier flew into a rage, ablaze like a torch, and hied home. Jabbar had just finished his meal and put a betel into his mouth, when the Vizier reached home and seized him by the ears. He took off the shoes from his feet and struck Jabbar on his head. Jabbar fell down on earth and rolled about in pain. He had his ears chopped off at the Nawab's command; his father, the minister, had a broom, fastened to his neck. Subjected to these indignities, Jabbar made his escape from the country. Nobody knew whither he had gone. (Ll. 1-56.)

(6)

Let me now relate to you what happened next. Lāl Bai fell ill and was reduced to the state of bed-ridden prostration. She began to wither like a flower, dropped from its stock. Her mother's tears now became incessant. Lali—the image of gold—did not recover. Shedding her last tears before the near and dear ones, she passed away into heaven. Loud wailings rose up in the sky and rent the atmosphere. Her father wept violently, beating his breast with the hands; her mother, too, vented her unbearable grief by striking her breast against the earth and tearing off her hair. The female attendants and maids of the house retired to a corner and shed silent tears. The neighbours and kinsmen, too, shared in their piteous lament. The whole forest-dominion joined in the mournful chorus of bewailings for the loss of that maidenly paragon of beauty.

Listen, then, my audience, to my account of what happened next. The last remains of that youthful figure were carried to an open space, where they were duly interred.

In the meantime, a horrible deed was going to be perpetrated by villainous Jabbar. He called one of his companions and after having held a consultation with him, came up to the burial ground during the night. There the wretch indulged in numerous wild thoughts, all of which cannot certainly be recounted here. His beastly propensities became kindled again. He became resolved to exhume the dead body and commit violence upon it for the satisfaction of his carnal desires. Planning thus, they began to dig the grave. Nizam came to learn about this. He faltered in the course of his recital of the sacred formula and suddenly rose up with a start. "A hundred victims, less only by one, used daily to lose their heads at my hands; but even those misdeeds of mine are surpassed in heinousness by this villainous outrage." Thus musing within himself, Nizam made up his mind and hastened to the spot with the iron stick in his hand. The rogues had, in the meantime, disinterred the body. Nizam first recoiled at the sight. But when the scoundrels were about to take off the sheet which covered the dead body, Nizam, the quondam dacoit, forgot himself. He took the iron stick in his hand, and for a time, sobriety of temper quitted him. He brandished the club and struck the two villains on their heads. The blow of the club rent their skulls and killed them on the spot.

Nizam now returned to his former place of worship. He fixed the stick to the ground and once again turned his eyes towards the tip of the same. Now he came to see the twigs of a creeper issuing from inside the club. The Fakir, too, made his appearance at this stage. Nizam stood up and did reverence to the Fakir, and then said, "Pardon me, Fakir Sahib, once more have I sinned; I have added two more names to the list of persons, slain at my hands. Forgive me, Fakir Sahib; O forgive me, my preceptor." Shaikh Farid, as he heard this, held him in deep embrace and pressed a thousand kisses on his brow. The Fakir then said, "You have reduced the period of your penance from twelve to six years by killing that scoundrel. If you can achieve such noble deeds, surely you would be carried to heaven in a celestial car." (Ll. 1-51.)

(7)

Let me tell you, my worthy audience, what transpired next. Nizam, this time, followed the Fakir. After having travelled through the *Digar* forest, they arrived at the bank of a river. Sheikh Farid paused there for a while and then took off the cap from his head. Having floated the charmed cap in the river, the preceptor and the pupil easily crossed the stream through grace of God. On the other side of the river, behind the market-place, an old woman had a shop of sweet-meat. Delicious preparations of cakes of many varieties the old woman used to sell. She was endearingly called 'aunt' by the local people. Now Farid and Nizam reached there and the woman *salaamed* the Fakir. The Fakir addressed her thus, "Hear me, aunt, this is my friend Nizam, whom I wish to consign to your care. Two meals you will give him daily, in return for which, he will tend your cows. If he can win your praise by carefully attending to his duties you may give him something more as his wages, but that would rest entirely on your own discretion." Saying this, the Fakir took leave of her. Nizam fell at the feet of his preceptor. The Fakir consoled him thus, "Do not fear, my child, you will surely have me by your side in times of need."

Nizam accepted service in the house of the woman. In the forenoon and in the afternoon, he grazed the herd in the neighbouring meadows. Indifferent to what passed around, he always looked distracted in mind; the neighbours took him to be crazy. He did not resent or cry, even if he was beaten. He drudged all day long without any sign of toil or fatigue and seemed almost insensible. Bearing patiently all sorts of harsh and abusive words, he would still devote himself, heart and soul, to the services of anybody who might demand them of him.

The old woman had a son, named Sundar. He was an exquisitely handsome lad, whose beauty put to shade even the lustre of the sun and the moon. Since the death of her husband the woman was rearing the child with all the warmth and tenderness of a mother's heart. The child was always jolly and cheerful at heart; the cowherd became his fast friend.

Now there lived a great Mahomedan Saint, named *Bara Pir Saha*, who was known for his great piety and spiritual attainments, for his unbounded compassion and wonderful self-possession. He had a great affection for the lad Sundar, whom he loved and caressed as if he were his own child. The house of the woman, who owned the shop, was graced by the presence of the Fakir, who came there frequently to see the child Sundar. Sundar was indeed a very fortunate child, as it was his personal attractions that brought the saint to his mother's cottage, which became now a habitual resort of the Fakir.

One day the old woman called the cowherd Nizam to her and he appeared shortly, before her. She asked Nizam how much he would demand of her as his wages. Nizam replied, "No money do I want, mother. I have no attachment for matters terrestrial. My mind is like unto a dry sea, it craves for an abundance of water. I seek one favour of you, mother. The great Pir Saheb visits your house frequently; he is the prince of Saints and a hundred *salaams* do I make at his feet. My one desire is to sit at his feet and receive instructions from him. If you are propitious, mother, then alone will my desire be fulfilled." At these words of Nizam, the old woman asked him, "Whose son are you? Tell me all about your family and parentage." Nizam replied, "I am Nizam, the dacoit. Long years have I spent slaughtering people in the *Digar* forest."

The old woman was struck dumb at the reply. She had no words to utter, courage failed her for the moment. She began to shiver violently, as if she had a sudden attack of a malignant fever. What did then Nizam do? At once he threw himself at the woman's feet and exclaimed, "You are my foster-mother, and more respected than she who bore me in the womb. Many a sin have I committed in my life. Save me, mother; O, save me from those."

Just at this moment, the great Pir made his arrival and announced himself by a shout. The woman hurried there and made her *salaam* to the Fakir. The Pir said, "Where is Sundar? Bring him in my presence without delay, as I shall depart soon to-day." The woman replied with a smile, "He is laid down with illness. Please come early next morning, when I shall arrange your meeting." The Pir then said, "Do not deceive me. Why do you object to my seeing him to-day?" She replied, "First promise me a boon; then I shall show you my darling." The Pir said, "What may your needs be, which make you a supplicant before me! Why this falsehood, then? And whence this hesitancy again?" The woman replied, "I have another son, whom you must admit as your disciple." The Fakir said, "Yes I may initiate him into the mysteries of spiritual life, if he has the inspiration of the Prophet at heart."

The woman then opened the door and pointed to Nizam, at which the Pir exclaimed, "Oh my God! he is the dacoit."

With folded palms did Nizam recite the sacred formula. The old woman then addressed the Pir thus, "A confirmed marauder, he has now become a real Fakir. Let me now relate to you the whole of his past history." The Pir said, "No need of that, I have heard of him from Sheikh Farid. Besides, Nizam dacoit has attained notoriety enough and is widely known." The old woman said, "Know for certain, my father, this Nizam is dearer to me than my own child Sundar." Now the Pir was in a mental see-saw as to whether or not he would admit an old dacoit into his discipleship. Thus vacillating, the Pir became somewhat restless and the utterance slipped out of his mouth, namely that, "Nizam's *father* is admitted into the ranks of an *âuliâ* (a mystic saint)." Not satisfied with that, the old woman said. "I beseech you, father; once admit that *Nizam* is an *âuliâ*." The great Pir Sahib, on hearing this, made an utterance to the effect that Nizam's *forefathers* up to the seventh degree in ascent would be henceforward accepted as *áuliás* in heaven. Not even satisfied with that, the woman implored with tears, "No, that will not do. '*Niazm* is an *áuliá*' this you must utter." And the child Sundar, too, joined in his mother's prayer and imploringly clasped the hand of his beloved Pir. Just at this moment, Sheikh Farid, too, made his appearance and repeated what the other two had desired. So a triple alliance was formed and the request was pressed with their combined ardour,—which the Pir Sahib could no longer resist and thus, finally, came out of his lips the gracious pronouncement, "Nizam *himself* is an *áuliá*."

Scarcely had this declaration escaped the lips of the truthful Pir when Nizamuddin, who stood expectant by, melted into air. (Ll. 1-116.)

THE END.

ISHA KHAN MASHNADALI OF JANGAL BARI

INTRODUCTION

Our sources of information.

Regarding Ishā Khan Mashnadali, the most authentic source of information is the famous Ain-i-Akbari itself. Abul Fazl states that Ishā Khan's father was killed in battle by Salim Khan and Taz Khan of Bengal, and his two sons, Ismile and Ishā were sold as slaves. They were subsequently traced by Kutubuddin, Ishā's uncle, to be living in Turan whence they were brought back to their native province, and Ishā Khan soon became the ruler of Bhati and had twelve great Zeminders dependent on him. Hence he is called by Abul Fazl 'Mazban Bháti'—the governor of Bháti. Ishā Khan gave endless trouble to the Imperialists.[1]

Dr. Wise, Civil Surgeon of Dacca, contributed an article to the Journal of the Asiatic Society of Bengal in 1874 A. D. (pp. 209-14) in which he gave us a mass of information about this chief, who finally settled at Jangal Bāri in the subdivision of Kishoregunj (Eastern Mymensingh) and became the founder of the famous Dewan-family of that place. In another article on Chand Ray and Kedar Ray of Vikrampur, published in the Journal of the Asiatic Society of Bengal for 1874 A. D. (No. 3, pp. 202-3), Dr. Wise gives us some further details about Ishā Khan. Mr. H. E. Stapleton, in his notes "on seven sixteenth century cannon" (J. A. S. B., pp. 367-75, for

[1] Ain-i-Akbari, Vol. I., p. 342, n.

1909), discussed some historical questions relating to the Dewan family and their ancestry.

In a work, called the Mashnad Ali Itihāsa, written in Bengali by Munshi Raj Chandra Ghosh and Pandit Kali Kumar Chakravarti at the instance of Dewan Sovandad Khan and Dewan Azimdad Khan, and published at Dacca in 1298 B. S. (1891 A. D.), the writers have tried to trace a full history of the Dewans from Kalidas Gazdani, the father of Ishā Khan. The two scholars had access to the State-papers, preserved in the archives of the Dewan family at Jangal Bari and consulted the historical works on the subject, written by European and Mahomedan historians and gave a connected narrative of the Dewan family there.

We have got numerous ballads, in which we find accounts of the exploits of Ishā Khan and details about his descendants. First of all, we have an old ballad, which was composed by an anonymous poet probably in the 18th century. This is the most important of the ballads, mentioned above. The second one we have got was written by Munshi Abdul Karim of Galachipa in the subdivision of Kishoregunj, Mymemsingh, about seventy-five years ago. It is a fanciful work on the historical accuracy of which little reliance can be placed. The third ballad, written by the same author, chiefly describes the incidents of the life of Dewan Mannower Khan, a grandson of Ishā Khan and incidentally refers to the latter. The fourth ballad, composed by an anonymous writer, evidently a Mahomedan, is entitled 'The Songs of Dewan Feroz Khan.' In this ballad some account is given of Ishā Khan, the ancestor of the hero of the tale. Besides these four ballads, there are many songs incidentally bearing on the life of Ishā Khan, sung by illiterate rustic folk of Eastern Bengal.

The discrepancies.

I am sorry to say that the accounts given in the ballads do not always agree. We must try to trace the real history of the sturdy chief of Jangal Bari, the hero of a hundred fights, from these conflicting accounts and from those, given by Mahomedan and Christian writers. In 1586 Ralph Fitch visited Sonargaon. He remarks, "The chief king of these countries is called Isa Kan and he is the chief of all other kings and is a great friend to the Christians." From the Ain-i-Akbari we gather that Ishā Khan successfully withstood the invasion of the Imperialist General Shāh Bāz Khan in 1585. We have an account of his valiant fight with Man Singh, and all these indicate to the great power that he had acquired over East Bengal in the latter part of the 16th century. The 'Ain' frequently calls him "The wealthy Zeminder of Bengal."

The description of Ishā Khan's expeditions, of his memorable fight for independence and of his romantic abduction of Sona Mani (Subhadrā) is more or less familiar to the people of Eastern Bengal and though tinged with the colourings of rustic imagination, they have an undoubted historical background. But it is the question of his ancestry that offers us a puzzling problem.

The identity of Soloman Khan with Soloman Kararani disproved.

When Dr. Wise wrote to the Dewan Sahebs of Jangal Bāri in 1874 A. D. for accounts of Ishā Khan, they supplied him with the information that Kalidas Gazdani, the father of Ishā Khan, married a daughter of Hussein Saha. But in the history of Jangal Bāri, the Dewans must have latterly altered this view; for their protégés, the authors, declared that Kalidas Gazdani had married a daughter of Ghyasuddin, who ruled in Bengal

' J. A. S B. of 1874, pp. 209.

from 1560 to 1663. I suppose, I have been able to find out the reasons for their change of views in this matter, but I shall dwell on the point later on.

From the various accounts, available to us about the ancestors of Ishā Khan, it seems to be an undisputed fact that Ishā Khan was a son of Kalidas Gazdani, who had accepted the Islamic creed and assumed the title of Soloman Khan. Not only do the Dewans themselves attest to this view of their ancestory, but the fact of an ancestor of the Rajput Chiefs coming from Baiswara in the district of Oudh and settling in Bengal, and of Kalidas Gazdani's marrying a daughter of the reigning Mahomedan monarch, has had corroboration in various outside evidences. Mr. Stapleton writes, "Mr. B. Buru, C. S., Deputy Commissioner of Gonda, to whom I referred the question of Kalidas Gazdani's ancestry, suggests that he was a Bais Rajput of Baiswara. This is curiously confirmed by the note given at the bottom of p. 1. of the Itihāsa (Mashnad Ali Itihāsa) সোলেমান খাঁর পূর্ব্বপুরুষগণের আদিনিবাস অযোধ্যা প্রদেশান্তর্গত বয়েস ওয়ারা রাজ্যে।" (J. A. S. B., Oct. 1919, p. 370).

The first ballad gives some further details on this point. It says that Raja Dhanaphat Singh of Baiswara was a friend and powerful ally of the Delhi Emperor of his time. And Bhagirath, a scion of his family, came to Bengal with the object of visiting the shrines; he was very warmly received by King Ghiasuddin of Bengal. Kalidas Gazdani was descended from Bhagirath and latterly became a Mahomedan convert and having married the third daughter of that monarch, ascended the throne after his death in 1563 under the name of Sulaiman Kararani.

The older tradition of the family was that Kalidas having turned a Mahomedan convert and assumed the title of Sulaiman Kararani married a daughter of Hussein

Shah, who ruled from 1493 to 1520 A. D. Hussein Shah was succeeded on the throne of Bengal by the following Pathan rulers—Nasarat Shah (1520-1534 A. D.), Ghiasuddin Muhammad Shah III (1534-1536 A. D.), Sher Shah (1536-1545 A. D.), Muhammad Shah Gazi (1545-1556), Bahadur Shah (1556-1560), Ghiasuddin Jalal Shah (1560-1563), Sulaiman Kararani (1563-1572). I have taken this table with slight alterations from Mr. H. Nelson Wright's catalogue of coins in the Indian Museum, which is a reliable work, based on numismatic evidence.

Now the tradition that Sulaiman Khan and the notorious Kālā-Pāhār were both of them sons-in-law of the same Mahomedan sovereign is largely extant in this country. Babu Doorga Churan Sanyal's Social History of Bengal, though it may not deserve the credit of a reliable history, embodies a vast mass of the legends and traditions, preserved in the genealogical works of the Varendra Brahmins. He says that Kālā-Pāhār married a daughter of Hussein Shah, and gives an interesting account of this marriage, which is a love-romance. Such instances are not rare in the history of conversion and Cupid is admittedly the most powerful ally of the missionaries in the history of all religions.

Now if, as alleged in the family history of the Dewans of Jangal Bāri, Kālāpāhār and Kalidas Gazdani married two daughters of the reigning Mahomedan monarch of the time and if the tradition of the Brahmins be true that it was a daughter of Hussein Shah whom the Kālā Pāhār married, it must follow that Kalidas Gazdani also married a daughter of the same king. This tradition was in existence also in the family of the Dewans. Or how should it be explained that when Dr. Wise asked for information about thier ancestry, the Dewans furnished

39

the information that Kalidas had married a daughter of Hussein Shah?

But when, later on, a history of the family—Mashnad Ali Itihasa—was written, the authors consulted various English and Mahomedan histories, and probably inspired by the motive of establishing the identity of Sulaiman Khan with Sulaiman Kararani and thus proving the Dewan family to be directly descended from an Emperor of Gaur, made a statement that Fatema Bibi was a daughter of Ibrahim Malikul-ulma, who had married the first daughter of Jalal Shah (J. A. S. B. for 1909, pp. 37) and that Kalidas Gazdani had married the third daughter of Jalal. Had they upheld the older tradition of Sulaiman's marrying a daughter of Hussain Shah, it would not have been possible to prove the identity of the hero with Sulaiman Kararani. It is, therefore, evident that the old tradition of the Dewan family was changed in order to ascribe to their ancestor the status of a King of Bengal. When a new aristocracy springs up, such attempts to connect it with some time-honoured royal line are often made by the court-parasites and friends of the family.

Now it is proved beyond doubt that Daud Khan was a son of Sulaiman Kararani. We find it proved by the coins (Wright's Catalogue, p. 182). We find it mentioned in the history of Pratapaditya, written by Ram Ram Basu in 1801. This treatise, its author writes, was based on an early sketch of Pratapaditya, written in Persian. Pratapaditya's father Vikramaditya was a minister of Daud Khan, and in the family records of this valorous hero of the 16th century, many interesting accounts are given about Daud Khan. If Daud Khan were a brother of Ishā Khan, it would certainly have been mentioned by Ram Ram Vasu.

And curiously enough we find it stated in the 'Ain' distinctly that after Daud Khan's death, his old mother threw herself as a supplicant of the mercy of Khan Jahań, who had captured and killed her son. Can it be believed that the old lady would have done this, if Ishā Khan were his son? The 'Ain' mentions the names of some of the close relations of Daud Khan, but there is no mention of Ishā Khan there. On the other hand, that famous history traces the ancestry of Ishā Khan, describes the death of his father and relates the circumstance of Ishā Khan being sold as a slave and living for a time in that humble capacity in Turan. The early career of Ishā Khan, from this account of the 'Ain,' seems to be obscure. How he gradually rose to power and wealth may be traced from another authentic source. The Rajmala of Tipperah gives the narrative of the Kings of Tipperah very faithfully from after the legendary period when their connection with Yayāti of the lunar race is sought to be established. The tale of this pre-historic period is no doubt mixed with fiction. But the court historians preserved authentic records of the later administration, and barring some short accounts, where they now and then tried to extol the monarchs wilfully by giving them victories over their enemies, which they did not win, the general treatment of the family-history is quite reliable. Perganna Sarail keeps afresh the memory of Ishā Khan's exploits and fights with the Imperialists. There is no doubt that Ishā Khan for a time was a general of the Tipperah Raj and sought to please Amar Manikya in various ways. I will, later on, give in this discourse, an abridged translation of the texts of the Rajmala bearing on Ishā Khan. It must, however, be admitted, for the sake of truth, that the court-parasites, who wrote the book, probably made a wrong statement when they said that the title of Mashnad Ali was conferred on Ishā Khan by the Tipperah Raj. This might have been done evidently to pander to the vanity of the descendants of Amar Manikya under whose orders the latter part of the Rajmala was written. But in all other points, connected with the Moslem chief, the account of the book seems to be a reliable presentation of facts.

Now the family history of Jangal Bāri Dewans, as also the ballads, make no mention of the early career of Ishā Khan. These records bring him at once into prominence after the death of Sulaiman Kararani, as a warrior who fought against the Imperialists. His obscure and humble life is ingeniously brushed aside in order to present him in full glory from the very beginning. One of their objects for doing this may be also to shorten, by suppression of facts of Ishā Khan's youthful life, the distance of time, so that he could be represented as a son of Sulaiman Kararani. As we have already stated, the first ballad says that the ancestor of Kalidas Gazdāni was Dhanapat Sing, a Kshattriya Raja of Oudh; next it mentions that Raja Bhagirath, a descendant of Dhanapat settled in Bengal and that Kalidas Gazdani was a scion of his family. None of these later descendants is said to stand in the relation of father and son but mentioned as mere scions of a family, of which the great ancestor is Dhanapat. I believe these names to be historical; but the statement of the ballad-maker suggests that there were many names in the genealogy of the Baiswara Rajputs, left out from the list. In order, however, to make Kalidas Gazdani same as Sulaiman Kararani, he is made to be a minister of at least three Kings and still retain the youthful attractions of his person so wonderfully well that the youngest daughter of the last King falls headlong in love with him. There is evidently a good deal of patchwork in all these, which shows that Sulaiman Khan was hurried down to the time of Sulaiman Kararani to become identical with him. The similarity in the two names was certainly a fact, of which advantage was taken by the manipulators.

That this alleged ancestry of the Dewans of Jangal Bāri from Sulaiman Kararani was a point, neither firmly established in the traditions of the family, nor in the popular mind, is evident from the circumstance that Abdul Karim, who wrote a ballad about Ishā Khan at the instance of some of the later Dewans, states that Sulaiman Khan (Kalidas Gazdani) had married a daughter of Baber, the founder of the Moghul dynasty. In his zeal to sing the praises of his illustrious sponsors and extol them as far as he could by a stretch of his rustic imagination, he describes how, on the death of Baber, Ishā Khan usurped the throne of Delhi at a public Durbar, held on the occasion of Humayun's accession and how the latter, struck dumb by fear and surprise at this conduct of his brother-in-law, made a compromise with him by according to him the first rank amongst his allies and Feudatory chiefs, assembled there. These statements are not more authentic than the Arabian Nights' Tales and are scarcely worthy of any serious notice.

Another weighty objection to our accepting Ishā Khan as a brother of Dāud is the fact that though Ishā Khan achieved the status of an independent King of Eastern Bengal, he still prided upon the title of Dewan, inherited from his ancestors and called himself Dewan Mashnad Ali. Had Dāud Khan been his brother, he would have equal reasons for calling himself a Dewan, as all other members of the family, descended from Kalidas Gazdani, have chosen to call themselves. But "Dewan" Dāud Khan is unheard of. On the other hand, we find Dāud Khan mentioning his family-surname "Kararani" in the coins, whereas nowhere do we find Ishā Khan calling himself Kararani. Dāud Khan is not known as Ismail, except in the State-records of the Dewan family of a later period. Here the Ain's statement is in favour in our theory. The later chroniclers of the family give Dāud the name of Ismail to make him a brother of Ishā Khan and thus establish him as a scion of the Kararani family.

If we summarise the three different versions of Ishā Khan's ancestry, we find the following discrepancies. Dr. Wise states, on the authority of the information supplied by the Dewans, that the father of Ishā Khan married a daughter of Hussein Shah. The "Mashnad Ali Itihāsa," published at the cost of the Dewans, says, not long after, that Ishā Khan's father married a daughter of Ghiasuddin. And the Second ballad, alleged by its author Abdul Karim to have been written at the instance of some of the Dewans of his time, states that Ishā Khan's father married a daughter of Baber! Either all these three accounts should be discredited, or the first one believed, as it has some corroborative evidence to support it. The fact, however, remains proved that Kalidas Gazdani turned a Mahomedan, assuming the name of Sulaiman Khan and that he married the daughter of a ruling Mahomedan King. In this all the three accounts and other evidences agree.

Barring the question of ancestry, there is a general agreement as regards the episodes in the life of Ishā Khan, described in the "Itihāsa" and in the different versions of the ballads, though there are points in them, which received some colouring in the hands of the various bards and historians. None of these accounts, however, as I have already stated, noted the incidents of the early career of Ishā Khan, which, on the authority of the "Ain" and the Rajmālā, remain as outstanding facts of unquestionable authenticity.

I will, here, give a brief account of Ishā Khan's adventures in Tipperah from the year 1578, when Amar Manikya was the ruling king of that place.

It seems, on his return from Turan to Bengal, Ishā Khan did not at once rise to celebrity. He seems to have gathered a force and settled in Pergaṇa Sarail in the distruct of Tipperah. I will here pursue the narrative of his life in Tipperah, as given in the Rajmālā.

Amar Māṇikya asked Subuddhi Nārāyan, a son of Harish Chandra, as to the number of coolies, supplied by each of his allies and tributary chiefs for excavating the "Amardighi," which he had undertaken to construct at Chouddagrām, on the west of the Udaipur Hills in Saka 1504 (1582 A. D.).

Subuddhi Nārāyan replied:—

"The Zeminder of Vikrampur, Chand Ray, has supplied us seven hundred men. These men are all hard-working and clever. The Vasu of Bāklā (Buckergunje) has sent seven hundred and the Zeminder of Bhowāl (Jaydevpur, Dacca) has supplied one thousand men. We have received five hundred men from Ashtagrām and another five hundred from Bāniāchung (Sylhet). We have got one thousand men from Raṇa-Bhowāl and *one thousand men have been supplied by Ishā Khan of Sarail.* We have got one thousand men from Balaram Sur of Bhulua (Noakhali)"............"We have thus secured 7,100 men from outside and these are engaged in excavating the tank. Some of these Rajas and Zeminders have supplied men out of fear and others out of love and respect for the Tipperah-throne. All the twelve Zeminders have thus come forward to help us with men. But the Raja of Tarap (Sylhet) has refused our demand."

Amar Manikya was highly incensed at the conduct of the Raja of Tarap and sent an army, 22,000 strong, under prince Rajdhar, to subdue Fateh Khan, King of Tarap. The prince defeated and captured Soddhorām, the general of Tarap-Raja, with his son. They were put into a cage and sent to Udaypur. The Tipperah-army next proceeded to conquer the Pathan King of Sylhet (Tarap) *and Ishā Khan was placed at the head of the navy.*[1]

"At the command of king Amar Manikya, the Bengali soldiers *undertook the expedition under Ishā Khan.* They went ahead of the tide by the river Surma and reached Sylhet."

Then follows an animated description as to how the Afghan chief, Fateh Khan, was conquered by prince Rajdhar and Ishā Khan. The names of the Bengali generals, who fought under them, have been given with some details of their qualifications in the account. Fateh Khan surrendered himself and was brought to Udaypur on the 1st of Magh in Saka 1504 (about the middle of January, 1582). "The king publicly praised Ishā Khan for his valour and gave him a seat on the left side of his son-in-law, Dayāvant Narain," at a Durbar held to commemorate his victory.

Sometime after this an Amir of the Delhi Emperor (probably Shah Baz Khan) led an expedition into the very heart of Eastern Bengal and attacked Ishā Khan who seems to have planted himself firmly at Sarail and

[1] The italics are ours

the adjacent locality by this time. Ishā beat a retreat and sought the help of Amar Manikya at this crisis.

He consulted two generals of the Raja—Tāz Khan and Bāz Khan, as to how he could secure substantial help from the Tipperah Raja and was advised to apply to queen Amarāvati Devi for intercession in his behalf. "The King," they said, "was a devoted husband and listened to the counsel of his queen in all matters." Ishā Khan sent a petition to queen Amarāvati and addressed her as "Mother" in the letter. This sort of address to an Indian lady is sure to appeal to her tenderly and ensure sympathy for the supplicant. The queen, at the request of Ishā Khan, washed her breast with water and sent him a drop to drink, which the Muhammadan Chief did with all affection and respect. This act was tantamount to his sucking the breast of the queen in the manner of a child, and Ishā Khan was treated from this time as a foster-son of Amarāvati. Curiously Mr. Long in his abridged translation of the Rajmālā renders the Bengali passage in the following words :—

"He (Ishā Khan) also won the favour of the Rani who tested his sincerity by giving him the water with which she had washed her body. He drank it."[1] What a queer and monstrous idea! But a foreign writer may be excused for his mistake on a point like this. We wonder how a scholar like Babu Kailas Chandra Sinha could paraphrase the verse in the following rendering! "অমরমাণিক্যের রাজ্ঞীও ঈষা খাঁকে পাদোদক প্রেরণ করিয়া বলিয়া পাঠাইলেন," etc. He calls it the water in which the king's feet were washed. He was evidently afraid of referring to the breast of the queen, lest it should offend the delicate sense of decency of our educated countrymen, imbibed by them from the western people. This is, however, a

[1] Analysis of Rajmālā by Rev. J. Long, p. 16.

sacred convention with the Asiatic races and there is nothing unholy or indecent in referring to the mother's breast at least in the eyes of the Oriental people.

Ishā Khan thus succeeded in ingratiating himself into the confidence of Amar Manikya, who was already predisposed in his favour for his past services in the interest of the State. The king granted him fifty thousand soldiers. As soon as Ishā Khan reached Sarail with this army, the Delhi General retreated from the field without venturing an encounter. It is stated here that Īshā Khan got many tokens of royal favour from Tipperah; but when we find the author of Rajāmālā, mentioning in this connection, that the title of 'Machalandani' was conferred on Ishā Khan by Amar Manikya, we feel that the court-parasite was perhaps trying to humour a descendant of that Raja, at whose order the history was written. But here, also, we reserve our judgment for reasons stated in the foot-note.[1]

Ishā Khan was now the master of 52,000 soldiers, as we find in the account of Rajmālā. He probably conceived from this time the idea of establishing his independence in Bengal. He could not have possibly

[1] Curiously the fit title of Ishā Khan, inscribed on his gun is not "Mashnad Ali," but, barring the 1st letter, which cannot be deciphered (probably a mere scratch) and which Stapleton reads as ব with a sign of query, the word reads Masenandalwi (মসেনন্দালি). The reading of this word by Mr. Stapleton as "বমসনদী ফি" is evidently incorrect. The word "মচলন্দানি" (the চ and স have similar sound in ordinary spoken Bengali and the ন, the last letter in the word, may have been confounded with ল by the Bengali copyist) seems very much similar to মসনন্দালি of the gun. Is it the Bengali form of the word Mashnad Ali? That the title of Mashnad Ali was granted to Ishā Khan by Akbar, is not known, so far as I am aware, from any other source than the State-record of the Dewan family itself. The repeated attempts of the historians of Jangal Bāri to connect the Dewans with the emperors of Delhi in all matters make us view this point with some suspicion. What is the reason for their having obliterated all facts relating to Ishā Khan's dealings with Amar Manikya, the king of Tippera? It should be stated here that the Khilat, if it was conferred on Ishā Khan by Akbar, has not been preserved in the family.

A Cannon of Ishā Khan with inscription. P. 314

Laksman Hazra's Capital reduced to a swamp. P. 315

achieved this end, remaining in the district of Sarail, for there he could only hold the status of a Feudatory Chief under the Tipperah Raja. Besides some other developments took place at Sarail, which made his position there not a very enviable one. Prince Rajdhara in one of his hunting excursions, found Pergana Sarail as abounding with jungles—a resort of buffaloes, bears, tigers and antelopes. The game attracted him and crossing the Titāsh, he wandered through the 42 villages of the Pergana, placed in the midst of a great wilderness and conceived the idea of founding a country-house at Sarail, from which he could go out a-hunting and extend his dominions by cutting down the jungle (the Rajmālā, p. 193).

Shah Bāz Khan was, in the meantime, preparing himself for a fight to avenge himself upon Ishā Khan for the affront the latter had given him with the aid of the Tipperah Raja. Ishā Khan, now master of a great army, wanted to find a secure place where he could be safe from the hands of the Imperialists and extend his power by new conquests. The details of his fights with the Delhi army and of his flight from the field are given in some of these ballads. It was at this time (1585 A.D.) that the unfortunate Coch Rajas, the brothers, Ram Hazra and Lakshman Hazra, were suddenly attacked by Ishā during the night. They fled by means of a tunnel in the palace—the relics of which are still in existence. The capital of the Coch Rajas, the Jangal Bāri (the Forest-home) became the chief seat of Ishā Khan's family.

In the ballad of Dewan Mannowar Khan, a grandson of Ishā Khan, we have got a reference to the palace the former had built at Dacca. The place where the stately mansion once stood, is still called "Dewan

Bāg."[1] In the survey-map the place is called 'Mannowar Khaner Bāg.' It is situate dnear the junction of the Akātiā Khāl and Sitalākshyā, seven miles north-east of Naraingunj. In the 'Dewan Bāg' seven brass cannon were discovered by some men, while excavating earth, sometime in February, 1909. Mr. S. E. Stinton, the then Magistrate of Dacca, made over the cannon to Mr. Stapleton for description. The latter has given a detailed account of these guns in the October number of the Journal of Asiatic Society Bengal, 1899. The first of these is tiger-mouthed and bears an inscription of Sher Shah, dated the 949 H. E. (1542 A. D.). The second, third and fourth are nearly of the same model and have tiger-heads on the top. This tiger may be taken as a symbol of Sher or tiger, in compliment to the King. The remaining three guns evidently belong to Ishā Khan. On the first of them is inscribed his name; the other two are of the same type. These seven cannon were undoubtedly the possessions of the Dewans. The inscription in Persian on the first gun shows that Sher Shah cast it in the year 1542; but it is noteworthy that at the other end of the gun, below the breech, is found, in Bengali, the word "Tarap Raja."

We have already found it, on the authority of the Rajmālā that Ishā Khan and prince Rajdhar led an expedition to Tarap and conquered the Pathan chief, Fateh Khan. This Fateh Khan must have secured Sher Shah's guns by inheritance or by force and when they became his property, he had, at least on one of them, the word "Tarap Raja" inscribed in Bengali, implying his present ownership. Sher Shah came from the northwest and hence his inscription was in Persian, the court-language

* 1. According to Dr. Wise, this garden-house coverred an area of 169 acres. See "Isha Khan Masnadali of Khizirpur". J. A. S. B. 1874. pp. 209-214.

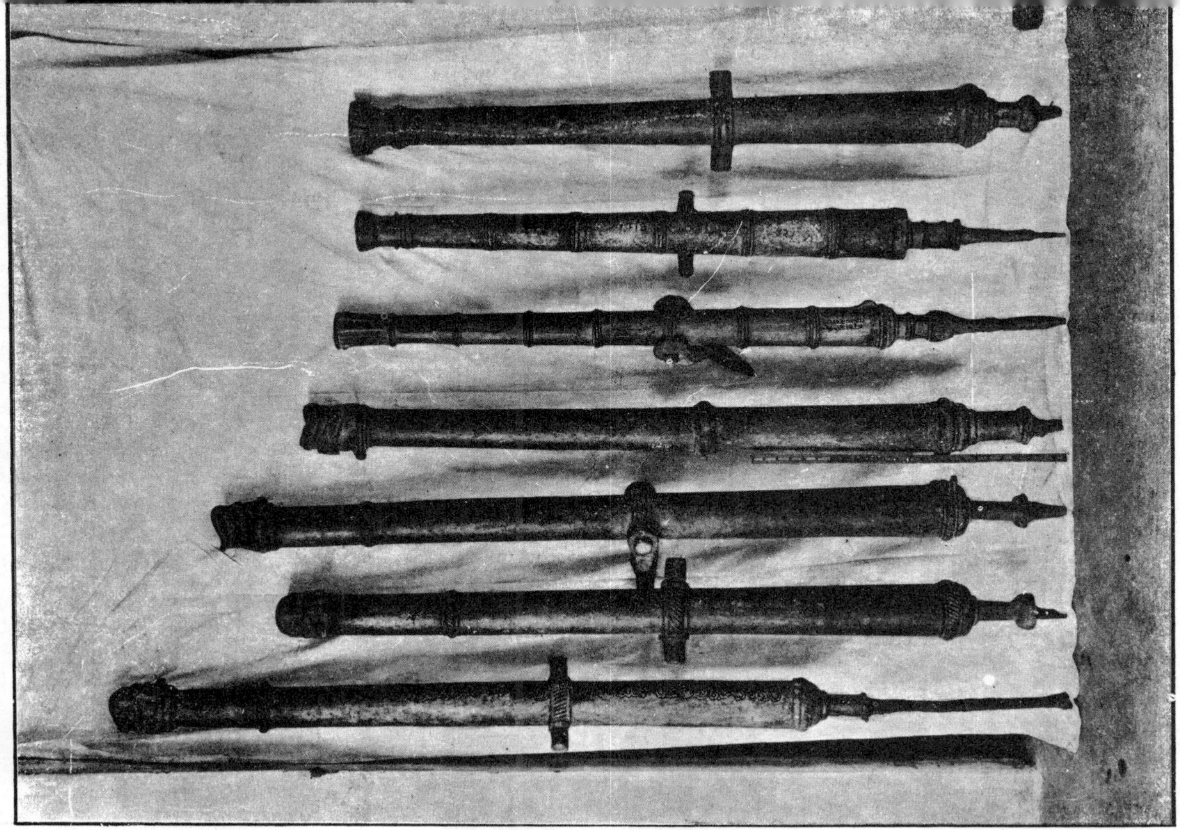

Ishā Khan's Cannon. P. 316

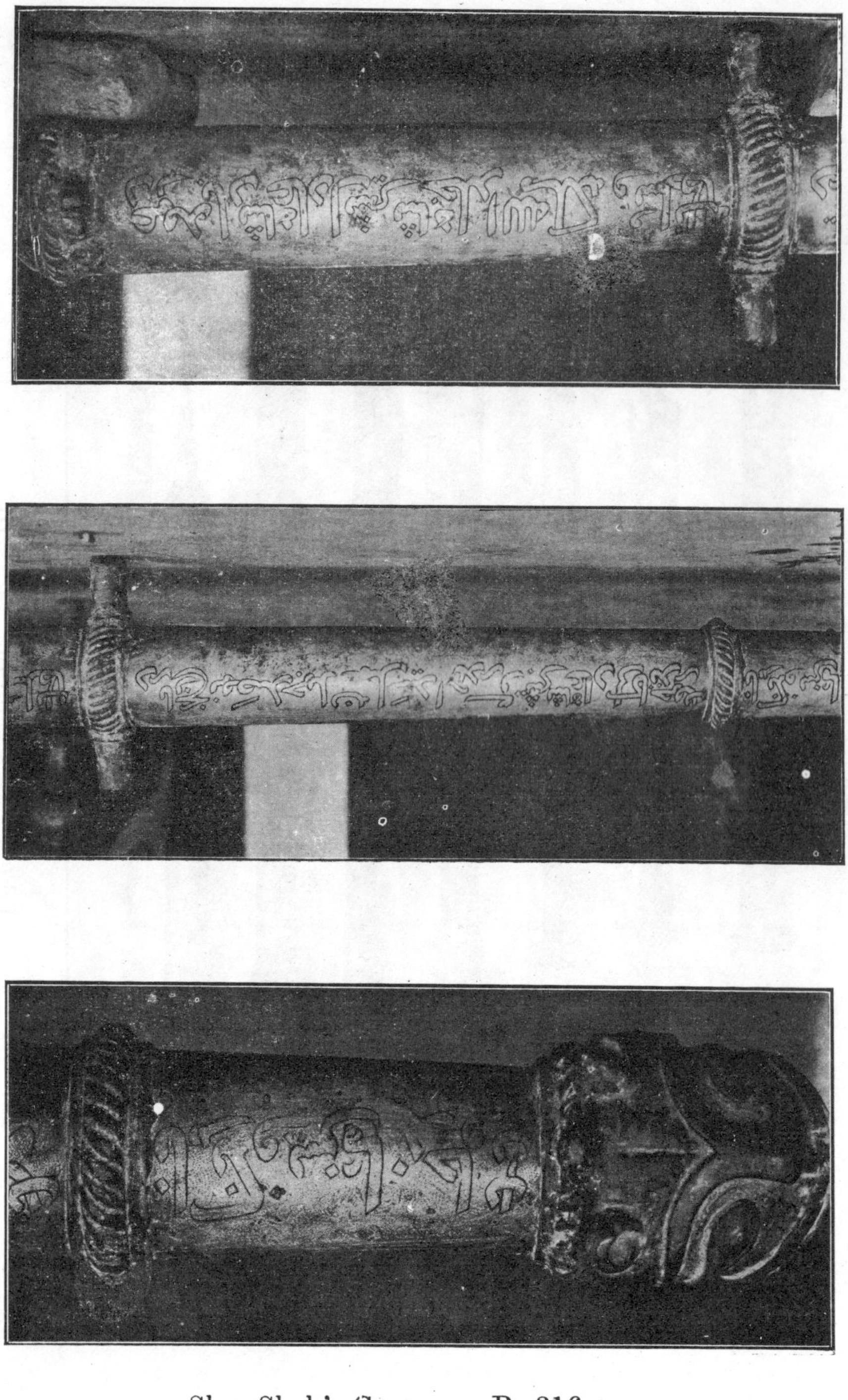

Sher Shah's Cannon. P. 316

of Delhi and other western provinces, occupied by the Mahomedans. But in Sylhet, Assam and Tipperah in Eastern Bengal, generally the court-language was Bengali during the 14th to 18th centuries, as is proved by the coins and copper-plate grants, issued by the rulers of these countries. This accounts for the fact that the fifth gun, bearing Ishā Khan's name, has its inscription in Bengali characters. We have thus found a sure clue as to how the four guns of Sher Shah came to the possession of Ishā Khan. Sher Shah was an Afghan and Fateh Khan of Tarap was also of the same tribe. So it is quite conceivable that Fateh Khan secured the guns of Sher Shah by direct inheritance or from some of his kinsmen. Ishā Khan obtained them by his victory over Fateh Khan. The remaining three guns belonged to Ishā Khan and no comment is necessary on them, except a historical point, involved in the date, inscribed in Bengali on one of them, to which I wish to draw attention. It is Hizra 1002 or 1593 A.D., the year when Man Sing was sent to conquer the redoubted chief of Jangal Bāri. It was evidently for the purpose of equipping himself for fighting with the Hindu General of Akbar that Ishā Khan cast some new guns and these three indicate the martial exigencies of the year.

Thus from the year 1578 when, as a landlord of some status, Ishā Khan sent one thousand men responding to a call from Amar Manikya to help in the excavation of the "Amar Dighi" near the Udeypur hills, down to the year 1593 when he fought battles with Man Sing and surrendered himself at Egara Sindur to the latter after a strenuous warfare, which evoked the admiration of Akbar and led him to order his release and confer a grant of twenty-two Perganas on him, we have a connected narrative of Ishā Khan's life, gathered from different sources. The first part of his career was ignored by the bards and chroniclers, who were appointed to write the history of Jangal Bāri by some of the Dewans themselves. But, for the detailed account of the latter part of his life, we have enough material in those treatises and ballads, though the reader must always be cautious in accepting the accounts as correct in their details.

The State-records, and following these, Dr. Wise have declared that Kalidas Gazdani was convinced of the superiority of Islam by the learned lectures of the court-minister of the reigning Moslem King and renounced Hinduism in his sincere faith in the new creed. But the first ballad relates a romantic love-affair. As it is certain that he married a Moslem princess, the greater possibility is that he favoured Muhammadanism because he loved a Muhammadan princess. He was a Hindu of the orthodox type. He gave away every day an elephant, plated with gold, to Brahmins, for which he was called "Gazdāni" (of course the elephant was far from being life-size). We are not inclined to believe that such a devout Hindu, as he was, could give up his religion at once, listening to the discourses of a Mahomedan minister, who is not known to have been an inspired prophet. A greater probability lies in the other direction where the omnipotent deity, presiding over the heart of human beings, found an opportunity to aim his dart. The State-papers of Jangal Bāri have very solid reasons for giving this shape to the story. They would naturally try to suppress anything that might look like a family scandal, as in Indian homes these points are so delicate that a very slight matter often proves damaging to the honour of a household. At the same time one point may be urged by way of discrediting the accounts of the ballad-makers that it is very usual with them to introduce a love-tale, wherever they find a margin or blank space in the body of the narrative, where they can conveniently manage to do it. With these remarks, I leave the readers to form their own judgments. The Dewans of Jangal Bāri once wielded great power over Eastern Bengal, but in spite of it, they were looked down upon by the genuine Mahomedan family, who had come from the north-west and settled there. In the ballad of Dewan Ferōz Khān, we find how a proposal of his marriage with a princess of Kella Tāzpur was indignantly rejected by her father Omar Khan. He called the Dewan family of Jangal Bāri *kafirs*, and infidels, guided by Hindu tastes and having Hindu blood running in their veins.

The name of Kedar Ray's daughter, as given in the ballad, is Subhadrā. She is, however, traditionally known among the Hindus by the name of Sonā or Sonāmani, which our writers sometimes turn into its Sanskritised form 'Swarnamayee.' It is not unlikely that amongst her own people, she was known by her more familiar pet-name of Sonā or Sonāmani, and when she entered the Mahomedan harem, she assumed her more dignified name Subhadrā. Difficulties have sometimes arisen in respect of the names of many of the personages, mentioned in these ballads. The popular ballads have sometimes given the more familiar names, quite different from those used in official documents. Amongst strangers, whom latterly Sonā adopted as her own, it was most natural for her to give up her undignified pet-name and use the classical word 'Subhadrā' instead. All accounts agree in stating that the Mahomedan name she adopted was Niyāmat Jān.[1]

We do not find any mention of the sons of Subhadrā either in the 'Mashnad Ali Itihāsa' or in the genealogy, given of the Dewan family by Mr. Stapleton in his article. But the names of Adam and Birām are quite familiar in the literature of the ballads, dealing with the history of the Dewan family, mostly written by Mahomedans. We find a good many incidents of their lives described in these ballads. There seems to be no reason to doubt that Ishā Khan got two sons by the Hindu princess and that they were called Adam and Birām. Of course they were familiarly called by these names. They had certainly some dignified names, used in official records, to which we have not been able to get a clue. Babu Durgacharan Sanyal gives an account of Sonamani's (Subhadrā's) return to her father's home on the death of Ishā Khan and living an ascetic life, as an outcaste. He says that the Dewans of Haibatpur were descended from the sons of the Hindu Begum of Ishā Khan.[2] I do not know how far the statement is true.

Of course, the orthodox Mahomedan writers would not like the idea of tracing the descent of a noble Moslem family from a Hindu and hence it might be quite possible that some of them would try to obliterate all trace of a princess of Kayastha family from the genealogy of the Dewans. We all know that Jahangir was a son of Jodha Bāi and there were many

[1] We have recently come across a ballad evidently composed by a Muhammadan in which she is called Sonai and not Subhadra.

[2] Printed as Sahabatpur, but corrected in the author's own handwriting in the margin of the copy, presented to me, as Haibatpur.—*Sanyal's Social History of Bengal*, p. 443.

such cases in the aristocratic Muhammadan families of India. But an Emperor of Delhi could assimilate foreign elements in his home, and he was too high to be criticised. Besides, when a point was an undisputed fact of history, there was no help but to admit it. But in smaller communities, and where one could easily wipe away all signs of a foreign connection, it is not unlikely that such a thing should happen. A Mahomedan nobleman may be naturally looked down upon for being descended from a Hindu wife, by orthodox people amongst Muhammadans. In the face of the existing circumstances, however, there is no clue to discover if any of the numerous branches of the Dewan family has wilfully blotted out the name of the princess of Sripur from their genealogical accounts. We attach no importance to what Mr. Sanyal says about the Haibatpur branch being descended from her, as the writer gives no authority for his statement. Dr. Wise mentions that there is a curious custom in one of the branches of the Dewan family, settled at Harishpur in Tippera, that the eldest son of the Zaminder is always styled 'Thākur.' This merely proves the existence of a Hindu custom in the family. And it should be known that the title of Thākur is not confined in Bengal to the Brahmins alone; it is also found amongst the Kayasthas and some other high castes. I do not know if this title refers to any custom in the family of the abducted Hindu princess. The title may also imply that the particular line of the Dewan family, stationed in the Tippera Rāj, adopted the custom in imitation of the Tippera Rajas, whose eldest son inherits the Rāj and is called "Yubarāj" and the second son is called by the title "Thākur."

There is, however, another possibility, which I beg to suggest, in spite of its doubtful character, in the absence of any historical evidence.

It is a well-known fact that the residence of Ishā Khan at Baktiarpur was destroyed by the imperial troops under Shah Bāz Khan in 1583. Dr. Wise refers to this catastrophe in his article, already referred to. In one of the ballads on Ishā Khan, we find a curious story that one of the Dewans, after Ishā Khan's death, had set fire to the palace of Jangal Bāri and destroyed his whole family, because the Delhi troops had peeped into his Zenana. The sense of honour of the Dewan must have been so delicate as to verge on madness. But the whole thing seems to me to be a mere piece of fancy and nothing more than that. When we read a ballad, composed by an illiterate peasant, his accounts are generally found correct, at least his mistakes are *bona-fide.* But when a half-lettered villager garbles out a tale with the conscious effort of making a display, we cannot conceive to what extent he may show the monstrous range of his fancy by distorting facts. The author of the ballad in question seems to us to belong to that school. He tells us that as soon as Dewan Abdul heard that the Delhi troops, his own allies, had constructed a high ladder with bamboo-poles out of curiosity and peeped into his Zenana, having a full view of the ladies, he was covered with a sense of disgrace and ordered that all the gates of the inner apartment should be shut. He then proceeded to set fire to the palace, which was burnt down to ashes with its inmates, and only a poor baby of six months, Machoom Khan survived, having been thrown down by a maid-servant from over the roof into the basket of a fisher-woman, who saved the poor thing from death. All other members of the Dewan family and their attendants died in the conflagration as the doors were shut from outside; and this is the way in which the Dewan Saheb revenged himself upon the Delhi troops !

The whole seems to be a myth, pure and simple. But I refer to the story for one reason. May it not be taken as indicating some historical event, relating to an expedition of the Imperialists into Jangal Bāri and the subsequent destruction of the palace by them ? The incident is said to have occurred shortly after Adam and Birām had returned to the palace, having married the two daughters of Kedar Ray. If there is any grain of truth in this account, it certainly hints at a tragedy, in which the princes met with a melancholy end. There seems to have been some popular tradition of the Jangal Bāri palace being destroyed by the Moghul army and of the consequent destruction of many members of the Dewan family. Such a tragic event could not but have left an impression on the popular mind. But the author of the ballad would not like to describe an event, showing the defeat of the invincible Dewans, whose prowess he had extolled beyond all measure, —even to the extent of declaring that Ishā Khan had usurped the throne of Delhi and thereby struck terror into the heart of Humayun. Thus he gave out a version, monstrously distorted, in which he attempted to prove how delicate was the sense of family honour with the Dewans !

The ballad-maker also states that the army of the Moghuls was one thousand in number and that they had lived for six months at the cost of the Dewan Sahib. All this hints at some altercation in which the Moghul army suddenly besieged the palace of Jangal Bāri and setting fire to it, destroyed it with many of the members of the Dewan family. .t is also mentioned in the ballad that for fourteen years the Jangal Bāri palace was in a deserted condition and when Machoom Khan, the surviving scion of the family in that locality, grew to be a lad of fourteen, he was invited by the people to take the reins of administration in his hands and that he had the old mansion, thoroughly repaired, before he sat on the '*gadi*' of his ancestors.

The destruction of the residence of Ishā Khan at Baktiarpur in 1583 by Shah Baz Khan has already been mentioned by me. Through the vista of these tragical incidents in the family of the Dewans, we have glimpses of events, which may indicate some catastrophic end of the sons of Subhadrā. At the same time it must be admitted that the genealogical accounts of the Dewan family, that have been hitherto available to us, are neither exhaustive nor accurate. In Dr. Wise's table we find that the line of Haibatnagar is descended from a brother of Ishā Khan, whereas the genealogy, given by Mr. Stapleton and in the 'Itihasā' it is traced directly from Ishā Khan. Not only are discrepancies of this sort very common, but throughout Mymensingh, there are innumerable families, who claim their descent from Ishā Khan. Some of these are undoubtedly "Nazar Marichar Chhele" or descended from the beautiful Hindu maidens, brought into the harem of the Dewans in lieu of "Nazar Marichā" or marriage-tax. I have written about them in full in my Introduction to the first part of the ballads. These children of "Nazar Marichā" not only inherited their paternal property but were called Dewans by courtesy. None of these lines would now admit that they are descended from Hindu women in that way, for reasons I have stated in connection with Subhadrā. It is impossible to collect a genealogical account of the different branches of the Dewan family, some of whom have sunk into abject poverty and low status and lost all touch with the main stock. In the face of these difficulties, it is not possible to find out any clue as to the immediate descendants of Âdam and Birām, if they lived long enough to have issue. But as I have already stated, it seems certain that they were sons of Ishā Khan by Subhadrā and that their uncle Kedar Ray had tried his best to revenge himself upon the innocent lads for the fault, if any, of their mother, who, instead of committing suicide by 'Jahar Brata' or courting death in some other way, had clung to Ishā Khan as a devoted wife and thus brought a great disgrace on the Rāj family of Sripur.[1]

[1] Babu Swarup Chandra Ray in his 'Suvarna Grāmer Itīhāsa,' published in 1891, gives some interesting facts about Sonāmani. He says that Sonāmani was abducted by Ishā Khan with the help of a treacherous officer of Chand Ray, who had been bribed by the Dewan. It is said that a good many bloody wars were fought between Chand Ray and Ishā Khan over the great insult, done to the noble Hindu family. Chand Roy seriously damaged the fort of Ishā Khan, built by him at Kalaigachha and devastated the town of Khijirpur, which had once been the capital of the Moslem Chief. It has been further stated that after Ishā Khan's death, Chand Ray plundered the town of Jangal Bāri and tried various other ways to take revenge on his family.

It is also related that Sonāmani met a tragic end. She fought hard against the Burmese marauders, who had laid seize to the fort of Hazigunj, in which she had taken refuge. But being unable to hold her own, she courted death by throwing herself into fire, for fear of being captured by the enemy. We find, also, a statement to the effect that the Tipperah Raja joined with the Burmese and Kedar Ray of Vikrampur in attacking Jangal Bāri and plundering it after the death of Ishā Khan. We have already referred to the fact, on the authority of the Rajmala, that Ishā Khan was once a great ally of Raja Amar Mānikya. That latterly there was an estrangement of feeling between the Moslem Chief and the Tipperah Raja may be inferred from the fact that no notice was taken, even by the ballad-makers of Mymensingh, of the hard fight which Ishā Khan had once fought in the interest of the Tipperah State. They wanted to obliterate all memory of Ishā Khan's association with Tipperah. According to the "Suvarna Grāmer Itīhāsa," Ādam and Birām had no issue. Like one or two other historical accounts, this Itīhāsa states that Sonāmani was *a daughter and not a sister* of Chand Ray.

In the account given by the Dewans, we find Mānsing's wife, appealing with tears to Ishā Khan to agree to accompany her husband to Delhi. The plea was that if he would not comply, the Emperor was sure to behead her husband. And Dewan Ishā Khan, taking pity on her, gallantly agreed to be taken as a captive to Delhi and allowed himself to be thrown into prison there with the noble purpose of saving Mansing's life from the wrath of the autocratic Emperor. This story evidently exaggerates the valour and other noble qualities of Ishā Khan at the cost of Mānsing, who is represented here as a general of no high merit, if not altogether a coward. Dr. Wise has believed in this story furnished by the Dewan family. But the popular version, written by a Mahomedan ballad-maker, gives a more reliable account. It glorifies Ishā Khan without lowering Mānsing. The valour of the former is praised ; he is represented as holding his own in the fort of Egar Sindura like a brave hero that he was. It, besides, gives details of the stratagem, employed by Mānsing to make him a captive. The whole thing appears quite natural. It does not diminish the glory either of Ishā Khan or of Mānsing and describes the situation very well in which both these warriors found ample opportunities to discover, and appreciate their respective merits in the battle-field, eventually leading to the release of Ishā Khan from the prison of Delhi and to the bestowal of great favours on him by the Emperor through the intercession of Mānsing.

Some historians have recorded that Kedar Ray died of the effect of an wound, received in battle with Mānsing. The ballad, however, gives a totally different account. Mānsing came to Bengal to subdue some of of the refractory chiefs of Bengal and he no doubt fought with Kedar Ray. It is not unlikely that the latter was wounded in some affray with the great general of Akbar. If it was true that Karimulla actually killed Kedar Ray, as stated in the ballad, it would still be quite possible for Mānsing to have appropriated the credit to himself in his report to the Delhi Emperor. The reputation of Karimulla, a village hero, could not have possibly gone beyond Bengal. In the ballad of Manoowar Khan, we find that Sripur was destroyed by the army of Jangal Bāri with the help received from Delhi. So the heroic exploits and successes, achieved by Karimulla, might have been ignored by the great generals of Delhi, in their accounts, sent to Delhi, in order to appropriate the entire credit and full share of glory to themselves.

Ishā Khan, it is indicated in the Muhammadan chronicles, reigned "from Ghoraghat to sea." It is not true that the other eleven sub-lords of Bengal admitted him as their feudal lord. It may be said with some certainty that he was the most powerful of them. Kedar Ray reigned at Sripur, which once stood on the banks of the Padmā. On the bank of that river was Khijirpur, once the principal seat of Ishā Khan. The grandeur of the city of Sripur is on record and Kedar Ray seems to have wielded a great power over the tract of land from Sripur to Dacca. Karimulla, the famous general of the Dewan family, found himself safe from his jurisdiction, while reaching the latter city, where a strong Mahomedan power was stationed, as we come to learn from the ballads. Kedar Ray and Chand Ray reigned over the large and important Perganna of Vikrampur, "and between Ishā Khan of Khijirpur, whose strength was on the opposite bank of the Ganges (Padmā) and the two brothers, there was constant warfare." The historic temple at Rājbāri which was reckoned as one of the typical monuments of Bengali sculpture and which Dr. Wise has described in detail, has recently been washed away by the treacherous river, on the bank of which it stood. The temple was associated with Kedar Ray. But the temple evidently bore signs of Pre-Muhammadan art and showed many features of Buddhist sculpture. Dr. Wise, while assigning its foundation to Kedar Ray, remarks, "The walls are eleven feet thick, larger than those found in Mahomedan buildings of the same age, being eight inches square and one and a half thick." The massive walls are of the pre-Mahomedan period and the vast reservoir in front of the monument, called "Keshaber Mār dighi" is probably indicative of some forgotten lady, at whose order the *Math* was founded. We cannot endorse Dr. Wise's statement on the authority of an absurd rustic story that the *Dighi* was constructed by one of the servants of Kedar Ray. The *Math* and the tank are always constructed together by the same person. My belief is that the *Math* was built in the Buddhist times and that Kedar Ray and Chand Ray had it thoroughly repaired and associated it latterly with their own names. Its archæological features have led us to derive this conclusion. With this historic edifice, Eastern Bengal has probably lost one of her noblest of monuments of the Buddhist age.

After the settlement of Bengal in Akbar's reign, Ishā Khan is said to have possessed 22 pergannas in Eastern Bengal, the names of which are mentioned in the body of the texts. The original residence of the family, as has already been stated, was at Baiswari in Oudh. Mr. Stapleton says "Bais and yāra" written without spaces on either side of the "৩" is simply Baiswara. The name Baiswara has apparently reference to 22 pergannas, held by these Rajputs, and the fact that Ishā Khan was also granted the same number of Pergannas in Eastern Bengal may be regarded as some actual proof of his descent from the Rajputs of Baiswara."

The ballads give accurate details of customs and manners prevalent in Eastern Bengal in the 16th century. They refer to the artistic designs, with which bungalows were constructed in the district of Mymensingh in those days. The feathers of the crane, of the king-fishers and of the pea-cocks were used in plenty for the purpose of decorating the roofs. It was a fashion to erect a number of crystal pillars in the mansions of the nobles and chiefs. The relics of such pillars are to be found even to this day in the débris of the palatial buildings of Mujlis Jelal. We also come to learn from these ballads that the big boats, which still go by the name of "koshā" in Eastern Bengal is suggestive of the fact that in olden times, a whole fleet would be so large as to cover two miles—a *krosha.* Of course Ishā Khan's 'koshā,' though undoubtedly a very big one, was far from being the monster-ship of the ancient Hindus and only proved the tradition of the old-world trading vessels. In ancient times it was the fashion to construct huge things. The Babylonians and Egyptians were famous for building gigantic monuments. This fashion was preserved till much later times in India. Huen-tshang saw, in Northern India, many huge figures of the Buddha, one of which stood as high as the Ochterloney monument, and that is a matter of the seventh century A. D.

We come to know from the ballads that the Muhammadan ladies of high rank used to wear Persian '*saris*' in those days and young Moslem noblemen favoured coats, made in Egypt. They wore caps made in Arabia, and used gorgeous shoes and slippers, inlaid with jewels, made by Persian artists.

Dr. Wise refers to the three Sanads, preserved by the Jangal Bāri family.

The first is from Shah Suja and is dated the 21st Julas of Shah Jehan A. H. 1057 (1647 A. D.) It directs Ahmad and Iwaz Muhammad, members of the family, to pay the revenues of the estates, jointly held by them to I't Quid Khan.

The second is dated A. H. 1059 (1649 A. D.) and is sent by Shah Suzā to the Munsabdars and other officials to make over some dockyards, which had previously been built by the government.

The third is dated 1700 A. D. and is an order from Azim ush Khan requiring Haibat Mahomed to keep in readiness 37 koshā-boats with 32 boatmen in each and to pay Rs. 10,267-7, the revenue of the Pergannas Budak'hāl, etc.

The ballad of Manowar Khan, which, for some reasons, we cannot publish in this volume, scarcely possesses any rural simplicity or directness, which is the most important characteristic of this class of songs. In it we come across the pedantry of a half-lettered village-poet, reminding us often of the age of Bhārat Chandra, when amorous subjects carried to abnormal excesses, received favour. But in Bhārat Chandra, his inimitably finished style, the classical dignity of words and their wealth of music invest even the most erotic matters with a literary fineness which, to some extent, hides the nudity of a disgusting scene. Many of his imitators, however, without possessing the grace and scholarship of the great master, imbibed his faults to a point outrageous to decency. Though this ballad may be charged with some of these blemishes, it no doubt gives us some real accounts of Manowar Khan and his dealings with Shah Sujā, from which the historian will be able to trace the later career of that unfortunate prince, now covered with a mist, which hardly leaves a vista to give some glimpses into the real facts of that period of his life. This account, coupled with that to be found in one of the works of the celebrated Mahomedan poet Alwal are perhaps the only source from which an account of the later events of Shāh Suza's life may be gleaned.[1]

In these historical ballads, we can hardly expect to meet with much poetry. But still the ballad of Ferōz Khan gives a picture of a real epic grandeur towards the end in the death of Sakhina,--a picture which, more than brass or marble, is a lasting memorial to that great heroine, presenting her unique and sublime martyrdom for love in the rude but simple language of the rustic poet.

We have noticed the episode fully in our Introduction to the first volume. Though lacking in poetry, these ballads do not lack in interest. In most of these, the reader follows the incidents described, with ardent curiosity and these descriptions have none of that haziness, which characterise the flamboyant and frothy style of some of our modern writers, but are vivid and always relevant to the point. Conciseness is generally the special quality of the ballads and their authors seldom use two words, when they can convey their idea by one.

[1] We have just received information from Babu Ashutosh Chowdhury, one of our ballad-collectors, that he has heard some ballads describing the love of a daughter of Sāh Suza with a Burmese prince. The ballad-maker humourously asks the Moslem princess as to how she would wear *lungi* in the place of her gown and adapt herself to other curious ways of Burmese life. The ballad was sung to Ashu Babu by some Bediyas of Chittagong.

A Comparative Review of the Genealogical Records of the Dewan Family.

We subjoin here three genealogical tables which we have got of Ishā Khan's family. Of these the one given by Mr. Stapleton in his article published in the Journal of Asiatic Society of Bengal for 1909 is based on the Masnadali Itihas written by Munshi Raj Chandra Ghosh and Pandit Kali Kumar Chakraborty. We give Mr. Stapleton's table below.[1]

Kali Das Gajdani *alias* Solaiman Khan = 3rd daughter of Jalāl Shāh Sūri. Ruler of Bengal 1561-1563, A.D.

- Ismail
- Ishā d. 1599
  - Musa
    - Machoom (alive till 1667 A.D.)
      - Manwwar (conquered Chittagong in 1666).
        - Sharif
          - Fatima Bibi (M. Haibat Khan)
        - At least four other sons
          - Latif
          - Mahbbat
          - Adam and Masum
  - Muhammed
    - Iwaz Muhammed alive in 1650
      - Hidayat
      - Hayāl
        - Haibat (founder of Haibatnagar near Kishorgunj)
          - Abdullāh
    - Ahmad

[1] The table is given with good many omissions, specially in respect of the matrimonial alliances contracted by the family.

(2) Table given by Munshi Abdul Karim of the village Galāchipa in the Subdivision of Kishorgunj (Mymensingh) in his Ballad of Manwwar Khan.

Kali Das Gazdani, m. a daughter of Babar
alias Solaiman
Khan
|
Dewan Isā Khan
|
Abdul Khan
|
Machoom Khan
|
Manwwar Khan

In the ballad of Ishā Khan, Abdul Karim says that Machoom Khan had five sons, *viz.*, Manwwarali, Latif Amirali, Lātif Khan and Haibat Khan.

(3) The genealogical table given in 'the Subarna Gramer Itihas' by Swarup Chandra Roy, published by Lalit Mohan Das from the Sakha Press, 33, Musalman Para Lane, Calcutta, in 1891.

Kali Das Gazdani
|
Ishā Khan
- Adam Khan, Biram Khan
- Abdul Khan
  - Machoom Khan
    - Latif Khan
      - Khodadad Ali
    - Mahammed Khan
      - Ali Noaz Khan
    - Manwwar Khan
      - Bulban Khan
        - Alimurdan Khan
          - Lal Khan
          - Kamarali Khan
            - Omedali Khan
              - Hasan Ali
                - Umed Ali
              - Enait Ali
              - Ehadali
          - Samshor Khan
            - Bahadur Ali, Kumar Ali and Jamsher Khan
    - Sarif Khan

The two tables, *viz.*, the one given by Itihāsa and the other, for the most part, copied from it by Mr. Stapleton are practically the same, though the latter has the value of important footnotes by that scholar. But from a comparison of the other three tables and references to the genealogy of the family in the article of Dr. Wise, it appears that none of these has any substantial claim to reliability. The table given by Babu Swarup Chandra Ray was no doubt, collected from a branch of the Dewan family, settled in some locality near Suvarnagrām and reveals names, which are mostly not to be found in the other tables. The fact is that the descendants of the Dewans, legitimate and illegitimate, all called Dewans by true lineage or by courtesy, are so numerous and their status so varied that each of these families has a different record of its own, sometimes manipulated by the members in such a way as to enable them to establish their claims on direct descent from the main stock by lawful marriage. It is difficult to find out a real and accurate record from the forest of genealogies, supplied by ignorant and illiterate people.

Mosque and ruins of house of Ishā Khan's immediate descendants. P. 335

Dewan Isha Khan Mashnad Ali.

Chorus :—

"Let the drum beat in honour of Ishā Khan."

(1)

In the Western country there was a Raja named Dhanapat Singh. He was a great chief and his riches were immense. His slaves and maid-servants were innumerable. He was on terms of great intimacy with the Emperor of Delhi, who protected him at the hour of danger—as does the shadow of a tree the weary passenger scorched by the rays of the sun.

In the family of Raja Dhanapat Singh was born, in course of years, Raja Bhagirath, the worthy scion of an illustrious aristocratic family, who, for the well-being of his subjects, was ready to sacrifice every interest,—nay his life. Raja Bhagirath in course of his travels, visiting the Indian shrines, came last to the province of Bengal. After he had seen different parts of the country, he visited Gour—its capital, where Sultan Ghyas Uddin was reigning at that time. The Sultan received the Raja very warmly in his court and treated him with every mark of respect. It is only the noble heart that can appreciate nobility in others. Says the poet—"To the dog clarified butter has no taste or value."

The Sultan began to admire the noble qualities of Raja Bhagirath and with earnest entreaties persuaded him to accept the post of his Prime Minister and to stay at his capital. So Raja Bhagirath settled at Gour and by his piety and administrative talents soon made himself esteemed of all. The subjects of the Empire he treated as his children. No one ever saw him indulge in pride, though he held such an exalted position. His fame soon spread far and wide in the country.

From him was descended Kālidas, who, in his turn, held the rank of the Prime Minister of the Sultan of Gour. Jāinuddin was at that time on the throne of of Bengal.

Now, Kālidas, the Prime Minister, was a youth of exceedingly handsome appearance,—in fact, among the youthful members of aristocratic rank none was equal to him in personal attractions. He shone, as it were, with the brilliance of the sun. If the minister stood in a dark chamber, it appeared that its darkness was dispelled in an instant. Even Madan, the God of love—husband of Rati, was no match for him in personal grace and beauty.

He was, besides, known for his extensive charity. The poor people and the Fakirs daily received gifts at his hands. His court was a resort of scholars and ascetics. With their advice the minister performed the duties of his responsible office. At his order the figure of an elephant used to be cast in gold every morning, and this he gave as a gift to the Brahmins daily. For this, Kalidas, the minister, was popularly known by the title of 'Gajdāni' or 'the giver of elephants.' In his eyes there was no distinction between the Hindus and Muhammadans. There was no envy or spite in his soul. Every year he performed with great *eclat* the ceremonies of Dol—the swinging ceremony of Krishna—and the Durgotsava (the well-known Pujas held in October). Besides these, he performed all other ceremonies mentioned in the Hindu almanac, omitting none. He kept in his palatial house a collection of all kinds of rare things, some as curiosities and others for luxury or use. If any of his friends wanted anything from him he offered it with sincere love to oblige him. If a foreigner became a guest at his house, he was hospitality itself, while entertaining him. And until the guest was served he never tasted a morsel himself. In a word, there was scarcely another man in the country as conscientious, honest and good as Kālidas Gajdāni.

Bahadur Shaha had died without leaving any issue after having spent large sums on religious purposes and in charity. And on his death, Jainuddin (Jalaluddin) was installed on the throne of Gour, and young Kālidas as Prime Minister was at the head of the administration of Bengal. (Ll. 1-56.)

(2)

Jālāluddin had a daughter named Maminā Khātun, beautiful as the moon. Many young princes came to Gour seeking her hands but she did not choose any of them. So they went away disappointed. No young man did she find as accomplished as could win her heart. So the world lost all its charm for her. Now brethren, allow me a little time to describe her beauty. Like a living flame in a lonely place, her charms unfolded themselves brightening the Sultan's harem. Her long hair flowed down her waist in profuse curls. Her face was like the moon and her eyes were lovely as those of a gazelle. The fairies, when they beheld her, felt ashamed of themselves and readily admitted their inferiority. Youth had just dawned on her. With her attending maids did she spend her time gaily in sweet talks. When she walked, it seemed that a flood of beauty flowed on the earth. She appeared too delicate to bear the burden of her growing charms. Alas, who is that fortunate soul for whom God had created this maiden, exhausting all His artistic skill!

One day she happened to go to the bathing *ghat* of the river, surrounded by her maidens. And there on the way she saw Kālidas the minister. As soon as she saw him the surprising beauty of his person maddened her soul. She forgot herself and stood transfixed to the spot, glancing at his noble form.

From that day she did not relish her daily meals, and the whole night she lay on her bed without sleeping for a moment. At last she took a desperate step. She wrote a letter to Kālidas Gajdāni and handing it over to one of her maids said, "Go with this to Kālidas Gajdāni." The letter ran thus, "I have been yearning for you. From the day I saw you first, I have been feeling as if I should leave my house, kinsmen and all and join you. I should like to be your slave though I am a princess. I value you, dear lord, as does the blind man his eyes that he has regained."

The maid-servant started with the letter and reached the place of the minister. She unloosed it from the edge of her *saḍi* wherein she had tied it, and handed it over to him.

The minister read the letter attentively; a smile was observed on his lips as he finished reading; and then he returned to his private chamber and cautiously wrote a reply to this effect:—

"Esteemed princess, listen to my advice and do not take me amiss. I am indeed very sorry for you. You are a Muhammadan and I am a Hindu. How can there be a marriage between us unless we profess the same religion? By my life, I cannot give up my faith and turn a Muhammadan; your beauty I do greatly admire, but this valuable thing I should not purchase at the price of my religion. Rather should I beg alms from door to door and turn a Fakir, than forego my religion by marrying a Muhammadan. Were I born a Muhammadan, there could be nothing to obstruct our union. If I forego my religion, my *shastras* say that I shall have to pay the penalty of great sufferings in seven future lives. So, do please accept my advice, esteemed princess, change the course of your mind and do not entertain the sort of feeling that you are now indulging in."

With this letter the maid-servant returned to the princess. (Ll. 1-58.)

(3)

When she read the contents of the letter, the face of Maminā Khātun reddened in humiliated pride and deep shame. She spent her nights and days absolutely without a wink of sleep in her eyes, she did not eat her daily meal, nor drink water, when thirsty. She took the silent vow of starving herself to death to hide her disappointment and shame.

But at a second thought she devised a plan, and resolved to destory the caste of Kālidas by a stratagem. She privately called the cook of the minister to the palace and contrived the following plan; she would have meals prepared at the palace and trust it to the cook. The minister would confidently partake of it without suspecting any foul play. If the cook could successfully carry out this plan, he would be rewarded with the grant of one *pura* of land; besides a beautiful bride would be secured for him and provision would be made for the maintenance of the couple, so that he would no longer have to earn his living by serving others. The cook was gratified at this prospect and assented to the princess's wishes.

A rich *Kabab* was prepared with the meat of goat and beef. *Kurmā* and *Koptā* and various other dainties were also prepared and sent from the palace to the minister's cook who served him the meal at dinner-time. The cook told his minister that some special preparations had been made by him that day with great care. Kalidas was pleased with what he ate and had a pleasant sleep in the night. In the morning the cook appeared before his master and said, "I took recourse to a stratagem and made you eat beef last night. You saw the beef with your own eyes and ate the forbidden meat. I was employed to adopt this device in order to destroy your caste and I have succeeded in doing so."

Not a moment did he tarry after this short speech but instantly bolted away from the place. (Ll. 1-34.)

(4)

The minister began to lament and say, "Who is the person at whose instigation the fellow dared to ruin me thus?" He struck his head with his hands and said again and again, "Who is such an enemy of mine that has thus ruined my position in society?" He bitterly lamented his fate and turned half-mad with grief. Finally he determined to put an end to his life and said, "What is the use of this cursed life? When my caste is gone, I will tie a halter round my neck and commit suicide".

When the minister in deep anguish abandoned his home and wandered about in the streets like a mad man, the Emperor Jalaluddin called him to the palace privately and gave him some good advice. He said, "The decree of God is inviolable. Is it not your good luck that you have turned a Muhammadan ? If you behave like a mad man what good will you reap from such a course ? Give up despair and try to compose yourself. I may now call you a Muhammadan as you have lost your religion, why not marry my daughter ? She is a beautiful girl. I propose that you do marry her. You know that I have no son. So after my death you will inherit all that I have. All my riches and property will be yours. So you see that you lose nothing but gain much by becoming a Muhammadan."

When the minister heard these words of the Sultan, he thus thought within himself, "Indeed, why should I act like a mad fellow ? Now I have practically become a Muhammadan being an outcast and it is not in my power to become a Hindu again. What is the reason that I should give up all the good prospects of my life ? I shall marry the princess and accept the proposal of the Sultan. And then in due course when I shall be the Sultan of this province, there will be nothing to regret in future."

Now hear me, my learned audience, what happened next. The name of Kālidas was changed into Sulaman Khan. He performed the 'Jumma' ceremony at the sight of the young moon. The marriage of Sulaman with Maminā was duly performed. It was stipulated in writing that all the property of the Sultan would, on his death, pass on to Sulaman. Sulaman was pleased with this marriage and the prospects that it gave him. He lived happily with Maminā Khātun and in course of time had two sons by her. He gave them the names of Dāud Khan and Isā Khan respectively.

For fifteen years Sulaman reigned in Gour and then departed from this world. Dāud Khan succeeded him on the throne of Gour and in great pride stopped paying revenue to the Emperor of Delhi. The latter sent one of his officers to Dāud with a mandate for immediate payment of his arrears.

Dāud heaped insults on him and then turned him out of the court. The officer returned to his master in Delhi and conveyed to him the news of the treatment he had received from the Sultan of Bengal. He added in conclusion, "Oh my Master, my life was spared, but I was so severely beaten that my limbs seem to have been paralysed. Such an enemy should at once be killed either in an open battle or by some stratagem." The Emperor was greatly enraged, and sent an army to Gour. A severe fight took place between the army of the Emperor and that of Dāud Khan with the result that the latter was killed. (Ll. 1-56.)

(5)

Isā Khan succeeded him on the throne of Gour. He ruled his subjects with affection and was ever ready to undergo great personal sacrifice for them. After three years Isā Khan too stopped paying revenue to the Delhi Emperor. The Emperor on hearing this, sent five *kahans* of soldiers to Gour with the order "Get Isā Khan up here, bound in chains, forcibly or by some stratagem." Shahabaj Khan, the Foujdar, well-known for his martial abilities far and near, was placed at the head of the army to conduct the expedition. There was none in the country to match him in the battle-field. He crushed all the enemies of the empire wherever they mustered strong. When such a great champion appeared in the field, Isā Khan being well-equipped, stood facing him with firm resolve. Isā Khan, the hero of a hundred fight, killed countless enemies and Shahabaj fought with equal valour. In fact, they looked like Hassen and Hossen. The army of Ishā Khan was extirpated and he alone was left in the field. At this crisis he saw no other course left to him than to retreat from the place. He crossed canals and rivers and fled through forests and dales and thus saved himself from the enemy. He reached Chittagong safe. There was none amongst the enemy who had the courage or tact to overtake him. From Chittagong, he came to the city of Dacca and spent his nights in the forests. In course of his flight from Chittagong he had brought some cats with him. He had nothing with him to feed these poor creatures. In a jungly land he let these cats loose. When they pursued some rats, curiously the latter seized the cats and killed them. Ishā Khan wondered at this strange sight and declared that he had never seen rats killing cats anywhere. "Here shall I settle with bag and baggage. Here I shall be able to make the impossible happen. I must build my residential house here in this jungle."

In that forest there dwelt two chiefs named Ram and Lakshmana. They were brothers and belonged to the *Koch* tribe. In the depth of night, hiding himself in darkness, Ishā Khan attacked their palace with the object of killing the brothers. They had, however, been apprised of their danger beforehand and fled from the place in precipitous haste and were never heard of in that part of the country again.

Ishā Khan had the jungle cleared and founded a city which he called Jangal Bāri. He prepared plans of a palace and other buildings with the help of experts and constructed the city in the most approved methods of that age.

He had beautiful houses raised in the inner compartment. The roofs were covered with the picturesque feathers of king-fishers. Each room was furnished with glass-doors. The pillars were made of crystal which sparkled in the rays of the sun. The outer houses had their roofs covered with the milk-white feathers of cranes. The palace was surrounded by a ditch. The audience—Hall was a *bunglow* with roofs decorated with peacock-feathers. Ishā Khan used to hold his *durbar* in that hall. Many garden-houses were built with beautiful tanks dug inside them, some of square and others of a circular shape. Formerly it was a jungle infested with tigers and bears, now it was made a flourishing city retaining its old name Jangal Bāri, or the Wood-land Palace. Brilliant and smiling was the city like the moon, having no place to match it in the whole world.

Enthroned there in his new city, Ishā Khan now set his whole heart to extend the jurisdiction of his kingdom. He increased his army, which now consisted of innumerable soldiers. Many forts were constructed in various centres. The report of all this procedure reached, in course of time, the ears of the Emperor of Delhi who sent one of his officers in order to summon Ishā Khan to Delhi. On receiving the summons the Chief of Jangal Bāri had the officer arrested and placed a heavy stone on his breast. He kept him confined in this condition, in his prison. One month—two months, the whole year passed but the officer never returned to Delhi. The Emperor consulted the almanac and fixed an auspicious day when he sent an army placing Raja Mansingh at the head. There was none who could cope with the Raja. The enemies of the Emperor he used to destroy with the ease with which one cuts the *kusha* plant (a species of esculent roots).

The first battle was fought at a place called *Bukāi.* Ishā Khan was made to retire from Bukai to Sherpur. He was pursued and pushed his way from Sherpur and took refuge in the fort of Dewan-bāg. Thence he went to Murapara. Thus the chief of Jangal Bāri moved from fort to fort; and Mansingh pursued him all the while driving him from all his strong positions. But still the Raja could not overtake him till he was tired by his pursuit. He took recourse to a stratagem to catch hold of the wild hero. The last place where Ishā Khan had taken refuge was the fort of Egaro Sindur. From here he heard a report that Mansingh, weary of pursuing him, had resolved to return to Delhi. Right glad at this news, Ishā Khan, with the generals of his army, passed the night in merriment and glee. Now, Mansingh had constructed strong iron cages which he placed at the several gate-ways of the fort of Egaro Sindur. So any one who attempted to come out would be caught in the trap. The Raja now set fire to the fort. The inmates could no longer stay but tried to escape and in their attempts, found themselves entangled within the cages placed at the gate-ways. Ishā Khan shared the fate of his followers and was thus caught by the Raja. The cage in which Ishā Khan had been put was now carried to Delhi on the back of an elephant.

One day—two days—a week passed; no one took any notice of the prisoner. His position was exactly like that of a lion fallen into a snare. No proper food was given to the chief who suffered intensely from hunger and thirst. He thus reflected within himself, "If I could but once make my escape from here, I would see how the Emperor reigns supreme in future."

One day the Emperor Akbar with his viziers and other courtiers sat in his *durbar* and called Mansingh to his presence. He asked the Raja to give him a report of war. Mansingh was pleased at this order and said, "Many a battle have I fought, Oh monarch, many a great wrestler and sturdy soldier have I seen, but I never saw a valorous champion in the field like Ishā Khan. I think there does not exist a second hero in your realms, possessed of such superior skill and valour as this chief. Your Majesty has cruelly deprived him of his usual meals and ordinary comforts of life. He has been suffering greatly. Such a handsome man as he is, he now looks emaciated and pale. If your Majesty would place him under an obligation by a show of courtesy that a hero of his merit deserves, he may render valuable service to the state in future. If your Majesty can subdue the enemy by good treatment, he will be eventually won over to your side. It is well-known that this Ishā Khan is not an ordinary man; if he can make his escape, he may be a source of trouble to the Empire in future. It will be well if your Majesty talks with him face to face. I am sure, it will lead to a mutual understanding, removing all feelings of hostility.

The Emperor, on hearing the words of the Raja, himself paid a visit to the prison and said to the prisoner, "I am very sorry that your dress is so unseemly and bad. I repent my cruelty towards you. I am going to release you from the prison"—saying so Akbar with his own hands, released the chief.

The chief, regaining his freedom, fell at the feet of the Emperor and bending low on the ground craved his Majesty's forgiveness. The Emperor was right glad at the conduct of the chief and lifting him up from the ground, embraced him. The Emperor then made Ishā Khan sit by his side at the *Durbar* and showed him great marks of honour before his courtiers. He, moreover, conferred on him the title of "Mashnadali" with a *sanad*—granting him the ownership of 22 perganas on an annual revenue of Rs. 10,000. The names of the perganas are as follow—'Sherpur,' 'Joyan Shai,' 'Alapsingh,' 'Joarsai,' 'Nashir-u-Jiral,' 'Mymensingh,' 'Khaliajuri,' 'Gangamandal,' 'Paitkara,' 'Baradakhat,' 'Svarnagram,' 'Baradakhatmanra,' 'Husen sahi,' 'Bhawal,' 'Maheswardi,' 'Katrar,' 'Kurikhai,' 'Sinda,' 'Hajradi,' 'Darjibazu,' 'Goair,' 'Husenpur.'

Ishā Khan started for Jangal Bāri with the Emperor's *sanad.* He had constructed a ship at Delhi, which was a curiosity, drawing admiration from people far and near. It was 150,000 yards in length and 2,000 yards in breadth and 100 yards high. The ship moved covering an area of 2 miles (a krosh), hence it was called 'Koshā.' The ship was manned by 2,000 oarsmen. The captain of the ship was a man named Shadhan, an inhabitant of a village on the banks of the Padmā. When the oars were plied by thousands of hands, the ship flew swiftly like the wind. It seemed, as if it could, if it wished, run on dry lands. Ishā Khan came on board this ship which was decorated with flags and *ensigns* and started homewards. The Emperor embraced him before he parted and sent with him twelve officers of his court to escort him. With the speed of the wind, pushed by sixteen thousand oars the ship moved on like a bird in the air.* In a moment she passed many a lake, many a river and many a canal and last of all reached the great river Padmā. Downstream the ship marched, spreading her sails and in her front, lay the city of Sripur, where Kedar Roy reigned. He had hundreds of officers, courtiers and ministers and the people of that country held him in great esteem. His wealth was unbounded and his palace abounded with

* This ship is a evidently myth, but there is this substratum of truth in the that story, Isha Khan had really constructed a gigantic ship which took the shape of this wild and monstrously exaggerated picture in rustic fancy.

innumerable servants and dependents. The city smiled with many a temple and building. A staircase made of white stone descended from the city to the river, and here and there peeped from the forest-groves brick houses of varied colour. There were many three-storeyed and four-storeyed houses in that city and as the '*kosha*' of Ishā Khan passed by the river, favoured by the currents, people gathered on her banks to see it, (Ll. 1-176).

(6)

From the ship the Moslem-chief observed a fair maiden sporting with her gay companions on the roof of a three-storied building. It appeared that the whole mansion was lit up by her beauty. Ishā Khan had never seen a maiden as beautiful as she. The chief fixed his gaze at her, awaiting the prospect of exchanging a glance. She was playing "Palā buji" with her maids. Suddenly her eyes fell on the waters of the Padmā where she beheld the handsome chief gazing at her. Eyes met eyes at an auspicious moment. Love thus sprang in both the hearts. Four eyes met and the sequel was fraught with important historical developments. Oh my audience, listen to what happened later on, as the result of this love.

The maiden and her companions wondered at the size and grandeur of the ship, which seemed to have covered the whole river as far as they could see. They all beheld the ship with curious eyes but she cared not to see what they so eagerly saw, keeping her gaze fixed on the handsome person of the master of the ship. As she beheld the youth, her eyes were tinged with passion ; she lost not a moment, but entered her bed-room and hastily wrote a letter which she put inside a cork. Then she went to the bathing ghat. The ship was moored to the bank and there she sported with her maids who were never weary of admiring

Ishā Khan

"She came, as expected, for bathing, a short while after." P. 351.

the ship. But her thirsty eyes sought the figure of the noble chief. Just at that moment Ishā Khan stood on board the ship in the mid-stream and four eyes again met. Casting her glance at him, she floated the cork in the current. The chief saw that something was thrown into the river, meant for him. The cork, meanwhile, came floating near the boat and he instantly took it up in his hand. He now drew the letter out and began to read it. When the maiden saw this, she returned homeward with her companions.

The contents of the letter were as follows :—

"Oh stranger, my heart has become mad for you. You saw me when I was bathing,—my mind yearns for you,—I care not for my religion or for my society. In you I will find all that is dear to me. If you feel any compassion for me, hasten to meet me. In the month of Chaitra (April), on the eighth day of the waxing moon, I will come to the landing ghat of the Padma for bathing again. Come with a strong army on that day with your ship and carry me by force. Come with a large number of oarsmen, so that the ship may go with the utmost speed. Bear this in mind that if my brother can overtake the ship, destruction will befall all of us."

The chief went to Jangal Bāri but his whole soul yearned towards Sripur, (Ll. 1-52).

(7)

On the eighth day of the waxing moon in the month of Chaitra, the chief ordered his ship to be ready. He took a strong army with him and started for Sripur. He cast anchor on the landing ghat at Sripur and sat on board the ship awaiting the approach of the fair maiden. She came, as expected, for bathing, a short while after. She too was restless and wanted to be at once united with the youth.

The maids—her companions, were with her as usual. A camp of canvas was stretched round a part of the Padmā and therein she sported with her gay friends. Her heart, however, was not in the sport. She only thought, how soon she would meet the lord of her heart. The chief perceived a brilliance through the *Padmā*; it seemed to him like a glow of fire reflected from the canvas and knew that the maiden had entered therein. He leaped out from his ship and catching hold of her from the midst of her attending maids, sprang on board the ship and at once ordered a speedy march homewards. The oarsmen plied the ship with all their might and it flew like a bird on the air.

The message at once reached Kedar Roy, whose sister Ishā Khan had thus carried off. With hundred boats, each carrying a strong army, he pursued the enemy but the *Kosha* of the Khan went with a speed, which could only be compared with that of a bird, and the Raja could not overtake the abductor of his sister. His boats remained two miles behind the "Kosha" of the Moslem Chief. In great despair he called aloud to Ishā Khan and exclaimed, "What city is there that will give you shelter, protecting you from my wrath after such an insult done to my family? If but once I can catch hold of you I will kick your head out and humiliate you like a slave; whether you hide yourself in the depth of water or in the air, I will one day catch you. Even if I cannot do so, my wrath will be visited on your sons; so that any how I must have full retaliation for this wrong. I take this solemn oath in the name of God." With this threat the Raja traced his way back to Sripur and Ishā Khan with his precious booty safely landed at Jangal Bāri. A short time after, he married her. Her Hindu name Subhadrā was changed into Nyāmat Ján, and the chief became greatly attached to her. So deep was their love that they remained together night and day and never separated from one another. Three years after, she gave birth to a son. In the lap of the mother, the baby looked bright as the moon. It was a thing so beautiful, that words fail to give an idea of its charming appearance. The baby filled its mother's heart with affection and they gave him the name of Adam Khan Mashnad Ali. Three years passed and another son was born to Isha Khan. He was as beautifulas Adam and they gave him the name of Birám. Now listen, oh my audience, to what happened next. (Ll. 1-58.)

(8)

When Adam reached his fifteenth year, Isha Khan Mashnad Ali passed away from this earth. This world is a vain show, my brethren,—none is one's own on this temporary stage. No one will travel with you to that unknown region,—be the person your wife, or son, or your own brother. They will readily take a share of your earnings and enjoy, but none is there who will be your fellow-traveller in the path of eternity. So all is vanity and one born must inevitably be a prey to death.

"Alas! who could fill up the gap created by the death of Isha Khan at Jangalbari?" Everybody who heard the news of his death, asked this question to himself. And the news was heard by the people of the neighbouring countries. In course of time Raja Kedar Roy also heard the report of Isha Khan's death. This wicked man thought it to be an opportune moment. He made fourteen of his best-equipped pleasure-boats laden with sweets and delicacies and led them to Jangalbari. He went direct to the palace of Isha Khan and paid a visit to his sister. The widowed sister was overjoyed at the visit of her brother and gave him a warm welcome. They sat together and passed some hours in pleasant conversation. The Raja, in course of his talk, said to his sister, "Oh my dear sister, you have been very happy, though you gave up your caste. Isha Khan was certainly a more prosperous man than myself. You are besides happy in your two sons, I am right glad to see them. I had a great mind to see Isha Khan up here, but it was not my good fortune to fulfil that wish. I was extremely sorry to hear the news of his death. God has granted me two daughters. I do not find suitable bride-grooms for them. I am much worried over the question of their marriage. Your house is certainly a noble one, and I have come here with great expectation. I am quite willing to marry my daughters to my two nephews, if you would agree to this match. I may, in that case, take my nephews over to Sripur for performing the marriage ceremonies. What do you say, my dear sister, to this proposal of mine?"

The sister began to tremble in fear as she heard the words of her brother.

"My brother," she thought, "has come here to ruin me. His heart is still beating with a spirit of revenge and he has come with the object of retaliating the wrong done to my father's family. He is trying by his artful words to win my heart; he will sacrifice my sons at the altar of Goddess Kālī. That assuredly is his object. The two birds of my affectionate heart, he has come to tear off from me." She was seized with great fear and thought within herself as to what means she should adopt to save the children at this crisis. But she hid her fears and said, "I see no objection, dear brother, to the proposed match. But how, being a Hindu, can you think of marrying your daughters to your nephews?" The Raja said in reply, "Amongst Mahammadans, there can be no objection to marrying cousins. So there is possibly no objection on your side, and I will make matters smooth as far as we are concerned. Don't entertain any doubt on this point."

Then at this critical point, she was at her wit's end to devise a plan as to how to get rid of this enemy of a brother, and slowly collecting herself, she said, "You propose that the marriage should take place at your house, but that is not the custom with this family. My sons cannot go to your house before marriage, which is to be celebrated here." The Raja said in reply, "My mother, dear sister, wants to see your sons. They are her grand-children, I have no objection to the marriage being celebrated in your palace, but before the marriage takes place, it is my mother's wish that she should see your sons. Her bereaved soul will draw a great consolation from seeing the faces of the lovely boys."

The sister, after a moment's pause, replied, "I feel, oh dear brother, the presentiment of some evil in sending my sons to your palace. My heart throbs at the thought of some evil which I cannot fully express, but which, my mind tells me, may happen if they leave are allowed to this city." (Ll. 1-70)

(9)

The Raja understood his sister's mind and taking leave of her came to his boat. He now thought about this matter and sent invitation-letters for dinner at his boat to all people of Jangalbari, high and low. The minister, the high officials, the land-holders, the citizens, the army and the police force were all invited. The great warrior Karimulla was also among them. The two nephews of course got the most cordial and special invitation.

They all took their repast and returned home after dinner. The wicked Kedar Roy sat with his nephews in the boat and had a pleasant conversation. They were charmed with the affectionate conduct of their uncle and forgot the hour when they should have returned to their palace. Evening passed away, even then the conversation between the uncle and the nephews did not cease. It was now 10 P.M. The nephews became anxious to return home. The wicked Kedar Roy said, "It is not a stranger to whom you have come! Why are you feeling restless? Am I not your nearest relative? Do you really take me for a stranger? What harm if you pass one night with your uncle? Don't be anxious, lads, remain here this night. In the morning you will return to your palace." They were charmed with the show of affection from their uncle and slept on the boat after a lively conversation. When they had fallen into a deep sleep at mid-night, the Captain sailed the boats homeward under the Raja's orders. The sails were all unfurled and aided by the favourable wind and skill of oarsmen, the boats travelled in a day what in ordinary course it would take three days to travel. (Ll. 1-32.)

(10)

In the morning the two brothers Adam and Birám rose from their sleep and asked their uncle as to where the boats were going. "Why not, oh uncle, land us here so that we may go and meet our mother. She is no doubt very anxious for us." The Raja said that the palace of the brothers where their mother lived was not far off. They would very soon reach it. Under such

Ishā Khan

" Kedar Roy sat with his nephews and had a pleasant conversation." P. 356.

pretexts he took them to Sripur which they reached in two and half days. The boats laid anchor at the landing ghat of the Padmā where the city of the Raja stood. Immediately by his orders the brothers were put under chains. They were imprisoned in a dark room, and the Raja in the presence of his officers abused the brothers in the filthiest language referring to their parents. "You have come here to marry my daughters. I will shew you what sort of marriage I meant"—saying so he ordered the brothers to be laid down with a stone weighing 40 lbs. on the breast of each. They began to cry 'Allah, Allah' in great distress. Their lament would melt a stone. "If our mother get the news of this,"-they said weeping, "she will die of grief. we are like the two ribs of her heart. How can she for one moment feel a sense of relief as our father is dead and she has none to call her own except ourselves." They almost fainted crying helplessly. "Alas," they said, "who is here to feel compassion for us ? If brother Karimulla would have been here, with his huge club, he would pursue our wicked uncle and send him to the region of death. Oh God how cruel is thy decree! we are going to die here in this utterly helpless manner !"

Now, my audience, for a moment let me leave the topic of Sripur and revert to an account of the events that took place at Jangalbari. The invited guests, one by one, returned to their house. Niamat Jan, the mother of the princes, anxiously awaited their return in her bed-chamber. But the night passed and it was dawn when still the lads did not return. Her soul, as it were, left the body in great fear. "Where have my two sons gone!" She thought. "Surely Kedar Roy has done some mischief." She called the great warrior Karimulla to her presence and told him that her sons had not returned after the dinner given by her brother. Karimulla became anxious at the news; he ordered a slave to go to the river-ghat and bring information as to why they did not return in the night. The slave went and found none on the river-bank,—the fields there were deserted and there was no human being to be seen. The princes were not there nor was there any trace of Kedar Roy and his fourteen boats. When this news reached Niamat Jan, she bitterly lamented and was almost mad with grief. Unable to bear the lamentations of the bereaved mother, Karimulla roared like a lion and said, "Do not cry, oh venerable lady, remove all grief from your heart. I take the vow of bringing to you the decapitated head of Kedar Roy. I will restore your sons to you. Do not weep, I take the solemn vow, that so long I cannot bring back the princes, I will not return to the palace."

This is the great warrior Karimulla. No one ever heard that he had been defeated anywhere in any battle. If a thousand men attacked him, all together, with strokes of his huge club he would send them all to the regions of the dead. His stature was tall as it was heavy, so that he looked like a hillock; his colour was deep black and flashes like embers of fire emanated from his eyes, when he got angry; his limbs were like the trunks of a fig tree; on his shoulders he bore a club, twenty maunds in weight. With that club thrown over his right shoulder, the warrior marched in great haste. "Wherever I shall find that wicked Kedar Roy, I will crush him to death like a fly by a stroke of this club"—thus did he muse within himself, as he proceeded on. In three days he reached the city of Sripur. When he heard about the sorrowful condition of the two princes, he turned as one mad. He began to kill and assault any one and every one whom he met. Kedar Roy heard this and

Ishā Khan

"Do not cry, oh venerable lady, I take the vow of bringing to you the head of Kedar Roy." P. 358.

became very sorry at the destruction of his people by the mad giant. He ordered his army to capture him. The whole army surrounded one man. He began to beat and assault them as best as he could—but how could he continue such an unequal struggle for long? When he found himself quite helpless, he hastily fled away to save his life. He came running to the landing ghat of the Padmā but was pursued by Kedar Roy's army. He plunged himself into the waters. The river was full, but he swam across under the waters raising his head only thrice over the river to draw his breath. He thus crossed the Padmā unseen by others. They all concluded that he must have been swallowed by a crocodile. The army returned from the river-ghat.

On the other bank of the river lived a boatman named Sadhan. In the depth of night Karimulla called him out and gave full account of himself. Hearing all from the beginning to the end, the boatman fed the warrior sumptuously. The menu consisted of one maund of *chira*, fifteen seers of sugar, two maunds of curd, with one seer of salt. He exhausted all this and Sadhan with his swift fishing boat, led Karimulla through the Padmā to Jangalbari which they reached in a day. Having come back to his city Karimulla took the whole army of the palace on the Kosha and started for Sripur. It flew like a bird helped by the wind.

Now, let us resume our story of Sripur. The two daughters of Kedar Roy came to know that their cousins of Jangalbari had been brought there on the false pretext of marriage with themselves. They put their two heads together and discussed the matter fully. "These princes," they said," have been given hopes of getting us for their wives. Now it behoves us to accept them as husbands. As our father has pledged his word, if we do not become their wives, ill will it fare with our parent in the next world. It is our duty to save these youths from danger. My parents may do things on the impulse of anger, but we should take a quiet view of matters and try our best to help the princes." They took rice and other food in golden plates and, when the night was advanced, paid a visit to then in the prison. They said with great tenderness, "Our father has brought you here on the pretext of giving us in marriage to you. You were, no doubt, pleased at the proposal and have come here joyfully. How happy would it be also for us to get you as our husbands. We will try our best to please you by our whole-hearted and life-long devotion. It does not matter what my father will do. Pray, do not take us for your enemies. Whether you marry us or not depends on your will; as for us, we assure you, even though one should cut our throats, we would not agree to seek our bridegrooms elsewhere. We have elected you as our lords and for your sake, dear ones, we are here, prepared to give up our parents."

On hearing this Adam replied, "We will not marry you stealthily, so please go back home. We give you words, we will marry you openly, if Providence grants the day for it. We will take meals prepared by you—but not to-day. Take back the plates full of rice. If God be willing, you will serve us meals in our palace, and we will gladly partake of the same on some future day."

The girls were sad at heart at the words of the brothers and returned to the inner compartments of the palace, in a dejected spirit. This event was like a great fire that overtook the Sripur palace that day and it was not extinitguished till it burnt all happiness of the house, not sparing the life of Kedar Roy himself. (Ll. 1-150.)

(11)

On the tenth day, the 'Kosha' led by Karimulla reached Sripur. He landed there with his army. They raised the cry 'kill,' 'kill' and attacked the palace. Kedar Roy perceived that it would be impossible to make a successful stand against the vast number of enemies assembled there. Finding himself helpless he ordered the princes to be taken to the temple of Kali for sacrifice. Some soldiers hastily took them there at the Raja's order. The daughters of Kedar Roy heard the news from their inner apartments and made constant enquiries as to what was happening but could not obtain any further news. They became maddened with grief. Each of the princesses took a sword in her hand and paid a visit to the temple. They saw the young lads tied to the altar—and a man whetting his weapon to give the final stroke. One of the girls forthwith ran and with a stroke of her sword killed the man. They did not stop there, but killed another servant of the temple, so that all the people fled from there. They thus saved the life of the brothers, and stood in the gate-way ready with their swords. Whoever tried to enter the gate with the object of sacrificing the princes at the altar, was killed by the sisters in the same way. The army of Jangalbari in the meantime surrounded the city of Sripur and set fire to the houses of the citizens. The golden city was destroyed in this way. Men and women fled in all directions in precipitous haste, and many were killed.

And now hear what happened to the wicked Kedar Roy next. He fled with his life, and Karimulla with his utmost vigilance could not find out the place where he had hidden himself. The warrior resolved to kill him, "for," he thought, "if he be spared, he may form some plot in future to endanger us all. I will kill him wherever he may have hidden himself, and I will not return home until I have taken his life."

Now the daughters of Kedar Roy with the princes came where Karimulla was; and they all were highly rejoiced at the sight. The daughters said, "It will not be safe, Oh Karim, to spare the enemy. Even if he be a saint he must be killed. If he be spared none of us will be safe. We know where he is. We will give you the information. You are to go there and kill him with your own hands. When attacked by the enemy, he seldom stays at his palace. In the forests of Asua, there is a nice building under-ground. The surface of it is covered by a thick jungle; it is connected with the river by a tunnel and thither does he retire at the hour of danger. The house has nine gate-ways and a big hall, and there he reposes on a couch. Karim was right glad at the news and forthwith went to meet the enemy. Asua was five *Rashis* from Sripur. The place was covered with an avenue of tamarind trees. On the southern side of the forest, Karimulla discovered the mouth of the tunnel and straightway he entered it and found nine gate-ways which he crossed one by one till he reached the Raja's hall where he was found sleeping with a feeling of absolute security. Karimulla, as soon as he saw him, roared like a lion. The Raja's sleep was gone and he held fast a sword that lay near him. But before he could aim a stroke with it, Karimulla smashed his head with the huge club that he carried with him. Then with the sword he cut off his head, and carrying it in his hand, came back to Sripur. His army greatly rejoiced at this victory. Karimulla next started for Jangalbari and arriving there, made preparations for the marriage of the brothers. The Moulvi of the Court fixed an auspicious day during the period of the waxing moon. The city of Jangalbari was beautifully decorated, and it smiled like a second heaven. Bonfires were lighted and guns were fired. Thousands of respectable men assembled. On the marriage day, the brides and bride-grooms wore bridal costumes and ornaments after bath. The brides wore gorgeous *sadis* brought from Persia. Their dress was so rich and ornaments so beautiful that even the fairies could not cope with them. Adam and Bairam wore valuable Egyptian coats, and caps brought from Arabia. Their shoes were made at Persia. Kasturi, kumkum, attar and other perfumes were sprinkled over their persons. When after robing, they met their consorts, the whole city, as it were, shone with their beauty. Now came the pleader (উকীল) and asked the daughters if they willingly chose Adam and Bairam as their bride-grooms. The princesses assented to the marriage. Then Adam and Bairam also agreed to it. Thus the memorable marriage came to an end and a great feast followed worthy of the occasion. (Ll. 1-104.)

Another Short History of Isha Khan.

The Dewans of Jangalbari had a historical account of their family written by competent persons, which was some years ago published from Haibatnagar. The materials of this history were collected from the papers preserved in the archives of the Dewan family and were also drawn freely from the Aini-Akbari, the Akbarnama, Syer-ul-Mutakherin, Alumni and the historical treatises written by Marshman and other European writers. A large mass of material was also collected from the traditions current in the country and the compilers used their discretion in dealing with popular versions of the accounts of the administration of the Dewans, by rejecting such elements in them as were untrustworthy or could not be substantiated by other evidences. This treatise is, by no means, to be called a perfect or complete one as the writers could not lay hold upon the ancestry and other particulars about a considerable number of families who still live in Mymensingh and call themselves scions of the Dewan family. The main difficulty arises from the fact that along with the genuine Dewan families, numerous families have sprung up recognised as Dewans but whose claims to legitemacy are of a doubtful character. Some of the old Dewans used to fill their harems with fair-looking Hindu women carried by force. The children born of these women were called Dewans by courtesy. And in many cases they also inherited some property of the Dewans.

The historical treatise referred to above was undertaken, at the instance of Dr. James Wise, late Civil

Surgeon of Dacca, by Dewan Sovandád Khán. The Dewan appointed his chief officer Munshi Raj Chandra Ghose to collect information for the purpose. He was helped by late Muhammad Idris, the then manager of the State of Haibatnagar in collecting these materials. But as Dewan Sovandád Khán had died a short while after, the undertaking could not proceed and was inpeded for some time. But luckily Dewan Ajimdád Khán, the brother of the deceased Dewan, interested himself in the work and encouraged Munshi Raj Chandra Ghose in resuming his task. This gentleman in co-operation with one Kalikumar Chakravarty, the then Head Pundit of the Jangalbari School, compiled the historical treatise tracing it from the founder of the family. The Head Pundit had lived in that part of the country for twenty-one years and succeeded in collecting a large amount of historical information from various sources. The history of the Dewan family covers a period of nearly four hundred years and as no systematic account was preserved of them, the authors often found historical information scanty and had to depend on traditions current in the countryside. They would gladly wait for getting an opportunity to obtain fuller materials; but the pressing requests from Mr. Lowes, Commissioner of the Dacca Division, and Mr. R. C. Dutt, Magistrate of Mymensingh, made it necessary to publish the history hurridly and in a somewhat imperfect shape.

This book is divided into eleven chapters. Unfortunately, owing to the whims of one of the Dewans, many important documents of the family were destroyed. Dewan Haibat Khan, fourth in descent from Ishā Khan, separated himself from the main family and founded a town called Haibatnagar, six miles to the west of Jangalbari. Dewan Shaha Neoaj, who was fifth in descent from

Dewan Haibat and died in 1247 B. E., is said to have done a very queer and whimsical thing. It is said that he, opened one day, an old chest containing the Sanadas granted to the family by the Delhi Emperors and some other valuable State-papers and letters. Looking at these he exclaimed, " We are no longer what we were. These only serve to make us conceited." And he threw them into the Narshindha.

I give below a short summary of the history of the Dewan family as given in the treatise.

The Eastern part of Mymensigh is popularly known as Haibatnagar-Jangalbari. This includes, amongst others, the Perganas of Hajradi, Husain Sahi, and Nashir-u-jiral. Jangalbari proper, the site of the Dewans, was originally comprised within the village Kadir-jangal and covered a space of 50 bighas only. The people of the surrounding villages, however, to the extent of hundred miles on all sides, still call themselves, when they visit other countries, as inhabitants of Jangalbari."

There are two ports in this part of the country, *viz.*, Kishoreganj and Karimganj. From these ports are exported every year a large quantity of very fine species of rice, jute, sugar, molasses, clarified butter, mats and other articles to Narayanganj, Dacca and other western districts. This country produces fine clothes of a variety of textures manufactured at Sharfarali, Jangalkhasa Salman, and Abruagunj, Half a century ago, Jangal-bari was in utter darkness,—ignorance and superstition reigning supreme in it. Shortly after the creation of Kishoreganj as a Sub-divisional headquarters, a middle vernacular school was established there mainly through the efforts of Babu Nandalal Bose, Munsiff, and was called Haibatnagar Minor School. The establishment of a Brahmo Samaj was the next step towards the advancement of the people and the late illustrious Deputy Magistrate Rai Ram Sankar Sen Bahadur took a lively interest in the cause of local education and helped in the foundation of other schools. There are two high schools, one at Haibatnagar and another at Bajitpur; ten or twelve middle vernacular schools have since come into existence at Jangalbari and neighbouring villages.

Masnadāli.

Kālidās Singh Gajdāni, a Kshatriya by caste, became convert to Islam and assumed the title of Soleman Khan. The family originally came from a place called Baishwara in Oudh. Before he became the Sultan of Bengal he was an orthodox Hindu and used to give away a golden elephant to the Brahmins every day. Kālidās thus earned the name of Gajdāni—the giver of elephants. Kālidās was the Prime Minister of Bāhādur Shāh, the ruler of Bengal who died in 1570 A.D. His younger brother, Jelaluddin (popularly called Jainuddin), succeeded him. He had three daughters and a little son. The eldest of these daughters was married to Syed Ibrāhim ol-olelmā and the second to the illustrious (?) Kālāpāhār.

Syed Ibrāhim was known for his high character and piety and Kālidās Gajdāni often discussed religious matters with him. He was gradually convinced of the superiority of Islam and finally gave up his faith in Hinduism sometime between 1561 and 1565. The little son, Jelal, had died when a mere child and Kālidās Gajdāni who had married his third daughter and adopted the name of Soleman Khan now succeeded to the throne of Gour. He ingratiated himself into the confidence of the Emperor Akbar by offering him valuable presents and considerably increased his kingdom which now comprised Bengal, Behar, Orissa and portions of Allahabad.

Soloman Khan died about the year 1571 leaving two sons, Dewan Ismail Khan, popularly known as Daud Khan, and Dewan Ishā Khan.

Soloman had also a daughter named Shahen Shā. She was married to Tajiuddin Gada, a remote descendant of the illustrious king Haroun-al-rachid.

Dewan Ismāil, on ascending the throne, stopped paying revenue to the Emperor of Delhi. A battle ensued in 1575 when he was killed. His brother Ishā Khan succeeded him, but following the example of his elder brother, he also quarrelled with the Delhi emperor. A great battle took place in which Ishā Khan was defeated by the eminent general of the Mogul army—Shahabaj Khan. Ishā Khan, after his defeat, fled to Chittagong. The news of the victory of the Mogul army was communicated to Akbar by Munshi Abul Fajal. On page 119 of the treatise Almuni, written in Persian, the very words of Akbar expressing his delight at the event are quoted. They run thus—" A highly gratifying news has been received from Bengal. By the grace of God, Shahabaj Khan, our general, has conquered the vast tract of land from Ghorāghāt to Sāgar. Ishā Khan, who headed the rebels, has fled towards Sāgar after his defeat."

Dewan Ishā Khan after his defeat first paid a visit to Chittagong and then came to Jangalbari. At that time the place was an impenetrable jungle—infested with wild beasts. Hence Ishā Khan gave it the name of Jangalbari or the Wood-land Mansion. The inhabitants of the place generally belonged to the Koch tribe. Here stood the beautiful palace of Laksman Singh—the Raja of the tribe—surrounded by a ditch, 100 yds. in breadth. On the south a road, 15 yds. in breadth, ran leading to the palace. Ishā Khan with his army entered the Rājā's house with the object of killing him and made a great search to find him out. But the Rājā had made his retreat by a sub-terranean tunnel, made of bricks, which lay beneath the eastern part of the ditch.

Traces of the road and the ditch, with an area of 50 bighas of land containing debris of the ruined palace, are still to be seen.

Ishā Khan firmly planting himself at Jangalbari now made deliberate plans for extending his territories. He built forts at each of the following places :—Murapara in the district of Dacca, Dewanbag and Hajiganj (near Murapara), Egarasindur on the Brahmaputra, Sherpur, *Dasa Kahania* and Rangamati. Akbar in the meantime heard of Isha Khan's attempts to assert his independence and sent his famous commandar Mansingh to punish the rebel. Mansingh pitched his tent at Demrā in the district of Dácca, and he had a large tank dug in that place, which was filled with water from all the famous Indian shrines. He gave it the name of Gangasagar. The neighbouring place he called by the name of Rájárbág or 'the garden of the Raja.' Up to now the place is considered sácred, and hundreds of pilgrims visit it on the eighth day of the waxing moon during the *Báruni* festivities, and a large fair sits there on the occasion.

After Mansingh had arrived at Demra, he fought a battle with Isha Khan near the fort of Dewanbag. The latter was defeated and retired to the fort of Egarasindur. Here a most sanguinary battle took place lasting for three consecutive days, in which considerable armies on both the sides were destroyed. This made both parties willing to settle matters by a duel fight. When according to mutual agreement, Isha Khan came out on his war-horse challenging Mansingh, the latter instead of appearing himself in the field took to the device of sending his son-in-law who accepted the challenge.

The son-in-law was a good warrior but though he fought well for a long while, he could not maintain his position up to the end. He fell struck by the sword of the Dewan. The soldiers of Isha Khan thought that it was Mansingh who had been killed and raised the cry of victory. Mansingh in wounded pride and grieved at the death of his son-in-law, now appeared in the field, "angry as a serpent struck on the head by a club." The two warriors fought with a skill which raised a feeling of wonder among the spectators, and for a long time no one could foresee who the victor would be. In the evening the sword of Mansingh broke, struck by that of Isha Khan.

Isha Khan requested the Raja to take another sword, but the Raja without giving a reply came down from his horse. Isha Khan thought that the Raja wished to fight the duel by wrestling. So he too left his weapons and horse, and stood facing him. The Raja at this stage, expressed his wish to desist from the fight altogether and extended his right hand to Isha Khan as a sign of friendship. Isha Khan shook hands with him in joy. There was for some time great rejoicings in the camps. Now, the time came for parting. The wife of Mansingh interviewed Isha Khan privately and said, "If you do not accompany us to Delhi, a great danger will befall us, for, the order upon my husband is very severe. He must take you with him to Delhi; otherwise the punishment of death would be visited on him. Now if you sincerely wish that I should not be made a widow, kindly accompany us to Delhi." The importunate tears of his friend's wife moved Isha Khan whose nature was generous and he forthwith agreed to go to Delhi in Mansingh's camp. On his arrival at the great city of the empire Isha Khan was unscrupulously thrown into prison.

A short while after, through the intervention of Mansingh and his sister—the queen of Akbar, Isha Khan was released from the prison. When the Emperor heard from Mansingh the account of Isha Khan as to how bravely he had fought and how nobly he volunteered to be taken to Delhi, he was exceedingly pleased and gave him a seat on his right in the court as a mark of special honour. He conferred on Isha Khan the title of Masnadali and the grant of 24 Parganas as a rent-free gift. He moreover placed four Gajis, four Asahebs and four Majlishis under him and made him the head of these twelve sub-lords. The descendants of Isha Khan still bear the proud title of Masnadali.

With these new honours and title Isha Khan returned to Jangalbari. The four Asahebs were given lands at Tārāp and other villages of Sylhet where they settled. The Majlishis settled at Khaliajuri in Pargana Nasir-u-*jiral* (Jian), the Gazis settled in Parganas of Bhowal and Sherpur where their descendants are living up to now. The descendants of the four Majlishis are to be found even now at Panch Kahaniá and Fatepur in Pargana Nasir-u-Jiral. The ruins of the famous palatial buildings of Majlish Jalal are still to be seen at Rowail—the native villlage of the chief—with their fine crystal pillars and artistic designs carved on the walls.

Ishā Khan, the Lord of 24 Parganas, had now a firm footing at Jangal Bāri. He married his cousin—a daughter of Syed Ibrahim—Malik-ul-ulma. Ishā Khan got two sons by her, Dewan Musha Khan and Dewan Mahammad Khan. Ishā Khan died in advanced years. His grave is still to be seen at Baktiārpur in Pargana Bhowal.

The Names of the 24 Parganas.

(1) Atia, (2) Kagmari, (3) Barabaju, (4) Sherpur, (5) Jayan Shahi, (6) Alapsing, (7) Mymensingh, (8) Jafarshah, (9) Nasir-u-jiral, (10) Khaliajury, (11) Gangamandal, (12) Paitkura, (13) Bardakhat, (14) Swarnagram, (15) Baradakhat mándrá, (16) Husainsahi, (17) Bhowal, (18) Maheswardi, (19) Katrar, (20) Kurikhai, (21) Jour Husainpur, (22) Singdha, (23) Darjibaju, (24) Hajradi.

The Genealogical Tree of the Dewan Family.

Raja Dhanapati Singh of Baishwara in Oudh

Raja Bhagirath Singh.

- 1. Kali Das Gazdani (Solomon Khan)
  - 2. Daud Khan
  - 2. Isha Khan
    - 3. Musha Khan
      - 4. Mosum Khan
        - 5. Manwar Khan
          - 6. Sharif Khan
          - 6. Mahabat Khan
            - 7. Asalat Khan
            - 7. Molaim Khan
            - 7. Multaf Khan
              - 8. Ajjor Khan
          - 6. Adam Khan (Manai Khan)
            - 7. Eoz Mahamood (D. 1241 B.E.)
    - 3. Mahamad Khan
      - 4. Eoz Mamood Khan (1059-1078. B.E.)
        - 5. Hayat Khan
          - 6. Haybat Khan
            - 7. Abdulla Khan
              - 8. Mamood Khan
                - 9. Jolkaran Khan
                  - 10. Shaba Newaz Khan (D. 1247. B.E.)
                    - 11. Khoda Newaz Khan (D. 1266 B.E.) at Shachi Pan Daripa Dacca
                      - 12. Rahim Newaz Khan
                    - 11. Nabi Newaz
                      - 12. Elaha Newaz Khan (D. 1279 B.E.) (1872 A.D.)

I shall here jot down a few notes in connection with some of the Dewans.

1. There are two grants of Shah Jahan written in brilliant golden letters to Dewan Eoz Mahamad Khan preserved by his descendants.

2. Dewan Haybat Khan founded a town called Haibat-Nagar six miles to the west of Jangal Bāri.

3. Reference has already been made as to how Dewan Shaha Newaz Khan destroyed some of the important documents of the Dewan family.

4. Dewan Khoda Newaz had for a time turned a Fakir and then returned to resume his duties as a worldly man.

5. Dewan Ibrahim Khan spent Rs. 50,000 in getting the whole Epic of Mahabharat recited and explained by competent pundits to the people of Mymensingh.

6. Dewan Rahim Dād Khan, at whose order, the historical treatise about the Dewan family first began to be written was a person of rare talents, whose taste and proficiency in Arts are still admired. He could make fine figures with ivory and prepared many beautiful musical instruments such as *Setar*, *Bin*, *Echraj* with his own hands, himself being a master of Indian musics. He was an expert calligraphist, and specimens of his skill are still preserved in various parts of Mymensingh.

The last scion of this distinguished Dewan Family is Dewan Azim Dād Khan, a brother of Dewan Rahim Dād Khan. He is a young man of great promise and noble character.

The Dewans in the past were regarded as heads of both Hindu and Mahomedan Communities of Eastern Mymensingh. Without their permission no religious festivity such as the Dol or the Durgotshab could be performed in Hindu homes. They even ruled over the tastes and fashions of the people. For using particular ornaments, dress and costumes, their permission was necessary. Up to now the lower class of people in the district seek the permission of the Dewans for building certain kinds of houses.

SURAT JAMAL AND ADHUA.

PREFACE.

The poet Faïzu Fakir, who describes himself "blind from birth", is the author of this ballad. We find his name in the colophon at the end of some of the cantos; it occurs altogether five times. Beyond telling us that he had no father, no mother and no brother, he does not give us any further account of himself. And Chandrakumar Babu has not been able to illuminate us any more on the life of the poet. Getting information about this ballad Babu Chandrakumar left his native village of Aithor in the district of Mymensing on the 26th of Chaitra, 1327 B.E., and reached Baniachang in Sylhet about the first week of the next month. He stayed at Roybagan (Aṭharabari P.O.) at the *Gadi* of one Narayan Babu and collected this ballad from three different rhapsodists who were quite innocent of any knowledge of letters.

The Dewans of Baniachang, like those of Jangalbari, were originally Hindus. In he fourteenth century Dewan Govinda Khan, the Brahmin Raja of the place, turned a Mahomedan convert and assumed the name of Habib Khan. Baniachang is one of the largest,—if not the largest village in the district of Sylhet. It has still a population of thirty thousand. Habib Khan was not only the lord of the place but acquired possession of the neighbouring kingdom of Laur, and of altogether 24 Parganas of the district. Baniachang is situated in 24° 31′N. and 91° 20′E. In the jungles of Laur there are still to be seen the ruins of a fort known as "Baniachang Habeli," attesting to the power once exercised by the Dewans of Baniachang over Laur. The line of the Dewans still continues in shrivelled and decayed glory, and Dewan Ajem Raja, who is living, is its present representative.

The ballad relates a story about this Dewan family. I could not get the names of Alal Khan, Dulal Khan and Jamal Khan in the genealogy of the Dewans. One Jamal Khan's name I find as 5th in descent from Habib Khan—The famous convert to Islam. But the father of this Jamal Khan in the genealogy is Ahamad Khan and not Alal Khan as found in the ballad. So the two Jamal Khans do not seem to be identical persons. The Dewans, however, had their pet names by which they were more familiarly known in the country, and the poet, it is quite possible, might have used these rather than the more dignified names of the chiefs to be found in documentary writings.

I sought the help of my friend Babu Achyutcharan Chaudhuri of Maina, Kanaibazar, Sylhet, for the solution of this problem. He is now the greatest living authority on all questions regarding the old history of Sylhet.

I shall quote here a portion from his letter dated the 1st of Agrahayana, 1329 B.E., dealing with my queries at some length.

"What will you do with Alal and Dulal of Baniachang? My work on the history of Sylhet has recently been published in four volumes, complete in two thousand pages. There is an account of Baniachang in this work. But the names of Alal and Dulal do not occur in the genealogy of the Dewans. The descendants of the Dewans cannot give any information on the point. It is besides not unlikely that these are Hindu names adopted by the Moslem Dewans. In the countryside they still call a child spoilt by indulgence as

"Alaler Gharer Dulal." It is quite likely that the two Dewans in question had enjoyed a good deal of indulgence and favour of their parents and were hence popularly called by these names. I am inclined to think that the Dewans, known as Jamal Khan and Kamal Khan, might have been popularly called by the names of Alal and Dulal. In the time of the old Dewans, instances of pet names being used by the people are not wanting. We have got a document, dated 1749 A.D., in which a Dewan of the name of Adam Khan is mentioned, but in the genealogy no such name of a Dewan is found. In the period referred to, we find two Dewans living. They were Ahmed Khan and Mahmud Khan. There can be no doubt that the pet name of this Ahmed Khan was Adam. There is one incidental proof leading to the conjecture that Jamal Khan and Kamal Khan might have been popularly known as Alal and Dulal. A tradition exists here that the two Dewans had contracted a great friendship with a Raja of Dakshinbhag named Dubaraja. The name Dakshinbhag originated about this time. It is a station on the A. B. Railway and is only thirteen miles from Sylhet.[1] Though Dubaraja's name is now forgotten, yet some historical facts relating to this Raja were once known in the countryside and thes refer to a period about 200 years ago. The origin of the name Dakshinbhag is associated with some social incidents which are of a considerable historical interest.

"Dubaraja is not an unfamiliar name in Sylhet. One of the Vaisnava poets of Sylhet is known by this name. He composed a poem called "Nimai Sanyas" 200 years ago. It is a fountain of devotional feelings and pathos. The poem treats of a visit of Chaitanya's

[1] It is about 36 miles from Badarpur, 216 miles from the western-most point of the railway-line, and 26 miles west of Karimganj.

parents to Sylhet before he was born. I got a MS. of this poem 12 years ago. It is still unpublished. This poet Dubaraja was a Vaisnava saint. It may be that the saintliness of his character attracted the admiring love of the Dewans Kamal Khan and Jamal Khan. There is an agreement in the point of time which leads to the conjecture that Alal Khan and Dulal Khan you speak of were probably identical with the Dewans Kamal Khan and Jamal Khan respectively.

"Sylhet was at one time famous for the ballads and songs of the *Bhats.* The fame of the *Bhats* of Baniachang particularly had spread far and wide. The songs of Makaranda, the prince of these Bhat-poets of Baniachang, are still on the lips of many, and are justly admired.

"Have you got any ballad in which there is a reference to the friendship of the Dewans Alal and Dulal with Dubaraja ? If you have got any, please do not doubt the historical value of such a ballad. Many important and historical events of our country lie hidden in the ballads of these unassuming country-poets, mostly unlettered and unknown to outside fame." (*Translated from Bengali.*)

My friend Mr. Achyuta Charan Chaudhuri Tattvanidhi has yet had no knowledge of this ballad. Without entering into the details of the historical questions involved, I quite agree with my friend's views expressed in the last para of the above extract. Stirring historical events often moved these "inglorious Miltons" of the countryside to compose ballads of this type. They gave the popular versions of the events which, though sometimes marked with a crude humour, are often more reliable than the records of scholarly historians, generally biased by party-feelings and anxious for the favour of their patrous.

But there is often a tendency in these ballad-mongers to mix up folk-stories with historical facts. The present ballad suffers from this drawback. The earlier portion seems to be pure folk-lore. We have heard times without number the stories of princes put in sub-terranean regions by the freaks of astrologers' calculations and of monarchs who would not see a child's face lest some great mishap should befall them, as predicted by wise men. But while discarding this portion of the ballad as incredible, the latter portion narrating the love of the princess "Adhuya Sundari" for Jamal Khan, and other subsequent developments of the story, cannot be dismissed by us as a mere fiction. These form the pivot round which the whole story, mixed up with fiction and rustic fancy moves. It had, no doubt, its origin in historical facts. It is true, that ignorance, superstition and want of culture have led to a distortion of the narratives in various ways, but still through the vista of popular narration, glimpses of social condition and torn pages of lost history may be revealed by future research. It will help, let us hope, in threshing out the grain from the chaff in future.

The Muhammadans often took fancy for Hindu maidens, and many disastrous wars were fought "for amorous causes" of this nature, as will be seen from many of the other ballads collected by Babu Chandra Kumar from neighbouring localities.

I have stated the reason in my Introductory notes to one of these ballads published in Vol. I, and I take the liberty to refer to it again. Most of these Muhammadan Dewans and chiefs belonged to families converted from Hinduism to Islam. They were guided by Hindu tastes and preserved naturally a predilection for the Hindu society, which, however, regarded them as 'untouchables.' This contemptuous treatment of a people, who held the power, often gave rise to a sense of wrong, for which retaliation was sought for by application of force. The Baniachang Dewans were Brahmins before their conversion. The treatment the old minister received from Raja Dubaraj, as described in the ballad, would naturally create a fiery animosity between any two unconcerned peoples. But here both the families were originally of the same stock; hence the sting of insult was felt all the more. Jamal Khan seems almost justified in our eyes in leading an expedition to carry the maiden Adhuyā by force.

Such causes would probably have never arisen if genuine Muhammadan families, recruited from Persia or other western homes of Muhammadans, had settled in the country and lived as neighbours of the Hindus. They would not have cared to covet Hindu wives in the way described in the ballad. True, in the history of Rajputana the contrary facts are sometimes observed. But that is because the Emperors of Delhi wanted to subjugate the proud Hindus of martial races, and took recourse to all manner of oppression with that primary object in view. In peaceful state of political atmosphere such aggressions did not generally take place. The history of Mymensingh and Sylhet literally bristles with such instances. The reason seems to be that both the parties involved in such dissensions had the same blood running in their veins and were besides governed by almost the same tastes and ideas. It was for this that the Hindu girls had a particular charm in the eyes of their Muhammadan cousins, who though vested with power and political superiority, were treated with contumely by the Hindu community from a social point of view.

The language of the ballad is a mixed one. But though the number of Persian, rather Urdu, words is greater in it than in most of the other ballads written by Hindus, still it is very far short of what we find in the "Musalmani Bangla" in which the Battala presses of Calcutta publish the Islamic folk-lore and other poems. The Urdu element in the present case is not atrocious, but just what we find mixed in the dialect spoken by the Muhammadans in the country-side. There is very rarely any word over which the Hindu readers would halt. It is but fair that the Urdu words that have crept into our spoken dialect, understood by the Hindus and Muhammadans alike, should be given a currency in writing in order to make our language a common vehicle for literary purposes of the two sections of our community. But our Sanskritists scrupulously avoid Urdu words in writing, though in their colloquial dialect they cannot avoid using them. Such, for instance, are the words সল্লা (wicked advice), বকসিস্ (reward), লাখেরাজ (rentfree), গোলাম (slave), আপশোষ্ (regret), বাঁদী (female-slave) সয়তান (Satan, wicked man), দুষমন (enemy), বদ্ (bad), মুস্কিল (danger), ওস্তাদ (teacher), দুনিয়া (world), আস্‌মান (sky), জমি (land), আখের (end), দরিয়া (river), আছান (cure), বেইজ্জত (insult), হাওলি (apartment), বেইমান (ungrateful). These and a number of similar words are to be found in the ballad, most of which we use in our colloquial dialect, though we try to avoid them in our literary writings, in our enthusiasm to use Sanskritic words. I have dwelt on this point in my Introductory notes to Vol. I, at some length.

It is to be noted that the blind poet, as also the absolutely illiterate ones, generally give us words exactly as they are spoken in the country. This certainly deserves the attention of the philologists. The blind and the illiterate never see words as they are written with their eyes, but always hear them with their ears. It is for this reason that our blind poet has so wonderfully reproduced the phonetic sound of the words, and the rhapsodists without any knowledge of letters have so truly handed us down the poet's version. Most of the writers, who have any knowledge of alphabets, would conform to their conventional use in writing. But the blind man here dictated his poem to the illiterate singers, true to the sound, without caring for literary or grammatical convention, as they were unaware of any. Thus in this ballad we find ছোড়ু for ছোট, পর্‌জা for প্রজা, চাঁন্ for চাঁদ, অইবে for হইবে, ছোন for শোন, ছাহা for সাহা, ছোক্ for শোক, বৈছান for বসানো, ছভা for সভা, পুন্ন্ for পূর্ণ, মাডি for মাটী, ছাহেব for সাহেব, ছফর for সফর, কাঞ্চা for কাঁচা, বচ্ছর for বৎসর, ছাথে for সাথে, ছমাচার for সমাচার, দুক্কু for দুঃখ, বির্দ্ধ for বৃদ্ধ, হাঁচা for সাঁচা, ছিডাইল for ছিটাইল, সুরুয for সূর্য্য, তিরভুবন for ত্রিভূবন, শর্য্যায় for শয্যায়, পাত্থর for পাথর, লিয়া for লইয়া, অইব for হইব, রাজত্তি for রাজত্ব, পরনাম for প্রণাম, স্ত্রিরী for স্ত্রী, যৈবতী for যুবতী, and আনল for অনল।

It will be seen from the above list that the স of the Bengali alphabets still retains the sound of ছ amongst the peasantry, especially the Muhamamdans. Though amongst the gentle classes of Bengal the distinction in the pronouciation of শ, ষ and স has been practically lost and totally ignored. Another curious point to note is that what apperantly strikes us as an anomaly in rhyming in regard to certainwords used in the ballad, is not really so. For instanceছোক (শোক) and কুল (কোল) are given in the text as rhyming with মুখ and বোল. The actual pronunciation of the words in the district of Sylhet and Mymensingh are not শোক and বোল but শুক and বুল. So there is nothing that jars in our ears in the rhyme which retains its harmony when the poem is recited by the people of those districts. In one place বাপ is made to rhyme with তাক্. This also is perfectly rhythmical, the abrupt ending of ক্ and প্ gives almost an identical sound to the two letters.

There are curious instances of verbal inflexions in the songs which will show a striking affinity with প্রাকৃত forms. Such as আইয়াম=আসিলাম, দেউখাইন=দেখুন as also দিউন, বইছান=বসান, ছাইড়িয়া=ছাড়িয়া, আছুইন=আছেন.

Compared with most of the other ballads collected by Babu Chandra Kumar, this one lacks in poetry. Though there is no lack of animation and interest in the story described, there is hardly any passage showing striking artistic beauty or poetical excellence. The poet in spite of his profuse use of colloquial words sometimes assumes an air of rustic pedantry specially when describing beautiful women. And in this his failure is of course obvious as he has no command over the artistic language of the classical poets, while the crudeness of patois often makes his style verge on the ridiculous. We do not find in this poem the simple rural charm and the direct epigrammatic style, so much in evidence in Mahua, Malua Chandravati and other poems. Shek Faizu's descriptions are often diffuse and monotonous, requiring a pruning here and there. Besides Fakir Faizu shows a strange lack of consistency by making contrary statements in various places of his poem. In one place he says that it took a man seven days to travel from Baniachang to Dakshinbhag, in another place he makes it five days and in the last canto the Dewan orders that the Raja of Dakshinbhag should be produced before him in less than 12 hours. The march of the army from Baniachang to Dakshinbhag and their return to the former city were to be covered by this "less than 12 hours!" In one passage Mecca is described as requiring six months to reach from Baniachang and in another Delhi is mentioned as of equal distance from that city. These discrepancies might have been made by the singers, for, it is hard to believe that the poet who could give such a sustained interest to his story, was guilty of such obvious mistakes.

The earlier portion of the story, as I have already said, is pure folk-lore affixed to a historical ballad.[1] But even in folk-lore, the writer must subject himself to some limitations. The architect Tera-lengra in one passage travels to Hailaban in a day, though in a previous passage it was stated that it would take one six months to do so. Such gibberish is intolerable even in folk-lore. One thing however, should be always borne in mind that these ballads were composed, and sung, by men without any knowledge of letters. These anomalies are therefore not altogether unexpected.

Another fault that strikes us is the author's repetition of the same idea in different places. When a mishap takes place, the whole country becomes merged in sorrow; the men and women of the city cry and weep; the birds lament by their chirps, and horses and elephants shed tears in the stables. When Alal Khan, the old Dewan starts for Mecca, this happens first; the same thing is repeated when young Jamal is sent to Delhi. We find again a similar account when Alál leaves the city for good at the end of the tale. This song, I beg to repeat,

[1] We find similar accounts in some folk stories, this makes us surmise that the first portion of the story was a folk-lore; but instances of inhuman cruelties committed on children and women due to astrological predictions, are not quite rare. Pratapaditya was ordered to be murdered when he was a mere baby, for such a cause and owed his life to the intervention of his uncle Basanta Ray. The throwing of little children into Sagar was a practice which continued till quite recent times. The folk-story itself might have been based on some historical facts and such facts might not have been probably out of date during the time of the narrative. Events slightly similar might have been adopted from some folk-tale and dovetailed to a really historical account.

lacks in artistic and literary beauties which characterise the songs collected from Mymensingh. It has, however, historical interest and discloses certain social conditions an during Muhammadan reign which are interesting. The life in prison is graphically described. The cruel punishments mentioned are no exaggerations. The wrath of the chiefs, who on flimsy grounds ordered wholesale murder and made towns and villages desolate, show how helpless the country sometimes was at the hands of its autocrats. The people seemed to have no hand in administration and they suffered the utmost from such oppressions. But occasionally they asserted themselves by revolting against the tyrants. I have referred to this point in my Introduction to Vol. I. Chandra Kumar in a short note addressed to me, accuses Fakir Faizu of fabricating a story of a Hindu girl of aristocratic Brahmin family falling in love with a Mahomedan youth. But Sheik Faizu, it must be said to his credit, was never actuated by any ill-feeling towards the Hindus. He represents his views justly without any advocacy or partiality for his Moslem brethren. The indignation of the Raja at the offer of a proposal of marriage for his daughter by Jamal Khan has been described from the Hindu standpoint, and the letter Jamal Khan wrote to Adhuya was couched in a courteous language showing no aggressive or atrocious spirit which Moslem orthodoxy would suggest. In the prologue his benediction falls on the Hindus and Muhammadans alike in a truly cosmopolitan spirit, and if he described the love of a Hindu girl for a Muhammadan, it was perfectly in conformity with the inevitable law laid down by that blind god, who does not recognise any Hindu or Muhammadan in his jurisdiction, but inspires all who come in his way.

One word more and I have done with this preface. Throughout the poetical literature stamped with the spirit of the Pre-Renaissance school, we often come across the name Tera-lengra. In Mainamati songs, in the Dharmamangal poems and even in some works written in honour of Manasha Devi we come across this name every now and then. It seems to imply the nomenclature of a special class of servants privileged to go to the inner apartments of a palace. Tera literally means a man with a crooked glance due to some natural deformity in the eye, and Lengra means a lame man. We have heard of eunuchs, as chartered servants in the zenanas of the Moslem chiefs. It seems the Hindus were averse to the cruelty of maiming persons in that way. In the place of eunuchs they employed men who were naturally deformed and maimed and therefore safe and trusted parties to act as message-bearers in the Zenana.

The Tera-lengra in this ballad is an architect who had an access to the inner apartments for doing works of building and repair.

Surat Jamāl and Adhua.

A Love-tale and Tragedy

BY

FAIZU FAKIR.

Prologue.

First of all I bow to Allah—The Unknowable One. And then I bow to my Guru, who has given me a taste for spiritual life.

Tell me, oh my Guru ! where was I, when the sky was not, the earth was not and the sun and the moon were not.

Tell me, oh my Guru ! how could grain enter the husk and oil into the mustard seed and how could life enter the egg and where is the door by which death enters it ?

In the universe I have no other friend than Allah. He is my only friend and I have none other.

When my Hindu brother dies, they carry him to the river-ghat, and when a Muhammadan dies they bury him.

The sky is black, the land is black and deep black roll the waves of the river. But he who does an evil deed in return for good is even more black than they.

Says Fakir Faizu, "Oh my Allah ! I am humble and poor. From my birth thou hast deprived me of my eyes. No friend have I, no parents and not a brother ! May my soul find rest at thy feet in the end."

ADHUĀ.

The Begum sent to a sub-terranean house.

At Baniachang there lived two brothers. Here am I to-day to relate their story. I charge my audience to listen to me with forbearance and patience. Of the two brothers the elder was Dewan Alal Khan and the younger one was called Dulal Khan.

Both the brothers ruled the State together as Dewans. The elder brother was reputed for his high character, magnanimity of soul and many noble qualities. His subjects were pleased with his administration. In fact, for soundness of his judgment, they considered him as a second Rustum. His charity was as unbounded as that of Hatem. Language fails to describe adequately the great virtues of that noble man.

The wife of Dewan Alal Khan was Fatema Bibi whose beauty far exceeded that of any fairy or nymph of heaven.

One night she dreamt that the full moon had entered her womb. She awoke with a start and related this to her husband. The Dewan said that the meaning of the dream was that a beautiful son would soon be born unto her. In due course she conceived and was about to give birth to a child. The astrologer calculated the position of planets and said that it would be a male child, worthy of his illustrious father in every respect. He however stopped here and said with sorrow again, "I am afraid to tell the truth, but I cannot help doing so. If within twenty years of the birth of the child, you happen to see his face you will meet with a great mishap. Not only this but if within this period any man or woman living in your city, happens to see the face of this boy, he will be doomed to premature death."

When Dewan Alal Khan heard what the astrologer said, he sat down on the ground, stupefied by grief. He asked his dear brother Dulal Khan to convene a meeting of his chief officers.

The ministers, Nazirs and the police prefects all assembled together and began to discuss the matter at the Dewan's bidding. They at last arrived at a certain decision and the chief architect Tera-lengra was sent for. This man had elephantiasis in both his legs, which looked as heavy as the trunks of a banana-plant. His grand-sons, nephews, sons-in-law and other kinsmen numbered twelve thousand. He was a great architect, far superior to any that lived in the kingdom. This man, with his train of kinsmen and followers, occupied a large part of the city of Baniachang and daily consumed 12 maunds of *Ganja* drug. The great smoke spread all over the city and fully clouded the sky.

Dewan Alal Khan said to the architect, "You Lengra, you must be prepared to carry out my orders immediately. By the grace of God, you stand unrivalled in your profession. A child will be born to my wife in a week hence, as the astrologer has foretold, and one day is about to pass. To-morrow early in the norning you are to proceed towards the forest known as the Haliaban.

"There build a subterranean palace for me. It should be made of stone. You are to finish it at once. You will have ample rewards from me, and I will see that you are pleased with them." When the day dawned Lengra with his host of grandsons and kinsmen hurried towards the forest known as the Haliaban. In usual course it would require a man six months to cross that wild region so large a tract it was. Lengra with his people hurried on; he had with him twelve thousand *Kodalias* (men who worked with spades). They levelled the ground with their spades and the architect laid the foundation of the house with stone. Stair-cases were also made of stone. After having built the house Lengra returned home. He got 22 *puras* of rent-free land as reward for his labour, and for the rest of his life hoped to live happily with his sons, grandsons and kinsmen on the income of this extensive land.

The Dewan, in the meantime, sent his wife with one single nurse to live in this newly built sub-terranean house. Food, raiment and other articles for daily use were stored there that would last for twenty years.

(Ll. 1-72.)

(2)

The Dewan turns a Fakir.

With his ministers and other officers the Dewan, as usual, held the helm of his State. But his mind lost all peace after having sent his Begum away. His city and palace looked void and he wept at whatever he saw around.

One day Alal addressed his younger brother and said, "No longer, brother, do I like to be the Dewan of this region. My city, my realm, my palace, and all I will give up, and go away to a remote shrine. What good, dear brother, will the possession of all these bring unto me? When I shall die, not a *cowri* will go with me. In the dead silence of the burial ground will this body of mine rot and worms will eat my flesh. Sons, daughters and friends all flock round one who is able to bear their burden, but they will not be your companions in that solitary walk of life which every one must travel alone. I will henceforward take refuge in Him. I will turn a Fakir to sing His holy name. I am going to pay a visit to Mecca, where traces of the divine foot-prints still lie in the dust. I charge you, my brother, to rule this land as Dewan during my absence for twenty years. If I outlive this period, I will return home.

So did the Dewan take the Fakir's staff in his hands, put on a turban and dedicated himself to Allah. He went alone leaving his palace; and all the people mourned for him in bitter grief. The ministers and officers, his relations and friends silently wept. Even the dumb animals of the stall—the elephants and horses—shed tears as he left the palace. The ministers and others gathered round him on the eve of his departure and asked him to allow them to accompany him. "We are your loyal servants," they said. "Do not leave us, we pray." But Alal Khan said, "I am resolved to go alone without taking even a *cowri* from the State." Thus did the Dewan start for Mecca all alone like a beggar. (Ll. 1-32.)

(3)

The Prince discovered by his Uncle.

Now let me revert to the topic of the poor Begum who, with a single nurse, lived in the jungly lands of Hamila. On the expiry of ten months and ten days from her conception she gave birth to a son. She, who had been accustomed to sleep on a golden couch, now lay on a mat spread on the floor of that dismal subterranean house. She had countless female attendants in the palace, but here one single maid-servant ministered to her comforts, serving food, when hungry, and offering water, when a-thirst. On the expiry of six days of her coming to that place which she had spent in sorrow and hope, a son was born unto her, bright as the full moon. She became so happy on getting the child on her lap that she forgot the loss of the palace, of her attendants and a hundred other comforts. She shed tears saying, "If the Dewan would have heard the news of his son's birth, he would have emptied his whole treasury, spending all on charity. But now this poor gem of mine shines in this dark cave here, having none to look at it. Ah me! how miserable am I!" A bright necklace of pure diamonds hung on her breast. She took it off and made a gift of it to her maid-servant, saying, "Oh my solitary attendant, I hold you dear as a parent—or a sister. In the sea of unfathomable grief into which I have fallen, you are my sole refuge and guide."

One—two—three months passed. The child grew like the waxing moon. By the grace of God, one year passed. The child crawled in the court-yard and sometime lisped the word "mother" in half-broken syllables. To her he was dear as a rib of her heart. She gave him the name of Surat-jāmāl.

Now one day Dulal, the younger brother who ruled the kingdom as Dewan Saheb in the place of his elder brother in Baniachang, went to that forest for hunting purposes with a large number of followers. It looked like a regular sea of human heads flooding the land as they entered the forest Hailaban. The Dewan saw wood-cutters hewing wood, helped by their young children. When these young urchins helped their elders in cutting wood, Dulal Khan stopped a moment and was astonished to find amongst the dusky sons of wood-cutters, a bright boy shining like the full moon. "Whose son may he be, beautiful as a cherub?"—he thought within himself and as he looked closely the resemblance that the child bore to Alal, his father, became apparent, and the junior Dewan began to think, "Such a handsome boy in this forest amongst the dusky wood-cutters,—he cannot be any other! No doubt he is Fatema's son—bright as the moon. He seems to be a lad of seven years. I never saw a lad as handsome as he." And he calculated the period and found that Fatema had been sent to the forest seven years ago.

"Now after seven years I meet him for the first time. The astrologer had predicted that should any of us see him before he attained his twentieth year, there would be a dire disaster.

"I do not know, Oh Allah, if the astrologer was right. But what is to befall me is inevitable now. Let me think no more"—he thought in this strain and returned to his city with his followers. (Ll. 1-54.)

(4)

The Conspiracy.

Now Dewan Dulal came back to his palace and summoned all his courtiers. The old minister hastened to meet the Dewan; the Karkun, the Munshi, the Nazir and other officials assembled in the palace. The Dewan told them what he had beheld in the forest. All of them put their heads together and devised plans as to how the little child, the son of Alal, should be killed. They said, "You are now the master of the country—our popular Dewan Saheb. You are the legitimate owner of all that you have been long enjoying. Your brother became old and left the country in your charge. He is far off and there is no knowing if he still lives or is dead already. Rule this kingdom, oh revered lord, so long as you live and exterminate the enemy's brood." The Dewan said, "But how can I kill the child? Devise some well-matured plan if you would wish it."

The ministers, Nazir and others discussed the matter seriously and sent for Tera-lengra, the architect, who duly arrived at the town and paid his respects to the Dewan.

The Dewan said, "Hear me, oh old architect, I have fallen into a great trouble and hope to get over it by your help. I will make you a gift of the extensive Hāmila forest; cut down the jungle and live there happily with your children making suitable dwelling-houses. Now listen to what I want you to do. You remember that you built there the subterranean house for Fatema Bibi some years ago. You know where it is. You are to cover the same with earth in such a manner that the lady with her son may be buried alive."

When the old Prime-minister heard this order passed on the architect, he retired to solitude and rained tears in silence.

Forty *puras* of land, no joke! They are to be all rent-free. The reward is great. So Tera-lengra marched thither quickly with his men.

The old minister lost not a moment and applying whip to his horse hurried to the Hamila forest and arrived there in the shortest time.

He called Fatema Bibi aloud and when she presented herself to the trusted officer of the State, followed by her maid-servant, the Minister wept like a child as he delivered his message.

The Minister.

"Your happy days, dear lady, are over. Dulal Khan is now your enemy. He has resolved to kill you with your son. Tera-lengra, the architect, is coming here with 10,000 men. They will cover this house with earth and bury you alive."

When she heard the news, she helplessly wept and could not speak for some time. The young prince just returned there from the play-ground in the forest. He was hungry and demanded food from his mother. But as he looked up, he saw his mother weeping, resting her head on her hand. He asked the maid-servant, "What is the matter with my mother ? Why is she weeping and who is this stranger in our house ? "

The mother embraced her child and said weeping, "My heart breaks to tell you the story. I left my kingdom and have been living in this dismal place, but greater woes are awaiting me. Your uncle is now your enemy and our old minister has brought us very bad news."

The young prince saluted the old minister and then sorrowfully asked his mother as to what had happened. "I know no one whom to call my own "—said the prince turning to the minister, " I have been seeing my mother's tears ever since I can recollect the past. I asked her many a time, but she would not tell me where my home is. If I have my father living or I have any brother or relation,—would you, revered sir, unravel the mystery of my life to me. The minister related to him all that had happened in the past,—what the astrologer had predicted, how the subterranean house was made in the forest where his mother was removed, how his father unable to bear the grief of parting with his queen went to Mecca and how latterly his uncle resolved to kill him. " Oh young prince, your uncle is your sworn enemy. He has already sent Tera-lengra with orders to bury you and your mother alive." He added, " You are to leave this forest-home within the remaining hours of night. Don't tarry a moment."

Jamal Khan, the young prince, began to cry helplessly saying, "alas ! Alas ! We have no sympathiser, no friend in this country. To whom shall we go ?" The mother and the son embraced each other and shed tears of despair. Jamal said, "Mother, where are we to go in this crisis ?"—and she answered helplessly, "Allah is our only refuge. None other do I see." They sought the old minister's advice and he said, after a moment's pause, "Your father, oh prince, had a great friend. He is the ruler of a western country. His name is Dubraj. Leave the forest to-night and proceed towards his dominions. Far off from this place is his capital and you will have to walk night and day. I myself will introduce you to the Raja." (Ll. 1-92.)

(5)

In the City of his Father's Friend.

They started at once and the faithful minister became their guide on the way. The prince prayed for the welfare of the young wood-cutters, his play-fellows, who held him dear as their life. The Begum was accustomed to journey in State-palanquins and Tanjams but now had, in this hour of great peril, to walk on foot. She went a few paces and then sat down to take rest; and slowly did they travel in this way so that they could reach the capital of the Brahmin Raja on the seventh day.

It was mid-day and they had become quite exhausted with hunger and fatigue. The prince Jamal now with his mother and the minister reached the city of the Raja. The place looked so beautiful that it appeared to them as a land of fairies. At that hour the Raja was seated on a cushion in his private room. The young prince and the minister saluted him as a mark of respect as they approached him.

The Raja was struck by the handsome figure of the young boy and with a curious look enquired as to whence he came and whose son he was. He ended with the query, "What it is that has brought you here, boy?" The old minister burst into tears unable to control his feelings, and then slowly wiping them away with his hand he thus introduced the prince to the Raja, "Alal Khan, Dewan of Baniachang was Your Highness' friend. This lad is his son. He has fallen into a great distress and come to you for help. Lady Fatema, his mother, is also here. She has accompanied us to this city. The boy's uncle has become his enemy. He sent his soldiers to murder him a few days ago."

When the Raja heard all, he embraced young Jamal with great affection and gave him a seat near his own on the cushion. He ordered rich meals for his guests; and his men sprinkled rose-water and *attar* on the prince's person.

A beautiful bungalow was raised in the outer apartments for Fatema Bibi and her son. The old minister also lived with them.

It became a custom with young Jamal to stroll in the southern part of the Raja's city every day for the sake of pleasure. A beautiful tank was there with landing *ghats* on its four sides, made of marble. Over each of these *ghats* gorgeous golden flags lay unfurled, and the young prince was pleased with the sight. He enjoyed all that he saw, and thus pleased with the city, he lived a happy life in his new home. One day, he softly spoke thus to his mother, "I shall tell you, oh good mother, of my resolve. I will go in the guise of a Fakir and visit Baniachang. I must see my father's kingdom with my eyes. Be kind, oh my good mother, to give me permission." The mother wept and said, "My cup of suffering has been full to the brim, I will not court new ones. I will not allow you to go to the city of our enemies. I have no ambition. Rather I would beg alms from door to door and live on them."

Jamal Khan said a good deal but his arguments could not convince his mother. He could not secure the permission inspite of his eagerness and solicitude.

Now, shortly after this, the young prince came out of his house in the dead of night and with some of his picked friends and play-fellows proceeded towards the forest Haliaban. On reaching the place he found that all the trees there had been cut down. Lengra was now the master of the whole land. He had brought a host of low-caste labourers with him, who settled there. He had got 40 *purās* of rent-free land as his reward and he was living there with his people in prosperity. Arriving there, Jamal Khan saw the neighbouring localities all made desolate by the oppressions of Dewan Dulal Khan. The ryots were found bewailing their lot in great despair. Dulal Khan on some pretext or other, inprisoned their headmen. For arrears of rent he very often passed capital sentence, killing the men himself with his sword. They were often thrown into cages where the lions were kept or into prison-houses where chillies were burnt continually creating a burning smoke which choked their breath. Their beard was tied to posts so that they could not move their heads one way or the other. Wives and mothers of the ryots were brought to the Dewan's place and insulted. They often fled in numbers from their native country, leaving their house and property. (Ll. 1-74.)

(6)

Jamal Khan becomes the Dewan of Baniāchang.

The prince returned and informed his mother of all that he had seen and heard. He was now sixteen years old and resolved to acquire a training in the art of war. He joined the soldiers and began to practise with his shield and sword. In that kingdom of the Brahmin Raja he soon achieved fame for his cleverness in handling weapons. When he was twenty he sought the permission of his mother one day to go on a hunting excursion. "I am bound," he said, "for the Hamila forest for hunting purposes. I have got a large and well-equipped cavalry with numerous foot-soldiers, horses and elephants, from the Raja. Now do not, oh mother, stand in my way." Lady Fatema began to cry and she prayed to God that He might protect the lad from all dangers. He was the sole delight of her unfortunate life and was like the prop of a blind person—her only stay.

Now Jamal Khan, shortly after, started for the Hamila forest with his army. He attacked the whole host of Lengra, killed many of them; and the rest of his people, about 10,000 men, took fright and fled away. The prince got Lengra arrested, and had him bound hand and foot with iron chains. Now, he marched to the city of Baniachang. The people of that large city looked with curiosity at them and wondered who might be the young hero who came with such a magnificent array of elephants and cavalry.

The prince applied whip to his noble steed, and through the dust raised by its hoofs the people caught a glimpse of him bright as the sun. But as soon as they heard that it was their own prince Jamal who had come, they joined his army in a body and laid siege to the palace. Dewan Dulal Khan, the enemy, fled by the back-door.

So the young hero took possession of his father's dominions and sent a message to the old minister at Dakshinbhāg. He, besides, sent the stately Tanjam of the palace to bring his mother back home. Lady

Fatema came in due course, and the Brahmin Raja Dubraj was right glad at what had taken place.

Jamal Khan, our new Dewan, began to rule the kingdom judiciously. Fakir Faizu says, "In all these affairs the Divine hand is to be traced. Jamal Khan had been but a beggar in the forest. But by His grace he now became a Dewan and see also how his uncle behaved! Oh my chorus, sing this Járee song keeping the time with your feet.[1] Now I will leave this topic and begin another. Many learned people have assembled to hear our song. Let me now sing the story of Adhuá. (Ll. 1-50.)

(7)

Adhua in Love.

Raja Dubraj had a daughter named Adhua Sundari. The fairies and nymphs of heaven were ashamed of themselves at the beauty of this princess. When she opened her large eyes and gazed at the sky, the sun hid itself behind the clouds in shame. She was the darling of her mother, and her five brothers held her in great affection. The couch whereon she slept was made of solid gold and she chewed betels of the colour of rose as she reclined on her couch for rest. Her five sisters-in-law with pretty hair-combs of mica bound her long hair into a chignon. One who beheld the glance of her large eyes, never cared to admire the dark clouds of the sky nor the dark waters of a river. She used to wear a *saḍi* transparent and white like the waters of the Ganges. No fairy, no nymph would dare stand near her when she decked herself in her fine apparel. When she walked, her long hair almost kissed the ground and one who had but

[1] The singers dance as they sing.

once seen her would never be able to forget her in life. Youth had just dawned on her as she was barely sixteen. People said that in the whole *pargana* of Dakshinbhāg, there was not a second girl as beautiful as she.

Once Adhua went to the palace-garden to pluck flowers. She saw Jamal passing by the road bright as the moon. She admired his manly form, and thought that there was not another young man in the whole world so handsome. She stood and gazed at him. Each time she felt as if a thousand moon-beams shone from the place. One—two—three days passed in this way. All this time she did not leave her bed. The five sisters-in-law made enquiries: "Have you, dear one, fallen in love? Who may be the person who has captured your young heart?" The mother, father and the five brothers made kind enquiries and tried to soothe her mind by sweet words. But she uttered not a word and remained in bed day and night, weeping all alone. Her mother often remained with her in her room, but the love-sick daughter dreamt only of Jamal, while her mother made a hundred enquiries without knowing her mind. One morning she rose up and gathered the finest flowers from the garden. She wove them into a garland and then she wrote a short note and wiped away her tears again and again while reading it herself. She called one of her maid-servants into her room and told her, "A boon, oh dear Swapan (*lit.*—a dream, the name of the maid), I have to ask of you. Please go to the city of Baniachang with this garland and letter of mine. Give them to Jamal Khan and tell him how much I am suffering for him." Swapan departed and on the seventh day arrived at Baniachang. The prince was riding a carriage drawn by four horses. The maid interviewed him on the way.

She saluted him and gave him the garland with the letter. He asked her as to what it was that had made her travel all the distance from Dakshinbhāg and come to his city.

She said, "Your Highness, I am a stanger to you. In the country of Dakshinbhāg there lives the fair damsel Adhuā. No fairy is a match for her in point of beauty. She is indeed like a living flame at the dawn of youth. She is deeply in love with Your Highness and has sent me to you with these tokens. She has desired me to say that you lived there for eighteen years; you have got a kingdom now and forgot the country which gave you shelter at the time of your distress. Indeed, men are so forgetful and cruel. Adhuā requests you in her letter to pay a visit to Dakshinbhāg at least for a day and thus give her an opportunity of seeing you. This garland she wove with the choicest flowers that grow in the garden-city of Dakshinbhāg. Kindly accept this as her present and read the letter."

He read the letter and felt as if he was shot by an arrow. He dismissed the maid with a few words and said nothing to his mother nor to anybody else, but stepped into his own private chamber all alone. (Ll. 1-73.)

(8)

The Interview.

On the landing steps of the river lay the beautiful pinnace of the Dewan on anchor. In the morning the young Dewan ordered the boatman to be ready for a trip to Dubaraja's city. The wind was against the tide and carried the boat with all her sails unfurled in utmost speed, and Jamal Khan reached the landing *ghat* of the river facing Adhua's residence in three days.

The boat was moored there and the young Dewan seated on the roof appeared resplendent as the sun.

In the mornning Adhua with her maids went to the landing *ghat* for a bath. Her five sisters-in-law accompanied her. They talked and smiled gaily on their way. Their long and curling hair was scented with oil. They had each a golden pitcher in her hand. Some went in a playful gait, the weight of the fresh charms on their persons making their steps gracefully slow. Some had their hair bound into a knot, others with dishevelled hair, hanging down in curls. One had a beautiful garland of Champa flowers on her breast and another with eyes beautified by the black dye *kajjal* cast her quick glances around, and all had red powder of luck that brightened their forehead. A maiden wore a waist-belt from which the golden pendants made a merry sound. Some had silken robes and others clothes that shone with the colour of the sky. The damsels gaily dressed came to the bathing *ghat*. Amongst them there appeared Adhua as does the moon among her attendant stars.

Stricken with love she looked thinner, but still her beauty shone like a spark of fire. She cared not for her hair, which uncombed, had become knotted. Still her face looked fair as the moon. She stood on the landing *ghat* and saw the stately boat anchored there. On the roof sat Jamal who appeared like the sun peeping from the east at the dawn of the day. Flowers of various hue and size appeared in their full bloom from the banks of the river and over these hummed a hundred bees. From his boat Jamal looked at Adhua and was wonder-struck at her beauty, but he concealed his emotion and ordered the boatman to ply their oars and go homeward. On the eve of his departure they had however exchanged mutual glances full of love's message. And the bee thus left the flower before it could have the pleasure of a mere touch.

When she returned home she could not suppress her emotion. It became apparent in her tears which she vainly strove to hide. The mother as usual made kind enquiries, but she gave no reply, and leaving her couch lay on the bare floor, brooding over some unknown grief. "You are the darling of the whole house, my daughter," said the sorrowful mother, "held in great affection by your brothers. What can be the reason of your sorrow ? When your soft lips gently utter the word 'mother' I feel thrice blessed. Tell me what ails you. Has any fairy cast her spell on you or did you see any bad dream last night, my child ? Do not let any unhappy thought weigh on your mind, but tell me freely what it is that causes you pain" ?

Fakir Faizu says, "No mother, it is not on account of any fault of yours that your girl is grieving. She has loved,—love is a great pain." (L. 1-60.)

(9)

The Proposal.

What do you think the young Dewan did, returning home ? He called his old minister to his presence and said, "Here is this letter; carry it personally to Raja Dubaraja. He has a beautiful daughter fair as a nymph of heaven. Go to the court of the Raja and hand over my letter to him. You will first orally communicate my message and tell him, "Hindus and Mahammadans are the children of the same God. Prince Jamal Khan offers to marry Adhua—Your Higness's daughter. I come with this message"—saying so, deliver the letter."

With the letter in hand, the minister marched towards Dakshinbhāg. He went with a large number of followers, some of whom rode elephants and others horses. He took with him a number of valuable jewels as dowry. It took him five days to reach the place. He presented himself at the Durbar of the Raja and having scented the letter with *attar* communicated the proposal verbally, and respectfully handed the letter over to him. (Ll. 1-18.)

(10)

Insult to the Minister.

The Raja was a Hindu and, besides, a Brahmin. As soon as he heard the proposal, he burst forth into a terrible fit of anger and became like burning fire. He ordered the public executioners to throw the old minister into a dark prison. He was kept there for a week with a heavy stone on his breast. A regular array of ants was let loose to plague him in bed.

All his beard was plucked by force and he was made to roll and whirl like a ball, being pushed from behind. One of his ears was cut and his body was scorched in several places by means of hot iron. After seven days, he was turned out of the city, being driven by the neck.

The minister in that sorry plight reached Baniachang and related the story of his insult to the Dewan with tears in his eyes. He concluded by saying, "It is for you, my lord, that I have lost one of my ears and been put to such grievous insult in the presence of all." (Ll. 1-16.)

(11)

Retaliation.

He became like fire, inflamed by wind at this report and ordered his army to be ready for war. The soldiers all cried, "Allah, Allah" and made preparations for an expedition. The elephants and horses were gaudily caparisoned and the soldiers showed great enthusiasm armed with their spears, arrows, swords and shields. They looked terrible as death, as they marched on.

The dust raised by the hoofs of horses created clouds in the sky. All who claimed any connection with Nabi assembled on this errand and they raised the war-cry, "Allah, Allah" which, so to speak, rent the sky. The citizens wondered at the brilliance of the army, as they saw Jamal Khan marching at the head of them mounting a noble steed. (Ll. 1-12.)

(12)

The Two Brothers.

Let us refer to the topics of Dulal Khan, brother of Alal, whom Jamal had driven from his *gadi.* When his nephew took the reins of administration in his own hands driving Dulal from the country, the latter turned a Fakir and after travelling six months on foot reached the shrine of Mecca. He met his elder brother Alal in that sacred city and bowed to him with all humility. He actually cried when he thus gave an account of himself: "Hear, my esteemed brother, the tale of my woes caused by your wicked son. He has turned me out from our city and I am no better than a Fakir to-day as you see. The subjects have taken fright at his conduct. He does not spare the womankind in his sweeping oppression. There in his harem are to be seen old and young women of respectable families bound in iron-chains. There is no man whose honour is safe in his kingdom. You are away from the country and live in Mecca letting such a son to reign in your place!"

When the old Dewan heard all this he became so angry that he could not speak for some time. He accompanied his brother homeward and first came to Daskhinbhāg, the place where his friend Dubaraja reigned. The two friends met after a long time and they embraced each other in great affection. Alal Khan asked of him a report as to the conduct of his son. It should be remembered that Dubaraja had, now, become an enemy to Jamal Khan. He gave a false report, nearly confirming all that Dulal had said.

Now, Alal Khan with his friend the Raja, who led his vast army, went to lay siege to the city of Baniachang. It was a vast army looking like surging waves at a time when a storm breaks. They looked menacing and grand as they proceeded onwards with swords and shields,—with elephants and horses.

Like two great streams rushing forth from cliffs and infernal regions and meeting one another, the two armies met and stood facing each other in a menacing attitude. The army of Baniachang stood ready for fight and displayed a great enthusiasm. But when young Jamal came to know all, he laid his shield and sword on the ground. He left the army and humbly walked to meet his father. The father and the son met in the open field. The old man became incensed at the sight of his son and looked like dry leaves that had caught fire. He planned to give order for the immediate execution of the young hero. At his order, they bound Jamal hand and foot with hard iron-chains. His glory was eclipsed likc that of the moon under the demoniac power of Rahu. Alal Khan, after this act, arrived at the city of Baniachang. For seven days Jamal Khan was kept in a dungeon with a heavy stone on his breast.

Helpless as he was, he cried for the mercy of God. After seven days, judgment was to be delivered on him.

Such are the mysterious ways of Providence. Let me describe the incidents that followed. (Ll. 1-52.)

(13)

The Contents of the Mysterious Letter.

One would take full six months to travel on foot from Baniachang to Delhi. The monarch of the great Empire resided in that great city. From there a letter came to the Dewan. But none could decipher its contents. Both the pages of the folio seemed blank, and the Dewan Alal Khan was at his wit's end to make any meaning out of the message conveyed by the royal communication. The ministers and other officers of the State each tried his best, but none could discover any alphabetical sign in the letter. Alas! who was the person that had played such a deception! The penalty for not complying with the royal order would be death. What should they now do at this crisis? The news spread in the city and there was none there who had not heard it. It became a gossip with the house-holders and soldiers alike. Prince Jamal heard of it from the prison. He became curious to see the letter and sent one of the jail-constables to his father asking him to show him the curious document. Alal Khan accompanied by his officers and friends himself went to the prison with the letter.

The letter was handed to Jamal in the dark cell in which he was, and a man was sent to bring a light there. Jamal Khan, in the meantime, had opened the letter in the dark and held it before his eyes. In darkness the letters of the epistle sparkled brilliantly and

Jamal at once read out its contents before his father. He said, "Oh my revered father, the great Emperor wants an army from you. He wants ten thousand soldiers and a good number of horses. His command is that within seven days the army should reach the city. Non-compliance with the orders will subject you and your children to a sentence of death."

Alal Khan was on the horns of a dilemma at this stage. "How can I go to the field within seven days?" he thought within himself. "But if I fail to carry out the order, the risk will be the loss of life, inflicted on myself and on the whole family." (Ll. 1-34.)

(14)

Jamal sent to War.

He asked the ministers and other officers to state their opinions as to who should be sent to Delhi. Just at that moment Raja Dubaraja thought, "If Jamal be not sentenced to death by the Dewan, there will be no retribution at all. So far as I can see, the father's affection may prevail and he may be discharged after a mockery of trial; this is the opportune moment to send him to the fatal war."

Thinking thus he said to Alal, "My dear friend, why do you worry yourself on this point? Send Jamal with an army. He is skilled in the art of war and I am sure he will come back a victor."

Alal approved of the suggestion and said to Jamal, "Now dost thou go, oh Jamal, and save our family and children."

He bowed to his father respectfully and became ready to go to Delhi at the head of an army to fight for the Emperor.

In the inner apartment the Begum Sahebā heard the news. She was afraid and called her son to her presence. He came fully equipped and dressed as a soldier for bidding her adieu. She said, "Alas, oh my son—" but could not complete the sentence. Then controlling herself she said, "Are you going to take leave of me? Oh, what words of consolation would you give to your poor mother at this hour of parting? You are the light of my eyes. How shall I live without seeing your face bright as the moon,—without hearing your words sweet as honey,—without hearing that affectionate address 'mother' from your lips? A mother alone knows the pangs of a mother's heart. How can others know that? If you go away whom shall I have left in this world to call as mine own? [I know not whose garden full of ripe fruits I destroyed or whom I robbed of his wealth for which I have deserved this sentence from Providence. When I shall rise in the morning how shall I bear the long day without seeing your moon-like face but once?"

The lady lamented long in this strain. Jamal Khan said affectionately, "Bless me, oh mother, so that I may return victor from the field. Do not lament and cry at this hour."

The mother blessed the brave child, and taking leave of her, Jamal started for the great city of the empire.

(Ll. 1-50.)

(15)

Letter to Adhua.

Now listen, oh brethren, to what happened to Adhua. On the way Jamal ordered his army to halt and take rest for a short time and at this interval he wrote a letter to Adhua which ran thus :—

"Do you, oh maiden, still recollect poor Jamal ? I am summoned to Delhi for joining the war that is raging there. Probably I go never to come back to my native land. You are, I am sure, unaware of this. Surely you will feel a gap in your heart for me. Is it not a pity that I am not allowed to meet my love and take the gift of sweet betels from her dear hands even once in my life ? I am now a Fakir and leave my home for ever. Adhua, my bitterest grief is that I shall not see your face bright as the moon and never again shall we meet in life. Great hopes had I that I would be happy in life, securing you for my bride. But that is never to be. I could not personally take a final leave of you. This grieves me most. But if, by the grace of God, I ever return to my country I shall do all in my power to get myself united with you in wedlock."

He closed the letter and wiped away his tears that had sprung from his eyes. He took off the diamond-ring from his finger and sent it along with the letter to Adhua.

With his ten thousand men, he next proceeded towards Delhi. He saw many bad signs on the way. On the left side, some one sneezed as he started. A fly blown by the wind sat on his eye-lid. His noble war-horse stumbled and got a hurt in the leg. He saw wood-men carrying loads on the way and as he turned back, he heard the cry three times, 'Stop, stop, stop.' At this point he saw a corpse being borne on the shoulders of men for cremation. It appeared to him that some one was lamenting in the air as he went on. All these omens were observed and he became pensive and sad, and weeping prayed to Allah to save him from all trouble and danger. (Ll. 1-38.)

(16)

The Tragical End.

One—two—three months passed, after which a letter came from the Emperor of Delhi. It contained the sad news of Jamal's death. All the old affection for the child returned to the Dewan at the report and he fell down on the bare floor struck by grief and looked like a banana plant blown down by a November storm. When restored to consciousness he began to cry and the Uzirs and other officers shared his great grief. The whole city of Baniachang mourned the loss of their beloved prince. Even the elephants and horses of the stall shed silent tears ; and the birds that lived in the forest or flew in the sky, stopped their gay notes for a time, stunned by grief. The flower-women lamented loudly. For whom, alas, would they weave garlands of flowers? Loud lamentations were heard throughout the great city. And Faizu Fakir, the poet, says, " Don't grieve, oh citizens, but pray to God to restore peace to your mind."

When the dire news reached the inner apartments of the palace, Fatema Bibi fell senseless on the ground. The attending maids nursed her, but it was of no avail ; for, on the third day she expired.

Dewan Alal was lamenting over the Begum's dead body when the old minister came there and told him the whole history of his son's case. He said, " It is through your fault that you have brought ruin upon you." And then he related how, after the Dewan had gone to Mecca, Dulal Khan became an enemy of his son and sent ten thousand men headed by Lengrā with orders to bury Jamal Khan and the Begum alive. How they escaped death by the grace of God and how, like a beggar of the street, Jamal went to Dakshinbhāg imploring the Raja's mercy with tears in his eyes; how he spent years in the city of Dubaraja; how he destroyed the town founded by Lengrā in the Hāmilā forest, and how he fought a hard battle and eventually he recovered his lost kingdom; how Dubaraja's daughter Adhua, a maiden fair whose beauty put to shame that of any fairy, got enamoured of him and herself first offered her love to the prince without his seeking it; how the old minister himself went to the court of the Raja with a proposal of marriage; how at his orders his police-staff arrested him and cut off one of his ears and insulted him in various ways, and how owing to this proposal the Raja got incensed at Jamal Khan, turned his enemy and advised the Dewan to send him to battle.

The old Dewan's wrath kindled like fire on hearing the story and his grief for his son's death increased tenfold. He called his generals and ordered them to bring the Raja to him, bound hand and foot, in the course of the night. His order was "fire is to be set on his city and the citizens are to be indiscriminately killed, their dead bodies rolling in blood are to be thrown into river; no house, no tree of that city is to spared; a regular river of blood should flow there, striking terror into the hearts of all."

The army naturally delighted in war and all martial operations went on in full speed, like fire while burning a forest. (Ll. 1-58.)

(17)

Poor Adhua

What did the princess Adhuā do when she received Jamal's letter? She hastened to the temple of Chandi and wiped it by her flowing hair. Her attending maids made preparations for worship. Rice dried with the rays of the sun, clarified butter, bananas and sugar, sandal and vermilion and other articles were brought in plenty. She sat in a worshipful attitude before Chandi and prayed to her like a devotee. Just at that hour the army of the Dewan reached Dakshinbhāg. They seized the person of the Raja and dragged the princess out from the temple. In the morning they reached the city of Baniachang with the captives. In the way she heard loud lamentations near the city and learnt that Jamal had been killed in the battle. Under her thick curling hair she had hidden a small box of poison. She opened it now...............

They brought her out from inside the palanquin at the order of the Dewan. The Dewan said, "Kerumulla is the groom of my horses. Adhuā must be married to him. My grief will be assuaged by this insult." They dragged her out by her long hair but found her unconscious by the effect of the poison. Her long and curling hair lay there besmeared with dust. She looked like the full moon, come down from heaven to the earth. The Dewan's heart burst in grief at the sight of the beautiful princess and the memory of his lost son grew afresh in his mind. He saw a letter bound to the curling locks of the maiden. Alas! it was the one Jamal Khan had written on the eve of his departure. He also saw the diamord-ring of his son on a finger of the girl. "How could she get the ring of my son?"—he wondered. Then Alal brought his friend Dubaraja to his presence and related all that had happened. The two friends became once more united in common grief and cried embracing one another. Both had lost their children and both were stupefied by grief.

The old Dewan called his brother Dulal to him and said, "You wish to be the permanent Dewan; well and good; be what you wished; I shall again leave this place and turn the Fakir that I was. I shall never again come to Baniachang. The grief for my son is consuming me like fire."

He took leave of his minister and other officers and turned a Fakir, bound again for the holy city of Mecca. The ministers and other officers silently wept and the inhabitants of the whole kingdom were merged in grief at the renunciation of the Dewan; in the forest the birds lamented by their warbles; and the tears of the fish were merged in the river; the slaves struck their heads with their hands as a mark of sorrow; the people of the city sat stupefied with their heads bent downward and wept.

Dubaraja who was such an orthodox Brahmin, turned a Mahomedan convert, and started for Mecca.

The ministers and officers, as they saw the two friends start for Mecca as two Fakirs, were struck with vehement grief. "Alas, alas," they said, "behold the Dewan of an Empire goes away like a street-beggar!"

Faizu Fakir says, "What is the good of all these lamentations? Allah has written with his own hand the luck of each man—what he will do and what he will be—and this is unalterable. Take the name of Allah, my friends, for my story ends here. This world is vain; the name of Allah alone is true." (Ll. 1-64.)

THE END

FIROJ KHAN DEWAN.

PREFACE TO DEWAN FIROJ KHAN.

The name of the author of this ballad is not known, though there can be no doubt that he was a Muhammadan.

The name of Firoj Khan does not occur in the genealogical tree of the Dewans, so far as it has been available to us. As I find it to be the case in many of these ballads, I am convinced that the Muhammadan chiefs generally adopted dignified classical names on assuming the reins of administration.

Their more popular names, however, are to be found in the ballads. And there can be no question that this ballad, like some others about the Dewans of Jangalbari, embodies a good deal of historical facts.

Firoj Khan probably was one of Isha Khan's grandsons, he cannot be further removed from the great chief. As will be seen from the genealogical tree and the State-records of the Dewans, the property was afterwards divided amongst numerous scions of the family and the later Dewans, who were mere landlords of some status, could scarcely think of fighting with the Emperor of Delhi for independence.

Firoj Khan, as appears from the ballad, was a daring chief with his head full of notions of the glories of his ancestors. He was a lineal descendant of Isha Khan and occupied his *gadi* in full-fledged power and glory. We find it distinctly mentioned that "he was born in the family of Isha Khan." Such a reference would not be consistent, if he were a son of the illustrious founder of the family.

Isha Khan had two sons,—Musha Khan and Muhammad Khan. Musha Khan had a son named Machum Khan and Muhammad Khan's son was Eoaz Mahammad. For reasons already stated, we are reluctant to go down beyond the latter two names for finding out Firoj Khan in the genealogy of the Dewans. The genealogy of the Dewan-family supplied to us is neither exhaustive nor very accurate. We have elsewhere found the names of not only Abdul Khan as son of Isha Khan but of Adam and Biram, his two sons by his queen Sonamani—the Hindu princess of Sripur. Kellatajpur was a seat of another line of Dewans who probably came from the north-west and represented genuine Moslem blood. The vast field known as the Kellatajpur Maidan lies to the south of Netrakona, on the river Patkhora. Traces of the ditch and bricks of the old palace are still to be found in this tract of land.

Chandrakumar collected this ballad from three singers —(1) Sayabali Gayen of Fajilpur, (2) Sadir Gayen of Chandratala and (3) Rahaman Gayen of Katikhali. He got a portion of it from an old blind Fakir who begged alms from door to door and earned his living by singing. The above three singers were the pupils of the famous Ajib Gayen of Kabichandrapur in Pergana Nasir-u-jial. But the name of Jogir Gayen of Baraibari Jigatala in Pergana Susang, from whom Ajim had learnt the ballad is still famous in the country side as a singer of uncommon power. There is another singer named Madan Byapari who sings another version of the ballad which is evidently distorted. He has introduced much of the old folk-element in it and described Sakhina as fighting with a club, 80 maunds in weight and performing other miracles like a Druid priest or a Tantrik Siddha.

The ballad keeps up a sustained interest, though it is not characterized by much poetry. The last scene redeems the prosaic narration of the preceding cantos and gives the whole song an almost epic grandeur. Sakhina's enthusiastic hopes of giving a reception to her lord on his return from the battle-field as a victor, are smothered by the cruel tidings which Daria communicates to her after some hesitation. But she bears the dire news of her husband being taken as a captive with the patience of a saint and her incessant fight in the field for 30 hours, dressed in man's attire, shows more than her martial skill and bravery—the supreme triumph of love. But a woman's heart, however strong, has a vulnerable point, and there she would scarcely be able to support herself even if the stroke be as soft as that of a flower. She who could fight like a lioness for a full day and night in the face of grim death roaring from the mouth of the enemy's cannon in the hope of rescuing her husband, and was looked upon by friends and foes alike to be indomitable in the field, dies of failure of heart, when the messenger comes running and shows her the letter of divorce by which her lord had brought on an amicable settlement with the enemy. She only pauses for a moment to look at the seal and signature of her husband to be too sure of it, and then drops down dead on the spot.

The ballad refers to facts which occurred in the latter part of the 19th century and must have been originally composed not much later than that time.

The ballad of Firoj Khan is complete in 238 lines.

Firoj Khan Dewan.

(1)

First of all obeisance to Allah. Let us next narrate the history of Jangalbari.

The founder of the family was Kālidās Gajdāni who was so powerful that within his jurisdiction tigers and buffalloes drank from the same fountain without daring to quarrel with one another.

In his court Pirs, Fakirs and scholarly Brahmins daily assembled and discussed learned subjects. He made small figures of elephant plated with gold and distributed them amongst Brahmins. For this he was popularly called Gajdani or "giver of elephants." Heated were the discussions that took place in his court between the Muhammadan and Brahmin scholars. As a result of this continued discourses the Dewan's mind was purged of all evil thoughts, and gradually the right sense dawned on him; he gave up his infidel faith and turned a Muhammadan.

Kālidās Gajdāni had two sons,—of these two, I shall relate to you the story of Isha Khan. He revolted against the Emperor of Delhi who sent an army against him. Who was there so powerful as could cope with the royal army? Isha Khan was defeated at Douj Ghat. He crossed the Jayantia hills and fled. The army of the Emperor pursued him. They could not overtake him as he took refuge in the dense woods, and he then went upstream and landed at Jangalbari. In that city two brothers, Ram and Laksman, ruled at that time. Isha Khan now went down stream and laid siege to their capital with his force. The two brothers fled from the city, which Isha Khan conquered. There the Dewan family became settled. And I will here relate to you the history of Jangalbari founded by Isha Khan. Great wrestlers came from different countries and bowed their head to Isha Khan with whom no one could cope in the strength of his arms. He measured forty *puras* of land there and built a new city on the plot. He had many large tanks dug in his city with landing *ghats* made of stone. In the bungalows with twelve gateways that he built, the doors were plated with gold. The windows, big and small sparkled in the sun as its rays were reflected on the glasses. Indeed the city with its smiling flower-gardens looked like a fairy land. The houses were equipped with crystal pillars, and gold was used in such profusion in the buildings that they shone with splendour from every corner. From the tops of the houses waved picturesque flags decorated with golden embroidery, and long staircases were all built with stone. The city shone as the moon, and the Dewan ruled the country from his magnificent palace.

Firoj Khan was a scion of this distinguished family. His fame had spread far and wide. One day his learned courtiers sat round him in his bungalow with twelve gate-ways. His ministers and high officers were there. And he addressed them thus : "At every stage of my life am I reminded of my glorious ancestors who had fought with the Delhi Emperors. The founder of the Dewan family, Isha Khan, was so powerful that even the Emperor of Delhi could not cope with him. I cannot forget for a moment that I am his descendant. Now hear me, my officers, what I have resolved to do. God Almighty has created me. It is He who has sent me to

Jangalbari. But I have so long kept my place as Dewan by sending half of the revenues that I gather from my subjects to Delhi every year. I do not care to retain my Dewanship on such a humiliating condition. Now listen to what I have been thinking of in my mind. I will henceforth cease sending revenue to Delhi. I will no longer attend the Durbar of the Emperor. Let the army of the Emperor do whatever they like. I will fight by the will of God and I am ready to court death if indeed that is the luck to which I am doomed. This is my resolve. I will myself call death to my doors."

Just as he had finished his address, a maid-servant came from the inner apartment. She said, "Your Highness' mother, the old queen, wishes you to see her immediately." The maid-servant after conveying this message saluted the Dewan and stood awaiting his reply.

The Dewan said to his officers, "My mother has sent for me, so let the Durbar close to-day ; I will settle everything to-morrow." (Ll. 1-88.)

(2)

Saying so, the Dewan entered the inner apartment and was instantly in the presence of his mother. The maid-servants offered the Dewan cool drinks of sweet *sharbat*. He drank and was refreshed and then reposed himself at his ease on a cushion. The maid-servants with fans decorated with mica fanned him and the mother gazed at his handsome person bright as the moon reclining on the couch, and she took pride in his manly features. The Dewan saluted his mother and said, "What is it, good mother, that made you send for me ?" She slowly said, "Do not be cruel, dear son, to your old mama. As often as I see your face, I feel a pain in my heart which is not to be removed until you consent to marry. You are now in your full youth but you say that you will not marry. Will you not comply with my repeated requests? My days on earth are short, and I may soon go to my grave. My ardent wishes will be fulfilled if I can see the face of a beautiful daughter-in-law in this palace before my death."

The Dewan listened to the words of his mother with every mark of respect but said, "Can you feel, oh mother, what a pain I bear in my heart? The chief man of our family was Isha Khan with whom the troops of Delhi could not cope. The Emperor honoured him because he was a hero who could not be subdued even by his most valorous generals. In our illustrious family many a hero was born in the past. Now, hear my resolve. I will live an unmarried life. Day and night the thoughts of my State are uppermost in my mind. I have resolved not to send revenues to the Delhi Emperor any more. I will no more attend the Emperor's Durbar."

When the mother heard tha words of her son, she was struck with fear and sorrow and solicitously entreated him to change his mind.

Meantime, when the mother and son were engaged in serious talk, a picture-seller came there. A maid-servant offered her a seat in the room. She opened her chest full of pictures and the maids stood surrounding her, when the pictures were brought out one after another. The old queen asked her son to purchase a good one, offering to pay the price herself. The Dewan looked into the pictures and selected one. He was evidently struck with it and asked the woman, "What fairy of Behest is so beautiful? Will you pray tell me whose picture is this ? I have seen pictures of fairies whose colour is all crimson and those whose colour is beautiful blue, and in fact, the whole host of those who dwell in the fairy land, but I never saw a fairy like this ? Where does she live ? Who, alas, is her fortunate mate ? " The picture-seller smiled and said, " Listen to me, my young prince, she is not a fairy. She is the daughter of Omer Khan, Dewan of Kella-Tajpur. She is a grown-up girl but is not yet married. She will marry if she gets a groom after her choice."

Firoj Khan selected this picture and kept it. When the woman wanted the price, the old queen was so very pleased that she presented her with her own necklace. The picture-seller was right glad and tock betels from the queen's hands along with the necklace and departed saluting her. (Ll. 1-76.)

(3)

Chorus.—" The river of love went upstream and with it his mind."

The Dewan kept the picture with his mother and went to his own room. He reclined upon his couch and thought within himself, " I never saw a woman of such exquisite beauty. There is none amongst the mortals to match this figure. It seems that God-Almighty sat in a lonely place and bestowed His whole thought in modelling her lovely form ; her limbs are fair and round as if worked out by the finest chisel. The colour has the glow of a ripe banana and at this dawn of youth her face looks like a water-lily. If one sees her but once, one's eyes are charmed. Yet it is but a likeness. I wonder how the figure itself would look ! My mind, it seems, is losing its balance, and

I cannot think of anything else. Who is the fortunate one for whom God has created this sweet creature ?"

Firoj Khan became thus absorbed in wild and romantic thoughts and cared not to attend his administrative duties. The ministers and other officers could not make out the reason of this change. The Dewan neither took his bath nor his meals in proper time. There was evidently something wrong in his head. Meantime the revenue due to Delhi fell into arrears. The minister called on him and acquainted him with this and other important affairs of the State. The Dewan said, "Hear me, oh my trusted officers, the position that I hold has no more any charm for me. I want to take leave for some time. You are to act in my place during my absence. Govern the country well and justly. I shall be absent for a little while and go on a hunting excursion."

The Dewan, shortly after this, saw his mother and asked leave of her. "I am going away," he said, "for hunting and shall be absent for a short while. The forest of Sonakandi is the abode of wild beasts. Large tigers and bears infest these woods and every year make a havoc amongst my subjects in the locality. The people there are in a constant state of alarm and many have deserted their homes in fear. The wild buffaloes of the place are no less ferocious and they also kill my men every now and then. My heart melts in compassion for my poor subjects, and I am determined to save them from their danger. I have come to you to ask your permission to set out with this object for Sonakandi." The mother wept and said, "How can I live, dear son, without you in this palace ? You are the candle of my house and the light of my eyes. The whole world will appear dark to me during your absence from home." Saying so, she wiped away her growing tears. She prepared meals with five curries with her own hand and affectionately served him on the eve of his departure.

Firoj Khan started with his army.—The dust raised by the hoofs of horses covered the sky. The soldiers were maddened by enthusiasm in the prospect of a chase and the Dewan pitched his tents at a place near the down-stream of the river flowing in the locality. He halted at the forest-side for some days. But hunting was a mere pretext. He was planning to visit the city of Kella-Tajpur all the while and could not for a time settle what path he would follow to reach that city. He called his Foujder (general) one day and said to him, "Stay here for twenty-four hours. I will go away and will be absent for one full day and night." The Foujder saluted him and departed. Now the Dewan was thinking of nothing else excepting Sakhina—the daughter of the Tajpur Dewan. In the mid night he disguised himself as a Fakir with Daspanja(?) in his hands befitting a fakir; he proceeded on his way counting the sacred beads. He walked with a great speed, journeying in three hours what in normal state would take twelve hours to travel. Thus did he reach the city of Kella-Tajpur in the shortest time and take his seat under a tree, reciting the name of Allah like a true Fakir.

The people who had been going by the road were attracted by the appearance of the Fakir and sat surrounding him under the tree. Some of them wanted medicine for the diseases they suffered from; some stretched their hands before him believing that the Fakir knew something of palmistry. Some wanted him to examine their forehead and foretell what was written in their luck; others, who were childless, prayed for using his miraculous powers so that they might get children, and promised him *sinni* or religious gifts as reward. Others again abused him saying that he was a rogue under the guise of a Fakir. Some took compassion on him and spoke affectionately regretting that in his early youth he had cut off all ties with the world and turned a Fakir. They wanted to know what was the trouble or disappointment that had made him so disgusted with the world that he abandoned it in early youth.

Omer Khan, the Dewan, ruled over that place with his ministers and officers. Sakhina was his daughter, whose beauty dazzled all eyes, and attracted by which many princes and sons of Nawabs had come there seeking her hands. But she chose none of them and they went away disappointed. It was the picture of this Sakhina that had turned the head of Firoj Khan who came there struck by her beauty, leaving his capital.

At this time Dewan Omar had fallen very seriously ill. Many a physician and Fakir failed to give him relief, though they had tried their best. The Dewan heard of the young Fakir and sent for him. When Firoj Khan received this invitation he was overjoyed at the opportunity thus given him for entering the Dewan's harem. Fakirs and Darbeshes were supposed not to know the wily ways of the world and had free access to Zenana.

Sakhina sat on the landing steps of the tank within the palace when Firoj Khan went thither responding to the Dewan's call. She was busy washing the red dye from her lovely feet. Her form reflected in the tank sparkled like the moonbeams on the waters. He at once recognised the maiden whom he had seen in the picture. "But the real is as remote from the picture as heaven is from earth," he thought. "It is not in the power of an artist to draw her exact likeness." Her beauty seemed like a lovely stream flowing down on all sides with its playful charms. When the young Fakir had come near the bathing *ghat* Sakhina turned back and beheld him, "Ah me," she thought, "what a pity that this young man has renounced the world and turned a Fakir and left no chance for my making a choice!" She gazed at him with her insatiate eyes.

The maiden came up to him instantly and saluted him with the respectful folding of hands as was becoming before a Fakir and said, "Tell me, oh young Fakir, who you are! What disappointment did you suffer in life that has made you cut off all worldly ties and turn a Fakir? Where was seen a person of your tender age, who ever turned a Fakir? My heart melts in compassion for you. How could your parents allow you to leave home in this way? I wonder that they did not follow your track with the speed of a bird! Why is it that you have entered our harem?" Firoj Khan said in reply, "Your esteemed father, oh maiden, is seriously ill. He sent for me and I am here to try to cure him. It is by luck, fair maiden, that some people become kings; my humble lot is to be a Fakir. So you see I travel from one country to another as such."

Saying so he entered the hall where the Dewan Omer Khan lay in his bed. He gave him a charmed locket. Firoj Khan, after this, joined his army and shortly after returned home. (Ll. 1-146.)

(4)

After coming back he became a lover of solitude. He indulged in all sorts of reveries about the maiden Sakhina. He neither attended the Durbar nor did his duties as Dewan and hardly came out of his private chamber. One day he called the maid-servant Daria to his presence. Daria was a young girl of a lively temperament and looked bright with her smile when she spoke. She wore on her feet anklets of an artistic pattern call the 'Bakmal' and a necklace which in the countryside they called 'Hasli.' Her steps were graceful and she often laughed without a cause. She asked the Dewan as to what was the matter with him that he looked pale. "What a pity," she said, "that insects are already at work in such fine green bamboo-shrubs! If your lordship is willing to marry, I will travel all over the world to find a lovely bride for you. You have now stepped into youth, why should you thus deceive your own mind and deprive yourself of the pleasures which it is fit in the nature of things for you to enjoy"?

When the merry slave-girl thus delivered herself, Firoj Khan slowly said in reply, "Hear me, Daria, I sincerely believe that there is none in the world who sympathises with me more than you do. I have known you from childhood and I can place absolute confidence in you. I am going to open my mind to you to-day. I am feeling extremely miserable over the thought of my marriage. If you can help me to the attainment of my object I will reward you well. I will myself choose a good bridegroom for you and give you five maid-servants to wait upon you and minister to your comforts.

"You are to go from here to Kella-Tajpur in the guise of a picture-seller. There lives in that city princess Sakhina, the daughter of Dewan Omer Khan. You are to enter her harem with the pictures I will give you. Show her all of them one by one and last of all produce this picture of a Fakir and submit it for her inspection with due courtesy." Saying so the Dewan offered her a basketful of pictures which she took in her arms and was about to depart—after having salaamed him. The young Dewan asked her to stop for a moment and gave some further directions. He said, "Go to the harem of Dewan Omer Khan, seeking a moment when Sakhina will be all alone in her room. Open your basket and let her know what she may be curious to learn from you. When you will show her the picture of the Fakir, keep your eyes fixed on her and study her face, closely observing what impression it makes on her. If she asks you anything in regard to that picture, tell her, 'I am a mere picture-seller and do not know much about him. I have only heard that he belongs to the family of Dewans. I have no detailed knowledge of the pictures that I sell, they are very numerous. I buy and sell them—that is my interest in them. I visited Delhi, Agra and other cities and last of all have come to Bengal. This picture of the Fakir I purchased on my way. I heard that this young man was a Dewan but has turned a Fakir enchanted with the beauty of a maiden named Sakhina, who it is said, lives in this very city—I have heard that he has been wondering from place to place like a Fakir maddened by her beauty.'

"You will say these words and observe if the colour of her face changes at this report."

Daria disguised herself as a picture-seller and started for Kella-Tajpur with the basket. It usually took a person three days to reach the city of Kella-Tajpur. Alone the slave-girl went all the way. She saw from afar the city with her crest of towers rising aloft to the sun and sparkling with their golden hue. The city covered a *pura* and a half of land. Every now and then did she see from distance blue-coloured tiara-shaped crests of Musjids fading as it were on the horizon. She admired the artistic skill and the plan of the city. The horses and elephants marched in the street with their riders on their gaily caparisoned backs; with eyes full of curiosity she observed everything as she proceeded.

On entering the palace she lost not a moment but instantly stepped into the harem and and saw Sakhina in her compartments. She was at that moment seated on a sofa in her room. Her dishevelled hair looked like broken clouds falling in profusion on the arms of the sofa. Daria beheld that unmatched beauty with wonder, and said to herself, "What is his fault? Even a woman would fall in love with such a maiden. How can a man resist such charms? I never saw a woman so beautiful. I wonder if in the land of fairies there is any to match her! How lovely are her feet decorated with the red dye! How exquisitely fine are her eyes painted with *surma*! With these eyes if she looks at any man he is sure to be maddened by her glance."

She saluted the princess and approaching her opened the basket of pictures. She first showed her the pictures of great emperors and kings and of great warriors. Next she showed her those of Nawabs and their Begums; and last of all she brought out from the basket the picture of the Fakir. She wiped away the dust and made it look bright. Then where the feet of the fair maiden decorated with the red dye *alta* rested on a foot-stool, she placed the picture with care.

She was startled at the sight, like one who had got a golden apple in dream or had met a very dear friend a real sympathiser—after the lapse of long years. And then keeping her eyes fixed on the picture she addressed Daria and said, "Now tell me, maiden, where did you get this picture? You have no doubt wandered about many strange places. Where is it, oh picture-seller, that such a one could be found? Who is the artist that has drawn this picture? And who is the person whose likeness it is? It seems that I once saw this Fakir. Tell me the plain truth without hiding anything."

She saluted Sakhina several times and said, "I will tell you, oh noble princess, all facts about this picture. My profession requires me to visit many places. I had been to Agra, Delhi and other countries. Last I came to Jangalbari where a merchant sold me this picture. I have heard from him this account of the Fakir. His name is Firoj Khan, he is the Dewan of Jangalbari. Oh my noble lady, this young Dewan is wandering about like a madman in the guise of a Fakir. At his absence the city of Jangalbari is in the deepest sorrow. The fair processions which on festive occasions attracted people from all countries to the city are no more to be seen there. The minister and high officers of State are all sad for their beloved Dewan. The subjects who love him dearly—the poor widows and others who live upon his charity—mourn for him shedding tears day and night."

Sakhina interrupted her in the midst of her speech and said, "I feel a deep compassion for the Fakir at what you have said, though he is a perfect stranger to me. Now, picture-seller, tell me if ever you met the Fakir and if you ever have heard why he has turned an ascetic. My heart weeps at the sorrows of the young Dewan. Will you tell me why he has left his palace and turned a Fakir? Tell me the whole story. I am purchasing the portrait with this my necklace. I will feel no rest until I hear the whole story."

Daria said, "I will tell you, oh princess, all that I have heard. This Fakir was formerly the Dewan of Jangalbari. It is said that in this fair city of yours there is a damsel named Sakhina, daughter of one Omer Khan. The young Dewan of Jangalbari struck with her beauty has turned a Fakir. What a pity that the Dewan is now a Fakir for the sake of a waman, when he has just stepped into his youth!"

As she heard this account she became maddened with grief. She wiped away her tears with the edge of her *sadi*. Her mind became steeped in deep love. The *hasuli* which she wore on her breast was worth a lakh of rupees. She took it out from her neck and offered it to the picture-seller as reward. Daria saluted her and departed.

She held the picture close to her bosom and remembered the Fakir whom she had seen but once. She gave up her meals, her sleep and all joys. It seemed that her compartments looked dark without her smile. No more did that sweet smile play on her lips and no more did she sing sweetly like a bird! On her couch no more did she allow flowers to be spread! Her attendants—the maid-servants—were alarmed at the strange change that had come upon her. They could not guess what was it that weighed so heavily on her heart.

Thus the two lovers pined away for one another. And now I am going to relate to you the story of their marriage. (Ll. 1-174.)

(5)

Firoja Bibi, the mother of Firoj Khan, marked that her dear son was indifferent to the affairs of State and she called him to her presence. She said, "I have told you my mind times without number. I am resolved that you should marry now. If you do not marry, your line will end here and in this palace the evening lamp will not be lighted. This illustrious house of the Dewans, already looks gloomy, its splendour will go if you do not leave a scion behind you. Marry as you would like, no one will interfere with your choice. But do not give pain to the poor old mother's heart. Do as I wish."

This time he did not oppose his mother. Silently he heard all that she said. He was inwardly pleased. He retired into the chamber and there he had a talk with the minister, he said to him, "I will open my mind to you to-day, oh Vizier. My mother is pressing me for marriage. Tell her that though I resolved not to marry, I will break my resolve for her sake. Tell her that there is a maiden named Sakhina, daughter of the Dewan Omer Khan of Kella-Tajpur. I am ready to marry her with the consent of my mother. If this maiden is not to be had as my bride, I will know that it is not the will of God that I should marry. So I will bear the pain of my heart secretly till I go to my grave."

On this errand did the minister seek an interview with the old queen in her apartment. He entered the inner apartment and saluted the old queen. She asked him what it was that had brought the old minister there. He saluted her again and said, "The young Dewan has at last given his consent to marriage. Omer Khan, the Dewan of Kella-Tajpur has a beautiful daughter named Sakhina. If this daughter could be secured for him, he would marry. If not, he would live a bachelor all his life."

The old queen after a pause said in reply, "Minister, I am really puzzled at this proposal. The Dewan of Tajpur, Omer Khan, is our sworn enemy. How can I make a proposal to him ? How can I think of making the daughter of our enemy the bride of this palace ? Go and tell this to Firoj. I will get for him a bride far more beautiful than Sakhina. My heart does not feel any pleasure at the thought of this match. It will not be a happy one. I feel a misgiving. Tell him, oh minister, if he will allow me to choose a bride elsewhere. I shall be most happy to do so."

The minister saw the prince again and told him all that his mother had said and added, "If you marry this daughter of our enemy, all honour and status of your high position you will lose." The young Dewan replied, "You need not talk a good deal. If I cannot get Sakhina for my bride, I will remain a bachelor. I have turned like one mad after her. Her beautiful face is ever fresh in my memory. I do not want any other girl. And how can I do it? She is like the cool drink of my thirsty soul—the light of my eyes and the necklace of my breast. I want her. I do not want any one else. Tell my mother, if Sakhina is not to be had, here ends my life in the palace. I will go away turning a Fakir."

The Minister carried the message to the old mother. She fully realised the pain of her son's heart and thought within herself. "This son of mine is my sole stay. If he goes away, not a moment shall I be able to stay in the palace. For his sake, I can give up my life itself. Why should I stand in the way of his happiness? I will not oppose this marriage."

Thinking in this way the queen sent the old minister to Omer Khan, the Dewan of Kella-Tajpur with the proposal of marriage. It took the minister three days to reach the city of Dewan Omer Khan. He interviewed the chief who asked him, "From what country have you come here, oh Mian? What business have you with me?"

The old man saluted the Dewan Sahib of Tajpur respectfully and said, "I am the minister of Firoj Khan,

Dewan of Jangalbari. His mother Firoja Bibi has sent me to your Highness. It is known all over the country that you have got a very beautiful daughter named Sakhina, who has attained her marriageable age. Our young Dewan Sahib, Firoj Khan, for personal qualifications, handsome appearance and manly qualities, is second to none in the country. Firoja Bibi, his mother, wishes to ask you if you would consent to this marriage. I have been sent to you to make this proposal."

Omer Khan got angry at his words. Before the whole court he said in an indignant tone, "These Dewans of Jangalbari were originally Kafirs. They do not observe Roja (fast) and Namaj (prayers) like true Muhammadans. And indeed I do not count them as such. This proposal comes from a Kafir and hence I take it as an insult. This surely deserves a punishment." Saying this Omer Khan roared like a lion ; and instantly servants came from all sides to execute his order. He said, "Hold this old man by the neck and turn him out of the court."

Thus insulted the old man returned to Jangalbari.

(Ll. 1-116.)

(6)

Firoj Khan, the young Dewan Sahib, heard this story of the insult. As if the whole sea was set on fire, the young Dewan flew into a fit of rage, and at his command his officers made the public drums to be beaten in the city-markets ordering people to be ready with arms. "To-morrow they must be prepared for a great fight." This was the command. The generals came forward from all sides with their armies. The war-horses were caparisoned and bedecked with jewels and made ready. The army started and the sound arose in their ranks "seize and kill." With a vast army Firoj Khan reached Kella-Tajpur the next day. They laid siege to the palace all on a sudden and forcibly entered it and seized the Dewan Sahib, his Uzir and other officers by their necks and drove them out from the city. The path was now quite clear and they entered the inner apartments. From her couch Firoj Khan raised Sakhina, imprisoned her and brought her to his own capital at Jangalbari. He was quite happy now and married her with her consent. Each was pleased with the other. They sat together and talked, walked together and were perfectly happy in one another's company. If one was sad, the other had no rest without sharing a part of it. They became steeped in love and enjoyed their nuptial life greatly at Jangalbari.

Let us drop here this topic and revert to the story of Dewan Omer Khan. (Ll. 1-26.)

(7)

Insulted and defeated by Firoj Khan, Omer approached the Emperor of Delhi. The Emperor was holding his Durbar as usual with his minister and high officers, and Dewan Omer Khan presented himself before him without any previous notice. The Emperor asked, "How is it, Dewan, that you are here all on a sudden ? Your garments are not quite clean and your face looks pale and dark like a *kesar* fruit. Evidently you look worried. Now, tell me the reason of your sudden visit to our capital."

The Dewan saluted the monarch and said, "I have come here to lodge a complaint before Your Majesty. Be graciously pleased to hear all that I am going to submit. The present Dewan of Jangalbari is Firoj

Khan. He is born of a Kafir family; but still he was so bold as to seek the hands of my daughter. He sent his minister with the proposal, and, as a matter of course, I dismissed him with refusal. He returned to Jangalbari and reported the matter to his chief. As a result the Dewan of Jangalbari laid siege to my capital with an army of 60,000 soldiers. My family, the members of my personal staff were all put to great humiliation. But this is not all. The worst that happened I am going to relate to Your Majesty. He drove away the female members of my house from the inner apartments and carried away my daughter Sakhina by force. There was none to save the poor girl from this disgrace. He married her by sheer force. With my heart as if pierced by an arrow I have come to lay my hard case before Your Majesty. I have no language to give adequate expression to the sense of my wrong. Maddened by grief I have come to the Durbar. I pray to Your Majesty to judge my case fairly. If I do not find justice here I will starve myself to death in this very palace of Your Majesty. It does not become one to live in this world after being so wantonly insulted by a Kafir."

The Emperor was angry at what he heard. His Majesty said in a loud voice before his court, "The Dewan of Jangalbari has, I see, become greatly conceited. He has ceased paying revenue to the State which is now in arrears for years. He does whatever he likes. Now, there should be an end of all such things. I will destroy him, his family and all, not sparing the children. Hear me, my ministers, send as large a force as available at this moment. The Dewan must immediately be arrested and brought here as a prisoner. When he will come here as a prisoner I will pass what judgment will be considered fit. (Turning to

Omer Khan) "You lead the army and go there to avenge yourself on the wrong committed on you."

The cavalry became ready and the warriors, riding elephants and horses, started with a vast following of foot-soldiers. The cry went on amongst the soldiers, "Be ready, start at once." The army consisted of a lakh of soldiers. The dust raised by their feet and horses' hoofs covered the sky. Some rode horses, others elephants; even the foot-soldiers vied to run apace with the cavalry. Omer Khan had the command of the army and rode foremost of all. The one lakh of army was a compact body, obeying their leader like one man. They all reached the precincts of Jangalbari and pitched their tents there.

On hearing the report of the arrival of this army Dewan Firoj Khan ordered the drums of his palace to be beaten, summoning his generals. They presented themselves before their chief in all haste with their armies. Firoj Khan robed himself as a warrior and went to the inner apartments to take his mother's permission to go to fight. (Ll. 1-62.)

(8)

Chorus—"Behold Firoj goes to the battle-field his mother's heart is pierced by the arrow of grief." He salutes his mother and says, "I am bound for war. Grant me permission, good mother. My town is under siege. Omer Khan has come down with the army of the Emperor determined to take revenge. Give me the dust of your feet, mother, and bless me. Don't, oh mother, detain me by your laments, lest the enemy takes advantage of my delay and enter the town."

The mother sorrowfully said in reply, "Don't, oh my son, go to war. Call your generals to the palace and order them to fight. You are dear to me like the ribs of my breast. I shall not be able to live here alone sending you to the battle, I feel a misgiving that all will, perhaps, end in a disaster, and my heart throbs with fear at the thought of your going to the fight."

He hastily cut short the conversation by saying, "No mother, that cannot be. I must go to the battle myself. If I do not go, there is little hope of victory, My army will not be able to make a stand in the field in my absence. I assure you, I will come victor, my army will feel a new life if they see me at their head and fight to the best of their power. With a heart full of love for me they will zealously fight for their motherland and come out victorious. If I show them an example of cowardice, what will remain there to inspire them with courage in the field? Defeat will be sure at the hands of the enemy." Saying so he saluted his mother and touched her feet and, bidding adieu, left her presence.

Next, Firoj Khan went to the apartment of Sakhina to take leave. He addressed her saying, "Look here, dear lady, your beloved father has come here with the Emperor's army and I am bound for a battle with him. I have come to bid you farewell on the eve of the war. Take care of yourself. Pray, console my grief-stricken mother—what more can I say? The time is short—I must be off instantly."

On hearing this, Sakhina took a handful of sacred dust gathered from the shrines of five saintly men. He gently touched this sacred dust with his forehead. She then prayed that he might win the battle and come back without delay. The prince said, "By the grace of God, before the day closes, I will once more come back to your arms, dear Sakhina, as victor of the field."

Saying so he took leave and passed from sight. Sakhina looked at him from behind so far as she coulp stretch her eyes. Tears flowed from her eyes and she softly murmured, "Alas, I have made my heart stiff as stone, to allow him to go to the fight."

With his army, Firoj came to the field. For two incessant days the fight continued and the number of the dead was equal on both the sides. No party won, no party lost. On the third day, Firoj was made a prisoner. The enemy got hold of his person and carried him to Kella-Tajpur. The people of Jangalbari made loud lamentations at this issue of the war.

Chorus—" The horse returned with the flag unfurled on its back, stained with blood. When the lady saw this, her heart was about to break."

Sakhina lay on her couch, when all on a sudden, Daria, the female attendant, entered her room. When she saw Daria, she addressed her saying, " Day before yesterday, in the morning, my husband went to the field and now listen to me, oh friend Daria, gather the choicest of roses and champa flowers to weave garlands When he will return as victor, I will offer garlands as my presents of love.

" In the gold-plated toilet room, keep in reserve water for *auzu*, keep ready fans decorated with mica. We shall need offer him our services, when he will come back, a victor fatigued by fight.

"Keep in store rose-water and scented oil, and in golden cups keep sweet betels for my husband. Bring sacred dust, dear Daria, from the shrines dedicated to five saints. My husband, on return, will need bow to the sacred token.

"The wives of the saints have sent their blessings and assured me of my husband's victory."

As she said this her face brightened with a smile.

But she stopped a moment and said again, "Why is it, oh Daria, that you do not smile to-day? You look pale. But take my word, you will be happy on his return to the palace as victor."

Then Daria could no longer control herself but wept and said, "Now, lady, your luck is gone. The war-steed has returned with our flag, tinged with blood. It no longer becomes you, esteemed lady, to sleep on the couch."

"Come down and make your humble bed on the floor. Remove the red mark of luck from your forehead and the valuable rings from your ears. Change your costly *saḍi* for a plain one and cut off your long flowing hair. From to-day you are to wear clothes befitting an ascetic.

"Remove your bracelets and other ornaments of the arm, and that bright necklace of diamond from your breast. The anklets with pendants should no more adorn your feet and you should also remove the jingling pendants from your belt. No more does that sweet smile befit your lips. Your beauty, your youth are now in vain. Alas, they are like flowers that bloom in morn to drop their faded petals in eve. News has come, dear lady, that your husband is now a prisoner at Kella-Tajpur."

When she heard this from Daria, she stood up in great emotion. It seemed to her that the sky itself had broken and fallen on her head. It was like a thunder-bolt falling on a garden of roses. The smile from her lips was gone and her heart seemed about to break. Her flowing tresses, unbraided, carelessly fell behind her back almost touching the ground. The maid-attendants, as they saw her grief, cried, 'alas, alas.' She addressed Daria and said, "My good luck, oh Daria, is gone. But never mind, whatever may befall me, I do not care. Bring our war-horse instantly. I must see who is that enemy that could make *my* husband a prisoner. Make ready the horse for war and order the soldiers, the bow-men and the sepoys to be ready to follow me. I shall ride. I am a woman bound for war. This, please, oh Daria, keep secret for the present. If they ask you, 'Who it is that is going to lead us?' Tell them that a cousin of the Dewan is going to fight."

The elephants were caparisoned, the horses became ready. 'Be ready, be ready,' was the cry heard everywhere and the soldiers put on their war-robes in response.

Now Sakhina went to the apartment of her mother-in-law to take leave of her. She had left her couch and in great grief lay like one stunned on the floor. She consoled her mother-in-law by tender words, "Your hair is dishevelled and your face looks so pale, dear mother," Arise from the floor and give me permission to go to the battle-field at Kella-Tajpur. I will see what sort of hero is he,—who has dared lay hands on my husband and made him a prisoner. I will fight him and know his worth. Bless me, mother, that I may be a victor in the field and bring back your dear son home." The dowager queen wiped her tears away and addressing Sakhina said, "Grieved am I to hear of your resolve. My son, a warrior and a man, has become a prisoner, and you, a tender woman, will go to the battle! Who is it that has counselled you to take this mad course? You are the lamp of my house, precious to me as the prop is to the blind. For a moment I would not like to part with you.

I shall cease grieving for my son, drawing consolation from a sight of you. I cannot allow you to go to the battle-field."

Sakhina softly repeated her request for permission to go to the field saying, " Don't object, oh mother, but grant me this boon ; I assure you, I will come back a victor accompanied by my husband. If my luck turns hostile and I die in the battle-field—no grief, no sorrow will I feel in dying for my husband. For his sake I will give up my life. Adieu, dear mother, accept my humble respects at the hour of parting."

The mother-in-law and the daughter-in-law stood weeping, locked up in each other's arms for a moment. It seemed as if the golden city of Jangalbari became veiled in darkness.

The great war-horse Dulal, gaily caparisoned, stood ready in the inner compound of the palace and Sakhina jumped up on its back and rode with the speed of a flying bird. The van-guard rode in advance and other soldiers followed her, and the cloud of dust raised by horses' hoofs and the feet of the infantry covered a portion of the sky. The sun and the moon could not be seen in their proper time owing to the mass of dust raised in the sky. The birds left their nests and the animals ceased to graze in great fright. The journey which usually took a day was finished in 20 minutes as they proceeded on, and now before them stood the city of Kella-Tajpur. " My father is my enemy now," she thought and ordered the army to lay siege to the city. For two days and a half the parties fought with no decisive result. And Sakhina at this stage ordered her men to set fire to the city. Big palatial houses, great arches and doors were reduced to heaps of ashes. It was a great shame for the Emperor's troops that they became defeated at last. The afternoon passed and the sun peeped out from the western horizon. She was still fighting from the back of the war-horse with undaunted zeal.

At this moment came a messenger from the fort of Tajpur. He salaamed her and said, "A formidable warrior art thou, greater than Hanif himself. I come from Jangalbari, the enemies have destroyed the palace there. We do not know who you are, fighting in the interest of that ill-fated city. Here is a document which will shew the terms of amnesty signed by Dewan Firoj Khan who has sent me to you. He has asked me to convey the report to you that he has divorced the woman Sakhina for whom the golden city of Jangalbari has been ruined. He will meet all the rest of the demand made by the Emperor in course of a week. The war is at an end. This is the news which I have been ordered to communicate to you." Saying so, he handed her the document of divorce and she saw on it the impression of Firoj Khan's great seal.

A moment she took to read the document and then as if stung by a snake, she fainted and fell unconscious from the back of her horse. The golden crown on her head broke to pieces as she fell on the ground, and the great horse Dulal shed tears standing by her side. The soldiers began to cry and lament. Her seat a moment ago was on the back of her horse and now see her lying on the bare earth. It was as if the evening star had fallen on the earth from the sky. The city of Jangalbari now actually became covered with darkness. Her long dishevelled hair fell unbound on all sides. From her body fell the male's attire. The generals and soldiers at once recognised their queen and began to lament loudly. In the fort of Tajpur the report quickly spread, and Firoj Khan accompanied by Omer Khan at once visited the place. They came and saw the full moon—the golden moon—lustreless on the ground. Omer Khan took her in his arms and just as a child cries taking the broken toy in his hands, began to lament over the body of his dear daughter. He said, " My doubts have all been cleared to-day. Had I known that things would come to such a pass, I would have myself sought for this marriage and taken the lead in all matters. Had I known all this I would have given the kingdom of Tajpur to Firoj Khan as dowry, and would have myself carried you to Jangalbari and offered you to its lord.

Dewan Firoj Khan addressed his minister and said, " I do not know what I have done to deserve this great calamity. Why should she have left me thus ! But I shall turn a Fakir for her sake. How can I console my poor mother ? No, here ends my connection with Jangalbari. No more would I care for the exalted position of Dewan Sahib. I am a Fakir to day. I shall sing songs in your praise, my love, and beg alms from door to door ! " He wept and said to his minister again, " Try to console my mother as best as you can. I am not going there. Her burial place will be mine too. I will sleep the eternal sleep there ; until I do so, I cannot think of getting any peace of mind." The minister wept and the great army cried in sorrow. Even the beasts of jungles and the birds of air shed tears at his sorrows.

The brave warriors sat down on the field of battle struck with grief and the report of this reached the city of Jangalbari.

Twenty-two spades-men dug a grave and after having performed the due rites such as the recitation of *Jánejá* they buried the body of Sakhina there. After burial they returned to their respective homes, carrying a deep sorrow in their hearts.

This song is finished and my audience may now depart. If I live I will come again next year to sing to you, gentlemen, a new song. I do not know how to keep time, nor have I any musical instrument. I am afraid, my song will be found faulty in many ways. With my poor knowledge how can I expect to please such a distinguished audience as yourselves? Those who have sung chorus are all novices in the art of music, untrained and without any knowledge of the musical science. They have not been able to keep time and often struck discordant notes destroying the effect of the song. O, my esteemed President of this august assembly, forgive me for all my shortcomings. I bow down to you with great humility.

The master of the house, who bears the expenses of to-night's performance is Rang Miah. His name has justly got famous. He is a lucky man and is an inhabitant of Kajalkona. His great sympathy drew us to his home. I have received a reward from him, for singing this ballad of Firoj Khan. I have got *Dhuti* and *Chadar* and rice, —I beg to offer my thanks to him. May he flourish in wealth and may his children be long-lived and may he be happy with his sons and grandsons. May the fourteen *arahs* of land that he possesses yield rich crops from year to year. I pray for God's blessings on you, gentlemen. I shall now return home. May God fulfil your desires, amen! *Allah ho Akber.*

(Ll. 1-238.)

THE END.

Fig. I. A "Gadhu" boat.

Fig. II. The "Sarenga" boats at the Cháktái Ghat, Chittagong.

Fig. III. Modern Sloops built by the Bálámis.

Fig. IV. Modern Sloops built by the Bálámis.

Fig. V. Modern Sloops built by the Bálámis.

Fig. VI. Modern Sloops built by the Bálámis.

Fig. VII. Modern Sloops built by the Bálámis.

Fig. VIII. A Bálám boat of Chittagong.

INDEX.

INDEX

A

Abdarpur—264, 270.
Abdul (Dewan)—322.
Abdul Karim (Munshi)—35, 302, 309, 310, 334.
Abdul Khan—334.
Abdulla—283, 333.
Abdulla—373.
Ābir (red dye)—20.
Abruagunj—367.
Abul Fazl—301.
Abu Raja—131, 132, 135, 157-58, 163, 165, 168, 170, 172, 173, 175, 176, 178, 179, 181, 182, 186.
Achyut Bharan Tattanddhi—380, 382.
Adam (Khan, Mashnadali)—320, 325, 333, 353, 356, 360, 363.
Adam—381.
Adhar Chandra—189, 195, 205, 211.
Adhua—383, 389, 404, 406, 417.
Adunā—23.
Afghan—317.
Aguru—193.
Ahammad—330, 381.
Aini Akbari (also Ain)—301, 303, 307, 311, 365.
Aithor—79.
Ajib Gayen—424.
Ajjor Khan—373.
Aem Raya—370.
Akbar—314, 317, 327, 328, 347, 348, 368, 362, 370, 372.
Akbarnāmā—365.
Alangher char—186.
Alap Singh—349, 372.
Alal Khan—380, 388, 392, 393, 394, 411, 412, 413, 416.
Alaler Gharer Dulal—380.
Ali—283.
Alimurdian Khan—334.
Ali Noaz Khan—334.
Allahabad—369.
Alumni—365.
Āmāni—243.
Amarāvati (Rani)—313.
Amardighi—311, 317.
Amar Manikya—307, 308, 311, 312, 313, 314, 317, 325.
Amina—283.
Amir—217, 225.
Ananda Bazar Patrika—281.
Annals of Rural Bengal—261.
Aparājitā (flower)—10.
Arabia—329.
Arabian Nights' Tales—309.
Arabic—38, 363.
Ārāhs (measuring of land)—41.
Arang—58.
Asahebs—372.
Asalat Khan—373.
Asharia Mandal—35, 37, 51, 55, 56.
Ashraf Hossain (Muhammad)—122.

Ashtagrām—311.
Ashtamangal—120.
Assam—39, 137, 317.
Asutosh Chowdhuri—275, 331.
Atasi (flower)—19.
Atia—373.
Attar—363.
Auliā (Moslem Saint)—279, 281, 297, 298.
Azim Dād Khan (Dewan)—302, 366, 374.
Azim Ush Khan—330.

B

Baber—309, 310.
Babylonians—329.
Bacon—218.
Bahadur Ali Khan—334.
Bahadur Shah—305, 339, 368.
Bāhātiā—127.
Bāilākhāli—237, 238.
Baisakh—245.
Baiswara—304, 308, 328, 329, 368, 373.
Bajitpur—368.
Bāklā—311.
Baktiarpur—322, 324, 372.
Balarām—37, 42, 43, 44, 45, 50-54.
Balarām Sur—311, 314, 379, 383.
Barabaju—373.
Bana Durga—59.
Bangshidas—280.
Baniāchung—311, 384, 387, 388, 392, 393, 399, 411, 412.
Baradakhat—349.
Baruni—370.
Baradakhatmaura—349.
Bāramāsi—121.
Bara Pir Saheb—277, 295.
Bashkuli—263.
Baz Khan—313.
B. Buru—304.
Bechārām—266.
Bediyās—330.
Begum—320.
Behar—369.
Behari Lal Ray—215.
Bel—203, 234.
Benares—90, 92.
Bengal—34, 37, 122, 260, 294, 305, 307, 308, 311, 326, 329, 334, 369.
Besar (nose-ornament)—59.
Bhagirath Singh—304, 308, 337, 373.
Bhāndi-forest—270.
Bharāi—74, 86.
Bharāinagar—93, 104, 116
Bhāratchandra—330.
Bhelua—33, 34, 129, 131-32, 135-41, 145, 147-48, 150, 152, 153-70, 172-73, 175-85, 187-88.
Bhowal—40, 311, 349, 372-73.
Bhulna—311.
Binni (paddy)—239.
Biram (Khan)—320, 323, 325, 356, 363.
Ben—374.
Birbhum—259.
Birsingpur—270.
Boāl (fish)—230.
Boālkhāli—275.
Boragar—270.
Brahmadaitya—221.
Brahmaputra—216, 221, 223, 232, 370.

Brahmins—136, 277, 321.
Brahminic Renaissance—122.
Brahmo Samāj—368.
British—216.
Buckergunje—311.
Budak'hal—320.
Bukāi—346.
Bulban Khan—334.
Bungalow—133, 346.
Burmese—39.

C

Candray—114.
Chai (plant)—240.
Chaitanya Bhāgavat—218.
Chaitanya Deva—218.
Champā (flower)—9, 10, 49, 59, 63, 128, 199.
Chānd—140, 151.
Chand Ray—311, 325, 327, 328.
Chandi—124, 417.
Chandidas—7, 8, 34, 167.
Chandrakumár De—6, 33, 40, 79, 191, 192, 379, 383, 387, 388.
Chandrakumar Sarkar—40.
Chandrahār (ornament)—128.
Chandrāvati—280, 387.
Chāpati—242.
Char Sambhuganj—6.
Chil (bird)—10.
Chirā—359.
Chirar moā—241.
Chittagong—33, 38, 57, 71, 72, 137, 275-78, 280, 331, 333, 345.
Chouddagrām—311.
Chou gangā—132, 172, 173, 175, 177-78, 184.
Christians—303.
Chua (perfumery)—208.
Chudder—234, 236, 245.
Cornwallis, Lord—960.
Cowrie—44, 216, 222.
Cupid—3.

D

Dacca—277, 301-2, 311, 315-16, 327, 345, 366-67.
Dakshinaranjan Mitra Majumdar—134.
Dakshin Bhag—381, 387, 405, 406, 409, 418.
Dargā—277, 278.
Darga Munshi—266.
Daria—425, 448, 450, 451.
Dāru—248.
Dāruk (tree)—80.
Darwesh—287.
Darzibazu—349.
Dasakāhaniā—222.
Dasamangal—120.
Daśamī—204.
Dashu—223.
Daud Khan—306, 307, 309, 310, 343, 344.
Dayāvanta Narain—312.
Delhi—193, 309, 317, 321-23, 325, 327, 344, 346-47, 369, 371-72, 388, 412, 413, 423, 429.
Demra—370.
Dewan *bāg*—316, 347, 370.
Dewan Bhābna—195.
Dewan family—301.
Dewans—305, 307, 309, 322-63, 365.
Dhananjaya—172, 187.

Dhān Durvā—156.
Dhanpat Singh (Raja)—304, 308, 337.
Dhoṛā—250.
Dhruva—84.
Dhuti—187, 245.
Digher-forest—285, 294, 296.
Dighi—328.
Dina Gopa—6.
Dingādhar—33, 35-37, 39, 41-45, 50-58, 69, 71, 73-76.
Divisional Commissioner—262.
Doā (fruit)—241.
Dôl (ceremony)—338.
Dôm (caste)—179-80.
Druid priest—425.
Dulal Khan—380, 382, 39?, 393, 396, 403, 410, 411, 416, 417, 419, 451.
Dubaraja—381, 382, 404, 413.
Dulu—255-56.
Durbur—15, 109, 309, 346-48.
Durgā—162, 175, 204.
Durga Charan Sanyal—305, 320-21.
Durgā Pujā—42.
Durgotsava—338, 374.
Durvā—174.

E

Eastern Mymensingh—301.
Egāra Sindur—317, 326, 347.
Egypt—329.
Egyptians—329, 363.
Ehadali—334.
Enait Ali—334.
Eoz Mahamad—374, 424.
Echraj—374.
Essem Khan—119.

F

Fakir—53, 54, 285-90, 296-97, 341.
Fakir Faizu—379, 387, 408, 419.
'Farid's Spectacles'—278.
Fariduddin—280.
Fajilpur—424.
Fatehpur—40.
Fateh Khan—312, 316-17.
Fatemah Bibi—283, 306, 333, 392, 416.
Fengu Raja—33, 38.
Feroz Khan (Dewan)—217, 302, 319, 423, 424, 426, 432, 443, 444, 446, 447, 448, 453.
'Folk Literature of Bengal'—79, 134.

G

Gāchhuni Shaikh—40.
Gadi—324.
Gajadāni—318, 338, 368.
Gajamati—124.
Gajis—372.
Galāchipā—35, 302.
Gandharāj (flower)—154.
Ganeswari—128.
Gangamandal—349.
Ganjer Ghat—221, 238, 246, 253.
Ganjer hāt—222, 223.
Gangasagar—370.
Ganges—203, 327.
Garo (hills)—192.
Garos—39, 74, 81, 98, 193.
'Gari Tambi Mansavi'—193.
Gaur—337-39, 343-44.
Gayā (Shrine)—90, 92.
Gayā (name of a person)—40.

Gayāıām—263.
Ghatak—152.
Ghorāghāt—327.
Ghyasuddin—303, 304, 310, 337.
Ghyasuddin Jalal Shah—305.
Ghyasuddin Muhammad Shah III—305.
Gilā (seed of scandre)—64, 199
Gilliatt—114.
Gitikathā—79, 134.
Goair—349.
Godhā—15.
Golak Viswas—40.
'Golden Book of India'—192.
Gonda—304.
Gopalgrām—40.
Gopis—8.
Governor General—262.
Govinda Dās—34.
Govinda Khan—279.
Gujir (ornament)—233.
Guno—123.
Guru—227.

H

Haibat Muhammad—330, 333, 334, 367, 374.
Haibatnagar—333, 365-68.
Habib Khan—379.
Haibatpur—320, 321.
Hajradi—367.
Halia ban—388, 393, 398.
Hanuman—269.
Hāoldar—267.
Hara Chandra Varmā—79.
Harikāl (birds)—247-48.
Harish Chandra—311.
Harishpur—321.
Haroun-al-rachid—369.
Hashan Ali—334.
Hayal—333.
Hazigunj—315.
Hazradi—349.
Hidayal—333.
Hijal (tree)—63, 66.
Hijra—317.
Himalayas—283.
Hindu—33, 38, 83, 136, 235, 276-77, 280-81, 319-21, 324.
Hinduism—318.
Hiraman—143.
Hiran—131-32, 162, 165-73.
'Holy Grail'—195.
Huen-t-shang—329.
Humayun—309, 323.
Hunter—261-62, 264.
Hussenpur—349.
Hussen Shah—304-06, 310.
Hussen Shahi—349, 367.

I

Ibn Batuta—278.
Ibrahim Khan—374.
Ibrahim Malik Ulema—306.
Ibrahim Ol Olema—368.
Ibrahim, Syed—372.
India—321.
Indra—211.
Ishā Khan (Dewan, Mashnadāli)—35, 299, 301-04, 306-18, 320, 322-23, 325-29, 333-45, 337, 343-53, 365-66, 423, 424, 427, 428, 429.
Ishāmati—284.
Ismail Khan—333.
I't Quid Khān—330.

Iwaz Muhammad—330, 333.

J

Jabbar—279, 291-93.
Jadunath Sarkar (Prof.)—281.
'Jahar Brata'—325.
Jaidhar Bāniya—119, 122.
Jainta (hills)—139, 162, 165.
Jainuddin—338-39, 368.
Jaiteswar—163-65, 168, 170, 175, 184.
Jalal Shah—306.
Jalal Shah Suri—333.
Jalaluddin—339, 342.
Jamait Ulla—217, 219, 246, 251.
Jamal Khan—381, 382, 384, 388, 389, 399, 403, 404, 406, 410, 412, 413, 414, 418.
Jamsher Khan—334.
Janakinath Mallik (Raja)—191-93.
Jangal bari—427, 428.
'Jangli Patsah'—290.
Jarail (wood)—285.
Jasimuddin (Munshi)—119.
Javā (flower)—65, 285.
Jaydevpur—311.
Jehangir—193, 320.
Jessamine—155.
Jhumkā (flower and ornament)—59, 233.
Jigā (hill)—97.
Jigatala—424.
Jnāna Das—34.
Joarshai—349.
Jodhbāi—320.
Jogir Gayen—424.
Journal of Asiatic Society, Bengal—301, 306, 316, 333.
Joyan Shai—349.
Jugaddal—40.
Jumma (bār)—252, 343.
Jumma—281.
Jungalbāri—299, 301-03, 307, 315, 317-19, 322-25, 330, 345-47, 349, 351-53, 355, 357, 359, 361-62, 365-70, 372.
Jungal Khara—367.

K

Kābab—342.
Kadamba (flower)—101.
Kadvi Jangal—367.
Kafirs—319.
Kāhan—222, 344.
Kaichar bāk—171.
Kailas Chandra Sinha—313.
Kajal Kona—454.
Kajjal—128.
Kālāpāhār—305.
Kāli—164, 270, 277, 354, 361.
Kālidas Gajdāni—302-06, 308-10, 318, 333-34, 338-43, 368, 427.
Kali Kumar Chakravarti—302, 333, 366.
Kalpataru—:27.
Kamal Khan—381.
Kalu—250, 252-54, 256.
Kahe Shaikh—2(9.
Kāma—140.
Kāmākhyā—74.
Kamalādighi—191.
Kamalā rāni (Rani Kamalā Devi)—180, 191-93, 196-97.
Kamalāsāgar—191-93, 205.
Kamarali Khan—334.
Kambojis—136.

Kamoonir desh—39, 74.
Kanchan—[5, 11, 14, 21, 23, 24, 26, 28-30, 340] ; [80-82, 108-15].
Kanchanmālā—[3, 9, 10-13, 15, 16, 19-21, 26] ; [77, 79. 84-86, 92-99, 103-07, 109, 115].
Kanchannagar—131, 139, 141, 151-52, 156-58, 164, 176, 179, 183, 185.
Kanchanpur—126.
Kanu—225-32, 236, 249-50. 252-56, 290.
Kapistak—263, 266.
Kapta—342.
Kararain—310.
Karimgunje—367.
Karimulla—327, 355, 357-59, 361-62.
Karnafuli—277.
Kārtikeya—42, 151.
Kasturi—363.
Katghara—40.
Kati Khali—424.
Katrai—349.
Kausalyā—158.
Kavikankan—218.
Kāyastha—320-21.
Kazi—255.
Kedar Ray—301, 319, 323, 325-28, 349, 352-53, 356-62.
Kellā Tazpur—217, 319, 424, 451-452.
Kenārām—280.
Kenduā—79.
Kangu Raja—75, 76.
Keoā (flower)—121.
Kerumulla—418.
Keshaver mār Dighi—3 8.
Khai—243.
Khaira—250.
Khaliajuri—349.
Khalisha (fish)—240, 243.
Khichuri—253.
Khilāt—314.
Khizirpur—316, 325, 327.
Khodabad Khan—334.
Khoda Newaz—374.
Khorāi—3, 17, 23, 28.
Killan Sadāgar—128.
Kishoregunj—40, 301-02, 333-34, 367.
Kirtankhola—6.
Koch—225, 227, 248.
Kai (fish)—240, 242.
Kóran—283.
Koshā—329, 349-50, 352-53, 361.
Krishna—8, 283, 338.
Krishnadas—264, 270-71.
Krishna Saha—268.
Krithivāsa—278, 280.
Krosha—329.
Kuch—238.
Kukis—39. 74, 81, 98.
Kulá—235.
Kulin—140, 151.
Kullar Abbas—40.
Kulpur—6.
Kumrabad—269-70.
Kunjalatā—81, 82, 98-105, 108, 110, 113, 115-16.
Kunkum—363.
Kurālyāmurā—284.
Kurikhai—349.
Kurmā—342.
Kusha (plant)—346.
Kushai—223.
Kutubuddin—301.

L

'La bella mal maridada'—122.
Lal Bāi—191-92.
Lal Khan—334.
Lakshman Hazra—315, 427.
Lakshman Singh—369.
Lakshmi—42, 59, 95, 140.
Lakshmindara—151.
Lalit Mohan Das—334.
Langal—266.
Laṇkā—269.
Latif—333-34.
Laur—269.
Lengra—390, 393, 394, 416, 417.
Lethbridge—192.
Līlā—84, 119.
Long (Rev. J.)—313.
Lowes, Mr.—366.

M

Machalandāni—314.
Machoom Khan—322, 324, 333-34.
Madan (God of Love)—338.
Madan—131-32, 139, 141, 143-44, 146-52, 156-58, 161, 163-66, 168-73, 177-79, 184-88.
Madan Byapari—425.
Madina—84.
Madhur Bāp—6.
Mahabat—333.
Mahesh Chandra Sarkar—40.
Maheswardi—349.
Mahomedan—33, 38, 136-37, 218, 273, 276-80, 302, 305, 313, 319-21, 327-28, 340-41, 343, 352, 354.
Mahamud Khan—381.
Mahomet—283.
Mahuā—33, 195, 387.
Mainamati-songs—276, 390.
Mainda—236.
Maishāl Bandhu—33.
Majhiya Shaikh—40.
Majlishi Jelal—372.
Majlishis—372.
Mālādhar—187.
Mālati (flower)—149, 154.
Maldah—162, 165.
Malilk-ul-ulma—372.
Mallikā (flower)—121, 154.
Maluā—84, 387.
Mamina Khatun—339, 341, 343.
Mān (esemlent plant)—12.
Manasa Devi—390.
Manshā Puja—121.
Mangal Chandi—45.
Manik—131, 139-40, 146-47, 151-52, 164, 171.
Maniktārā—215, 220, 236, 238-39, 244, 248-50, 250, 254, 255.
Mannowar ali—334.
Mannowar Khan (Dewan)—302, 315-16, 317, 330, 333-34.
Mannowar Khan Bāg—316.
Man Pavan—162, 165, 170, 175, 177, 179.
Man Singh—303, 317, 326, 328, 346-47.
Marichāli—79.
Marshman—365.
Mashnadāli—308-09, 314, 349, 368.
Mashnadali Itihāsh (Itihāsa)—302, 304, 306, 310, 320, 324, 335.
Match-maker—55.
Math—328.
Matiar Rahman—275.

Maulavi—362.
Maulvi Sahidullah—279.
Maurakshi—263, 265, 267.
Māydula—40.
Maynā—36, 73, 76.
Mazban Bhāti—301.
Mecca—387, 399, 410, 416.
Mecha (country)—199.
Medina—283.
Mediterranean—276.
Meghna—33, 39, 57-59, 71-76.
Menakā—132, 135, 166-68, 171-72, 176, 179-82, 184-85, 187.
Milton—133.
Mithā bish—219.
Moghul—309, 323.
Mollah—277.
Muga (pees)—243.
Muhammad—333.
Muhammadanism—318.
Muhammadan rule—216.
Muhammad Idris—366.
Muhammad Khan—372, 424.
Muhammad Shah Gazi—305.
Muhammad Toghluk—281.
Mujhis Jelal—329.
Murai—138-39.
Murapara—347.
Murari—131, 143, 146-47, 150-52, 156.
Murari Gupta—218.
Murighanta—243.
Musa—333, 424.
Mymensingh—6, 33, 39, 40, 80, 191-93, 215, 277, 302, 324-25, 329, 334, 365-67, 384.

N

Namasudra—40.
Nandalal Bose—367.
Nanoor—7.
Nārada—278.
Narayan Babu—379.
Narayangunj—316, 367.
Narsindha—367.
Nasaral Shah—305.
Nashir-u-Jilal—349, 367.
Nasirabad—278.
Nava Durga—88.
Nawapara—284.
Nazar Marichā—324.
Nazar marichar chhele—324.
Nelson Wright (H.)—305, 306.
Neter khuti—251.
Newaz Khan—374.
Nidhur Vyāpāri—40.
Nim—234.
Nimai Sanyas—381.
Niyāmat Jān—320, 352, 358.
Nizam (Dacoit)—273, 275-76, 279, 281, 283-90, 293-98.
Nizampur—278.
Nizamuddin—279, 281, 298.
Noakhali—277, 311.
Noapara—277.

O

Ochterloney Monument—329.
Omar Khan—319, 430, 442, 443, 444, 446.
Omedali Khan—334.
Orissa—369.
Oudh—304, 308.

P

Padmā (Manasā Devi)—174, 176.
Padmā (river)—327, 350-52, 359.

Patkara—349.
Palabuji—350.
Palasbari—252.
Pān—222.
Pancha—245, 255.
Panchamrita—88.
Panch Kahama—272.
Panchlish—278.
Pāpiyā (bird)—121.
'Paradise Lost'—133.
Pārul (flower)—128.
Pathan—312.
Patsah—291-92.
Payār—119, 216.
Pearpur—119.
Pererpur—263.
Permanent Settlement Act—260.
Persia—363, 384.
Persian—38, 306, 316, 385.
Phul bātāsā—239.
Phul Kumar—96, 100, 102, 110, 115.
Pir (Pir Saheb)—182, 277, 296-98.
Pirer kāndā—23.
Piriti—291.
Prāgjyotishpur—39.
Prahlād—84.
Pratapāditya—306.
Prologue—85.
Puja—200, 277.
Purah (measure of land)—161, 341, 402, 428.
Puranas—84.
Puthi (fish)—240.

R

Rādhā—47, 283.
Raghunath—192, 284.
Raghunath Singh—19 -93.
Rahaman Gayen—424.
Rahim Dad Khan—374.
Rāhu—14.
Rajanikanta Bhadra—6.
Rajarbāg—370.
Rajbāri—327.
Rajchandra Ghosh (Munshi)—302, 333, 336.
Rajdhara (Prince)—312, 315-16.
Rajdighi—251.
Rajmālā—307-08, 311, 313-14.
Rajmohul hills—264, 268.
Rajtikā—93.
Rajvamshis—136.
Rakshasa—60, 74.
Ralph Fitch—303.
Rama—83.
Rāmāyana—278, 280.
Ramgopalpur—192.
Ram Hazra—315.
Ramkumar Mistri—79.
Ram Lakshman (conch-bracelet)—126, 345.
Ram Ram Vasu—306.
Ram Sankar Sen (Rai Bahadur)—368.
Rana Bhowal—311.
Rangamati—370.
Rang Miah—454.
Rāngchāpur—39, 131-32, 157-58, 165, 167.
Ranjan—277.
Rashis (distance)—362.
Rati—140, 149.
Ratnakar—78.
Rāunya—284.
Rāvan—180.

Rāyer Bazar—40.
R. C. Dutt, Mr.—366.
Renaissance—136.
Robikul—283.
Rosul—283.
Rowail—372.
Rui (fish)—240.
Rukmini—5, 18-21.

S

Sadar Ali Gāyen—275.
Sadgopas—269.
Sādh—88.
Sadhu—87, 89.
Sadhu Das—269.
Sadhu Sil—236, 239-40, 242-45.
Saḍi (also spelt *sari*)—50, 51, 54, 57, 59, 64, 67, 73, 74, 96, 160, 179-81, 199, 201, 203, 207, 209, 211, 233, 237, 329, 340, 363.
Sadipur—266.
Sadir Gayen—424.
Sahajiyā—122.
Sākhinā—217, 331, 425, 447, 451.
Sāl (wood)—208.
Sāli (harvest)—17, 121.
Salim Khan—201.
Salukā—152-54, 164-65, 180, 182, 184-86, 188.
Samsher Khan—334.
Sanad—348-49.
Sānāi (flute)—56.
Sankanda—6.
Sankar—179.
Sankha (river)—284.
Sankhapur—131, 138, 146-47, 150-52, 156, 183, 186-87.
Sankhini—250.
Sannyāsi—82, 91-94, 104, 107-08, 111-13, 277.
Santal—257, 259-71.
Santi—117, 119-20, 123-28.
Sarail (Pergannah)—307, 311-12, 314-15.
Sāri (bird)—149, 152-53, 155, 162, 165, 168-71, 178, 182-83, 185, 200.
Sati (rites)—191.
Saturn—139.
Satyayuga—193.
Saurendra Kishore Ray Chaudhuri—192.
Sayabali Gāyen—424.
Sepoys—263.
Sepulveda's collections—122.
Setar—374.
Seyāt (vessel)—205.
Shadhan—349.
Shahbatpur—320.
Shah Baz Khan—303, 312, 315, 322, 324, 344.
Shah Jehan—330.
Shah Neoaz (Khan, Dewan)—366.
Shah Suja—330-31.
Shahen Shah—369.
Shaikh Farid—278, 285, 288-89, 294, 297-98.
Shail (fish)—230.
Shakespeare—121.
Shāknaibāttā—6.
Sharfarāli—367.
Sharif—333-34.
Shastras—341.
Sherpur—222, 346, 349.
Sher Shah—305, 316-17.

Shylock—35, 37.
Simul (tree)—237-38.
Sinda—349.
Singākhāli—39, 41, 45, 52-53.
Singāpur—39, 42, 44, 53, 56.
Singi (fish)—241.
Sitā—60, 107, 284.
Sitaghāt—284.
Siva—74, 203.
Siva Ratan Mitra—259.
'Social History of Bengal'—305, 320.
Sodhorām—312.
Sohāgi—40.
Soloman Khan—369.
Somai—199.
Someswari—192.
Sonakandi—432.
Sona Mājhi—230.
Sona Mani—303, 319-20, 325, 424.
Sonārgāon—303.
Soorma Valley—137.
Sovan Dad Khan (Dewan)—302, 366.
Spanish ballad—122.
Sripur—325, 327, 349, 351-52, 354, 357-62.
Stapleton (Mr. H. E.)—301, 304, 314, 316, 320, 324, 328, 333, 335.
Suā—207.
Subādār—267.
Subha Babu—262, 265, 268.
Subhadrā—303, 319-20, 324-25, 352.
Subuddhi Narayan—311.
Sujati—33-35, 39, 46, 50, 54-57, 59, 60, 76.
Suka—143, 146-49, 153, 162, 178, 182-83, 185, 200.
Suktā—243.
Sulaiman Kararani—304-07, 309.
Sulaiman Khan—305-06, 309-10, 333-34, 343, 368.
Sultan—343-44.
Sultan Bazed Bostani—278.
Sumāru—248.
Sundar—295-96.
Sundhā Methi—80, 97.
Suri—259.
Surmai—39, 57, 63, 74.
Susang Durgāpur—191-92.
Sutrakona—40.
Suvarna Grām—335, 349.
'Suvarna Grāmer Itihāsa'—325, 334.
Swarnamayee—319.
Swarup Chandra Ray—325, 334-35.
Syer-ul-Mutakherim—365.
Sylhet—122, 311-12, 317.

T

Tagar (flower)—155.
Tamshā Gazi—6, 23, 24.
Tārā—246-49, 251, 254-56.
Tarap—312, 316-17, 372.
Taziuddin Gada—369.
Taz Khān—301, 313.
'Tazkiratul Aulia'—280.
Tera Lengra—390, 393, 402.
Thakur—321.
'Thakurdadar Jhuli'—134.
'The Ill-married Lady'—122.
Tiārā (ornament)—128.
Tiler lāru—241.
Tinkari—218, 234.
Tipperah—219, 307-08, 311-15, 317, 321, 325.

Titash (river)—315.
Toghlakabad—281.
'Toilers of the Sea'—114.
Tokā—128.
Tulsi—234.
Turan—301, 307, 311.

U

Uchhigrām—40.
Udaypur—312.
Udaypur hills—311, 317.
Ujani—138, 143, 146-47, 151, 180.
Ulki—242.
Umad Ali—334.
Urdu—38.
Urumberia (a low caste)—55.

V

Vaishnavas—8, 34.
Vālmiki—278.
Varendra Brahmins—305.
Vashu—220, 223-25, 227-37, 239-46, 248-49, 251-54.
Venus and Adonis—121.
Victor Hugo—114.
Vidyādhara—98.
Vikramaditya—306.
Vikrampur—301, 311, 325, 327.
Vishnu—223-24, 239.
Vizir—291-92.
Vrindavana—283.

W

Washer-Maiden—1, 3, 6, 34, 195.
Western Bengal—259.
Wise (Dr. James)—301, 303, 305, 310, 316, 318, 321, 324, 328, 330, 335, 365.

Y

Yayāti—307.
Yuvarāja—321.

Z

Zeminder—50, 311.

OPINIONS

"HISTORY OF THE BENGALI LANGUAGE AND LITERATURE" (IN ENGLISH)

By

RAI SAHIB DINESH CHANDRA SEN, B.A.

Published by

CALCUTTA UNIVERSITY

Demy 8vo, pp. 1067, with illustrations. Price—Rs. 16.

HIS EXCELLENCY LORD HARDINGE OF PENSHURST in his Convocation Address, dated the 16th March, 1912, as Chancellor of the Calcutta University :—

"During the last four years also the University has, from time to time, appointed Readers on special subjects to foster investigation of important branches of learning amongst our advanced students. One of these Readers, Mr. Sen, has embodied his lectures on the History of Bengali Language and Literature from the earliest times to the middle of the 19th century in a volume of considerable merit, which he is about to supplement by another original contribution to the history of one of the most important vernaculars in this country. May I express the hope that this example will be followed elsewhere, and that critical schools may be established for the vernacular languages of India which have not as yet received the attention that they deserve."

HIS EXCELLENCY LORD CARMICHAEL, GOVERNOR OF BENGAL, in his address, on the occasion of his laying the

Foundation stone of the Romesh Chandra Saraswat Bhawan, dated the 20th November, 1916 :—

"For long Romesh Chandra Dutt's History of the Literature of Bengal was the only work of its kind available to the general reader. The results of further study in this field have been made available to us by the publication of the learned and luminous lectures of Rai Sahib Dineschandra Sen. * * In the direction of the History of the Language and the Literature, Rai Sahib Dineschandra Sen has created the necessary interest by his Typical Selections. It remains for the members of the Parishad to follow this lead and to carry on the work in the same spirit of patient accurate research."

SIR ASUTOSH MOOKERJEE, in his Convocation Address, dated the 13th March, 1909, as Vice-Chancellor of the Calcutta University :—

"We have had a long series of luminous lectures from one of our own graduates, Babu Dineschandra Sen, on the fascinating subject of the History of the Bengali Language and Literature. These lectures take a comprehensive view of the development of our vernacular, and their publication will unquestionably facilitate the historical investigation of the origin of the vernacular literature of this country, the study of which is avowedly one of the foremost objects of the New Regulations to promote."

SYLVAIN LEVI (*Paris*)—"I cannot give you praises enough —your work is a *Chintamani*—a *Ratnakara*. No book about India would I compare with yours......Never did I find such a realistic sense of literature......Pundit and Peasant, Yogi and Raja, mix together in a Shakespearian way on the stage you have built up."

BARTH (*Paris*)—" I can approach your book as a learner, not as a judge."

C. H. TAWNEY—" Your work shows vast research and much general culture."

VINCENT SMITH—" A work of profound learning and high value."

F. W. THOMAS—" Characterised by extensive erudition and independent research."

E. J. RAPSON—" I looked through it with great interest and great admiration for the knowledge and research to which it bears witness."

F H. SKRINE—" Monumental work—I have been revelling in the book which taught me much of which I was ignorant."

E. B. HAVELL—" Most valuable book which every Anglo-Indian should read. I congratulate you most heartily on your very admirable English and perfect lucidity of style."

D. C. PHILLOT—" I can well understand the enthusiasm with which the work was received by scholars, for even to men unacquainted with your language, it cannot fail to be a source of great interest and profit."

L. D. BARNETT—" I congratulate you on having accomplished such an admirable work."

G. HULTZUH—" Mr. Sen's valuable work on Bengali literature, a subject hitherto unfamiliar to me, which I am now reading with great interest."

J. F. BLUMHARDT—" An extremely well-written and scholarly production, exhaustive in its wealth of materials and of immense value."

T. W. RHYS DAVIDS—" It is a most interesting and important work and reflects great credit on your industry and research."

JULES BLOCH (*Paris*)—" Your book I find an admirable one and which is the only one of its kind in the whole of India."

WILLIAM ROTHENSTEIN—" I found the book surprisingly full of suggestive information. It held me bound from beginning to end, in spite of my absolute ignorance of the language of which you write with obviously profound scholarship."

EMILE SENART (*Paris*)—" I have gone through your book with lively interest and it appears to me to do the highest credit to your learning and method of working."

HENRY VAN DYKE—(*U. S. A.*)—" Your instructive pages which are full of new suggestions in regard to the richness and interest of the Bengali Language and Literature."

C. T. WINCHESTER—(*U. S. A.*) " A work of profound learning on a theme which demands the attention of all Western scholars."

From a long review in the TIMES LITERARY SUPPLEMENT, London, June 20, 1912—" In his narration, as becomes one who is the soul of scholarly candour, he tells those, who can read him with sympathy and imagination more about the Hindu mind and its attitude towards life than we can gather from 50 volumes of impressions of travel by Europeans. Loti's picturesque account of the rites practised in Travancore temples, and even M. Chevrillon's synthesis of much browsing in Hindu Scriptures, seem faint records by the side of this unassuming tale of Hindu literature—Mr. Sen may well be proud of the lasting monument he has erected to the literature of his native Bengal."

From a long review in the ATHENÆUM, March, 16, 1912—" Mr. Sen may justly congratulate himself on the fact that in the middle age he has done more for the history of his national language and literature than any other writer of his own or indeed any time."

From a long review in the SPECTATOR, June 12, 1912—" A book of extraordinary interest to those who would make an impartial study of the Bengali mentality and character—a work which reflects the utmost credit on the candour, industry and learning of its author. In its kind his book is a masterpiece—modest, learned, thorough and sympathetic. Perhaps no other man living has the learning and happy industry for the task he has successfully accomplished."

From a review by MR. H. BEVERIDGE in the *Royal Asiatic Society's Journal*, Jan., 1912—" It is a very full and interesting account of the development of the Bengali Literature. He has a power of picturesque writing...his descriptions are often eloquent."

From a long review by S. K. RATLIFFE in *India*, London, March 15, 1912—"There is no more competent authority on the subject than Mr. Dineschandra Sen. The great value of the book is in its full and fresh treatment of the pre-English era and for this it would be difficult to give its author too high praise."

From a long review by H. KERN in the *Bijdragen of the Royal Institute for Taal* (translated by Dr. Kern himself)—" Fruit of investigation carried through many years...highly interesting book...the reviewer has all to admire in the pages of the work, nothing to criticise, for his whole knowledge is derived from it."

From a review by DR. OLDENBERG in the *Frankfurter Zistung*, December 3, 1911 (translated by the late Dr. Thibaut)—" It is an important supplementation of the history of modern Sanskrit Literature. The account of Chaitanya's influence on the poetical literature of Bengal contributes one of the most brilliant sections of the work."

From a review in DEUTSCHE RUNDSCHAN, April, 1912 —" The picture which this learned Bengali has painted for us with loving care of the literature of his native land deserves to be received with attentive and grateful respect."

From a review in LUZAC'S ORIENTAL LIST, London, May-June, 1912—" A work of inestimable value, full of interesting information, containing complete account of the writings of Bengali authors from the earliest time...It will undoubtedly find a place in every Oriental Library as being the most complete and reliable standard work on the Bengali Language and Literature."

From a review in the INDIAN MAGAZINE, London, August, 1912—" For Mr. Sen's erudition, his sturdy patriotism, his instructive perception of the finer qualities in Bengali life and literature, the reader of his book must have a profound respect if he is to understand what modern Bengal is."

From a long review in the MADRAS MAIL, May 9, 1912 —" A survey of the evolution of the Bengali letters by a student so competent, so exceptionally learned, can hardly fail to be an important event in the world of criticism."

From a long review in the PIONEER, May 5, 1912— " Mr. Sen is a typical student such as was common in mediæval Europe—a lover of learning for learning's sake...He must be a poor judge of characters who can rise from a perusal of Mr. Sen's pages without a real respect and liking for the writer, for his sincerity, his industry, his enthusiasm in the cause of learning."

Extract from a long review by Sylvain Levi (Paris) in the REVUE CRITIQUE, Jan. 1915 ; (translated for the Bengalee)—

" One cannot praise too highly the work of Mr. Sen. A profound and original erudition has been associated with a vivid imagination. The works which he analyses are brought back to life with the consciousness of the original authors, with the movement of the multitudes who patronised them and with the landscape which encircled them. The historian, though relying on his documents, has the temperament of an epic poet. He has likewise inherited the lyrical genius of his race. His enthusiastic sympathy vibrates through all his descriptions. Convinced as every Hindu is of the superiority of the Brahmanic civilization, he exalts its glories and palliates its shortcomings, if he does not approve of them he would excuse them. He tries to be just to Buddhism and Islam; in the main he is grateful to them for their contribution to the making of India. He praises with eloquent ardour the early English missionaries of Christianity.

The appreciation of life so rare in our book-knowledge, runs throughout the work; one reads these thousand pages with a sustained interest; and one loses sight of the enormous labour which it presupposes; one easily slips into the treasure of information which it presents. The individual extracts quoted at the bottom of the pages offers a unique anthology of Bengali. The linguistic remarks scattered in the extracts abound in new and precious materials. Mr. Sen has given to his country a model which it would be difficult to surpass; we only wish that it may provoke in other parts of India emulations to follow it."

From a review in the ENGLISHMAN, April 23, 1912—"Only one who has completely identified himself with the subject could have mastered it so well as the author of this imposing book."

From a review in the EMPIRE, August 31, 1918—"As a book of reference Mr. Sen's work will be found invaluable and he is to be congratulated on the result of his labours. It may well be said that he has proved what an English enthusiast once said that 'Bengali unites the mellifluousness of Italian with the power possessed by German for rendering complex ideas.'"

From a review by F. G. PARGITER in the INDIAN ANTIQUARY, December, 1912—"This book is the outcome of great research and study, on which the author deserves the warmest praise. He has explained the literature and the subjects treated in it with such fulness and in such detail as to make the whole plain to any reader. The folk-literature, the structure and style of the language, metre and rhyme, and many miscellaneous points are discussed in valuable notes. The tone is calm and the judgments appear to be generally fair."

BANGA SAHITYA-PARICHAYA

OR

TYPICAL SELECTIONS FROM OLD BENGALI LITERATURE.

BY

Prof. Dineschandra Sen, Rai Bahadur, B.A., D.Litt.

2 vols, Royal 8vo, pp. 1914, with an Introduction in English running over 99 pages, published by the University of Calcutta.

(*With 10 coloured illustrations. Price Rs. 18.*)

SIR GEORGE GRIERSON—" Invaluable work......That I have yet read through its 1900 pages I do not pretend, but what I have read has filled me with admiration for the industry and learning displayed. It is a worthy sequel to your monumental History of Bengali Literature, and of it we may safely say '*finis coronat opus*.' How I wish that a similar work could be compiled for other Indian languages, specially for Hindi."

E. B. HAVELL—" Two monumental volumes from old Bengali Literature. As I am not a Bengali scholar, it is impossible for me to appreciate at their full value the splendid results of your scholarship and research, but I have enjoyed reading your luminous and most instructive introduction which gives a clear insight into the subject. I was also very much interested in the illustrations, the reproduction of which from original paintings is very successful and creditable to Swadeshi work.''

H. BEVERIDGE—'' Two magnificent volumes of the Banga Sahitya-Parichaya......I have read with interest Rasa Sundari's autobiography in your extracts.''

F. H. SKRINE—'' The two splendid volumes of Banga Sahitya-Parichaya I am reading with pleasure and profit. They are a credit to your profound learning and to the University which has given them to the world.''

From a long review in THE TIMES LITERARY SUPPLEMENT, London, November 4, 1915—'' In June, 1912, in commenting on Mr. Sen's History of Bengali Language and Literature, we suggested that work might usefully be supplemented by an anthology of Bengali prose and poetry. Mr. Sen has for many years been occupied with the aid of other patriotic students of the mediæval literature of Bengal in collecting manuscripts of forgotten or half-forgotten poems. In addition to these more or less valuable monuments of Bengali poetic art, the chief popular presses have published great masses on literary matter, chiefly religious verse. It can hardly be said that these piles of written and printed matter have ever been subjected to a critical or philological scrutiny. Their very existence was barely known to the Europeans, even to those who have studied the Bengali Language on the spot. Educated Bengalis themselves, until quite recent times, have been too busy with the arts and sciences of Europe to spare much time for indigenous treasures. That was the reason why we suggested the compiling of a critical chrestomathy for the benefit not only of European but of native scholars. The University of Calcutta prompted by the eminent scholar Sir Asutosh

Mookerjee, then Vice-Chancellor, had already anticipated this need it seems. It had shrunk (rightly, we think) from the enormous and expensive task of printing the MSS. recovered by the diligence and generosity of Mr. Sen and other inquirers and employed Mr. Sen to prepare the two bulky volumes now before us. The Calcutta Senate is to be congratulated on its enterprise and generosity."

From a review in The ATHENÆUM, January 16, 1915—" We have already reviewed Mr. Sen's History of Bengali Language and Literature and have rendered some account of his previous work in Bengali entitled *Banga Bhasa O Sahitya.* Mr. Sen now supplies the means of checking his historical and critical conclusions in a copious collection of Bengali verse......Here are the materials carefully arranged and annotated with a skill and learning such as probably no one else living can command."

From a review by Mr. F. G. PARGITER—in the *Royal Asiatic Society's Journal*—" These two portly volumes of some 2,100 pages are an anthology of Bengali poetry and prose from the 8th to the 17th century and are auxiliary to the same author's History of Bengali Language and Literature which was reviewed by Mr. Beveridge in this Journal for 1912......The Vice-Chancellor of the Calcutta University who was consulted, decided that the best preliminary measure would be to make and publish typical selections. The University then entrusted that duty to Babu Dinesh Chandra Sen; this work is the outcome of his researches. There can be no question that Dinesh Babu was the person most competent to undertake the task and in these two volumes we have without doubt a good presentment of typical specimens of old Bengali literature......The style of the big book is excellent, its printing is fine, and it is embellished with well-executed reproductions in colour of some old paintings. It has also a copious index.

THE VAISNAVA LITERATURE OF MEDIÆVAL BENGAL

[Being lectures delivered as Reader to the University of Calcutta.]

BY

RAI SAHIB DINESH CHANDRA SEN, B.A.

Demy 8vo, 257 pages

WITH A PREFACE BY

J. D. ANDERSON, Esq., I.C.S. (*Retired*)

Price Rs. 2

SIR GEORGE GRIERSON—"Very valuable book......I am reading it with the greatest interest and am learning much from it."

WILLIAM ROTHENSTEIN—"I was delighted with your book, I cannot tell you how touched I am to be reminded of that side of your beloved country which appeals to me most—a side of which I was able to perceive something during my own too short visit to India. In the faces of the best of your countrymen I was able to see that spirit of which you write so charmingly in your book. I am able to recall these faces and figures as if they were before me. I hear the tinkle of the temple-bells along the ghats of Benares, the voices of the women as they sing their sacred songs crossing the noble river in the boats at sunset and I sit once more with the austere Sanyasin friends I shall never, I fear, see more. But though I shall not look upon the face of India again, the vision I had of it will fill my eyes through life, and the love I feel for your country will remain to enrich my own vision of life, so long as I am capable of using it. Though I can only read you in English, the spirit in which you write is to me so true an Indian spirit, that it shines through our own idiom, and carries me, I said before, straight to the banks of your sacred rivers, to the bathing tanks and white shrines and temples of your well-remembered villages and tanks. So once more I send you my thanks for the magic carpet you sent me, upon which my soul can return to your dear land. May the songs of which you write remain to fill this land with their fragrance; you will have use of them, in the years before you, as we have need of all that is best in the songs of our own seers in the dark waters through which we are steering.''

The Vaisnava Literature of Mediæval Bengal. By Rai Sahib Dineschandra Sen. (The Calcutta University.)

"Though the generalisation that all Hindus not belonging to modern reform movements are Saivas or Vaisnavas is much too wide, there are the two main divisions in the bewildering mass of sects which make up the 217,000,000 of Hindus, and at many points they overlap each other. The attempts made in the 1901 Census to collect information regarding sects led to such unsatisfactory and partial results that they were not repeated in the last decennial enumeration. But it is unquestionable that the Vaisnavas—the worshippers of Krishna—are dominant in Bengal, owing to the great success of the reformed cult established by Chaitanya, a contemporary of Martin Luther. The doctrine of Bhakti or religious devotion, which he taught still flourishes in Bengal, and the four lectures of the Reader to the University of Calcutta in Bengali here reproduced provide an instructive guide to its expression in the literature of the country during the sixteenth and seventeenth centuries. The first part of the book is devoted to the early period of Vaisnava literature, dating from the eleventh century.

The Rai Sahib is filled with a most patriotic love of his nation and its literature, and has done more than any contemporary countryman to widen our knowledge of them. His bulky volume recording the history of Bengali Language and Literature from the earliest times to the middle of the nineteenth century is accepted by Orientalists as the most complete and authoritative work on the subject.

There is refreshing ingenuousness in his claim, 'my industry has been great,' and the 'forbearing indulgence' for which he asks if he has failed from any lack of powers, will readily be granted in view of the enthusiasm for his subject which somewhat narrows the strictly critical value of his estimates, but does not impair the sustained human interest of the book.

Chaitanya clearly taught, as these pages show, that the Krishna of the Mahabharata, the great chieftain and ally of the Pandava brothers, was not the Krishna of Brindaban. The latter, said the reformer, to Rupa, the author of those masterpieces of Sanskrit drama, the Vidagdha Madhava and the Lalita Madhava, was love's very self and an embodiment of sweetness : and the more material glories of Mathura should not be confused with the spiritual conquests of Brindaban. The amours of Krishna with Radha and the milkmaids of Bridaban are staple themes of the literature associated with the worship of the God of the seductive flute. But Mr. Sen repeatedly insists that the love discussed in the literature he has so closely studied is spiritual and mystic, although usually presented in sensuous garb. Chaitanya who had frequent ecstasies of spiritual joy, Rupa, who classified the emotions of love in 360 groups and the other authors whose careers are here traced were hermits of unspotted life and religious devotion. The old passionate desire for union which they taught is still dominant in modern Bengali literature not directly Vaisnava in import. As Mr. J. D. Anderson points out in his preface, the influence of Chaitanya's teaching may be detected in the mystical verses of Tagore."

From a long review in the TIMES LITERARY SUPPLEMENT, 26th April, 1918 :—(Mediæval Vaisnab Literature.)

" This delightful and interesting little book is the outcome of a series of lectures supplementing the learned discourses which Mr. Sen made the material of his 'Baisnava Literature of Mediæval Bengal' reviewed by us on August 2, 1917.

It is an authentic record of the religious emotion and thought of that wonderful land of Bengal which few of its Western rulers, we suspect, have rightly comprehended, not from lack of friendly sympathy but simply from want of precisely what Mr. Sen better than any one living, better than Sir Rabindranath Tagore himself, can supply.

It is indeed, no easy matter for a Western Protestant to comprehend, save by friendship and sympathy with just such a pious Hindu as Mr. Sen, what is the doctrine of an *istadevata*, a 'favourite deity' of Hindu pious adoration. In his native tongue Mr. Sen has written charming little books, based on ancient legends, which bring us very near the heart of this simple mystery, akin, we suppose, to the cult of particular saints in Catholic countries. Such for instance, is his charming tale of 'Sati,' the Aryan spouse of the rough Himalayan ascetic God Siva. The tale is dedicated, in words of delightfully candid respect and affection, to the devoted and loving wives of Bengal, whose virtues as wives and mothers are the admiration of all who know their country. Your pious Vaisnava can, without any hesitation or difficulty, transfer his thoughts from the symbolical amorism of Krishna to that other strange creation-legend of Him of the Blue Throat who, to save God's creatures, swallowed the poison cast up at the Churning of the Ocean and bears the mystic stigma to this day. Well, we have our traditions, legends, mysteries, and as Underhill and others tell us, our own ecstatic mystics, who find such ineffable joy in loving God as, our Hindu friends tell us, the divine Radha experienced in her sweet surrender to the inspired wooing of Krishna. The important thing for us, as students of life and literature, is to note how these old communal beliefs influence and develop that wonderful record of human thought and emotion wrought for us by the imaginative writers of verse and prose, the patient artists of the pen.

When all is said, there remains the old indefinable charm which attaches to all that Dines Chandra Sen writes, whether in English or his native Bengali. In his book breathe a native candour and piety which somehow remind us of the classical writers familiar to our boyhood. In truth, he is a belated contemporary of, say, Plutarch, and attacks his biographical task in much the same spirit. We hope his latest book will be widely (and sympathetically) read."

J. D. ANDERSON, Esq., retired I.C.S., Professor, Cambridge University :—"I have read more than half of it. I propose to send with it, if circumstances leave me the courage to write it, a short Preface (which I hope you will read with pleasure even if you do not think it worth publication) explaining why, in the judgment of a very old student of all your works, your book should be read not only in Calcutta, but in London and Paris, and Oxford and Cambridge. I have read it and am reading it with great delight and profit and very real sympathy. Think how great must be the charm of your topic and your treatment when in this awful year of anxiety and sorrow, the reading of your delightful MS. has given me rest and refreshment in a time when every post, every knock at the door, may bring us sorrow."

JULES BLOCH—" I have just finished the romantic story of Chandravati (given in the Bengali Ramayanas). May I congratulate you on the good and well deserved luck of having discovered her after so many others and having added that new gem to the crown of Bengali Literature.

I cannot speak to you in detail of your chapters on the characteristics of the Bengali Ramayanas and on Tulsidas, I had only to learn from what you say and thank you for helping me and many others to get a little of that direct understanding and feeling of the literary and emotional value of those poems in general and Krittivas in particular. I hope your devotion to Bengali Literature will be rewarded by a growing popularity of that literature in India and in Europe; and also that young scholars will follow your example and your direction in continuing your studies, literary and philological."

SIR GEORGE GRIERSON—"I must write to thank you for your two valued gifts of the " Folk Literature of Bengal " and " The Bengali Ramayanas." I delayed acknowledging them till I had read them through. I have been greatly interested by both, and owe you a debt of gratitude for the immense amount of important information contained in them.

I add to this letter a few notes which the perusal of your books has suggested to me. Perhaps you will find them useful.

I hope that you will be spared to us to write many more such books."

DR. WILLIAM CROOKE, C.I.E., EDITOR OF "FOLK LORE"—"I have read them ('Folk Literature of Bengal' and 'The Bengali Ramayanas') with much interest. They seem to me to be a very valuable contribution to the study of the religion and folk-lore of Bengal. I congratulate you on the success of your work and I shall be glad to receive copies of any other work which you may write on the same subjects."

H. BEVERIDGE—"Of the two books I must say that I like best the Bengali Ramayanas. Your book on Bengali folk lore is also valuable" (from a letter of 12 pages containing a critical review of the two books).

From the "*Revista Trimestrale di studi Filosofici e Religiosi*"

Rai Bahadur Dineshchandra Sen's Folk Literature of Bengal.

—"The University of Calcutta continues with every alacrity, the fine series of its publications thus testifying to the high scientific preparation (issuing out) of those indigenous teachers. This volume devoted to the popular tales of Bengal also constitutes a contribution of the first rank to such a subject. The tracing of the History of the Bengali language and literature in this University is one of the most well-deserved studies of Bengal. To it is due, in fact, the monumental and now classical History of the Bengali Language and Literature (1912);—in which, so far as our studies go, we value most the accurate estimate of the influence of Chaitanya on that literature—accompanied by the grand Bengali Anthology Banga Sahitya Parichaya, 1914, and then above all the pleasing and erudite researches on Vaishnab literature and the connected religious reform of Chaitanya.

A world wholly legendary depicted with the homely tenderness in most secluded locality of Bengal and half conceived in the Buddhistic epoch with delicate phantasy and fondness; the world in which Rabindranath Tagore ultimately attained his full growth is revived with every seduction of art in the luminous pages of this beautiful book. The author came in touch with this in his first days of youth when he was a village teacher in East Bengal and he now wishes to reveal it by gathering together the most secluded spirit and also the legend collected in four delicious volumes of D. R. Mazumdar, yet to be translated.

A spirit of renunciation in the devotion of wives in the love of tender and sorrowful ladies, in eagerness for patient sacrifice carry us back, as we have said, to the Buddhistic epoch of Bengal; it rises as an ideal of life and is transmitted to future generations traversed by the Mussalmani faith which also is pervaded by so many Buddhistic elements. Malancha, the sublime female incarnation of such an ideal—whose legend is translated in the last pages of this volume—the Lady wholly spiritual, a soul heroic in its devoted renunciation, mistress of her body who reveals in herself qualities that essentially belong to Idea, a creature of the soul, shaped by the aspiration to come into contact with the external world. Malancha loses her eyes and her hands, but so strong is her desire to see her husband that her eyes grow again and such is her desire to serve him that her hands also grow again.

In the popular narration the prose often assumes a poetic movement and metrical form. The archaic language that reminds us of remote antiquity is converted into lyric charm and becomes knotty in the prose, making us think pensively of the Vedic hymnology that entered the epic of Mahavarat." (Translated from the original Italian).

Extract from the Times Literary Supplement, April, 1921.

THE BENGALI RAMAYANAS

BY PROF. DINESCHANDRA SEN, RAI BAHADUR, B.A., D.LITT.

(Published by the University of Calcutta. Rs. 4 As. 2).

The Indian epics deserve closer study than they have hitherto received at the hands of the average Englishman of culture. Apart from the interest of the main themes, the wealth of imagery and the beauty of many of the episodes, they are storehouses of information upon the ancient life of India and a key to the origin of customs which still live. Moreover, they show many curious affinities to Greek literature, which suggest the existence of legends common to both countries. The Ring of Polycrates is reproduced in other conditions in the "Sakuntalá," the *Alcestis* has its counterpart in the story of Sávitri, and the chief of the Pandavas descends into hell in the manner of Odysseus, though on a nobler errand.

The main theme of these lectures is the transformation of the old majestic Sanskrit epic as it came from the hands of Valmiki to the more familiar and homely style of the modern Bengali versions. The Rámáyana, we are told, is a protest against Buddhist monasticism, the glorification of the domestic virtues, proclaiming that there is no need to look for salvation outside the home. The Bengali version, while reducing the grandeur of the heroic characters to the level of ordinary mortals, bring the epic within the reach of the humblest peasant; they have their own virtues, just as the simple narrative of the Gospels has its own charm, though it be different in kind from that of Isaiah's majestic cadences. Thus in the Sanskrit poem "Kauçalya", Rama's mother, is sacrificing to Fire when she hears of her son's exile; she does not flinch, but continues the sacrifice in the spirit of Greek tragedy, merely altering the character of her prayer. In the Bengali version she becomes an ordinary Bengali woman, giving vent to lamentations such as one hears every day in modern India. In the Nibelungenlied one sees the same kind of transformation from the old Norse sagas to the atmosphere of medieval chivalry.

The author approaches his subject in that spirit of reverence which is the due of all the great literature, and to him Válmiki's Rámáyana is the greatest literature in the world. The fact does not blunt his critical faculty; rather does it sharpen it, for, as he says in the preface, " historical research and the truths to which it leads do not interfere with faith," neither do they stand in the way of admiration. He sees more in the Rámáyana than the mere collection of legends into a Sanskrit masterpiece from which various versions have been made from time to time. He shows us how, as the centuries proceeded, each successive version was influenced by the spirit of the age, how the story became adapted to the purposes of religious propaganda, how in the interests of the Vaishnava cult the hero Ráma became the divine avatár of Vishnu, even at the risk of absurd situations. He takes us through the age of the Sákti influence, of Rámánanda's philosophy and its revolt against Mahomedan iconoclasm, of the flippant immorality of the eighteenth century. " These Bengali Rámáyanas," he says, " have thus quite an encyclopædic character, comprising, along with the story of Ráma, current theologies, folk-tales, and the poetry of rural Bengal of the age when they were composed." To him the Rámáyana is a yellow primrose, but it is something more; and if some of his theories seem over-fanciful, at least they have the merit of sincerity. To the student of folklore these lectures are to be recommended as an earnest and loving study of a fascinating subject.

From a Review in the " Folk-Lore."

" THE BENGALI RAMAYANA " : LECTURES DELIVERED AT THE CALCUTTA UNIVERSITY IN 1916. BY RAI SAHIB DINESCHANDRA SEN, B.A. Published by the University of Calcutta, 1920.

THE FOLK-LITERATURE OF BENGAL : LECTURES DELIVERED AT THE CALCUTTA UNIVERSITY IN 1917. By the same Author. Published by the University of Calcutta, 1920.

It is a matter of congratulation that the author of these two volumes of lectures an eminent Bengali scholar and author of an important work, *The History of Bengali Language and Literature*, has devoted his attention to the folklore of his country, and that a lectureship on this subject has been founded in the University of Calcutta. In the first series of lectures he considers the questions connected with the Bengali versions of the great Indian epic, the " Ramayana " the work of Valmiki. The first result of his analysis of the poem is that, as might have been anticipated, the poet used much of the current folk-tradition. Many incidents in the epic closely resemble tales in the Buddhist Jatakas. The second theory suggested is that originally the cycle of legends connected with the demi-god Rama and the demon Ravana were distinct, and that it was left for the poet to combine them into one consistent narrative.

The second course of lectures deals with a series of folk-tales current among Musalmans in Bengal, which evidently embody early Hindu tradition. The influence of woman in preserving these tales, and particularly the scraps of poetry embodied in them, is illustrated in an interesting way, and he makes an important suggestion that tales of the Middle Kingdom, or the Upper Ganges Valley, were conveyed by the crews of ships sailing from the cost of Bengal to Persia and thus were communicated to the people of the West long before any translations of collections like the Panchatantra or Hitopadesa were available.

The learned author of the lectures is doing admirable work in a field hitherto unexplored, and the University of Calcutta deserves hearty commendation in its efforts to encourage the study of Indian folklore.

Times Literary Supplement, May 13, 1923.

THE FOLK-LORE OF BENGAL.

THE FOLK-LITERATURE OF BENGAL : BY RAI SAHIB DINESH-CHANDRA SEN. (Calcutta University Press·)

Those who are acquainted (we hope they are many) with Mr. Sen's other works, the outcome of Lectures delivered to Calcutta undergraduates in the author's function, as Ramtanu Lahiri Research Fellow in history of Bengali Language and Literature, will know exactly what to expect of his present delightful excursion into Bengali Folk-lore. There is some honour, to begin with, in the odd fact that he should be lecturing to Bengali lads on Bengali nursery tales in English. Mr. Sen is not, and does not profess to be, one of those remarkable Bengalis who like Sir Rabindranath Tagore, for example, are perfectly billingual to the extent of being able to think with equal ease, and write with equal felicity and justness of expression, in both languages. Let not this be regarded as a sin in the Ramtanu Lahiri Fellow. He thinks in Bengali, he thinks Bengali thoughts, he remains a pious Hindu, though his Hindu ideas are touched and stirred by contact with many kindly and admiring English friends. He is the better fitted to explain Bengal to the outer world. For he loves his native province with all his heart. He has no doubts as to the venerable origins, the sound philosophy, the artistic power, the suggestive beauty, all the many charms of the Bengali Saraswati, the sweet and smiling goddess, muse and deity alike, the inspirer and patron of a long line of men of literature and learning too little known to the self-satisfied and incurious West.

A Hindu he remains, thinking Hindu thoughts, retaining proud and happy memories of his childhood and of the kind old men and women who fed his childish imagination with old world rhymes, with the quaintly primitive Bengali versions of the stately epics of Sanskrit Scriptures, with tales even more primitive, handed down by word of mouth by pious mothers, relics, perhaps, of a culture which preceded the advent of Hinduism in Bengal. What makes Mr. Sen's books so delightful to us in Europe is precisely this indefinable Hindu quality, specifically Bengali rather than Indian, something that fits itself with exquisite aptness to what he knows of the scenery and climate of the Gangetic delta where Mr. Sen was born, and where he has spent the whole time of his busy life as a student of his native literature. He began life as a village school master in Eastern Bengal, a land of wide shining meres and huge slow moving rivers, where the boatman sings ancient legends as he lazily plies the oar, and the cowherd lads on the low grassy banks of Meghna or Dhaleswari chant plaintive rhymes that Warren Hastings may have heard as he " proceeded up country " in his spacious " budgerow."

All these pleasant old rhymes and tale Mr. Sen loves with a more than patriotic emotion and admiration, and this sentiment he contrives to impart to his readers, even through the difficult and laborious medium of a foreign language. We can imagine his lectures to be pleasant by conversional than eloquent in the academical fashion. He tells the lads before him what life-long pleasure he has taken in the hereditary legends he shares with them. But in the present volumes, for example, he is driven to assume from time to time the austerity of a professional student of a comparative folk-lore, and so strays (unwittingly, we may be sure) into the region of heated controversy. Mr. Gourlay, distinguished administrator and student of the history of Bengal, has given Mr. Sen a friendly foreword. It is evident that this professional element in Mr. Sen's work has a little frightened his kindly sponsor. "When I read the author's enthusiastic appreciation," he says, "of Bengali folk-tales, the thought crossed my mind that perhaps the Rai Sahib's patriotism had affected his judgment ; but after I had read the translation of the beautiful story of Malanchamala, I went back to the first lecture, and I knew that what he said was true."

Mr. Gourlay has expressed a hope that Mr. Sen will make a collection of Bengali folk-tales. It must be admitted that the late Rev. Lalbehari Dey's tales may well be supplemented. But surely Mr. Gourlay knows Daksina Ranjan Mazumdar's four wonderful and wholly delightful volumes, one of them with a preface of appreciation by Sir Rabindranath Tagore himself. Mr. Mazumdar may well claim to be the Grimm of Bengal, and Mr. Sen has repeatedly acknowledged his debt to his unwearied diligence in collecting Bengali folk tales. The wonder is that no one has yet translated the marvels of "Thakurdadar Jhuli," "Thakurmar Jhuli," "Thandidir Thale" and "Dadamahasayer Thali." Appropriately illustrated, sympathetically rendered, they may yet be the delight of Western nurseries, and form the best, the most natural and easy of introduction to Indian thought and literature. There are other admirable works for the nursery in Bengali, such as Miss Sita Devi's "Niret Gurur Kahini" and the volume of Hindustani Fairy tales translated by her and her sister. But there is only one Mazumdar, and we heartily hope that Mr. Sen's version of his Malanchamala in this volume will draw the attention of European students of Indian folk-lore to the four excellent collections we have mentioned. Their style, subtle, archaic yet colloquial, may well puzzle the translator, for not every one of us has the pen of a Charles Perrault. But the task is well worth attempting. Meanwhile Mr. Sen does well to remind us that two of the best of La Fontaine's Fables are taken from the "Panchatantra."

Bengali Ramayanas by D. C. Sen. From a review in the *Journal of Royal Asiatic Society* by SIR GEORGE GRIERSON—

"This is the most valuable contribution to the literature on the Rāma-saga which has appeared since Professor Jacobi's work on the Rāmāyaṇa was published in 1893. The latter was confined to Vālmīki's famous epic, and the present volume, from the pen of the veteran author of the *History of Bengali Language and Literature*, carries the inquiry on to a further stage, and throws light both on the origins of the story and on its later developments.

The subject covers so wide a ground, and its treatment exhibits so wide a field of Indian learning that, within the limited space available, it is impossible to do more than indicate the mere salient points adduced by the author, and, perhaps, to add a few new items of information.

It has long been admitted that the core of the Sanskrıt Rāmāyaṇa—the portion written by Vālmīki himself—consists (with a few interpolations) of the second to the sixth books. The first and the seventh, in which Rāma is elevated from the stage of a heroic mortal to divinity, are later additions. The Rai Saheb, accepting these conditions, has been able to dispel part of the darkness which has hitherto enveloved the sources of Vālmīki's poem, and to trace its origin to three distinct stories, which the great poet combined into a single epic.

The oldest version is that contained in the Dasaratha Jātaka, in which Sītā is said to be Rāma's sister. Rāma is banished to the Himâlaya, being accompanied by her and Laksmaṇa—under much the same story of palace intrigue as that told by Vālmīki,—and returns to reign after twelve years. He then marries his sister Sītā, and they live happily ever afterwards. She is not abducted by any one, and there is no mention either of Hanumān or Rāvaṇa.[1]

The second strand of the epic belongs to Southern India, where there grew up a cycle of legends[2] about a grand and noble

1 This was long ago recognized by A. Weber. See *Indian Antiquary*, Vol. i, p. 121.

2 We find much of this in that portion of the Uttara Kāṇda which J.cobi calls the Ravanois.

Brahmana.[1] Most of these stories are said to be collected in the Jain Rāmāyaṇa of Hemachandra, a work which I have not seen, and which is described by our author as far more a history of Rāvaṇa than of Rāma. On the other hand, a Buddhist work—the Lṇkâvatāra Sūtra—narrates a long discourse which Rāvaṇa held with the Buddha, and claims him as a follower of Mahāyāna Buddhism! He was thus revered by Hindus, Jainas and Buddhists alike.

The third strand was the floating group of legends related to ape-worship once widely current in India. In these Hanumān was at first connected with Śaivism, and there are still extant stories telling how Śiva made him over to Laksmaṇa for service under Rāma. Even at the present day it is not only the devotees of Visṇu who adore him, and Śaivas, but the crypto-Buddhists of Orissa claim him as a powerful divinity.

From materials taken from each of these three sources Vālmīki welded together his immortal poem. He refused sanction to the ancient legend that the Sītā whom Rāma married was his sister, but gave no hint as to her parentage. This was supplied in later works, such as the Adbhuta Rāmāyaṇa—a wonderful collection of old and fantastic traditions—in which she is described as the daughter of Mandôdarī, the wife of her abductor.[2]

After thus discussing the origins of the Rāma-saga, and its development by Vālmīki, the Rai Saheb proceeds to the main subject of his work—the Rāmāyaṇas of Bengal. None of them are translations of the Sanskrit epic. Like the celebrated *Rāmacaritamānasa* of Tulasī Dāsa, each author tells his story in his own way, weaving into it his own thoughts and ancient traditions

[1] Numerous temples in Southern India are said to have been founded by Rāvaṇa (see Bombay Gazetteer, I, i, 190 454, n. 1; XV, ii, 76, 290 ff., 341). He is said to have performed his celebrated austerities at Gokarṇa in Kanara (Bombay Presidency), a district which abounds in legends about him. Some of these have spread to very distant parts of India. For instance, the story of the loan to him of Śiva's "self-*liṅga*" (Gaz. XV, 290)

[2] Vide J.R.A.S., 1921, p. 422. This story appears to have been widely spread. It reappears in the Kāshmīrī Rāmayaṇa popular in Kashmir. According to the Jaina *Uttara Purāṇa*, quoted by our author she was a daughter of Rāvaṇa himself.

current in his neighbourhood. They secured their general popularity by the thorough Bengalization of their theme. The scenery, the manners and customs, the religious rites, the very food, although placed in Lankā, are all those familiar to Bengal. The most famous, and one of the oldest, of these Rāmāyaṇas is that of Kṛttivāsa (fourteenth century). All these features are already found there, but later writers, falling under the influence of the Vaisṇava revival of Chaitanya, not only filled their poems with Vaisṇava doctrine and with theories about *bhakti*, but even transferred legends concerning Chaitanya to pseudo-prototypes in the war before Laṇkā.[1] Space will not permit me to mention all Kṛttivāsa's successors. Each had his own excellencies and his own defects. I therefore confine myself to calling attention to the incomplete Rāmāyaṇa of the Mymensingh poetess Candrāvatī. In one of her poems she tells her own beautiful and pathetic story, and there can be no doubt but that her private griefs, nobly borne, inspired the pathos with which her tale of Sītā's woes is distinguished. It is interesting that, like one or two other authors, she ascribes Sītā's banishment to Rāma's groundless jealousy. A treacherous sister-in-law, daughter of Kaikeyī, named Kukuā, persuaded Sītā, much against her will, to draw for her a portrait of Rāvaṇa. She then showed this to Rāma as a proof that his wife loved, and still longed for, her cruel abductor. This story was not invented by the poetess. It must have been

1 The Bengali version of the conversion of the hunter Vālmīki is worth noting for the light it throws on the connexion of Bengali with Māgadhī Prākrit. Nārada tried to teach him to pronounce Rāma's name, but he could not do so owing to sin having paraylsed his tongue. Nārada succeeded in getting him to say *madā* (pronounced *marā*, meaning "dead." This is the Māgadhī Prākrit *madā* (Vr. xi, 15). It is peculiar to the Bengali language, the more western word being *marā*. Nārada next got him to use this western pronunciation, and to repeat the word rapidly several times—thus, *marāmarāmarāmarā* It will be seen that in this way Vālmīki, without his paralysed tongue knowing it, uttered the word *Rāma*, and thus became sufficiently holy to become converted. *Apropos* of the *bhakti* influence, on page 127, there is a story about Nizāmu'd-din Auliā and a robber, which recalls the finale of the Tannhäuser. The robber is told that he cannot hope for forgiveness till a certain dead tree bears leaves. In process of time he does feel true repentance, and the dead trunk becomes at once covered with green leaves from top to bottom.

one of those long orally current, but not recorded by Vālmīki or by the writer of the seventh book of the Sanskrit poem, for it reappears in the Kāshmīrī Rāmāyaṇa to which I have previously alluded.

A few words may also be devoted to another curious version of the old tradition. Under various orthodox names Buddhism has survived in Orissa to the present day, and, in the seventeenth century, one Rāmānanda openly declared himself to be an incarnation of the Buddha and, to prove it, composed a *Rāma-līlā* or Rāmāyana. I have already alluded to the fact that Hanumān was worshipped by this Orissa Buddhists. It need not therefore surprise us that Rāmānanda stated that he wrote his book under the ape-god's inspiration.

I have drawn attention to only a few features of this excellent work in the hope that my remarks will induce those interested in the subject to buy the book and study it for themselves. It deserves attention, even if we do not accept all that its author wishes to prove. As a collection of hitherto unknown facts bearing on the development of the Rāma-saga in Bengal it is unique.

BENGALI PROSE STYLE
and
CHAITANYA AND HIS AGE

F. W. THOMAS—(Library, India Office, London):

"I have now, however, given myself the pleasure of perusing the two volumes, which are worthy additions to your already great contributions to the study of your country's language, literature and history. The story which you tell of the development of Bengali as a language of modern prose has an interest which is much more than local. It shows how at different times different tendencies may be deliberately fostered and yet in the end the language may succeed in deriving profit from them all and ultimately arrive at a style which exactly corresponds to its needs, and it also shows how important may be in such a development the influence of individual writers. The Sanskrit provided an admirable model of a classical speech, strong in logical structure and precision but by itself it was, no doubt, rather too cumbrous and inflexible for the variety and multifaraity of modern experience. I think that Bengali has been successful in its assimilation both of Sanskrit and of European influences. The points which you make concerning the non-verbal character of the rustic language and the old prose writings and concerning the varieties of grammatical forms admissible even in early writings of the nineteenth century are curious. Of course the nominal style became characteristic of Sanskrit also in its later developments and was no doubt due to ethnic factors. That the modern Bengali has returned to a full use of the verb and that it has made a choice among the varieties of inflextional forms, thereby fixing a literary norm, and that it took place in less than a century—these are facts highly creditable to the intellectuality and taste of the people, and of course, you have gone on to the finer developments and made your prose writing a real art, capable of reflecting not only the general level of thinking, but also the subtleties of the idiosyncracy of particular writers.

I have also found your 'Chaitanya' of great interest. Although I myself am by nature inclined to the *Jnana-marga* and little drawn to the Bhakti-cult for which reason I had hitherto regarded Chaitanya only from the outside—your book has enabled me to realize somewhat the intensity of his religious emotions, his goodness and the deep effect which these combined to produce. The fact that he commenced as a Pandit is highly important, since it shows that not undeveloped intellectuality but the overpowering impulses of his nature were what determined his mission.

M. Levi justly congratulates you on preserving your critical judgment, in the presence of so highly emotional an atmosphere, and inspite of the fact that your own feeling strongly responds thereto. I have taken note of some eloquent passages in which your personal sentiment is in fact distinctly helpful to the readers by enabling him to realize the matter from the inside. And your book seems to me indispensable both for those who approach Chaitanya from the scholarly side and for those who wish to understand the mind and history of Bengal."

CHAITANYA AND HIS AGE.

Elaborate notices of these works have appeared in many journals of Europe and India.

From a long review in *Journal Asiatique* for January to March 1923: "Among books published entirely under one signature and not noticed up to now, it is necessary to mention first those of the indefatigable Dinesh Chandra Sen. Everywhere we find the proof of the profound knowledge which Mr. Sen possesses of a subject which he has renovated by his discoveries and of his enthusiasm for that mysticism which borrows the language of terrestrial love to express the diverse phases of the Divine love. In the last book (Chaitanya and his Age) which is the most agreeable to read and without doubt the most important, after having described the life of Chaitanya......................... Mr. Sen has added a very interesting supplement on the various sects which according to him are only Vaishnavite in name......... the Sahajias, the Bauls, etc. These he believes to be the sects of disguised Mahajanism........." ("*Translated from French*").

EMILE SENART, PRESIDENT, ASIATIC SOCIETY, PARIS :—I thank you for the two volumes that you have sent me. I was getting ready in accordance with your wish to bring them to the notice of the readers of the Asiatic Journal. But I was anticipated by M. Jules Bloch: you will see his article in the forthcoming issue of the journal. But at least I want to tell how greatly I appreciate the powerful art which for many years you have put at the service of Bengali Literature and how much I really felt the charm of the biography of Chaitanya. Your warm enthusiasm for the mystic side of religion and the cult of Krishna expressed themselves in such a touching manner! You have not conceived it in a narrow way—in the manner of the West. So that for us it does not lose the interest and seems a continuation in the heart and in the imagination of the remarkable and emotional action of this man of religious contemplation.

Believe, dear co-worker, in the expression of my deep gratitude and devotion. (*Translated from French.*)

From a long review in the *Pioneer*—12th August, 1923.

"The author displays zeal, energy, and learning of no common order. He is filled with a passionate conviction of the truth of what he writes. Further, he is familiar with the apparatus criticus of modern scholarship ; gives full references and weighs his authorities with solemn impartiality...............Much care, learning and scholarship have been directed to the task of separating the historic from the legendary element in the many sources with which the author concerns himself. The result is a picture which, so far as the data from which it is constructed are concerned, leaves little to be desired........."

HIS EXCELLENCY LORD RONALDSHAY wrote a letter of appreciation. He pointed out some errors; his letter is, howver, quoted here with some omission. It will show the deep interest with which His Excellency reads all publications of the Calcutta University of which he was once the Chancellor.

"I need hardly say that I have read 'Chaitanya and his Age' with the utmost pleasure. It seems to me to give a vivid account of the time when there was a great flowering of the emotional temperament of Bengal, due in large measure, no doubt, to a reaction against the frigid intellectualism of the monistic school of Vedanta Philosophers—or as you call them—pantheists. We see the same thing, do we not, in the case of Ramakrishna Paramahamsa, of Dakhineswar, in that he laid stress upon the supreme value of the Bhakti-cult?

Your chapter on Sahajia is extremely interesting and recalled with great vividness the talk which we had at Barrackpur on that subject. But until I read your recent volume, I had not realised that there were so many sects of Sahajias or that the cult was so wide-spread. Nor, I think, had I realised how wide is the gulf between the mass of the people who have been untouched by western education and their western-educated fellow countrymen. Babu Parvaticharan Kabishekhar's ' Charu Darshan ' must be an interesting novel from this point of view, and I agree with you that it ought to be translated into English. Why not encourage some of your pupils to undertake this? In case you may be bringing out a further edition of ' Chaitanya and his Age ' at any time, I note down a few printer's errors that happened to catch my eye as I read it. (Here His Excellency refers to some mistakes.)

There are also some little discrepancies in connection with the date of Chaitanya's birth. Thus on page 102 you say that Jagannath Misra was 48 years old at the birth of Chaitanya and was himself born in 1435. This would make the date of Chaitanya's birth 1483. On page 103 you mention a copy of Mahabharata made in 1468 by Jagannath or 17 years before Chaitanya's birth. This would make the date of the latter 1485. Again on page 106 you say that Jagannath died of fever in 1506 when Chaitanya was only 20, which makes the date of Chaitanya's birth 1486. This latter date is the one which you tell us on page 109 is accepted by the Vaisnaba historians. These are all trifling matters and I only mention them in case it may be of use to you."

THE EASTERN BENGAL BALLADS

WITH A FOREWORD BY THE RIGHT HON'BLE LAWRENCE JOHN LUMLEY DUNDAS, EARL OF RONALDSHAY.

From a Review in the Oriental List, London (Jan.-March, 1924).

"*Eastern Bengal Ballads: Mymensingh*": Ramtanu Lahiri Research Fellowship Lectures for 1922-24 in two parts.

In these two volumes Dr. Dineschandra Sen has for the first time made available, both for English and for Bengali readers, ten typical ballads (gathas) sung by professional minstrels in the district of Mymensingh. The words of the ballads have been taken down in writing from the lips of those who sing them by one Chandrakumar De, who has travelled into many out-of-the-way places in East Bengal for this purpose. It was an extremely difficult task to which he set himself; he often found the professional singers whom he approached unwilling to disclose to a stranger the text of these songs, which had been handed to them as a private family possession; to recover the whole of a ballad he often had to make special journeys to several different places and to consult a number of different singers; and throughout his work he was handicapped by ill-health. It is to be hoped that the collaboration between him and Dr. Sen will continue and result in the preservation of many more of these ballads, which are of immense value both to the student of folk-lore and to the philologist.

The ballads mostly date from the 16th and 17th centuries, and throw a flood of light on the social, religious and political condition of Eastern Bengal in those days. The first volume (Vol. I, Part I) contains a valuable introduction by Dr. Sen, and an English translation (or more strictly a paraphrase) of the ten ballads. There is also a separate introduction to each ballad. The second volume (Vol. I, Part II) contains a Bengali introduction, the full Bengali text of each ballad, and a number of footnotes explaining obsolete words and provincialisms. There are eleven illustrations, and a literary map of Eastern Mymensingh. Embodied in some of the ballads are several interesting specimens of 'baramasi' poems—poems describing the twelve months of the year in relation to the experiences of the hero and heroine of the poem. The language throughout is the common village speech of the Mymensingh district, and is in delightful contrast to the artificial style of such writers as Bharatchandra, with its far-fetched conceits and high-sounding Sanskrit expressions.

Great as Dr. Sen's other services to the cause of Bengali literature have been, it is doubtful whether any of his previous work is a more valuable contribution to our knowledge of Bengali life and thought than this collection of ballads, which, but for his enterprise and the praiseworthy efforts of his collaborator, would in all probability in the course of the next few years, have been lost beyond recovery."

From a review in the Times Literary Supplement of 7th August, 1924.

"A writer needs more than merit in himself if his work is to attract wide notice; his subject-matter must have a quality of general appeal. Probably no scholar alive in India to-day has such a record as Dr. Dineschandra Sen, a record of patient, enthusiastic pioneer research, whose results have been valuable and full of interest. Fifty years ago, very little was known, even by Bengalis, of old Bengali literature, and if such ignorance no longer prevails to-day, it is largely because of one man who, in spite of poverty and obscure beginnings and ill-health, has toiled through many years to bring his own land's history and literature to light. His journeyings should become a legend, and the Bengali imagination, centuries hence, should see one figure eternally traversing the Gangetic plain, now beaten upon by the fierce sun as he makes his way across the red, deeply fissured fields of Vishnupur, now floating on the rain-swept rivers of East Bengal. He has coaxed a cautious peasantry into opening their store of traditions and memories, and he has persuaded them to part with hundreds of old manuscripts that were stuffed into palm-leaf roofs or between bamboo rafters. If he has not made a nation's ballads he has discovered a great many of them. If a small part of this service had been rendered to a better-known literature it would have made him famous. But Bengal is popularly supposed to have had no history; and it has certainly been without the dramatic or catastrophic events which strike the imagination in the story of many lands. Plassey, despite Nabin Sen's song of lament over it, was not a disaster to Bengali arms though fought in Bengal. Agra and Lahore, Delhi and Seringapatam, evoke more romantic associations than Dacca or Murshidabad. Aurangzeb and Akbar, Pratap Singh and Tipu Sultan, mean a good deal even to a European; but Lakshman Sen and Hambir Singh mean nothing at all.

Yet the records brought to light by Dr. Sen concern a population of fifty millions, who speak as expressive and beautiful a language as there is anywhere in India, and whose literature is a thing that Indians outside Bengal regard with pride, as an enrichment of their common heritage. That literature has been flowering with amazing exuberance for nearly a century now; and as the Bengali mind grows in consciousness of itself and its achievement, it must increasingly be interested in the beginnings of that achievement. In his latest book, Dr. Sen has reclaimed a whole province for scholarship and study, the ballads of the Mymensingh borderland. As we know, a debatable land, where races and interests meet and sometimes clash, has a vivid life which often takes on spontaneous and vigorous expression. And the Mymensingh swamps and spreading rivers, a refuge to fugutive kings and struggling independences, a region where Bengal and Assam, Aryan and Mongolian meet and merge, have sheltered through the centuries much more than moving and beautiful stories. A great deal of Bengal's forgotten and neglected history lies hidden in these ballads.

In his introduction Dr. Sen tells how his notice was first drawn to the ballads. Nearly a dozen years ago he was interested by articles in an obscure and local Magazine, and on inquiry found that they were by one Chandra Kumar De, a young man of no English education, in frail health and wretchedly poor. He had been employed by a village grocer, on a salary of one rupee (sixteen pence) a month, " but was dismissed on the plea of incompetence and inattention." Probably the employer had reason for his action, for the boy was dreaming of his own country and her past. He got new work, this time munificently paid by two rupees a month, the work of a rent-collector; he had to travel widely, and during his travels heard the old ballads. Dr. Sen persuaded Calcutta University to employ him; and by an expenditure of fifty rupees a month for three years over 17,000 lines of Old Bengali poetry have been recovered. Dr. Sen exultantly remarks :

" I would not have been more pleased if these lines were all gold. The songs perfectly artless, written mostly by Hindu and Muhammadan peasants, often show the real heart of poetry, and some of them at least, I believe, will rank next only to the most beautiful of the Viasnava songs in our literature."

He has found European scholars who share his enthusiasm. If other friends, both in England and Bengal, renew the charge that his enthusiasm for what is old is often like the uncritical joy of a man madly in love, he is unmoved. The charge is familiar to him, and he puts it by with a smile. The mass of work that he has now brought forward is too large for hasty assessment, and even on a first view much of it is manifestly poorer than he thinks it. But among these ballads are some tales so simple and appealing that they need only a more cunning literary presentation to win recognition outside Bengal. And Dr. Sen, throughout his long and successful career as discoverer, has never done his land greater service than by saving these stories that would so soon have faded out from the world."

Paris, 10th April, 1924.

MY DEAR FRIEND,

I am sorry I could not answer earlier your lovely letter, dated 10th January, 1924. I am growing more and more busy day by day since my coming back home. Still I cherished the hope of reading all your Ballads before writing you, and I kept them faithfully on my desk all the time. But I had to content myself with the first one and with your learned Introduction. To-day I am on the eve of Easter vacations, and I am confident I can now make time to enjoy a full reading of your delectable work. But I have read enough of it to anticipate the pleasure I can derive from it. Your enthusiasm at the discovery was fully justified. Your Eastern Bengal, you are so proud of, is positively an earthly replica of India's *Nandan*, a paradise of vegetation, sky, running water, a sporting place of Apsarases and Gandharvas, and you are another Narada coming to the world to repose above these celestial beauties, and in a way how attractive! This is the wonder of art that, owing to you, I could in the sad, dull, dim days of winter dream of a blue sky, of lovely rivers, of evergreen woods, of couples of lovers wandering amidst the wild beasts, indifferent to all dangers, raptured by their mutual love.

There is one dark side, the news you give me about your bad health. It may be that after such an unceasing strain of labour you had to suffer from a nervous depression. Even before I could meet you, I could guess that you are working in a constant strain of imagination and passion which overtaxes your bodily strength. I know that no sacrifice is of account to you for the love of your country. But India has not such a plenty of worthy worshippers that the loss of one of them may be indifferent. The work that you can do no one else can do or will do. Think of it and keep yourself ready for more work. This is a friend's wish and prayer.

But do not miss to send me a word that you are feeling better, and stronger, that you are recovering after this tremendous shock.

Believe me, my dear friend,

Ever yours,

SYLVAIN LEVI.

DEAR SIR,

Thank you very much for your kindness in sending me the first volume of your Mymensingh Ballads. My sister and myself (she is my interpreter in English) have read it with great interest. The subject it deals with touches all mankind; the differences with European stories are due to reasons which are much more social than racial. The good æsthetic taste that is felt in most of these ballads is also one of the characteristics of popular imagination in many of our Western countries: "Womeder Wehmuth" as a beautiful song of Goethe's, put into music by Beethoven, expresses it "The Pleasure of Tears."

It is true that with us French people, the people of Gaul, it reacts against this with our bold and boisterous joyful legends. Is there none of this kind of thing in Indian literature? I was specially delighted with the touching story of Madina which although only two centuries old, is an antique beauty and a purity of sentiment which art has rendered faithfully without changing it. Chandravati is a very noble story and Mahua, Kanka and Lila are charming (to mention only these ones).

The patient researches of Mr. Chandra Kumar De and your precious collaboration with him have brought to the historical science a valuable contribution to its efforts to solve the problems of popular literary creations. From where have these great primitive epics and ballads come? It seems very likely that they have always come from some poetic genius whose invention has struck the popular imagination. But the question is how much people deform his idea in putting it into the shape in which we find it? Which is the part of the collaboration of the multitude in this work of re-casting, which is continuous and spontaneous? Rarely has any one had the happy opportunity to seize an epic as one might say on the lips of the people who have given birth to it before writing had fixed it in some shape as you and Mr. Chandra Kumar have succeeded in doing in this case. I congratulate you sincerely for this beautiful work and I ask you, dear Sir, to believe in my high esteem and admiration.*

4th March, 1924. ROMAIN ROLLAND.

* Translated from French by Captain J. W. Petavel.

From a review by MR. E. F. OATEN, LL.B., M.A., published in the *Englishman*, dated the 7th of February, 1924.

It is not easy for an Englishman to hazard an opinion as to the reception which the ballad poetry of Eastern Bengal, recently rescued from oblivion by Dr. Sen, and now given by him to the world in the form of an English translation, will receive at the hands of literary Bengal. But one thing is certain. The measure of Bengal's appreciation of these ballads, not as mere historical or literary curiosities, but as living literature, will be some index of the extent to which her spirit is escaping from the trammels of artificiality in its effort to express itself not only in literature but in life. To the western critic, stumbling by good fortune upon Dr. Sen's Book, these ballads, straight from the unsophisticated people's heart, come fresh and stimulant as the breeze that revives the jaded traveller from Calcutta as he sits in steamer and ploughs across the monsoon gusts of Eastern Bengal. In them we escape, as regards the subject-matter almost entirely from the priest, as regards language, entirely from cultured artificiality, and as regards the most universal of human passions, altogether from that ideal of chastity which caused a poet of an earlier age to place the following words in the mouth of Sita, as a defence to her character: "Even when I was a mere child, I never came too close to a male play-fellow."

In the introduction which Dr. Sen prefixes to his translation, we learn that these ballads cover a period of 300 years from the sixteenth century onward, that they were known only and that orally only, solely to the class, rapidly decreasing, of professional village-singers or rhapsodists; and that he collected the ballads through the agency of a poverty-stricken and uneducated literary enthusiast, named Chandra Kumar De, to whom the real credit for first bringing these ballads to literary notice must be ascribed, though Dr. Sen's work in introducing them to a wider literary world, and inspiring the discovery of others, has been infinitely valuable.

Briefly stated, these ballads contain a picture of the state of society and the conditions of life, prevailing in Eastern Mymensingh in the 16th century and onward. The area in which the ballads rose and flourished was one into which the Sen Rajas with the Brahminic canons and arbitrary conventions were unable to penetrate; it was therefore for generations ruled by a different society and a different standard of moral and communal life; its culture was indigenous, natural, fresh, unartificial, in short, true original Bengali. It was a society not of dogmas, but of real life.

There are a dozen aspects from which these ballads, thus redeemed from rapidly approaching oblivion, are important. Lord Ronaldshay in his introduction emphasises their importance as the seed from which modern Bengali has sprung. They will certainly also prove valuable as a source of historical information. But one cannot but dwell here on their intrinsic value as literature, since it is to be hoped that Bengal will eventually value them most as such. As Dr. Sen writes, " these songs have features in them which have a universal appeal." Their language is that of a despised " patois," they describe Bengali men and women acting in ways that are not now conventional and are in some cases regarded as immoral; but they describe the great human passions, and chiefly the passions of love, working in social conditions that were, as compared with conditions to-day, strangely unrestricted by conventions. In these ballads women fall in love, and in no case blindly follow the selection of the guardian. They go through fire and water for the sake of the man they choose. They devise stratagems and slay his foes. They converse with strange young-men at the ghat and arrange future meetings. They receive love-letters. Yet ever they prefer death to dishonour, properly so regarded. Malua's scorn of the Kazi's overtures to her through a go-between, in her husband's absence, is characteristic. " The wicked Kazi has not the worth of my husband's toe. Take this insult from me and go to your Kazi and tell him all. I take him to be my foe and hold him as a dog. I hit his face with a broom from here."

In fact it may be said that woman, the Bengali woman, is the general hero of these ballads, so far as those hitherto published are concerned. By the side of her devotion, heroism and self-renunciation, the male characters are sometimes poor creatures, devoid of personality. In Mahua, Malua, Sunai and several others, not solely Hindu, the literature of Bengal receives on its roll many names of which it may be proud. It is therefore distressing to learn from Dr. Sen that these songs are losing public favour every day. Bengal needs these literary heroines, even though, or even possibly because their conventions are not those of to-day. Possibly Dr. Sen's book, and especially his enthusiastic and triumphant introduction to them, will restore them to public favour, and give them wider currency. It is clear at least from Dr. Sen's enthusiasm for the unconvetionality of the characters of the ballads, that it is not without meaning that he prefaces to his book the quotation that " if a man were permitted to make all the ballads, he need not care who should make the laws of a nation."

Lord Ronaldshay in an article entitled " What is it Nationalist India wants " published in " the Nineteenth Century and After " (July 1924) refers to Dr. Dineschandra Sen's " Eastern Bengal Ballads " in terms of high praise, with copious extracts from the book.

From a review by Mr. F. E. PARGITER, (I.C.S. retired) in the *Royal Asiatic Society's Journal* (October, 1924) :

Songs and ballads have been handed down orally and recited among the peasantry in the district of Mymensingh in North-East Bengal, and Chandra Kumar De, a poor man who had been fascinated by them during his local visits as rent-collector, began writing about them in the local Journal *Sourabha* in 1912. His notices attracted Dr. Dineschandra Sen, who then helped him and engaged him in 1919 to recover all the ballads that could be discovered there. This was done, often with great difficulty, because reciters did not always know the whole of a ballad, so that the portions were discovered piecemeal and sometimes confusedly. Dr. Sen has now edited ten ballads as a first instalment in this work, the ballads (Maimansingha Gītikā) in Pt. II and English translations in Pt. I.

The Bengali of the ballads is the peculiar dialect of East Bengal, which differs from that of Calcutta in various respects, and is of real interest and value in phonology and vocabulary, as the reviewer can vouch from personal knowledge, some results of which are shown in his *Vocabulary of Peculiar Vernacular Bengali* Works, published by the Bengal Asiatic Society. The English version is not a close translation, but a free rendering which gives the matter and spirit of the original. The ballads belong to the last three or four centuries. The dramatis personæ are Hindu and Mohammedan, chiefly Hindu yet not Hindu of the orthodox type, for the conditions are those of freer country life, and youth and maiden meet in true love episodes. The stories are charming, both happy and tragic, and are told generally in simple language, fresh with country scenes and feelings, and illustrated with pretty sketches by a Bengali artist. The characters are finely and often nobly delineated, and the heroines display the highest ideals of Bengali womanhood. Dr. Sen has discussed each ballad in a preface, and has prefixed to the whole a long introduction investigating their origin, variety, nature, recitation and value, and the political condition of that district. The ballads should stimulate interest among students of Bengali, and the English version will charm all readers.

Luzac's Oriantal List, London, Jan.-March, 1926.

Glimpses of Bengal Life. By Rai Bahadur Dinesh Chandra Sen, B.A., D.Litt. (Hon.), etc. In this volume, which consists almost entirely of lectures delivered to the Calcutta University in 1915 (and subsequently revised), Dr. Sen rambles discursively over a large range of topics connected with the old literature and life of Bengal, and, as might be expected from a scholar of his distinction, *nihil tangit quod non ornat.* The early part of the book is concerned with the high standard of rectitude and lofty sex morality which is revealed in the rustic ballads. The author passes on to discuss the system of espionage adopted by the ancient rulers ; costume ; the influence of Islam on the Hindu Courts; and the superior observation of nature of the old writers, as compared with modern Bengali poets. Then follow some stray notes on the curious Mainâmati songs and the story of Gorakshanath, and an examination of certain features of the life and teaching of the Vaishnava poet Chandîdâs. The next section deals with the story of Chaitanya's desertion of Nadia, as revealed in the usually neglected sayings of the Vaishnava poets. To many readers the most interesting part of the book will be the chapter devoted to humour in Old Bengali literature; and the description of Bharat Chandra's character of the sage Vyâsa, which is in the best style of comedy, may be recommended to all who are inclined to disparage Indian humour. The supplement is an excellent specimen of literary controversy, in which Dr. Sen convincingly champions the authenticity of the Karcha of Govinda Dâs.
